THE LIBERAL DEFENCE
OF MURDER

RICHARD SEYMOUR lives, works and writes in London. A research student at the London School of Economics, he runs the Lenin's Tomb website and is the author of *The Meaning of David Cameron* and *American Insurgents: A Brief History of American Anti-Imperialism.*

THE LIBERAL
DEFENCE
OF MURDER

◆

RICHARD SEYMOUR

VERSO

London • New York

This updated paperback edition first published by Verso 2012
First published by Verso 2008
© Richard Seymour 2012
ll rights reserved

The moral rights of the author have been asserted

1 3 5 7 9 10 8 6 4 2

Verso
UK: 6 Meard Street, London W1F 0EG
USA: 20 Jay Street, Suite 1010, Brooklyn, NY 11201
www.versobooks.com

Verso is the imprint of New Left Books

ISBN-13: 978-1-84467-861-7

British Library Cataloguing in Publication Data
A catalogue record for this book is available from the British Library

Library of Congress Cataloging-in-Publication Data
A catalog record for this book is available from the Library of Congress

Typeset by Hewer Text UK Ltd. Edinburgh
Vail

To Marie. With all my love.

We must study how colonization works to decivilize the colonizer, to brutalize him in the true sense of the word, to degrade him, to awaken him to buried instincts, to covetousness, violence, race hatred, and moral relativism; and we must show that each time a head is cut off or an eye put out in Vietnam and in France they accept the fact, each time a Madagascan is tortured and in France they accept the fact, civilization acquires another dead weight, a universal regression takes place, a gangrene sets in, a centre of infection begins to spread; and that at the end of all these treaties that have been violated, all these lies that have been propagated, all these patriots who have been tortured, at the end of all the racial pride that has been encouraged, all the boastfulness that has been displayed, poison has been distilled into the veins of Europe and, slowly but surely, the continent proceeds toward savagery.

– *Aimé Césaire*

CONTENTS

ACKNOWLEDGEMENTS

This is the first book I have written, and it could not have been completed without considerable help. Many thanks are due to the following, some of whom are quoted in the text, and all of whom provided important information and suggestions well beyond that indicated by the use made of the relevant interview material: Sasha Abramsky, Gilbert Achcar, Ian Birchall, Rony Brauman, Robert Brenner, Alex Callinicos, Vivek Chibber, Noam Chomsky, Alexander Cockburn, Philippe Cohen, Mike Davis, Alex de Waal, Peter Drucker, Liza Featherstone, Peter Gowan, Serge Halimi, Johann Hari, Corey Robin, Catherine Samary, Adam Shatz, Enzo Traverso, Dominique Vidal, Ellen Meiksins Wood and Gary Younge. Also extremely helpful in discussions were Dan Hind, Max Lane, Dragan Plavsic, Gáspár Tamás and Andy Zebrowski. I am grateful to Alberto Toscano and China Miéville for reviewing the drafts and providing insightful commentary. Whatever miscues remain in the text, their guidance has helped me to avoid the worst. The team at Verso have been accommodating and helpful throughout. Thanks especially to my editor, Sebastian Budgen, who provided an immense variety of invaluable material and assistance, checked my dubious translations from French to English, and facilitated most of the interviews. And a great thank you to Charles Peyton for his invaluable copy-editing work on the manuscript. I am indebted to dozens of friends and colleagues, too numerous to mention here, for providing references and forwarding useful material and commentary. This second edition has been emended to take note of several criticisms and corrections, some offered anonymously, some in sympathy and others in polemic. If a criticism hasn't resulted in a correction, it's because I disagreed with the criticism.

PROLOGUE: SEPTEMBER 11
AND *KRIEGSIDEOLOGIE*

> Watching the towers fall in New York, with civilians incinerated
> on the planes and in the buildings, I felt something that I couldn't
> analyze at first and didn't fully grasp . . . I am only slightly
> embarrassed to tell you that this was a feeling of exhilaration.
> — *Christopher Hitchens*[1]

This book seeks to explain a current of irrational thought that
supports military occupation and murder in the name of virtue and
decency. It will be recalled that those predictions of a cakewalk
towards a jubilant, free Iraq were not solely the product of the Bush
administration. What has sometimes been called the 'pro-war Left' – in
fact, a loose coalition of liberals, former radicals and ex-socialists –
has shocked and awed former colleagues and comrades, with bold and
strident claims about the great works that American military power
could achieve in Iraq, and elsewhere. It has been of great service to the
Bush administration that, in addition to the shock troops of Christian
fundamentalists, Israel sympathizers and neoconservatives, it could
boast the support of many prominent liberal intellectuals, some of
whom still claim an affiliation to the Left. (A number of them even
claim to represent the authentic Left against the 'pseudo-Left'.[2]) Some
of these commentators are close to Washington or to figures who have
been prominent in the Bush administration. Some have helped formu-
late policy, as when Kanan Makiya was called upon to help devise
plans for the 'New Iraq'. And they have all performed a role of
advocacy for the Bush administration and supportive governments.

The reasons why their support should have been so useful are
explored in more detail in the Conclusion. To put it briefly, they have

helped to screen the war-makers from articulate criticism. They have taken threat-exaggeration out of White House press briefings (where it would be regarded cynically), and the moral exaltation of American military power out of the realm of the Pentagon (where it might result in laughter). This coalition is historically far from unique, in many ways resembling the Cold War intelligentsia who pioneered 'CIA socialism'. And it plays a traditional role in castigating dissent among the intelligentsia, while the arguments of the pro-war Left reach wider audiences through journals, newspaper columns, television slots and so on. As well as acting as conduits for the distribution of policy justifications, the liberal pro-war intellectuals help frame arguments for policy-makers in terms more palatable to potentially hostile audiences. The arguments themselves are antique, and have not improved with age. They are symptomatic of the hegemony of what Jean Bricmont calls the 'interventionist ethic'.[3] If it were not for certain widely held assumptions about the remedial power of conquest, originating in the age of European empires, their arguments would make no sense to anyone. In the chapters that follow I will excavate the origins of these liberal apologies for empire, and track their development over the course of three centuries, on both sides of the Atlantic.

Disaster triumphant

Many of the current batch of liberal advocates of empire have a history on the Left, often abandoned at some point after the collapse of the Soviet Union. For all but recalcitrant Stalinists, the human prospect following the collapse of the Russian superpower in 1989 was supposed to be a promising one. Fukuyama's sighting of an 'end' to history was, notwithstanding his own dyspepsia, touted as a prospectus for universal accord. The one true model for society had been revealed by no less an authority than History, and that model enjoined free-market capitalism and liberal democracy. As Gregory Elliott observes, 'the locomotive of history had terminated not at the Finland Station, but at a hypermarket. All roads lead to Disneyland?' There were some outstanding problems, of course: in place of Stalinist dictatorships emerged new particularisms of a religious or national sort that, while hardly systemic threats, clearly posed problems for the 'New World Order' that Bush the Elder had vaunted. It was in the course of engagement with these problems that former left-wingers decided at various points to pitch in their lot with what the French Foreign Minister Hubert Védrine had referred to as the American 'hyperpower'.[4] The occasion for apostasy varied, but key moments were Saddam Hussein's invasion of Kuwait, the collapse of the former

Yugoslavia, and the attacks on the World Trade Center. In the absence of states purportedly bearing the historical mission of the proletariat, many former Marxists, including anti-Stalinists, either made peace with centrist liberalism or morphed into their neoconservative opposites. American military power was now an ally of progress rather than its enemy.

As the profile of political Islam has risen under the impress of 'al-Qaeda', a modish concern of pro-war intellectuals has been the chastisement of religion, and especially Islam, as a source of reaction and irrationalism. Similarly, the gurus of spiritualism, New Age mysticism, Western Buddhism and 'postmodernism' have been berated as agents of the Counter-Enlightenment. Predictably, anti-imperialism has been incriminated by association with the enemies of progress.[5] For figures such as Christopher Hitchens, the 'war on terror' is an urgent contest between the forces of secular humanism and Enlightenment, and those of medieval terror. To oppose it is to give succour to an implacable enemy. Sadly, as Adorno and Horkheimer observed at an incomparably graver moment, Enlightenment of this kind 'radiates disaster triumphant'. Nowhere has the brochure for humanist imperialism less resembled the practice than at the frontiers of the 'war on terror', whose bloody outcomes include violence of genocidal proportions in Iraq, and whose motifs include the resurrection of modes of torture abandoned by the enlightened despots of the eighteenth century, the mercenary armies of nineteenth-century imperialism, the ethnic cleansing and aerial bombardment of the twentieth century, and an unprecedented complex of global gulags. 'Progress' of this kind belongs in the annals of discredited ideas, along with Manifest Destiny, the civilizing mission, *Lebensraum* and the 'master race'. It happens to share its origins with all of these.

The strange death of irony

We were to hear a great deal after 9/11 that the response of the antiwar Left was 'delinquent', 'self-hating' and lacking in sympathy for its victims. The correlate to this supposed indifference was the claim by Jerry Falwell and Pat Robertson that the attacks were punishment from God for having allowed homosexual intercourse and abortions to take place. According to Paul Berman, the 'left-wing Falwells' called for the US government to stop 'trying to preserve the Jewish state' and allow 'Saddam Hussein to resume his massacres (thus eliminating America's other putative sins)'.[6] Rejecting the thesis of divine violence thus, somehow, implies the innocence of the American state. At the least, this petulant outburst conflates a critique of the American state's foreign policy with an assault on cosmopolitan liberalism. The irony is that Berman could have found no surer supporters of Israel or American policy towards Saddam than Falwell or Robertson, while they are as robustly critical of the Left for undermining America as he is.

As the historian of ideas Corey Robin points out, Robertson and Falwell were not the only ones to think that 9/11 terminated a period of decadence. Mainstream pundits, such as David Brooks of the *New York Times*, made similar noises without the religious cues. Perhaps one should have seen it coming. In 2000, Robin had interviewed a pair of disillusioned neoconservatives, irate at what they saw as Clinton's paucity of global ambition. Irving Kristol had reviled the 'business culture' of conservatism, lamenting the lack of an 'imperial role'. For William F. Buckley, Jr, the emphasis on the market had become 'rather boring . . . like sex'. The sighs of relief after 9/11 were palpable. 'What I dread now,' George Packer wrote, 'is a return to the normality we're all supposed to seek.' 'This week's nightmare, it's now clear, has awakened us from a frivolous if not decadent decade-long dream', added Frank Rich.[7] For William Kristol and Robert Kagan, neoconservatives affiliated to the Project for the New American Century (PNAC), the 1990s had been 'a squandered decade', and there should be no 'return to normalcy'. Lewis Libby, then a Pentagon advisor and now a convicted perjurer, complained of a lax political culture that made Americans appear morally weak and slow to defend themselves. The attacks on Washington and New York offered an opportunity for the moral resuscitation of the American empire, providing the Bush administration with a rationale for an audacious and aggressive project. Or, as then National Security Advisor Condoleezza Rice claimed, they 'clarified' America's role.[8]

On the day that the attack on Afghanistan began, former *New York Times* editor James Atlas told the paper's readers that 'our great American empire seems bound to crumble at some point' and that 'the end of Western civilization has become a possibility against which the need to fight terrorism is being framed, as Roosevelt and Churchill framed the need to fight Hitler'. The alarming ease with which 'Western civilization' is conflated with the American empire is matched only by the implication that nineteen hijackers from a small transnational network of *jihadis* represent a civilizational challenge, an existential threat comparable with the Third Reich. But this has been precisely the argument of neoconservatives and liberal interventionists: there is an 'extraordinary threat', hence the need for 'extraordinary responses'. Failure to recognize this bodes ill for 'civilization'.[9]

This civilizational motif occasionally shades into the 'chaos' motif, in which the structures of civilization are threatened by societal breakdown. These were prepared and argued over long before 11 September 2001, and two elite US thinkers in the field of international relations were decisive in the production of this ideology. One is Samuel Huntington, a Cold War intellectual who had justified authoritarian regimes in the Third World and American military aid to security apparatuses in those states, which he insisted was 'politically sterile' (not so, as Chapter 3 makes clear). Huntington maintained, in 'The Clash of Civilizations?', published two years after the final collapse of the Soviet Union, that the source of future international conflict would be civilizational fault-lines. A civilization, Huntington maintains, is a 'cultural entity': China is one such, while the Anglophone Caribbean is another. This unit is defined by 'language, culture, tradition and, most important, religion'. The power of 'the West' is driving a growth in 'civilization-consciousness', particularly given the eclipse of nationalism and socialism. This process is underpinned by growing economic regionalism. Conflict is thus defined in the new era by 'What are you?' rather than 'Which side are you on?'. Citing the Orientalist scholar Bernard Lewis, Huntington concludes that the most likely conflict is with Islam, enraged as it is by 'Judeo-Christian' expansion, and embroiled as it is in several bloody conflicts. 'Islam', says Huntington, 'has bloody borders'. Ideas such as 'individualism, liberalism, constitutionalism, human rights, equality, liberty, the rule of law, democracy, free markets, the separation of church and state' belong to 'the West' and have 'little resonance in Islamic, Confucian, Japanese, Hindu, Buddhist or Orthodox cultures'. Huntington finishes by adumbrating an emerging 'Confucian–Islamic Connection', characterized by the 'Weapons States' of China, North Korea and the Middle East. Huntington's thesis has been extremely influential, particularly in light of the growing profile of religion, and provides much of the intellectual backbone to Sam Harris's *The End of Faith*. Even critics such as Michael Ignatieff have, as I will discuss in Chapter 4, fallen for a version of Huntington's idea.[10]

Robert Kaplan's much-derided 'The Coming Anarchy' is, on the face of it, a contesting thesis. Kaplan's argument, though mocked as 'the New Barbarism Thesis', was allegedly placed on the desk of every US ambassador overseas at the behest of Bill Clinton. Focusing on state failure, criminality and atomization as the chief forms in which anarchic conflict arises, Kaplan attributes these to resource scarcity and environmental degradation. In the new social landscape of Africa he depicts, 'hordes' of young men wait around for economic opportunities, licit or otherwise, constituting 'loose molecules in a very unstable social fluid, a fluid that was very clearly on the verge of igniting'. 'Disease, overpopulation, unprovoked crime, scarcity of resources, refugee migrations, the increasing erosion of nation-states', the sinister augury goes on, provide the basis for conflict, as in Sierra Leone, where a 'premodern formlessness governs the battlefield'. Dense slums appear as a result of 'overpopulation', and disease spreads, creating a virtual 'wall' around Africa that undermines its economic competitiveness. Elsewhere, Kaplan concedes that Africa's condition may owe a great deal to slavery and its partition by European powers; but the main cause of its Malthusian decadence is a deficit of 'social ingenuity' which is, he maintains, unevenly distributed among societies.[11]

But Kaplan goes further: Fukuyama is right about the end of history, but only for the relatively privileged, highly urbanized groups of people living in sealed-off, gentrified societies. But with mass Arab migration everywhere else, and the rise of Islam as the alternative to nationalism, the shantytowns are turning Muslim, so that Israel will end up 'a Jewish ethnic fortress amid a vast and volatile realm of Islam'. At any rate, 'in places where the Western Enlightenment has not penetrated and where there has always been mass poverty, people find liberation in violence'.[12] This was the situation that the purportedly negligent posture of the United States in the 1990s had seemingly allowed to stew, and which would no longer be tolerated post-9/11.

Lean and mean patriotism was in, flabby moral relativism was out. After the attacks on Manhattan and Washington, wrote Judith Shulevitz in the *New York Times*, 'tolerance for people with dangerous ideas seems frivolous compared with the need to stop them'. This new 'sense of seriousness', as she chose to call it, allowed her to understand the 'urgent patriotism' of Steven Spielberg's 'Band of Brothers'. The invocation of Americans in a collective struggle with fascism was not incidental: Spielberg's focus on World War II, seen by many as a good 'liberal' war, had arguably been an effort to overcome the trauma of Vietnam and resuscitate liberal nationalism. Shulevitz continued: 'Somewhere deep in my heart, I have always longed for a catastrophe like the present one', as it would produce a 'collective purpose' comparable with World War II or the 'Velvet Revolution'. It would sweep aside all triviality, such as 'petty political squabbling' and 'enervating celebrity gossip'. An op-ed in the *Washington Post* mused that the hijackers 'decided to attack the symbols of American empire, financial domination, military hegemony, strangely ugly buildings housing the people who rule a strangely ugly world despite our soft hearts.' It was this softness, the failure to make this strangely ugly world beautiful, that had brought about such bloody consequences in Vietnam, Iran, Lebanon and Somalia.[13]

The neoconservative *Weekly Standard* carried an urgent appeal for a hardening of the American heart, urging policy-makers to 'restore our awe' and 'majesty' even if they had to 'scorch southern Lebanon'. However much violent revenge was contemplated, the stentorian call for a new seriousness echoed broadly. 'No longer will we fail to take things seriously', pronounced Roger Rosenblatt of *Time* magazine. Graydon Carter, editor of *Vanity Fair*, concurred: 'I think it's the end of the age of irony'.[14] Within less than a month of irony's departure, the United States Air Force was dropping food packages and cluster bombs on Afghanistan.

The hope that a nationhood retooled for war would restore collective purpose proved to be forlorn. The fixtures of American life, from celebrity gossip to school shootings, did not evaporate. By 2003, *Dissent* magazine complained that 'a larger, collective self-re-evaluation did not take place in the wake of September 11, 2001' – not as regards foreign policy, but rather the domestic culture that had formed during the 'orgiastic' preceding decade. An angry *New Yorker* article would later mourn the dissipation of 'simple solidarity' alongside the squandering of international goodwill by the Bush administration.[15] Yet the sense that America would, and must, experience a national rebirth, was to become an indispensable early component of the 'war on terror' doctrine.

For if, as Lewis Libby explained, the problem was moral weakness, many now took great pains to enforce a censorious 'moral clarity'. The previously disavowed bipartisanship of Congress and Senate was now ostentatious. At any rate Bush, like the Kaiser, no longer recognized political divisions. *Septemberlebnis* and *Burgfrieden* were accompanied by threats and repression. When Bush told the world, 'You're either with us, or against us', he did not omit Americans from this injunction. The PATRIOT Act was rushed into law by politicians who had scarcely deigned to read its contents. More than 1,200 immigrants were immediately rounded up and detained without cause; antiwar activists were spied on[16] and detained without justification, their activities disrupted by the FBI, and their message received poorly, if at all, by a hostile press.

Most of the intellectual class lined up behind the attack on Afghanistan, and the neoconservatives who had suddenly become spokespeople for the aforementioned 'moral clarity' (among them former crooks from the Reagan administration, as well as some entrepreneurial types who would try to elicit bribes from the Saudi monarchy and deceive federal investigators) were joined in spirit by a number of figures who had come from the Left. Christopher Hitchens, formerly associated with a strand of heterodox Trotskyism, repeatedly rallied to the defence of 'American' values, accusing the anti-war Left of 'fascist sympathies'. Todd Gitlin, once of Students for a Democratic Society, supported the war on Afghanistan, and upbraided progressives for anti-Americanism. Michael Walzer, faced with antiwar protesters, wondered aloud whether there could be a 'decent left'. Marc Cooper, also supporting war on Afghanistan, accused its opponents of 'self-hatred'. The 'liberal Marxist' philosopher Norman Geras compared the Left's assertion that the 9/11 attacks were caused in part by US foreign policy with Ernst Nolte's claim that the Nazi Holocaust had to be understood as a 'pre-emptive' anticipation of a threat from the Soviet Union.[17]

Those who believed that a different response from the left would have prevented the Right from gaining the early initiative, and somehow compelled Washington to fight a 'better' war, missed an important point about the underlying imbalance of political discussions. The anti-war Left did have a strong intuitive explanation for the attacks on 9/11, which was that they were likely to be at least partly a consequence of US foreign policy – a point hardly debated now – and that this very policy ought to be changed. Secondly, the left had a practical and prudential response, namely not to undertake any course of action that would make the problem worse while also causing enormous suffering for tens of thousands of people who had not asked to be involved in the conflict. From this perspective, any reaction should have been more akin to a police hunt than a war. One thing the left did *not* have access to was the kind of knowledge that would demonstrate plausible ways to disable organizations such as 'al-Qaeda' other than through belligerence, since this knowledge tends to be the exclusive preserve of states and experts. And it lacked the kind of 'visionary' answer to the atrocity that the neoconservative right was now offering. Since the neoconservatives thrive on catastrophe, and since their argument is always that the United States should be aggressively expanding its dominion – especially now that it was facing a greater challenge than its leaders recognized – 9/11 was heaven-sent. The neocons had a narrative, a plan, and an obsession with Iraq as the last remaining hub of a senescent Arab nationalism; they were energetic and had all the right entrées to power, while the left was still reeling from historic defeats. And finally, the claims of the antiwar left that these attacks would be used to justify a wave of aggression that was by no means connected with catching the 9/11 criminals fell victim to an intense emotional and intellectual fug.

The language of 'human rights' imperialism and American exceptionalism

Even as left-wing anti-imperialism was treated to the full range of invective, the language of imperialism became more openly bruited.[18] 'Given the historical baggage that "imperialism" carries, there's no need for the US government to embrace the term', Max Boot argued, but 'it should definitely embrace the practice'. The 'historical baggage' he referred to was the crimes of 'Old Europe', to which the United States was an exception. Similarly, Robert Kagan described his homeland as a 'behemoth with a conscience' pursuing a liberal world order utterly different from Old Europe. Republican right-winger Grover Norquist argued that America was exceptional, the 'successor to European civilization, not its extension'.[19]

But these claims were not restricted to neoconservatives: as in so many other things, they and the pro-war liberals shared a common vocabulary. Christopher Hitchens hoped that the 'new imperialism' would aim to 'enable local populations to govern themselves', that the era of the client-state must be over, and that, 'if the United States will dare to declare out loud for empire, it had better be in its capacity as a Thomas Paine arsenal, or at the very least a Jeffersonian one'.[20] Michael Ignatieff, who had long been an advocate of 'humanitarian intervention', travelled to Afghanistan and noted with approval that America was indeed an empire, but condemned Bush for not taking the empire seriously enough. The empire's 'grace notes', he later concluded, were 'free markets, human rights and democracy, enforced by the most awesome military power the world has ever known'. This stood in stark contrast to the 'colonies, conquest and the white man's burden' of older European empires.[21]

Many liberals across Europe were, if bemused by the language of empire, often more than satisfied with the conjoined lexis of human rights. In Germany, Gerhard Schröder's decision to participate in 'military operations to defend freedom and human rights and to create stability and security' was backed by his Green Party coalition partner and minister for foreign affairs, Joschka Fischer. The liberal British playwright David Hare 'strongly supported the American action in Afghanistan, not only as a legitimate act of self-defence but also as a humanitarian undertaking on behalf of a country desperately in need of relief'.[22] In France, Bernard-Henri Lévy (known commonly by his brand-name, BHL) distinguished himself as one of the most vociferous pro-American voices, supporting the occupation of Afghanistan, and was widely praised as a result.[23] Lévy had a lengthy background in the internal politics of Afghanistan, and was drafted to help support French diplomatic efforts in the occupied country. He has also practised advocacy as a journalist. For example, his widely praised but sensationalist book, *Who Killed Daniel Pearl?*, attempted on the basis of poor evidence – much of it gleaned from the claims of Indian intelligence and a caricatural understanding of Pakistan – to accuse the Pakistani state of the murder.[24] (Lévy has often been accused of treating the facts lightly.)[25] Similarly, his pro-American sentiments were elaborated in *American Vertigo*, a collection of journalistic essays based on a lightning tour of the United States that attempted to follow in the footsteps of Alexis de Tocqueville. Amid a clutter of cliché about American obesity and the co-existence of 'materialism' with fervid religiosity, and despite some criticisms of the Usonian model, Lévy's mission is to reassure his audience that the 'American dream' is admirable and real. In particular, he disparages 'The Myth of the American Empire', admires Richard Perle, discovers that he shares 'antitotalitarian' axioms with William Kristol, and expresses delight in the idea that in 'the most powerful democracy in the world there finally appears a generation of intellectuals who arrive close to the top and can concretely work for the universalization of human rights and freedom'.[26]

Fear and loathing in the Washington axis

Although the liberal supporters of Bush were confident that the same arguments applied with respect to an invasion of Iraq, the scale of the antiwar movement shook them. Salman Rushdie, in a widely published article, argued that there was an 'unanswerable' liberal case for regime-change, although he took issue with Bush's focus on weapons of mass destruction. The *Observer* columnist Nick Cohen was eager to see the Iraqi National Congress assisted to power by Washington, so that they could 'replace minority rule with a multiracial, devolved democracy which stands up for human rights'. Further, he wanted to know 'how Noam Chomsky and John Pilger manage to oppose a war which would end the sanctions they claim have slaughtered hundreds of thousands of children who otherwise would have had happy, healthy lives in a prison state'. He argued that the Stop the War Coalition was the biggest threat to Iraqi democracy, and that it consisted of enemies of 'Iraqi socialists and democrats' who fervently wished for war. And finally, when Baghdad fell, he remarked that 'for a few weeks, the

British Army was the armed wing of Amnesty International, whether it knew it or not.' This would have been a somewhat more plausible claim had not Amnesty International vociferously opposed the war on humanitarian grounds.[27]

American newspapers were nevertheless encouraged by the 'anti-anti-American' fraternity among French intellectuals.[28] André Glucksmann, Pascal Bruckner and Roumain Goupil, former left-wingers outraged by European governments opposed to the venture, signed a statement supporting war on Iraq. Glucksmann accused the governments of France and Germany of repeating 'the arguments of Stalin's "Peace Movements" during the Cold War'. Jose Ramos-Horta, the former East Timorese freedom fighter, explained that 'sometimes a war saves people', describing how he had 'rejoiced' at the US war on Afghanistan, and condemning the Spanish government for withdrawing troops from Iraq. In an interview arranged by the US ambassador to Poland, former Soviet dissident Adam Michnik told *Dissent* magazine that Polish forces were taking part in the war for 'freedom' and that 'we take this position because we know what dictatorship is'. He told readers of his pro-American Warsaw newspaper *Gazeta Wyborcza* that Saddam was part of an Islamist war against the 'godless West', and reminded them of the failure of 'appeasement' at Munich and Yalta. Ex-Trotskyist Iraqi exile Kanan Makiya argued strongly for the American war, and involved himself in the planning process for the post-invasion society to be constructed by America. Incensed by reports of Colin Powell's cautious attitude to war, Makiya described him as an 'appeaser' at a New York University debate in 2002. Describing the sound of bombs falling on Iraq as 'music to my ears', he later watched the fall of Baghdad on television in the company of President Bush.[29]

Christopher Hitchens, by then a good friend of Deputy Secretary of Defense Paul Wolfowitz and convicted felon Ahmed Chalabi, argued that there would be no war deserving of the name, that the attack would be 'dazzling' and would be greeted as an 'emancipation', and enjoined the administration to 'bring it on'. He promised readers that Saddam did indeed possess weapons of mass destruction, and that the Baathist regime was connected to al-Qaeda through Islamist fighters operating in the north of Iraq. He chastised the 2 million anti-war demonstrators who gathered in Hyde Park:

> the assortment of forces who assembled demanded, in effect, that Saddam be allowed to keep the other five-sixths of Iraq as his own personal torture chamber. There are not enough words in any idiom to describe the shame and the disgrace of this.

However, moral clarity was soon proving to be a taxing business. In March 2003, reporting the apostasy of Thomas Friedman, he explained: 'I am fighting to keep my nerve'. And again,

> the population of Baghdad was making a secret holiday in its heart as those horrible palaces went up in smoke, and this holiday will soon be a public holiday, and if we all keep our nerve we can join the festivities with a fairly clear conscience.[30]

Michael Ignatieff was uncomfortable about being on the same side as the Bush regime, but he argued that the 'case for empire is that it has become, in a place like Iraq, the last hope for democracy and stability alike'. Paul Berman, a champion of what he calls the 'anti-totalitarian' Left, argued that the war on Iraq was part of the same combat as that with al-Qaeda, because 'al-Qaeda . . . and Saddam's Baath Party are two of the tendencies within a much larger phenomenon, which is a Muslim totalitarianism'. (In fact, Michel Aflaq, the doyen of secular Baathism, had been the son of Greek Orthodox Christians, and all the Baathist parties contained non-Muslim members, including Saddam Hussein's foreign minister, Tariq Aziz.) The neoconservatives, Berman continued, were correct that 'something fundamental has gone wrong in the political culture of the Middle East' and that liberal democracy was the only solution. Distrustful of the neocons, however, he pleaded for

> a left alternative to the neocon vision . . . a left-wing passion for democratic and liberal internationalism, a left-wing passion for anti-fascism and anti-totalitarianism, a passion to try as much as possible to square the means with the revolutionary liberal and humanitarian ends.[31]

The British liberal commentator, and columnist for the *Independent*, Johann Hari, repeatedly claimed that Iraqis favoured intervention before the war, and (quite erroneously) that this was supported by research by the International Crisis Group.[32] While allegations about the threat of Iraq's 'weapons of mass destruction' and the alleged relationship with al-Qaeda were prominent within the 'left-wing passion' for war, especially salient was the argument that an American-led invasion would represent 'liberation' for the people of Iraq. The combination of arguments was exactly the same as that presented by the Bush administration – indeed, several of these commentators appear to have taken their cue from the press conferences and representations of figures in the executive.[33]

'Islamic nihilism' and American annihilism

The discourse of human rights and their preservation had been adequate to galvanize widespread liberal support for military intervention in the former Yugoslavia. However, the wave of aggressive American expansionism prescribed by Bush demanded something more. Wars that would accumulate a heavy body-count, and that would involve the use of weapons designed to maximize damage to the population, such as cluster bombs and daisy-cutters, required a suitably dehumanized enemy. American renewal in its combat with the enemy – 'Islamic fascists' as Bush eventually designated them – would combine domestic with international repression. And while the Bush administration was rounding up Muslims and erecting its network of secret prisons to complement the prison multi-complex that was being opened in Guantánamo, the Islamophobic demagogy of public commentators was swift and copious. It is of course a staple of American rightist bigotry that, as Pat Robertson recently put it, Islam is 'a worldwide political movement meant [*sic*] on domination'. The liberal media watchdog, Media Matters for America, has documented dozens of cases of this particularly egregious form of Islam-bashing from the right.[34] Yet some of the most sedulous efforts in demonizing Islam have emerged from Bush's liberal defenders.

BHL, who styles himself an opponent of religious fundamentalism, was a key signatory to the statement, 'MANIFESTO: Together facing the new totalitarianism' (the 'new totalitarianism' in question being the Islamic kind); and – while he makes a crude distinction between 'moderate' and 'extremist' Islam – he does not hesitate to attack the signs and symbols of Islam as such. Thus, essaying on the condition of Muslim women, he informed us, *ex cathedra*, that '[t]he veil is an invitation to rape'. Adam Michnik wondered about 'the relationship between the terrorists who appeal to the Islamic religion, and the reality that none of the leading religious leaders of Islam condemned the crime'.[35]

The claim that there was something specifically and uniquely wrong with Islam was widespread. For Hitchens, it was a psychological deviation, a triumvirate of

> self-righteousness, self-pity, and self-hatred – the self-righteousness dating from the seventh century, the self-pity from the 13th (when the 'last' Caliph was kicked to death in Baghdad by the Mongol warlord Hulagu), and the self-hatred from the 20th.[36]

Responding to claims that US foreign policy had motivated the attacks, Hitchens expostulated that the grievance and animosity predate even the Balfour Declaration, let alone the occupation of the West Bank. They predate the creation of Iraq as a state. The gates of Vienna would have had to fall to the Ottoman *jihad* before any balm could begin to be applied to these psychic wounds.[37]

One might note in passing that, according to the logic of such argument-by-reference-to-atavistic-spiritual-remnants, it would be difficult to object to someone bent on explaining the modern Zionist movement in terms of a Mosaic psychic imbalance stored in the collective unconscious of Europe's Jewish population.

Telling an audience that the claim that suicide attacks in Palestine are driven by despair was 'evil nonsense', Hitchens remarked that those who do it adore their 'evil mullahs' (even where the attackers happen to be secular, as is often the case), and their 'evil preaching' (and 'vile religion'), and further that the act is an 'evil, wicked thing'. Even if we consider this with large helpings of interpretative charity, this is a myopic argument. In most of the research on suicide attacks, the decisive factors are political rather than religious ones. For example, Robert Pape's study of suicide attacks notes that, until 2000, the vast bulk of such attacks around the world had been carried out by secular-nationalist or Marxist groups. The strongest correlation was between the incidence of suicide attacks and the presence of an occupying army. Luca Ricolfi's study of Palestinian suicide attacks finds that religion is an enabling factor, but does not 'mould individuals, forcing them to become martyrs'. Among the relevant motivations are constant humiliation and 'severe material deprivation' – a miserable condition in which 'reality has shrunk to a minimum', thus providing the maximum space for myth and the symbolic in politics. Neither pecuniary nor religious motives are adequate explanation in themselves. It is the crushing and suffocating reality of contemporary Palestinian society that drives some people to carry out these actions.[38]

To dismiss conclusions based on solid empirical data as 'evil nonsense', and to insist dogmatically on those that are incompatible with that evidence, surely betrays an attitude more befitting a fundamentalist preacher than a secular humanist intellectual. Yet supporters of the 'war on terror' have often presented their Islam-bashing as part of an enlightened war of reason against entrenched superstition. Christopher Hitchens, if relentlessly reductionist about the role of Islam in inspiring 'evil', is at least willing to attack other religions. *God Is Not Great* affirms the not-so-contrarian title of Hitchens's recent polemic, which seeks to hold religion responsible not only for the

theocratic tyrannies of ancient and modern times, without qualification, but also for the secular tyrannies of modernity. An obvious
ramification of Hitchens's strident anti-theism is his willingness to
blame the Islamic religion for the ruin of Iraq under the US-led
occupation; this alongside a complete failure to notice that sectarian
religious parties are the closest allies of the occupying forces that he
supports. Although it is true that Hitchens has always been hostile to
religion, this animosity has only recently been mobilized to whitewash
the crimes of American foreign policy.[39]

Sam Harris was widely celebrated for his book, *The End of Faith*.
Yet his central claim is that, while Christianity and Judaism have
largely foresworn their savage past, the key threat is Islam, the thrust
of whose doctrine is 'undeniable: convert, subjugate, or kill
unbelievers; kill apostates; and conquer the world'. He goes on to
add that

> 'Muslim extremism' is not extreme among Muslims. Mainstream
> Islam itself represents an extremist rejection of intellectual
> honesty, gender equality, secular politics and genuine pluralism
> ... Muslims intentionally murder non-combatants, while we and
> the Israelis (as a rule) seek to avoid doing so ... [T]he people who
> speak most sensibly about the threat that Islam poses to Europe
> are actually fascists.[40]

When Christopher Hitchens countered Sam Harris's 'irresponsible'
argument that fascists were the sole repository of good sense in respect
of the Islamic threat, he boasted: 'Not while I'm alive, they won't
[be]'.[41] An advocate of war against 'Islamic fascism', he thus now finds
himself competing with fascists of the non-Islamo kind for the most
'sensible' line about the Muslim 'threat'.

Islam's alleged incompatibility with 'Western' values is frequently
emphasized. Will Hutton, a liberal supporter of New Labour and
signatory to the Euston Manifesto, wrote following the verdict of an
'honour killing' trial that

> many Muslims want to build mosques, schools, and adhere to
> Islamic dress codes with ever more energy. But that energy also
> derives from the same culture and accompanying institutions
> that produced British-born suicide bombers. The space in which
> to argue that Islam is an essentially benign religion seems to
> narrow with every passing day.[42]

It is worth pausing to consider the proximate cause of Hutton's scepticism about the prospects for coexistence: he sensed that the 'honour killing' of a young woman by her father and uncle was not only 'alien' but also 'connected to the family's religion – Islam'. Honour killing, which the UN estimates claims 5,000 lives each year, is forbidden in mainstream interpretations of Islam, while the practise extends well beyond Muslim societies. It might be added that the murder of women is not at all 'alien' to the 'West' which, Hutton avers, must 'stay true to itself'.[43] But the theme of specifically Muslim repression of women, and the accompanying figure of Western militaries as emancipators, is one that frequently emerges in apologetic discourse on the 'war on terror'.

Martin Amis, like his friend Hitchens, makes the link between his sense of Enlightenment and his hostility to Islam explicit. In his memoir *Experience*, Amis remarks at least twice that he thinks about Israel 'with the blood'. He adds that he will 'never be entirely reasonable about her'. Indeed, blood comes up quite a bit: he pines for a lost love who has gone to 'give blood' for Israel. To declare openly that one will never be rational about a defining political issue of the day advertises a sort of fanaticism. Yet this is how the mysticism of blood and soil, the giving of life's fluid back to the land itself, is converted into a liberal apologia for Zionism. He is presumably still thinking 'with the blood' when he encounters a gatekeeper at the Holy Mosque in the Arab Quarter of Jerusalem and declares: 'I saw in his eyes the assertion that he could do anything to me, to my wife, to my children, to my mother, and that this would only validate his rectitude'. He repeated this charming little anecdote in an anfractuous and fatuous three-part polemic for the *Observer* entitled 'The Age of Horrorism', in which the story of Political Islam is retold as a pseudo-psychoanalytical drama, with sexually repressed Muslim males raging against the unwittingly attractive American female.

Amis told *The Times* in 2007, in spittle-lathered manner, that

> there's a definite urge – don't you have it? – to say, 'The Muslim community will have to suffer until it gets its house in order.' What sort of suffering? Not letting them travel. Deportation – further down the road. Curtailing of freedoms. Strip-searching people who look like they're from the Middle East or from Pakistan . . . Discriminatory stuff, until it hurts the whole community and they start getting tough with their children . . . They hate us for letting our children have sex and take drugs – well, they've got to stop their children killing people.[44]

This confession was later attacked by the literary critic Terry Eagleton in the introduction to his book *Ideology*, producing some exchanges that were invariably referred to as a literary 'spat'. The fact that Amis had been recruited to lecture at Eagleton's place of employment, the University of Manchester, provided an added frisson. When asked about his comments by the columnist Yasmin Alibhai-Brown, Amis offered obsequious observations about her Shia identity ('the more dreamy and poetic face of Islam, the more lax and capacious', it 'endeared you to me, and made me feel protective'), but was dismissive of Eagleton's criticism. With by now characteristic stridency, he insisted that he was only confessing to a momentary sensation, not recommending anything. So: 'Can I ask him, in a collegial spirit, to shut up about it?' Perversely, he added: 'The extremists, for now, have the monopoly of violence, intimidation, and self-righteousness.'[45] Since the term 'extremists' in this usage clearly excluded those who had invaded and occupied Iraq under a rhetorical mantle of self-righteousness, Amis's statement constituted a simple performative contradiction, but served to corroborate his earlier claim of Western innocence.

Innocence, or as Anatol Lieven calls it, 'original sinlessness', is certainly relevant here. George W. has outlined its dimensions: 'I'm amazed that there's such a misunderstanding of what our country is about that people would hate us. I'm – like most Americans, I just can't believe it, because I know how good we are.'[46] Of course, 'most Americans' do not devise American foreign policy, but the point about Bush's faux *naïveté* is that it is a performance that deliberately evokes childhood, that land of pre-sexual innocence. When American presidents mimic Little Orphan Annie, as Gore Vidal once put it, they are inviting audiences to forget everything and once more partake of an 'idealism' that would otherwise seem rather soiled by the accretions of memory and history. They encourage a psychological regression, in which listeners identify America with how they felt about it as a child – any criticism of it is therefore an attack on one's childhood memories, and draws a powerful defensive response. More than that, the evocation of childhood is itself a powerful reassurance of funda-mental ethical innocence.[47]

So it is that, as American-led military forces have invaded Muslim countries and Israel has bombarded its Arab neighbours, the argument has been raised that, in fact, Muslims and Arabs are themselves invading 'us' (because they are jealous of our freedoms). This has produced a batch of neologisms, such as 'Eurabia', the title of a polemic by the right-wing British writer Bat Ye'or, which argues that Europe is being taken over by Arab Muslims in a curious alliance with

EU state leaders, while also directing European leaders away from their proper alliances with Israel and America. And 'Londonistan', the name of a book by the British neoconservative Melanie Phillips, maintains that the UK is incubating a future Islamist terror regime, in which London is 'a global hub of the Islamic jihad', with thousands of British Muslims actively supporting terrorism, and hundreds preparing to strike the mainland. Neither author actually coined the phrases, but they have popularized them among supporters of the hard right, while overlaying them with racist dramaturgy.

'Londonistan', a contemporary equivalent of the old anti-Semitic term 'Jew York', has entered the lexicon of the 'war on terror', is used without apparent irony by defenders of Western liberalism such as Christopher Hitchens and Nick Cohen, and is now common parlance in American newspapers. The precise definition of the term is hard to pin down, its connotation exceeding its denotation. For Hitchens, it refers to the presence of a Muslim minority in London, many of whom are refugees from 'battles against Middle Eastern and Asian regimes which they regard as insufficiently Islamic'. They 'bring a religion which is not ashamed to speak of conquest and violence', says Hitchens, an author rarely ashamed to speak of conquest and violence.[48]

Similarly, as the American government arbitrarily detained thousands of Muslims,[49] while cultivating hostility towards them with its rhetoric, and kidnapped people all over the globe and subjected them to torture in secret prisons that easily out-do their Stasi precedents, it was not long before the argument was heard that Muslim countries are in fact resuscitating twentieth-century barbarism. In May 2006, a story appeared in the Canadian *National Post* that was subsequently picked up by a number of right-wing newspapers and websites, as well as some liberal ones. It claimed that Iran was planning to pass laws that would oblige non-Muslims to wear badges to indicate their ethnicity, so that they could be distinguished in public. Replete with 'Nazi' references and illustrated with photographs of Jews bearing the yellow stars imposed by the Third Reich, this story turned out to be completely false – and, to be fair, both the *National Post* and the *New York Post* have since removed the story from their websites. One effect of this ceaseless stream of anti-Muslim propaganda was revealed a few months later. A Gallup poll released in August 2006 found that almost four in ten Americans thought that Muslim Americans should be obliged to carry special ID, which at least hints at the idea that barbarism is not the exclusive property of non-Americans. In March 2006, it was found that negative impressions of Islam among Americans had almost doubled since 2002.[50]

Indeed, given the palpable hostility of these commentators, one would expect a seam of accompanying violent rhetoric. And that is what we get. Against this unspeakable enemy, Sam Harris mandates torture as a form of 'collateral damage' in the 'war on terror'. Nick Cohen has argued that anyone even suspected of terrorism by the intelligence services should be deported, even if they are likely to be tortured, and suggested that torture may be necessary under certain circumstances. Christopher Hitchens stops short of this, but is strangely drawn to eliminationist rhetoric. Following the November 2004 siege of Fallujah, Hitchens remarked that 'the death toll is not nearly high enough . . . too many [jihadists] have escaped'. Similarly, about the Islamists, he had this to say:

> We can't live on the same planet as them and I'm glad because I don't want to. I don't want to breathe the same air as these psychopaths and murders [sic] and rapists and torturers and child abusers. It's them or me. I'm very happy about this because I know it will be them. It's a duty and a responsibility to defeat them. But it's also a pleasure. I don't regard it as a grim task at all.[51]

He later told those present at the christening of the David Horowitz Freedom Center that 'it's sort of a pleasure as well as a duty to kill these people'. He also commiserated with his friend Martin Amis on his unfortunate desire to 'punish' Muslims: What does one do with thoughts like this? How does one respond 'when an enemy challenges not just your cherished values but additionally forces you to examine the very assumptions that have heretofore seemed to underpin those values?'[52] Will it be necessary to destroy liberalism in order to save it? It is quite something to witness liberals collapse into this kind of nonsense and still call themselves liberals or even leftists; but for them to claim that they have been coerced into it by the 'enemy', and complain about it as if it were only another burden for the white man to bear, is surely a matchless stroke of self-satire.[53] By a familiar alchemy, then, the manifest intolerance, prejudice and hostility of both liberal and neoconservative pundits towards Muslims is articulated in terms of *Islamic* intolerance, prejudice and hostility. Such projection is, as later chapters will further elaborate, a classic feature of imperialism, including in its most barbaric modes.

In a recent book, *Imperial Grunts*, Robert Kaplan compares the current multifaceted war against various selected Islamists to the nineteenth-century wars against Native Americans. In fact, he describes how soldiers in places as different as Colombia and Afghanistan

greeted him by welcoming him to 'Injun Country' – a quite commonplace reference in American imperial ideology. 'This is breathtaking',
said David Rieff. 'Here is a serious writer in 2005 admiring the Indian
Wars, which in their brutality brought about the end of an entire civilization'. Kaplan's book lauds the foot-soldiers of the empire, the
'imperial grunts' as he calls them, and celebrates the fact that 'by the
turn of the twenty-first century the United States military had already
appropriated the entire earth, and was ready to flood the most obscure
areas of it with troops at a moment's notice'. 'Islamic terrorism', he
maintains, has become 'the sharp edge of a seeping anarchy'. The
enemy, the barbarian, can thus be compared with the Indian tribes that
American civilization set out to exterminate. Kaplan exalts Rudyard
Kipling, the poet of empire, and his contemporary Frederic
Remington, whose paintings and sculptures captured the white man's
burden in action as the Native Americans were finished off. To them,
Kaplan remarks, the 'white man's burden' meant 'the righteous
responsibility to advance the boundaries of free society and good
government into zones of sheer chaos, a mission not unlike that of
post-Cold War humanitarian interventionists'.[54]

Kriegsideologie

Anatol Lieven, in his study of American nationalism, compared the
post-9/11 climate in the United States to the 'Spirit of 1914' that pre-
vailed across Europe on the outbreak of World War I. As Chapter 1
will discuss, recent historical findings have cast doubt on this 'spirit',
but the comparison is nevertheless perceptive. As Domenico Losurdo
illustrates in his *Heidegger and the Ideology of War*, that era also generated a striking martial discourse (*Kriegsideologie*), which insisted on
civilizational explanations for war. It was then mainly thinkers of the
German right who elaborated the discourse. Max Weber, though
politically liberal, argued that the war was not about profit, but about
German existence, 'destiny' and 'honour'. Some even saw it as 'a
religious and holy war, a *Glaubenswieg*'. Then, too, it was hoped that
war would restore social solidarity, and authenticity to life. The
existentialist philosopher Edmund Husserl explained: 'The belief that
one's death signifies a voluntary sacrifice, bestows sublime dignity and
elevates the individual's suffering to a sphere which is beyond each
individuality. We can no longer live as private people.'[55]

And in November 1917,

> Ideas and ideals are again in motion, and again find an open
> heart to welcome them . . . Death has once again regained its

original sacred right. It is here again to remind one of eternity. And thus again we have developed organs to see German idealism.

Nazism inherited *Kriegsideologie*, and this was reported and experienced by several of those closest to the regime as a remake of the 'wonderful, communal experience of 1914'. In *Philosophie* (1932), Karl Jaspers exalted the 'camaraderie that is created in war [and that] becomes unconditional loyalty'. 'I would betray myself if I betrayed others, if I wasn't determined to unconditionally accept my people, my parents, and my love, since it is to them that I owe myself.' (Jaspers, though a nationalist and political elitist like Max Weber, was not a biological racist, and his Jewish wife would fall foul of Nazi race laws.) Heidegger argued that '[w]ar and the camaraderie of the front seem to provide the solution to the problem of creating an organic community by starting from that which is most irreducibly individual, that is, death and courage in the face of death'. For him, the much-coveted life of bourgeois peace was 'boring, senile, and, though contemplatable', was 'not possible'.[56]

These are family resemblances, rather than linear continuities. The emergence of communism as a clear and present danger to nation-states, and the post-war conflagrations of class conflict, sharpened the anti-materialism of European rightists who were already critical of humanism, internationalism and the inauthenticity of commercial society. Their dilemma was different, and their animus was directed against communism – a political formation that barely registers in the United States today except as critique. But some general patterns suggest themselves. The recurring themes of *Kriegsideologie* were community, danger and death. The community is the nation (or civilization) in existential peril; danger enforces a rigorous moral clarity and heightens one's appreciation of fellow citizens; death is what 'they' must experience so that 'we' do not. We have heard from American commentators and politicians relishing a fight to the death, enlivened by an urgency and sudden sense of clarity, urging a new sense of solidarity guided by patriotism (with its implicit and explicit exclusions). These, I maintain – the barbarian virtues of the early-twentieth-century German right – have infused the lingua franca of American imperialism. But then, as Chapter 3 discusses, they were present all along.

In this prologue I have outlined some of the reactions to the attacks on New York and Washington on 11 September 2001. An ideology of war, both domestic and foreign, has since been elaborated, often coyly, but sometimes with brutal clarity. A refulgent American nationalism has frequently been its hallmark. Many of the supporters of Bush's expansionist policies would protest that they were imperialists long before 9/11, and long before it was again fashionable to call it imperialism. This is true. In the following chapters I intend to outline the historical roots and precedents of liberal and socialist support for imperialism – in particular the impact that centuries of European world-domination have exerted upon the consciousness of the inhabitants of both that continent and its colonial offshoots. In the concluding chapter I will weigh the claims for the humanitarianism of such ventures and for their consistency with left-wing, or even 'anti-totalitarian', principles.

1

FORGING OLD EUROPE

It is curious how all roads in England – liberalism, pacifism, socialism, etc. – lead to the maintenance of the Empire.
                                                    – *Jawaharlal Nehru*[1]

The tradition of imperial liberalism is almost as old and perplexing as liberalism itself. On the face of it, a doctrine that appears to stress human equality and universalism[2] ought to have nothing to do with a violent system of domination and exploitation. Yet, for many liberals, the virtues of empire were then very much as they are now for 'liberal interventionists': it promised pedagogy, cultural therapy, economic development, the rule of law, liberty, and even, sometimes, feminism. Later, it would become commonplace for imperial rule to be seen as the threshold for socialism too. To understand this is to grasp the deranging impact of centuries of organized white supremacy, and the increasingly triumphalist narratives that went along with it. It is also to touch on the strategies that European states elaborated for dealing with class conflict, and for integrating (or co-opting) dissidents.

Liberal Herrenvolk

Beginning with the subjugation of Ireland and the imposition of emerging capitalist property forms, the British colonization of the New World was soon underpinned by a slave-based labour system which gradually replaced the impressment and indenturing of domestic white labourers, and the extermination of native inhabitants of colonized land. Liberal ideas about the international order, drawing to a great extent on early-modern humanism and on Hugo Grotius in particular, provided a great deal of the ideological sustenance for the empire-builders. Grotius, the founder of international law *avant la lettre*, had been the Dutch republic's most auspicious legal authority on the right to colonize, just as the republic was waging an offensive war to colonize the East Indies. As Locke would go on to argue, Grotius maintained that the rights of the state derived from a delegation and aggregation of the 'natural rights' of any individual in the 'state of nature' (putatively, the condition of human beings before states emerged). These included not only the right to liberty but a perceived corollary right to property. One consequence was to justify the Dutch Revolt, which had overthrown King Philip II of Spain, as a legitimate assertion of man's rights. Another was to justify the wars waged by the United East Indies Company – since individuals bore the same rights as states, they could wield violence in much the same way in the absence of an authoritative state. Moreover, the Dutch had a perfect right to obtain property in the East Indies so long as they did not deprive others of their legitimately obtained property. Grotius's famous argument for the 'freedom of the seas' was an attempt to prove that the Portuguese could not legally obstruct the Dutch colonists, since they could not legitimately own the seas. Further, since it was permissible in the 'state of nature' for individuals to punish others who are offensive and immoderate, so he maintained that it was permissible for Dutch colonists to punish those who frustrated their activities – so not only was colonialism justified; piracy, including the theft of bullion from Portuguese colonists, was also claimed as a natural right. And when the Dutch turned from sea-borne imperialism to territorial expansion, Grotius began to argue that the military intervention of colonialists into societies with customs deemed barbaric was just.[3]

John Locke, who devised the principles that would underpin the British polity and property relations following the 'Glorious Revolution' in 1688, also formulated the principles justifying the British empire as it colonized parts of the Atlantic coast of the Americas and the Caribbean islands, and was a member of the Board of Trade and Plantations for some of that time. The basis for his defence was a theory of property expressed in *Two Treatises of Government*, in which a person might rightfully appropriate a portion of land on the basis of having mixed his labour with it. Radicalizing Grotius's conception of the right to acquire and defend property, Locke maintained that it was God's command that the goods of the earth be captured and cultivated, rather than wasted. Peoples and nations which break the 'law of nature' are subject to private punishment, including war. Colonists should not 'exterminate' the natives of colonized territory, by any means, but they have a right to constrain and punish them to prevent them from appropriating property wilfully.[4]

Land, as the chief form of property, might thus be lawfully acquired in 'barren' territories where no sovereign authority operated, and where it was deemed that rational, industrious Europeans could make proper use of it. And, in circumstances where property was a nebulous concept, it was possible to appropriate according to one's wants and deny others the ability to do so. Barbara Arniel writes, 'From its inception, the natural right to property is defined in such a way as to exclude non-Europeans from being able to exercise it'. Locke's participation in the slave trade perhaps seems odd for a philosopher of natural law and someone who had declared slavery to be 'so vile and miserable an Estate of Man' that ''tis hardly to be conceived that an Englishman, much less a Gentleman, should plead for it'. However, this expressed Locke's opposition to the enslavement of *Englishmen*, not of Africans. For Locke, colonial slavery could be justified in terms of 'the state of war continued, between a lawful Conqueror, and a Captive'. Not only did Locke plead for slavery, he profited from it. As Bernasconi and Mann suggest, 'to advocate, administer, and profit from a specifically racialised form of slavery is clear evidence of racism, if the word is to have any meaning at all'.[5] Liberal theories of international order would continue to bear the marks of racism throughout the colonial period and beyond.

When, in the late eighteenth century, the British Empire faced serial challenges from its former colonists in the Americas, the turn to India and the East, with its devastating effects on local populations, produced the first serious efforts to curtail its excesses and even challenge its legitimacy. The mass challenge to slavery is well understood, and sometimes the British abandonment of slavery and efforts to suppress the trade are themselves treated as noble examples of proto-humanitarian intervention at work. Yet, as David Brion Davis has suggested, that view is susceptible to robust challenge:

> If we take a quick snapshot of Britain in the late eighteenth and early nineteenth centuries, it is not the first country we would choose in predicting the leader of a vast crusade to stamp out the slave trade and liberate hundreds of thousands, or, through its influence, millions of slaves . . . Inequalities of power had shaped British society like a vast pyramid, with the nobility and great landlords at the top, in control of a highly decentralised government . . . Before 1832, suffrage was limited to a tiny minority, mostly owners of very substantial property . . . In Ireland, a small Protestant minority exploited the country as if it were a plantation. In far-off India the British drew extraordinary wealth from systems of exploitative labour that were arguably as bad as the slavery in the West Indies but that received far less publicity. (Indeed, it was not until 1860 that it became illegal in India to

own a slave.) In England itself, young men of the lower orders were vulnerable to being kidnapped by press gangs and forcibly conscripted into the navy, where the punishment of flogging was at least as common as on a slave plantation.[6]

Yet, despite certain reservations, and with growing regret and disillusion, the British state did suppress the slave trade (much to the annoyance of their former American colonists – see Chapter 2), and did not, as is commonly thought, stand to gain from more efficient labour as a result. Part of the explanation is that, although the anti-slavery movement was animated by sentiments of solidarity, the anti-slavery campaigners actively 'concealed all humanitarian motives' from the government when pushing for a Foreign Slave Trade Bill in 1806, and framed their argument in terms of profit and national self-interest. In doing so, they engaged with an elite that was increasingly optimistic about the prospects for a more efficient national economy through reform and social engineering – which is why the realization that slavery remained an extremely cost-effective form of surplus-extraction caused such consternation in the years that followed.[7]

Sankar Muthu has shown that, aside from criticism of the slave trade, the Enlightenment produced a brief, vivid critique of empire. Kant, Herder, and Diderot based their antipathy to empire on both a universalist humanitarianism and an insistence on respect for non-European cultures (the latter stance is often, in a confused way, condemned today as condescending 'relativism' that overlooks the negative aspects of those cultures). For example, Kant's conception of humans as cultural agents, whose activities are determined by a range of socially and environmentally conditioned choices, allowed for a broad conception of rationality that underpinned his opposition to colonial domination. Since humans were not naturally 'savage' or 'noble', their forms of life could be understood as inherently rational. Dispensing with his early biological hierarchy of races (in which he concurred with Hume that 'Negroes' might well be mentally below par), he also rejected Locke's conception of property, since 'developing land is nothing more than the external sign of taking possession' rather than a legitimate cause for doing so. He insisted in *Toward Perpetual Peace* on the rights of citizens of the world, as partaking of a 'universal state of mankind', and proposed, in place of imperialism, peaceful transnational relations between peoples. Importantly, not only did Kant oppose the means of empire (coercion), but he also criticized its ends (civilization, cultural transformation) on the universalist grounds of cosmopolitan freedom.[8]

Edmund Burke notoriously sought the impeachment of Warren Hastings, the first governor-general of British India, on account of the East India Company's depredations in India. He saw its violence, repression and corruption as systemic and not incidental, rooted in the failure to see Indians as fully human – a lapse of the moral imagination. Bentham would lambast both the slave trade and the colonies (although, as in the case of India, he did not always favour self-government). As Jennifer Pitts has argued, rather than being based purely on the calculation of interests, Bentham's criticisms embodied moral objections to the 'manifest injury' and 'manifest oppression' that empire necessitated. In contrast to much triumphalist thought about the superiority of British rule of law, he argued that the imposition of British law – so mediocre and vexatious in his analysis – on India was both unwise and wanton.[9] Despite its many limitations, this body of thought provided the basis for future critiques of empire and the racist codes that legitimize it.

Yet, by the 1830s at least, the sceptical attitude to empire elaborated by Enlightenment liberals had been replaced by an almost uniform support for the colonial enterprise among those who advocated the extension of self-government domestically. For example, John Stuart Mill, an advocate of extending the franchise to the working class in Britain, argued in his 1854 essay, 'On Liberty', that some societies were in such a backward state that 'the race itself may be considered as in its nonage' – thus, as the equivalents of children, they may be considered exempt from the doctrine of liberty. Further: 'Despotism is a legitimate mode of government in dealing with barbarians' – the sequel was crucial – 'provided the end be their improvement, and the means justified by actually effecting that end'. Until such time as they were improved, 'implicit obedience to an Akbar or Charlemagne' was their lot. Further to this humanitarian argument for colonial autocracy, which set a precedent that has not ceased to be imitated, there was the progressivist one: it was acceptable to use dominative relationships to nurture liberal democracies, since this would eventually result in a world composed of liberal-democratic states in which there would be no imperial powers. In 'A Few Words on Non-Intervention' (1859), he argued for a strict dichotomy between the legal and political standards one should apply to the 'natives' and those applicable to civilized nations. Though he was not a biological racist, and indeed condemned Carlyle's vituperations regarding congenital racial difference, he partook of a cultural supremacism and a self-congratulatory civilizational discourse that authorized colonial domination. What is particularly damning is his complete lack of interest in the truth of his assertions about the 'savage life', despite his deep involvement in the empire and his access to wide-ranging empirical study.[10]

Alexis de Tocqueville, whose wisdom is often tapped for contemporary commentary on democracy, is not as well known for his writings on empire. Though sometimes critical of the British empire's depredations in India, Tocqueville was nevertheless a great admirer of colonialism, and took part in several illuminating exchanges with John Stuart Mill on the topic. Perceiving colonies as an ideal solution to France's domestic problems and as a route to national glory, he urged the conquest of Algeria on the French. Like Theodore Roosevelt after him, Tocqueville perceived the materialism and egotism of emerging bourgeois societies as enfeebling. Although he argued that war was destructive of democracy and that it encouraged authoritarianism, he nevertheless believed that it 'enlarges the mind of a people and raises their character'. This may seem incongruent with Tocqueville's liberalism and approval of American democracy. Yet, as Jennifer Pitts argues, Tocqueville's support for colonialism throws his views on America into new relief – for instance, his sense that both Amerindians and African slaves were incapable of participating in democracy, and had to be excluded for it to thrive. Tocqueville constantly invoked the inferiority of indigenous peoples when justifying European colonialism. Thus, the coastal Arabs in Algeria were 'half-savage peoples' who 'honour power and force above all else'. Tocqueville was not always as hostile in his depictions of the colonized, but he did partake of Orientalist discourses, in which Arabs were viewed variously as static, ungovernable, sensual, shrewd, and inconstant. And however critical he frequently was of the methods used in conquest, which he commented ironically were 'more barbaric' than those of the Arabs, he did believe that it was the duty of Europeans to civilize non-Europeans. And he came to see empire and the frontier as being fundamentally intertwined with progress and democracy, rather than as merely incidental facts about democratic states.[11]

Like Mill, Tocqueville was directly involved in the building of empire. As a member of the French National Assembly, he was charged with drawing up a report with recommendations for French strategy in combating the resistance to colonial rule in Algeria. The report called for an uncompromising war, since 'our domination of Africa must be firmly maintained'. At no stage whatsoever should the colonized be allowed to think of themselves as 'our compatriots and our equals'. He generously stated, after visiting Algeria in 1846, that he did not wish to exterminate the natives. But he insisted that it was foolhardy to trust in the 'goodwill of the natives' or allow them a 'regular government', which they were not yet fit for. On grounds such as these, he would go as far as to advocate racial segregation for Algeria. Unlike Mill, who judged the colonies on the principle of utility, Tocqueville did not always feel obliged to qualify this with appeals to the amelioration of the colonized.[12] And whatever criticisms he had of the British, he was moved to remark, upon hearing of the Indian Rebellion: 'I have never for an instance doubted your triumph, which is that of Christianity and civilization'. 'Nothing under the sun,' he wrote, was 'so wonderful as the conquest, and still more the government, of India by the English.' Pitts remarks that the

> emergence of support for violent conquest and despotic rule of non-Europeans in the mid-nineteenth century, among thinkers normally celebrated not only for their respect for human equality and liberty but also for their pluralism, implicates the liberal tradition, at this moment in its history, in an inegalitarian and decidedly nonhumanitarian international politics.[13]

Perhaps the key turning point in the consolidation of triumphalist, racially arrogant imperialism was the Great Indian Rebellion of 1857, stimulated by a combination of racial arrogance on the part of the Company's British soldiers towards sepoy soldiers, religious affront, and the growing extraction by the company from the Diwani class that the sepoy foot-soldiers were from. It rapidly spread throughout the whole of Indian society, involving agents from every class and ethnicity. The British, confronted with the Rebellion, were not merely astonished and outraged at the ingratitude of the natives, who did not appreciate the civilization that governed them. They were so determined to annihilate their opponents that they descended into the most extreme depravities. Wherever they beat the rebels militarily, the British embarked on a wave of terror. Not only rebels, but suspected sympathizers were hanged. Children parading in rebel colours were strung up. Villages were shelled, burned and sacked. Women were raped to death. Estimates of sepoy and civilian deaths are alarmingly imprecise – the English did not do body-counts – but estimates have tended to include at least 100,000 sepoy deaths. A recent estimate of the total post-Rebellion mortality, including the ongoing 'vengeance' and the famines that resulted from repression, suggests up to 10 million deaths, a figure that is entirely plausible in light of the terrible record of famine and repression under the British empire. As Mike Davis points out, between 1872 and 1921, life expectancy in India fell by 20 per cent. Per capita income did not grow at all from the British arrival in 1757 to their departure 190 years later – in fact, there was a drop of 50 per cent in the latter half of the nineteenth century. Vivek Chibber writes:

> According to the most reliable estimates, the deaths from the 1876–1878 famine were in the range of 6 to 8 million, and in the double-barreled famine of 1896–1897 and 1899–1900, they probably totaled somewhere in the range of 17 to 20 million. So in the quarter century that marks the pinnacle of colonial good governance, famine deaths average at least a million per year.[14]

To justify this terror, it was necessary to exaggerate and invent sepoy atrocities. In a fashion typical of the cocktail of racism and misogyny mixed by empire-builders, the greatest outrage was reserved for the confected rape of white women by 'niggers'. When these fictions were exposed in the *Manchester Guardian* a year later, it made little difference.[15] Charles Dickens, a sentimental Victorian reformer who had previously been critical of some of the cruelties of the East India Company, wrote to Emile de La Rue in October 1857:

> I wish I were Commander in Chief over there! I would address that oriental character which must be powerfully spoken to, in something like the following placard . . . 'I, the Inimitable, holding this office of mine . . . have the honour to inform you Hindoo gentry that it is my intention, with all possible avoidance of unnecessary cruelty and with all merciful swiftness of execution, to exterminate the Race from the face of the earth, which disfigured the earth with abominable atrocities'.

He would later, in the afterglow of the Jamaican Rebellion of 1865, also crushed with unconscionable barbarity, marshal the discourse of scientific racism. The 'original African negro,' he said, 'is not a high moral type'. Further: 'Naturally improvident and indolent', he fell

> lower in the scale of humanity, not, however, without crying out against the oppressors who would not feed him in idleness, and not without repeated attempts at rebellion, in the senseless hope that by murdering those oppressors and seizing their property he would at last attain the goal of affluent indolence.[16]

Two important results of the insurgency were the imposition of direct rule from Britain, in the form of the Raj, and the growing prominence of the racist doctrine of 'Aryanism'. The Aryan idea has its origins in the heart of the British Empire. It was a result of the Company's growing control over revenue-collecting and the need to develop an understanding of the texts and languages of the colonized. Not merely a suppuration of imperialism, it became an important fact about the way the empire was organized, and eventually it was offered as the reason why the empire had come about. Essentially, it posited an Indo-European race based upon certain philological affinities between Sanskrit and the Greek and Latin languages. The thesis was that the world's populations could be divided into 'races' descended from Biblical figures – Aryan, Semitic and Tartar. The Aryan race had, it was maintained, invaded and inhabited India during the Vedic 'golden age' and formed a precocious civilization. The post-Vedic age in India had been a sustained period of degeneration: by contrast, the Aryans of Europe were in rude health. These categories not only provided an argument for empire; they also helped to cement British power with the caste system.[17]

The Indian Rebellion sharpened the argument over Aryanism, since it had suddenly become a pressing question whether Britons could really have descended from such savages. The response included both an intense, maddened loathing of dark-skinned people, and the spiritualization of race. Thus, in the promotion of Christianity as a marker of inherent cultural difference between the races, particularly important was the trope of 'fanaticism', as applied to both Hinduism and Islam: 'native fanaticism' was an artefact of an inherent spiritual corruption and degeneracy, not of colonialism. Since the English interlopers were supposed to belong to the same 'race' as those who had invented and practised 'authentic' Hinduism, the argument had to be that it had been exposed to a corrupting influence, and the blame was typically placed on Islam – a theme appropriated by Hindu nationalists.[18]

Imperialist racism was, of course, hopelessly muddled, and as a consequence was obliged to operate through metaphor. For example, if the Irish were not easily subsumed into the Tartar or Semitic 'races' – in fact, there was some feeling that the Celts had ancient connections with the Aryans – they nevertheless could be found to bear curious resemblances either to American Indians in their manner of habitat, or to 'human chimpanzees'. Carlyle's denunciation of Irish rebels thus included the demand: 'Black-lead them and put them over with the niggers'.[19] Nevertheless, the ideology of Aryanism was crucial both in the development of anti-Semitism and, in a complementary fashion, Orientalism. Arabs, referred to by Disraeli as 'Jews on horseback', were bracketed in the same 'Semitic' racial category as Jews. This supplies part of the explanation for the striking similarities between anti-Muslim and anti-Jewish racism. European race theorists such as Ernest Renan could slip between an essential 'racial' discourse about Arabs and depictions of an 'Islam' without history or development: 'No Semite advanced in time beyond the development of a 'classical' period . . . Every manifestation of the actual "Semitic" life could be, and ought to be, referred back to the primitive explanatory category of the "Semitic".' Most importantly, these categories were defended as part of a liberal, humanistic discourse. To Europe's rationalism, dynamism and liberty was counterposed the fanaticism, laziness and despotism of 'Mohammedanism' and the Orient. As Edward Said has put it,

> Underlying these categories is the rigidly binomial opposition of 'ours' and 'theirs', with the former always encroaching upon the latter (even to the point of making 'theirs' exclusively a function of 'ours'). This opposition was reinforced not only by anthropology, linguistics, and history but also, of course, by the Darwinian theses on survival and natural selection, and – no less decisive – by the rhetoric of high cultural humanism. What gave writers like Renan and Arnold the right to generalities about race was the official character of their formed cultural literacy. 'Our' values were (let us say) liberal, humane, correct: they were supported by the tradition of belles-lettres, informed scholarship, rational inquiry; as Europeans (and white men) 'we' shared in them every time their virtues were extolled.[20]

The threat of removing control from the East India Company prompted Mill, in his capacity as the Company's Examiner of Indian Correspondence, to compose a detailed defence of the Company's impact on India. As far as he was concerned, these included the suppression of 'Hindoo prejudice', particularly infanticide, sati (the burning of widows on the deceased husband's pyre), human sacrifice, and laws against remarriage. The claim of Company initiative in these cases is misleading, since the impetus for these reforms came from Indians themselves, but it has been a common fixture of Eurocentric histories that it was the impact of a modernizing colonialism that stirred the reformers into action. In fact these issues were important to the development of another strand of imperial ideology, for here too are some of the ingredients of what Valerie Amos and Pratibha Parmar have referred to as 'Imperial Feminism', by which they describe how a white, Eurocentric and colonizing discourse 'sought to establish itself as the only legitimate feminism in current political practice', and in which the mistreatment of women 'came to be seen as definitive of primitive societies'. Indeed, one of the earliest empire tracts, James Mill's *A History of British India*, viewing the condition of women as an indicator of social advancement, argued that 'nothing can exceed the habitual contempt which Hindus entertain for their women'. If Hindu women were seen as passive and Hindu men unnatural and barbaric, the British form of gender relation in which women were held to be house-bound adjuncts to their male partner in a family unit was held to be 'proper'.[21]

The origins of proto-feminist discourses favouring colonialism lie, Claire Midgely argues, in the anti-slavery movement. The white women who participated in the campaigns against slavery also challenged the treatment of those they referred to as their sisters in the colonized world. They used the same language – hence the campaign against the application of the 'Contagious Diseases Act' was described as a 'new abolitionism'. But, while professing their sorority with colonized women, they did not challenge colonialism: rather they sought to use it as the instrument of reform. They solemnly undertook the task of defending the 'helpless, voiceless, hopeless' 'dumb animal'. Though regarding non-white men as especially endowed with innate propensities for violence against women, they were 'wounded' to hear that these women were also being oppressed not merely by 'some half-wild, benighted Race' but 'by those who are connected with us by the closest ties'. Thus, the early feminist Catherine Macaulay saw nothing positive about the condition of women in non-Western societies, regarding it as a static affair, unchangingly oppressive and oppressively unchanging. Mary Wollstonecraft located in 'savage' African and 'despotic' Oriental societies a past 'night of sensual ignorance' which European women could escape from by becoming (and being allowed to become) more like rational European men. Their claim to fuller participation in public life was underwritten by their role as moral reformers of the empire. This was also true of some feminists in the German empire when it emerged – particularly those of the *Bund Deutscher Frauenverein*, who argued in favour of a 'peaceful imperialism' in which the Reich could undermine the internationalism of some feminists by integrating women properly into the nation. Aside from providing a basis for the claims of women in European societies, imperial feminism also supplied the animating illusion that, in stark contrast with those of non-white societies, white women were emancipated. Feminists in the British empire thus accepted the discourse of race, 'claimed racial responsibility' as saviours of the Anglo-Saxon race, and as a consequence believed themselves to be the highest female type.[22] Though many of the reforms they pursued were in themselves laudable, the imperial feminists, in effect, demanded a Human Rights Watch policy from an exploitative, murderous system whose right to exist they never questioned.

Arguably, nineteenth-century liberal imperialism reached its zenith with Gladstone's annexation of Egypt in 1882. Egypt had been an important strategic interest for Britain throughout the century, especially after the opening of the Suez Canal, in which the British government acquired a 44 per cent stake, and which provided a short route to India. Britain, alongside France, exercised direct control over the Egyptian economy, and therefore had a direct interest in its future. Gladstone had run his election campaign, the celebrated 'Midlothian campaign', beginning in late 1879, as a critique of Disraeli's imperialist policies towards Egypt and Afghanistan, the brutal repression of the Zulus and the annexation of the Transvaal in South Africa. Egypt, close to bankruptcy on account of the costs of the canal – which fell most heavily and brutally on the peasantry – was nominally under the rule of the Ottoman empire. However, it was sufficiently under Anglo-French control for Khedive Ismail, the ruler since 1863, to be overthrown in 1879 when he ceased payments on debts racked up under extortionate terms to British banks such as the Rothschilds. Even with Ismail deposed, the payments were difficult to extract. The payments had to come from taxation, and securing them required extreme brutality, torture and floggings. This stimulated mass resistance from the peasantry, and one of the figures held responsible for the disturbance was Sayyid Jamal al-Din al-Afghani, the Muslim reformer whose writings so influenced the development of contemporary political Islam. An opposition movement rallied under the slogan, 'Egypt for the Egyptians', against an administration that was dominated by Europeans.[23]

Gladstone was himself a co-owner of the debt and, whatever his criticisms of Disraeli's policy, showed no intention of allowing it go unpaid. But the revolt that took place gained the support of the army, which was threatened by the government's cutbacks. Colonel Ahmed Urabi, an army officer with a peasant background, came to head the rebellion. When the government tried to arrest him and several of his followers, it provoked open mutiny and a humiliating climb-down from the government. The army was therefore able to impose a nationalist administration on the government. This provided Gladstone with the reason he needed to occupy Egypt. The country, he declared, had to be saved from a military junta. Although the opposition was at this point demanding a constitutional government, which the Liberals supported in theory, in practise such an arrangement would deprive the British of control of the economy. They therefore leaned heavily on the Khedive against the nationalist claims of the Chamber of Notables, and forced the nationalists to rely increasingly on the army. Dispatching warships, the Anglo-French alliance demanded that the Khedive disband the nationalist Chamber and deport the Urabists. When the Egyptian government refused to hand over the control of forts at the port of Alexandria to the British, a sustained bombardment was perpetrated. As anti-colonial riots spread across Egypt, Gladstone argued that the bombing at least demonstrated that 'the fanaticism of the East' would not be permitted to kill Europeans 'with impunity', and therefore had hastened a peaceable settlement. As the British invaded, Joseph Chamberlain told the House of Commons that its sole purpose was 'liberating the national sentiment in Egypt', and won the support of the overwhelming majority of Liberal MPs as a result. Such liberation entailed the murder of thousands of Egyptians, repression of the peasant rebellion and the systematic use of torture. It would later take Britain to war against the 'fanatical' Mahdist insurgents in Sudan.[24]

Liberal imperialism thus constructed the colonial subjects at best as passive victims, needful of tutelage, capable of self-government only after a spell of European supremacy, and at worst as fanatics and murderers, racially degenerate peoples given to tyranny and unnatural practises, fit only for subordination. The imposition of highly exploitative systems on the colonized was seen not only as advantageous to them, but as natural – a logical step en route to civilization. If liberal supporters of empire had initially been optimistic about the prospects of raising the natives to lofty European heights, the experience of resistance and defiance, so bewildering to them, converted them to the belief that the colonized were savages in need of a stern hand of repression. It was a pattern that would repeat itself throughout the twentieth century.

Social democracy and empire

From the very origins of socialism and social democracy as unique currents independent of liberalism, strong pro-imperialist currents existed within them, including among those who claimed to owe their politics to Marx and Engels. Like their liberal antecedents, they drew upon Enlightenment ideals of progress, social engineering and humanitarianism to legitimize, rather than criticize, empire.

The example of Marx and Engels

'Marx believed the barbaric races should be civilised', Ward Churchill has written, so that they may be 'turned into workers because then they could become proletarian revolutionaries'. Similarly, according to Edward Said, Marx's writings on India bear the stamp of Orientalism. According to Said, Marx entertained an enduring and repeated conviction that colonial rule made social revolution possible, and therefore he was able to contemplate any kind of cruelty that might be visited on them.[25] On the face of it, nothing could be more obvious than Marx and Engels's support for colonial domination. Frederich Engels wrote of the conquest of Algeria in 1848:

> Upon the whole it is, in our opinion, very fortunate that the Arabian chief has been taken. The struggle of the Bedouins was a hopeless one, and though the manner in which brutal soldiers, like Bugeaud, have carried on the war is highly blamable, the conquest of Algeria is an important and fortunate fact for the progress of civilisation . . . after all, the modern *bourgeois*, with civilisation, industry, order, and at least relative enlightenment following him, is preferable to the feudal lord or to the marauding robber, with the barbarian state of society to which they belong.[26]

A year earlier, he had rejoiced at the conquest of Mexico: 'It is to the interests of its own development that Mexico will in the future be placed under the tutelage of the United States', since it had been 'forcibly drawn into the historical process'. Later, he wrote that the war had been 'waged wholly and solely in the interests of civilization', and was satisfied that California had been 'taken away from the lazy Mexicans, who could not do anything with it'. Marx himself was rancorous about Simón Bolívar, the liberator of Latin America, whom he saw as nothing more than a petty tyrant. In his writings on India, he claimed that 'Indian society has no history at all, or no known history. What we call its history, is but the history of the successive intruders who founded their empires on the passive basis of that unresisting and unchanging society.' Further, he maintained that England was, inadvertently, bringing about a 'social revolution' in India, without which mankind would not reach its socialist destiny, thus making the colonists 'the unconscious tool of history'.[27]

There is little doubt that both Marx and Engels, at different points, accepted more or less wholesale the prejudices of their day, precisely as some of their followers would. It was one thing to reject Rousseau's romanticism about pre-capitalist societies, and coolly insist on the possibility that morally grotesque actions could result in a 'progressive' outcome. It was quite another to dismiss Mexicans as 'lazy' and applaud war as a civilizing mission. If this were the end of the story, however, it would be hard to see how Marxism was to become the basis for the plurality of national liberation struggles throughout the world over the course of the twentieth century. Marx's writings, for all their impressive range and perspicacity, got a great deal wrong about India. His sense that Indian society, prior to the impact of colonization, was characterized by a network of languid village communes as the foundation for 'Oriental despotism', was taken directly from Hegel and bore no resemblance to the persisting social arrangements of Indian society. One of his early errors was to believe that, by building a network of railways across India, the East India Company would inadvertently, even in self-interest, bring economic development. As Gunnar Myrdal observed, since the railways were 'constructed primarily . . . with the aim first of facilitating military security and secondly of getting the raw produce out cheaply and British goods in', the railways did not exert 'spread effects' but rather 'served to strengthen the complementary colonial relationship and further subordinate the Indian to the British economy'.[28]

However, this does not justify Edward Said's claim that Marx's writing was inhibited by an Orientalist vocabulary which denigrated the value of the lives of 'Orientals'. Aijaz Ahmad has subjected Said's writing on this point – and his general theoretical work – to caustic treatment. While accepting that many criticisms of Marx's writings on colonialism in India are valid, he denies that they were original when Said emphasized them. Rather, Said's unique contribution appears to have been to contextualize Marx's writings in a discourse that putatively revokes the humanity of the colonized, which can then be seen as raw material for the Marxian version of progress. Moreover, there was much that Marx got right about India, especially regarding the barbarity of British rule, about which he was scathing: 'The profound hypocrisy and inherent barbarism of bourgeois civilization lies unveiled before our eyes'. The empire resembles a 'hideous pagan idol, who would not drink the nectar but from the skulls of the slain'. Discussing the Indian Rebellion of 1857, he described the alleged sepoy atrocities as 'only the reflex, in a concentrated form, of England's own conduct in India'. Marx rarely missed an opportunity to contrast British denunciations of atrocities with its own policy; and thus when discussing revelations about British torture in India, he commented that dispassionate and thoughtful men may perhaps ask whether a people are not justified in attempting to expel the foreign conquerors who have so abused their subjects. And if the English could do these things in cold blood, is it surprising that the insurgent Hindus should be guilty, in the fury of revolt and conflict, of the crimes and cruelties alleged against them?[29]

As early as 1853, he had insisted that Indians would not reap any of the benefits of a new society until either the British working class had overthrown its masters, or 'till the Hindus themselves shall have grown strong enough to throw off the English yoke altogether'. By 1881, Marx had evidently given up any hope that colonialism could be even inadvertently progressive, describing the railways as having been 'useless for the Hindoos' and Britain's mode of extraction as 'a bleeding process with a vengeance'.[30]

Both Marx and Engels were to revise their opinions on imperial conquest – recognizing, for instance, that the war on Mexico entailed an expansion of the domain of the slaveocracy of the southern United States, rather than of liberty. When French armies led by Louis Bonaparte took advantage of the American Civil War to invade Mexico in 1862, Marx and Engels hoped for a Mexican victory. At the same time, they urged Lincoln to transform a merely 'constitutional' war into a 'revolutionary' one. While Engels had cheered the French capture of the Algerian anti-colonial rebel Abd el-Kader in 1847, he was ten years later to write of the 'unceasing bloodshed, rapine and violence' that the French had unleashed. The 'barbarous system of warfare' imposed by the French was in stark contrast to the 'dictates of humanity, civilization and Christianity' claimed by the French as their rationale. In part, this change of perception may have been because the same troops, under General Louis Cardignac, that had suppressed the Algerian uprising were retained by Paris to do the same to its own proletariat in 1848. Marx, visiting Algeria during the last years of his life, was disgusted by the settler population's 'barefaced arrogance and presumptuousness vis-à-vis the "lesser breeds"'. He identified with the resistance to the occupation, but insisted that they would 'go to rack and ruin without a revolutionary movement'. Perhaps the most telling example of Marx's attitude to colonialism was the one that Lenin would insist on in his 1914 pamphlet, *The Right of Nations to Self-Determination*: that of Ireland. While recognizing the historically conditioned importance of the question of national self-determination, Marx came to argue that the English working class would 'never accomplish anything before it has got rid of Ireland'. The ordinary English worker, he maintained, hates the Irish worker as a competitor who forces down the standard of life. In relation to the Irish worker, he feels himself to be a member of the *ruling nation* and therefore makes himself a tool of his aristocrats and capitalists *against Ireland*, thus strengthening their domination *over himself*.

Marx compared this to the attitude of poor white Americans to African-Americans in former slave states. Not only was imperialism indicted for its obviously ruinous consequences for its victims, but the chauvinism it produced was 'the secret' of capitalist class power, and an enduring obstacle to real freedom for labour.[31]

Socialism and the 'non-adult races'

The heirs of liberal imperialism can be found in the Fabian Society, a middle-class socialist organization which openly advocated a paternalistic empire, and would later influence Labour's colonial policy at the highest levels. The Fabians were largely influenced by utilitarianism in their formulation of policy, and, although there was some dissent, largely backed colonialism. They cut their teeth on colonial matters during the Second Boer War (1899–1902), a battle which reflected the sometimes delicate racial dynamics of the empire. The war was the cumulative result of long-standing British policy: the Cape of Good Hope had been annexed from the Dutch during the French Revolutionary and Napoleonic Wars, since it was the only feasible route to India before the Suez Canal was opened. Disraeli, the Tory imperialist, had later annexed the Transvaal, and although Gladstone had spent much of his election campaign denouncing imperial acquisitiveness, his message to President Paul Kruger of the Transvaal upon the Liberal landslide success was that 'Our judgement is that the Queen cannot be advised to relinquish her sovereignty over the Transvaal'. But this betrayal, as it was certainly seen by the Boers, rebounded badly on Gladstone, since a successful uprising was launched on 15 December 1880, leading to a humiliating defeat for the British in January 1881. The Pretoria Convention afterwards conceded the independence of the Transvaal, thereafter known as the South African Republic.[32]

So it might have remained, had it not been for the discovery of huge gold deposits in 1886. A forlorn hope was entertained that the British might effect a 'peaceful commercial annexation' of the territory, due to the inquiry's expertise and commercial attractiveness. But the appointment as colonial secretary of Joseph Chamberlain – an imperialist who had split with the Liberals over their advocacy of Home Rule in Ireland

– led to a more aggressive policy. Chamberlain collaborated with the entrepreneur and empire-builder, Cecil Rhodes, in trying to stimulate a coup in the South African Republic. Aware of the controversy this would generate, they tried to frame the policy in humanitarian terms. The Uitlanders, a largely English-speaking minority of disenfranchized migrant workers in the Republic, could be used to stimulate a revolt that would then be led by British South African Police battalions (effectively Rhodes's private army), and the argument would be made that the putsch was necessary to defend their British birthright of free and equal citizenship. The coup failed miserably, and led to denunciations and demands for an inquiry, which was duly held – only for it to cover up for the guilty parties. The establishment closed ranks, the Uitlanders were rehabilitated, and a war of aggressive 'diplomacy' was launched. Kruger was invited to make a variety of impossible concessions to the British, as troops gathered to press the point home. Though he made a substantial offer on the factor supposedly motivating British pressure – the Uitlanders would be given a seven-year retrospective franchise – he was rebuffed. With 10,000 troops stationed in British South Africa, the war began in October 1899. It was a brutal affair, fought with a scorched-earth programme that intensified as it ground on, and finally the use of concentration camps. The irony is that, though they would stimulate the greatest outrage, these too were seen as a humanitarian response to a situation needlessly caused by Boer resistance. They were considered 'refugee camps', even though they involved burning thousands of people out of their homes and detaining them. In fact, given the racist assumptions about what black males might do to white Transvaal women and their children, the argument was offered that the wives of the selfish men who had put war before family had to be protected, and this was the only humane way. At their peak, the camps contained 160,000 people, but the disease and malnutrition caused by conditions in them meant that, by October 1901, deaths were running at 344 per thousand, leading to an overall total of 25,000 deaths. The subsequent British victory resulted in an administration concerned overwhelmingly with satisfying the demands of mine-owners for cheap labour by creating a racially ordered labour market, and thus provided the premises of apartheid in South Africa.[33]

The response of liberals and the left was mixed. Some, who came to be known as the 'Pro-Boers', opposed the war. Liberals set up a Transvaal Committee, while the journalist W.T. Stead set up a Stop the War Committee. The labour press was largely opposed to the war; some even went to fight on behalf of the Boers, in a manner that anticipated the International Brigades in 1930s Spain. On the other hand, this was an extremely unpopular position to take, and opponents to the war were subject to verbal and physical violence for stating their case. Until the Boer War, the Fabians had insisted on 'a clear line between socialism and politics', since '[s]ocialism was an economic doctrine and had nothing to do with other problems'. However, the divisions opened up on the left during the attack on the two Afrikaaner states prompted the Society to draw up a manifesto entitled *Fabianism and the Empire*, composed by George Bernard Shaw. It was a call for the rationalization of the empire based on utilitarian principles: their concern was 'not specially for the wage-earning class . . . but for the effective social organisation of the whole empire, and its rescue from the strife of classes and private interests'. 'The earth belongs to mankind', as their historian Edward R. Pease would later summarize their position, 'and the only valid moral right to national as well as individual possession is that the occupier is making adequate use of it for the benefit of the world community'.[34]

The first concern was to stipulate that under no circumstances could the democratic institutions that had flourished (for white subjects) in Australasia and Canada be applied to India or 'the Soudan'. Since 'we are no longer a Commonwealth of white men and baptised Christians', we must 'rule these vast areas and populations by a bureaucracy as undemocratic as that of Russia'. Local self-government for the whites would lead to 'black slavery, and, in some places, frank black extermination'. 'As for parliamentary institutions for native races, that dream has been disposed of by the American experiments after the Civil War. They are as useless to them as a dynamo to a Caribbean'. They are also 'impracticable in India', where the effort should be to harness local intellect and use rational economic measures to stave off famine. The Fabians argued that the natives should not be treated as children since this was offensive, but did not detect an inconsistency between such sensitivity and the alleged necessity of 'grandmotherly' tyranny.[35]

As for South Africa, 'neither democracy nor bureaucracy will serve alone, however modified' – again, having ruled out self-government for the indigenes, the Fabians could argue that they were defending the natives from white colonists. However, as Edward Pease recorded, they had simply recognized in their majority that 'the British Empire had to win the war and that no other conclusion is possible'. Recognizing British self-interest in the war, they lamented that a 'Federation of the World' had not yet been founded to internationalize such disputes. One day, they hoped, the 'Powers' would see the sense of taking 'concerted steps to use their armaments as an international police to suppress war' – in the meantime, they accepted the need for 'responsible Imperial federations'. The Boers, since they could not be ruled against their will, should be offered a constitution with some liberties, and British authority should be exercised in the interests of 'the whole of civilized society'. No nation, the Fabians insisted, had a right to do what it pleased with its territory regardless of the interests of the rest of the world. Thus, Britain's wars on China (the Opium Wars and the suppression of the Boxer Rebellion) enforced 'international rights of travel and trade'. The institutions of the Chinese empire were inconsistent with these rights and, 'accordingly, must go'. To this was added the humanitarian stipulation: the empire should improve the well-being of the Chinese. Opposing the principle of non-interference, they held it reasonable to conquer another state if it resulted in the liberalization of its institutions, and added the progressivist clause: 'The state which obstructs international civilization will have to go, be it big or little'.[36]

Sydney Olivier, a Fabian socialist employed by the Colonial Office, was one of the few dissenters. He was particularly alienated from the 'old gang' over the manifesto and their approval of the Boer War, and was increasingly opposed to colonialism, which he – like Hobson, his contemporary and co-Fabian – saw as a mode of economic extraction. However, even he was not immune to paternalistic arguments for empire, nor to the doctrine of race. Writing to fellow Fabian Sidney Webb after arriving in British Honduras in 1900 (today a tax haven for British businessmen known as Belize), he described the place as 'a nigger's paradise'. He accepted racial categories, contending that they were the work of environmental pressures and natural selection. If Africans were not biologically inferior, they were nevertheless 'backward'. Finally, he was in favour of a paternalistic empire, which would benevolently oversee the colonized. If he was realistic enough to recognize that, as 'presently constituted', the empire would not be a tool of rationalization and enlightenment, given the prominence of financial interests, he nevertheless maintained that the Colonial Office had once been the solicitous guardian of the colonized.[37]

The Fabians were particularly important in the long-term trajectory of the Labour Party's colonial policy. In 1919 they drafted the party's radical new policy programme, 'Labour and the New Social Order', which contained the following statement about colonialism:

> If we repudiate, on the one hand, the Imperialism that seeks to
> dominate other races, to impose our own will on other parts of
> the British Empire, so we disclaim equally any conception of a

selfish and insular 'non-interventionism' unregarding our special obligations to our fellow citizens overseas: of the corporate duties of one nation to another; of the moral claims upon us of the non-adult races; and of our own indebtedness to the world of which we are a part.[38]

Although the Fabians were a substantial component of the Labour Party when it was founded in 1906, and generally contributed the most pro-imperialist arguments, they were not alone. The SDF, a small Marxist sect run by the former Tory Henry Hyndman, was one of the original components of the Labour Party. Its leader, while favouring freedom for India and Ireland, was otherwise patriotically committed to the empire. The pacifists in Labour exhibited an early ambivalence. Keir Hardie criticised the Boer War as a 'capitalist war' for the interests of mining companies and investors, and campaigned for self-rule for India. Ramsay MacDonald criticized aspects of imperial governance in *Labour and the Empire*, but he did not propose to abolish it. Instead, the Labour Party should aim to use its influence to 'democratize the personnel of the Imperial machine' and 'develop native civilization along its own lines', allowing indirect rule and native administration – but always constrained by uniform standards imposed by London in the interests of 'human liberty' and 'justice'. Having visited India, he drew the impression that the only form of government appropriate to the Hindu religion was a 'ruling caste' 'retaining power by force and fraud'. The empire was seen by the party in general not as a system to be dismantled, but as a means by which to achieve reform. Thus, the 1918 Labour Manifesto called for 'freedom' for both India and Ireland, advocating 'the right of self-determination within the British Commonwealth of Free Nations'.[39] This self-determination, as it transpired, was something to be delivered gradually, following a necessary period of intelligent and enlightened rule in the interests of the colonized.

Republicanism and the civilizing mission

The colonization of Algeria in the 1830s was welcomed by much of the French left. The Saint-Simonian Philip Buchez argued that France should take the opportunity to dominate the Mediterranean, as it would provide a holding base for 'direct communications with the interior of Africa'. Charles Fourier had hopes that the communal societies he was proposing for Europe could be imported into Africa – a move certain to civilize the local population. One Fourierist paper declared that France's motto should be 'colonize everywhere and always'. The Fourierists in

Algeria declared in 1848 that the colonization of Africa was 'the providential destiny of France in the nineteenth century'.[40]

But it was particularly after the French loss in the Franco-Prussian war and the experience of the Paris Commune that the colonial idea really took hold. The Catholic Church provided much of the moral sustenance for French expansion, with 40,000 missionaries distributed throughout the world. Cardinal Lavigerie, who had become Archbishop of Algiers in 1868, addressed the novices under his supervision with an appeal to higher goals than those that politicians could conventionally espouse. 'No thought of self-interest or of glory spurs you on,' he told them. Rather, it would be 'the honour of France to see you completing her work by carrying Christian civilization far beyond her conquests into this unknown world'. Although many of those who ended up running the empire, such as the Republican Paul Bert, were profoundly anti-clerical, the clerics were far too useful to keep out of the venture: 'anti-clericalism would not be an export item'.[41] And at any rate, Lavigerie's pious, priestly rhetoric would soon tumble just as fluently from the lips of socialist politicians.

The main pro-imperialist bloc in France during the 1880s was the moderate wing of the Republican Party, known by critics as the 'opportunists', which included Léon Gambetta's Union Républicaine (Republican Union) and Jules Ferry's Gauche Républicaine (Left Republicans). Gambetta saw colonialism as a safety valve for society, an outlet for its bad elements, and a retardant of socialism; but he also saw it as a way to recoup the losses of 1870, when Bismarck had inflicted a stunning defeat on France. Jules Ferry, twice prime minister of France, was one of the most ardent colonialists in French political history and is credited – if that is the right word – with having produced a 'renaissance' in French imperialism. He led a powerful colonial lobby in parliament, and argued that colonies had humanitarian justifications as well as economic ones. He directed the conquest of the relatively independent Ottoman state of Tunisia in 1881, and later in his premiership sent an expedition to Amman-Tonkin (northern and central regions of Vietnam, respectively) to annexe the territory. The languages of race and rights were invoked coterminously – France had a *right* to empire, because of its *duty* to civilize the 'inferior races'. French colonization brought 'justice', 'material and moral order', 'equity' and 'social virtue', Ferry maintained.[42]

However, Ferry came under fire from both left and right towards the end of his rule. The left was agitating for nationalization and fuller democratization; but the main source of the crisis was opposition to the colonial policy, although this was not always principled in form.

Clemenceau's paper, *La Justice*, complained less about colonial aggression than about the worry that it had 'left Bismarck the master of Europe'. And even at the height of opposition to the war against China, in 1883, only sixty deputies voted against war credits. Nevertheless, by the mid 1880s, Ferry was forced to try to shore up his support on the right by explaining the economic rationale behind colonialism, which he did before the Chamber of Deputies on 28 July 1885. He explained that colonial policy was 'the daughter of industrial policy'. Because Europe had not managed a successful 'division of labour', Ferry maintained that the division of labour would have to be globalized. Any country with a high level of manufacture required export markets, without which it would experience 'a general decrease in prices, profits and wages'. He noted the economic crises that had struck Europe since the late 1870s, of which 'long frequent strikes' were its 'most painful symptom'.[43]

As the fear of Bismarck ruling Europe faded, radical socialist leaders, pacifists even, would go on to evince a similar enthusiasm for the colonies. Jean Jaurès, who was to work so hard to prevent World War I, was astoundingly nationalistic when it came to colonization. As France competed with England over ownership of East Africa, the military leadership sought credits to lead an expedition into Fashoda, a village in Sudan today known as Kodok, with the aim of making inroads on the British. Though it was a futile mission, they obtained the requisite votes, and it was Jaurès who silenced mild criticism from a colonialist about the difficulty of the mission by insisting that 'c'est un vote national'. Although Jaurès would sometimes criticize French imperialism in Algeria, his comments were largely to the effect that Arabs should be given political equality in the colonial system, not that the colony should be abolished. At the 1907 conference of the Second International at Stuttgart, he aligned with those who argued for a more humane management of the colonies, rather than their destruction. The Radical Socialists had come, by 1903, to accept the existing colonies, though they opposed their expansion, and by 1913 were calling for their preservation under humane rules guided by the Declaration of the Rights of Man.[44]

Not all of the arguments for colonialism were strictly humanitarian. One of the leading intellectuals of the Socialist Party (SFIO) was Georges Vacher de Lapouge, who was instrumental in the development and articulation of scientific racism. His argument was rooted in the Social Darwinism that had become prominent in the late nineteenth century. The French Revolution, from this perspective, had been an evolutionary disaster, putting the wrong race in power. His deeply melancholic view of racial struggle and selection led him to introduce Francis Galton's doctrine of eugenics into France. Calling for a ban on interbreeding and a 'socialist-selectionist' state, he declared: 'to the celebrated formula which summarizes the secular Christianity of the Revolution: Liberty, Equality, Fraternity, we respond: Determinism, Inequality, Selection!' His racial science, which stipulated that the Aryans constituted a superior race, while the Jews also constituted a strong, villainous opposite, would make a profound impact in Germany. In particular, German intellectuals were attracted by a racial doctrine that was not encumbered by vulgar hate-speech. His closest German colleague was Hans F. Günther, who would go on to become a key figure in the German National Socialist Party.[45]

Perhaps the most explicitly anti-imperialist socialists in France in the late nineteenth century were the Parti Ouvrier Français (POF), sometimes known as the Guesdists after their prominent spokesperson Jules Guesde. They derided French nationalism in favour of cosmopolitanism and a globally emancipated proletariat, and took a uniquely positive attitude to migrant labour. Parochialism – the preference for a particular people simply because of their location – was an 'absurdity': socialists 'have only one homeland – the social revolution'. They were quite prepared to make themselves unpopular in this by, for example, opposing 'revenge' for the losses to Prussian armies in 1871. They were also unremittingly hostile to the anti-Semitism that was a characteristic aspect of French chauvinism, to the extent of quite robust philo-Semitism. For example, Guesde, noting the prominent Jewish figures among German socialists, lamented that 'there are so few Jews among us here in France'. The POF were among the first socialists to debunk the stereotype held by the 'national socialists' of Jews as rapacious capitalists, insisting that 'classes exist within the Jewish race', that most were working-class, and that these Jewish workers tended to be the most exploited of all. Race theory was bunk, 'blood' explained nothing, and 'race war' would have to give way to 'class war'. As internationalists, they were opposed in principle to the colonial idea. Guesde had been one of the few on the Left to oppose the conquest of Tunisia, and the Guesdists would be one of the most articulate opponents of the colonial idea in the Second International. Despite their sectarian abstentionism on the Dreyfus Affair, the Guesdists had been the vanguard of anti-racism on the French Left. Yet the tidal pull of nationalism was strong enough that, by the summer of 1914, even Guesde was rallying to the French state, and would accept a post in the national unity government.[46]

German patriotism and militarism

Germany unity, a liberal project in the nineteenth century, had emerged not as a consequence of popular revolt but from a war led by the Prussian military, and as a consequence it had pronounced militaristic and chauvinist tendencies, which did not spare its internal dissidents. Many of the leading intellectuals of the German Social Democratic Party (SPD), such as Wilhelm Liebknecht and August Bebel, had been involved in the national movement. Though they were anti-militarists, they had to rely on the army to accomplish their goals, and therefore tried to elaborate an alternative militarism – a radical one based on popular militias on the Swiss model; though, in fact, as Karl Liebknecht pointed out, these had become a strike-breaking instrument after 1899. Since they had accepted the Prussian solution to German unity (an empire, with many German-speaking peoples excluded, and exaggerated power for the less democratic Prussian state), they also abandoned their opposition to annexation. Bebel called for 'Social Democratic patriotism', and the party as a whole – despite being demonized and outlawed for a long time by the state – accepted the Reich's institutions as legitimate. Increasingly, they rejected anti-militarism and the idea of disarmament – Karl Kautsky, the party's foremost intellectual, for instance, dismissed the idea out of hand at the 1898 Hague Conference.[47]

This militarism and increasingly conservative disposition was suffused with chauvinism. Many Social Democrats accepted Hegel's thesis about 'historical' and 'non-historical' societies, and the infancy of the East. Kautsky was also profoundly influenced by the Social Darwinism of Ernst Häckel. In 1882, two years before Germany launched its protectorate in South West Africa, Kautsky told Frederich Engels that '[i]n so far as they cannot be assimilated by modern culture, the wild peoples will have to disappear from the surface of the earth'. This statement is particularly striking in light of the fact that Kautsky would later be among a minority to take an anti-colonial position at the 1907 Stuttgart conference of the Second International, at a time when the leadership of the SPD was moving in a pro-colonial direction. August Bebel told the Reichstag in 1896 that '[i]n the East resides a lack of culture and a piece of barbarism . . . True culture finds its home in Central, Southern and Western Europe'. Eduard Bernstein, the most eloquent of the SPD's revisionists, later argued that the party should adopt a 'humane' and 'nonaggressive' colonialism, to promote democratization and the evolution of capitalism. He argued, in 'The Struggle of Social Democracy and the Social Revolution', that 'the subjection of natives to the authority of European administration does not always entail a worsening of their condition, but often means the opposite'. He added that 'under direct European rule, savages are without exception better off than they were before'.[48]

In the case of Bernstein, the pro-colonial attitude was related to his accommodation to the Reich and his belief that the course of capitalist development had disproved Marx's theory of crisis. The system seemed to be stabilizing itself, the middle class was growing – all indicators pointed to parliamentary gradualism. Instead of a revolutionary party, he advocated a left bloc in parliament, an alliance between the liberals and the social democrats, despite German liberalism – a 'stinking corpse' as he characterized it – having broadly capitulated to chauvinism. Bernstein was influenced in his belief in the possibility of a socialist-liberal coalition by his long stay in the UK, by his association with the Fabian left, but also with the ethical socialists of Labourism – Keir Hardie and Ramsay MacDonald in particular. Since Bernstein did not accept that capitalism was inherently crisis-prone, he could not accept the argument that colonialism was an attempt to remedy the crisis by providing markets for domestic capital – rather, for Bernstein, it was an agent of civilization and progress:

> every vigorous race and every robust economy, together with its cultural superstructure, strives toward expansion. In all ages this drive has been a potent factor in evolutionary progress . . . In principle, I am in full agreement with those preaching a crusade against colonial chauvinism. But I am of the opinion that this crusade is condemned to futility as long as endeavours to enlarge by colonial expansion the economic sphere of one's own nation . . . are not differentiated from the kind of colonial policy which is directed against one of the advanced nations of the civilised world. Only the latter merits thoroughgoing opposition.[49]

Predictably, a racialized version of Social Darwinism organizes Bernstein's perceptions. Humanity cannot yet forswear violence, and 'Where two civilisations clash, the lower must give way to the higher. This law of evolution we cannot overthrow, we can only humanize its action. To counteract it would mean to postpone social progress.' At any rate, 'the higher culture always has the greater right on its side', and where necessary it has 'the historical right, even duty' to subjugate lower civilizations. Bernstein's arguments for humanitarian empire, wherein he maintained that the purpose of colonialism could be attained without its abuses (and thus that any 'abuses' could not constitute an argument against colonialism), were drawn from the British radical tradition – especially from the Webbs and from the Shaw-drafted Fabian manifesto. In arguing for colonialism, he was opportunistic enough to cite alleged economic benefits to the working class, though he was himself sceptical as to their existence.[50]

After the Reich launched a wave of genocidal violence against the Herero people of German-controlled South-West Africa in 1904, Bernstein argued before the Stuttgart Conference of the Second International in 1907 that

[w]e must get away from the utopian notion of simply abandoning the colonies. The ultimate consequence of such a view would be to give the United States back to the Indians . . . Socialists too should acknowledge the need for civilised peoples to act like the guardians of the uncivilised . . . our economies are based in large measure on the extraction from the colonies of products that the native peoples have no idea how to use.[51]

Another SPD delegate, Eduard David, agreed, quoting August Bebel's appeal for an ethical foreign policy: 'If representatives of civilized countries come as liberators to the alien peoples in order to bring them the benefits of culture and civilization, then we Social Democrats will be the first to support such colonization as a civilizing mission'. Even Karl Kautsky, who argued that a 'socialist' colonial policy was a 'logical contradiction', accepted the force of the argument that Europeans had a 'civilizing role' vis-à-vis the 'primitive peoples'.[52] Bernstein's opposition to aggressive colonialism against 'advanced' states might suggest that the SPD would perform more creditably in the case of a European war, and for some of the time, they did – until, that is, a major European conflagration became imminent.

Among the allies of the German Revisionists at the Stuttgart Conference was Henri van Kol of the Dutch Social Democratic Workers' Party (SAPD), who had persuaded his colleagues to support colonialism both as a civilizing venture and on the grounds of the putative economic benefits that the East Indies brought to the Dutch working class. Van Kol argued that socialists could not 'abandon half the globe to the caprice of peoples still in their infancy'. Mocking the idea of assistance without colonial rule, van Kol said, 'Suppose that we bring a machine to the savages of central Africa? What will they do with it? Perhaps they will start up a war dance around it.' (The transcript records that this witticism was met with 'loud laughter'.) Van Kol's arguments carried great weight in the SAPD for a considerable time, and it only reconsidered its position with the development of powerful anti-colonial movements in the East Indies during the 1920s, and even then did not adopt the policy of immediate independence supported by its left-wing critics. The party still believed that the Dutch working class would suffer were the Indonesian state to become independent. The party's revisionist wing resented the concessions to anti-colonialism and the party's failure to be harder on communism. In fact, in its anti-communism it made the fatal error of arguing that the party was much too concerned about the developing fascist currents in the country – a complacency that received its answer when those same currents were empowered during the Nazi occupation of the country.[53]

The Stuttgart Conference, which was to determine a (rarely observed) colonial policy for the Second International, heard from only one Indian delegate, named Bhikajee Kama. To stormy applause, he argued:

> Each year India must pay thirty-five million pounds sterling to Britain, and not a penny of it finds its way back to India. This economic relationship causes the hunger and desperate poverty of an immense population, countless epidemics, and a death rate that has risen to an unspeakable level . . . What is socialism, if not justice? And if it is justice, why must millions of unfortunate Indians endure such agony? . . . Indians demand their human rights and autonomy. We want the right to self-determination, we demand justice and the right to govern ourselves.[54]

The anti-colonial motion was duly carried, and the appeal to self-determination would later form the basis of the Bolshevik anti-imperialist doctrine. But the political practice of socialists in the main colonial powers was not altered.

The very experience of the long-term domination of Europeans over non-Europeans deranged and corrupted egalitarian and libertarian thought of all kinds. The collapse of anti-imperialist critique was ominous not merely for the colonized. Imperialist tyranny had, as we will see, a way of extending back into the imperial 'centre'.

'The Spirit of 1914'

The collapse of left parties into support for their own governments as they raised armies for the unprecedented barbarism of World War I tore the Second International apart, and demonstrated the bind that most of the social-democratic parties were in. They were dedicated to class struggle, but increasingly integrated into their respective national states, hoping to secure improvements for workers in that context. The Second International had agreed at its Basel conference in 1912 that, in the event of war, they should demand a general strike. Forced to choose between class and nation, however, most chose the nation.

The British Labour Party, which had never preached class war (even if, as Kautsky cunningly argued, it practised it well enough to be admitted to the Second International), still considered the war harmful to the working class. Until 1914, whatever the limits of its criticisms of the empire, Labour had been mainly anti-war, and contained a strong pacifist current. It was operating, moreover, in increasingly propitious circumstances for the radical Left. The working class was insurgent: strike waves had begun in 1908 and, from 1910 to 1914, the average number of days lost to strike action increased from between 2,000 and 3,000 to 41,000. And as the government moved closer to war, committing itself to a defence of France in the event of its territory being compromised, it was fiercely criticized by Keir Hardie and Ramsay MacDonald. On 2 August 1914, Hardie and Arthur Henderson led a mass anti-war demonstration in Trafalgar Square. Nevertheless, on the following day, when Sir Edward Grey told the House of Commons that peace in Europe was unsustainable, Ramsay MacDonald replied that, although the government had produced no convincing proof that England was in danger, in the event of war, Labour would not act for it, but would not act against it either. On 5 August, Labour's National Executive Committee passed a resolution denouncing Grey for committing England to the defence of France. On the same day, however, the Parliamentary Labour Party supported the government's request for war credits amounting to £100 million, forcing MacDonald to resign in protest.[55]

Rapidly, an astonishing volte-face was effected by the party. Arthur Henderson took over the leadership and entered into a coalition government with the Liberals and the Tories, accepting a cabinet post. The Henderson-led party not only supported the war, but took part in recruitment campaigns and accepted an electoral truce throughout. The commitment to a general strike was forgotten, and in its 1914 manifesto Labour blamed the whole conflict on Germany, and decided that it was now an effort against the 'evils' of 'military despotism'. Most of the original components of the party were either on-side or severely divided. The trade union bureaucracy largely supported the war and agreed to suspend strikes in order to increase production. The Fabians were split between the old guard, represented by the Webbs, who supported the war, and younger members who agreed with the

Independent Labour Party's opposition. The ILP, which continued to organize anti-war protests with the Peace Society and the British Socialist Party, was sneered at by the Labour leadership, who claimed that, had anyone listened to them, 'the Germans would be here now'. The British Socialist Party, which was by then the main Marxist component of the Labour Party, was opposed; appropriately enough, Hyndman split away to form his own National Socialist Party and demanded a more vigorous prosecution of the war. By January 1916, Labour had moved from grudging acceptance of the war to outright support, together with condemnation of the 'atrocities committed by Germany' – which, it was soon learned, were largely fabricated.[56]

When, in December 1916, Lloyd George replaced Herbert Asquith as prime minister, he persuaded pro-war Labour members of parliament to join his cabinet, and Labour conferences twice backed the decision to enter the war cabinet. Until the February 1917 overthrow of the Russian Tsar, there was little dissent within Labour ranks over anything beyond specific measures, such as the attempt to introduce industrial conscription. When Arthur Henderson resigned his cabinet post in 1917, it was over the way he had been treated by cabinet colleagues rather than any concern over the war. But the growing proletarian unrest across Europe, and particularly the consummation of the Russian Revolution in October 1917, had an electrifying effect on the Labour Party. Nye Bevan recalled that it was regarded as 'one of the most emancipating events in the history of mankind'. The Party was driven to the left, and increasingly opposed the war, while the party's centre-right considered the threat of an emerging extra-parliamentary left sufficient to try to outflank its opponents while centralizing the structure of the party itself – a task to which Arthur Henderson devoted himself.[57]

It would be mistaken to reduce Labour's broad support for the war to the sudden upsurge of patriotism in the British working class. Although there was a carefully cultivated jingoistic atmosphere, and millions of volunteers signed up to fight under the illusion that the war would be over rather quickly, it is equally the case that millions did not. The average enlistment rate between August 1914 and May 1915 was 30.5 per cent of the male population across the country, and many of the motivations concerned – though usually couched in patriotic terms – were either pecuniary or involved the hope that war would be an adventure, an escape from the stultifying reality of Britain's domestic class structure. Until 1914, British elites had been largely unsuccessful with indoctrination programmes designed to boost army recruitment and highlight the Teutonic Threat. Britain was consumed with its brewing domestic civil war, conducted along the lines of gender and class, and also a growing conflict with the Irish over Home Rule. Even after the German invasion of Belgium, it was not clear that anyone beyond a minority of the cabinet supported British involvement in the conflict.[58] Those currents of the Labour Party that did enthusiastically support the war tended to be those that were already broadly in favour of the empire, and whose outlook was gradualist, reformist and – often – elitist.

The role of the German masses in World War I was for a long time occluded by official propaganda and mythology. Kaiser Wilhelm's declaration that 'I recognise no more parties: I know only Germans', is often depicted as having been greeted with overwhelming if not unanimous support. It is said to have crystallized a sense of national unity that 'led to the political truce of *Burgfrieden*'. It produced 'national enthusiasm' and 'considerable jubilation'. 'Even a considerable number of socialists at least formally supported the war effort.' Further, 'popular support for the war was not universal, but the relatively few voices raised against war were drowned by a chorus of approval in the popular press, in the churches and even among organised labour'. The socialists proved 'as German as their class enemies', in fact 'more assimilated – and patriotic – than they dared to admit'. And those who were not had to think about the danger of alienating the mass of the members who believed that conflict had been 'forced' on Germany. The satirical magazine *Simplicissimus* reflected the patriotic line, as did the left-liberal *Hamburger Fremdenblatt*: when the parties accepted *Burgfrieden* ('the truce of the fortress'), so did the press. James Joll writes of a 'mood of 1914' that represented a 'widespread revolt against the liberal values of peace and rational solutions of all problems'. Given these circumstances, perhaps it would seem less surprising that the SPD, the main internal foe of Wilhelmine Germany, voted for war credits on 4 August 1914. However, this image is founded on a myth which has been carefully demolished by the historian Jeffrey Verhey, who points out that the crowds in these images embodied a number of different attitudes: not only 'euphoria' or 'jubilation' but fear, curiosity, excitement at the escape from the humdrum and the mundane, and so on. Further, they were substantially outnumbered by larger anti-war rallies organized by socialists, which were censored from the national press. Finally, those most supportive of war tended to be the bourgeois elements, while those most critical of it tended to be agrarian strata and the working class: class and political tensions were at best only temporarily suppressed.[59]

To explain the SPD's support for the war is to grasp the continuity of their outlook. Certainly, the Social Democrats emphasized continuity with their principles. August Bebel had argued that German workers had a *class* interest in war with Russia, asserting that 'the German fatherland' belonged to the masses more than it did to anyone else, and therefore if Russia, 'the champion of terror and barbarism', were to attack Germany, the SPD cadre would resist. While anti-militarists demanded a general strike against imperialism, the leadership of the SPD declared that a '[g]eneral strike is general nonsense'. This stunning rapprochement with a political elite that had fought pitched legal and political battles against the party, and had considered it such a dangerous enemy that it had prepared military offensives to counter it, was partially a response to threatened state aggression: it was only when the chancellor was assured by socialist leaders of their loyalty that he persuaded army leaders not to arrest them.[60]

However, the rightward drift of a substantial segment of the SPD leadership, with growing prominence for Fabian-influenced reformists such as Bernstein, had been a long-brewing affair. The 1907 elections in particular had split the party on the colonial question, as Chancellor Bülow had succeeded in creating a conservative coalition, drawing in sections of the progressive middle classes over support for the idea of Germany as a 'world power'. The dramatic losses for the SPD pushed Kautsky radically to the left, while the revisionists were convinced that there was a 'reactionary mass' that could not be persuaded of a radical anti-imperialist stance. At the Stuttgart Conference of European socialists in the same year, it became clear that the revisionists were the strongest faction in the SPD. In addition, the imperial government intervened directly in the affairs of the SPD to help August Bebel bring the party into line, following a December 1907 injunction by the war minister against anti-militarism. Subsequently, while the conservative coalition broke down in 1909 over the intransigence of agrarian conservatives in opposition to fiscal reform, the SPD saw their best results for years in 1912, and were to prove instrumental in voting for tax increases to pay for military build-up in 1913. The party leadership now believed it could achieve reforms by cooperating with the war effort. Kautsky's response to the 1907 elections had been to wonder whether the state had finally found the answer to socialism in 'the fascinating effect of the colonial state of the future'. Arguably, it was rather the integration of a section of social democracy into the imperial project that was central in producing a temporary effect of fascination.[61]

Quite absurdly, the SPD tried to shirk responsibility for its support of the war by invoking the fantasy of a Russian invasion:

> The responsibility for this calamity falls upon supporters of this policy. We are not responsible. The Social Democratic Party has always combated this policy to the utmost . . . Our exertions have been in vain . . . The problem before us now is not the relative advisability of war or peace, but a consideration of just what steps must be taken for the protection of our country.[62]

Across Europe, in almost every country that participated in the war, the trend was repeated. The French Socialists (SFIO) abandoned their commitment to launch a general strike in the event of a war, the efforts of Jean Jaurès notwithstanding. Jaurès had argued for a pre-emptive strike – a European-wide effort to force political leaders to pursue arbitration rather than risk a continental revolt. But, like many in the party's gradualist wing, he also looked to a natural alliance between Britain, France and Russia, and was an admirer of what he saw as Britain's liberal foreign policy. Jaurès was assassinated before the war began, but the Socialists, citing the German threat to the republic, joined the coalition government. Initially calling for peace in their July 1914 manifesto, the Socialists nonetheless blamed the 'aggressive tactics of Austro-Hungarian diplomacy' for the threatened war, and held that the French government was 'sincerely anxious to avert or diminish the risks of conflict'. By 4 August, *L'Humanité* was declaring that the Socialists would vote unanimously for war credits if called upon, since France was clearly the victim of aggression. The party authorised two of its representatives, Jules Guesde and Marcel Sembat, to join the National Ministry of Defence, and refused to attend international conferences throughout the war, arguing that this would be seen as indirect negotiation with the Germans. The internationalists were in a minority in the party at least until May 1917, by which time the overthrow of the Russian Tsar and the evidence of growing revolutionary sentiment had convinced the formerly bellicose to join the internationalists in the National Council and vote to send delegates to the international peace conference in Stockholm.[63] The CGT, the syndicalist union which had also pledged itself to a general strike in the event of war, instead ceded to the threat of repression from the French state.

The right-wing press was baying for the blood of the anti-militarists, and the government had prepared for mass arrests of 'spies', and anti-militarists in particular. The assassination of Jaurès by a young French nationalist at the end of July 1914 suggested that the death threats issuing from such papers as *Action française* should be taken seriously. On the other hand, a preference for complicity in a Europe-wide war implied a set of moral judgements and evaluations that were somewhat divergent from the publicly avowed anti-militarism of the French left of the time, and the roots for this normative dissonance must be sought in the general acceptance of colonialism. After all, if one's own state is a worthy instrument for civilizing non-Europeans, it is but a short step to claim that it could also be used to chase away the Hun. It was the combination of mass strike waves across France and the revolutions in Russia and Central Europe in 1918 that eventually led to a split within the Socialists, with two-thirds of the membership departing to join a new Communist party (PCF) which accepted Lenin's commitment to Socialist internationalism and anti-imperialism.[64]

In Italy, where the government initially opted for neutrality, a pro-war 'democratic interventionist' current developed in the largely pacifist Socialist Party (PSI). Benito Mussolini, who became one of the leading advocates of 'democratic interventionism' by late 1914, initially made his name as an anti-war street-fighter during Italy's invasion of Libya in 1911. Italy's international agreements had enabled it to claim Libya as quid pro quo in the event of a change in the balance of power in North Africa. As France set out to consolidate its holdings in Morocco, the recently elected reformist administration of Giovanni Giolitti launched a war to occupy Libya. While the bulk of the PSI was against the war, the reformist wing of the party joined with Giolitti and voted for war credits. Very soon, having inflicted indiscriminate violence on the resistant population, including bombing of areas that could not be reached with bayonets, Italy declared the mission accomplished – all too soon, as the war was to last until 1919. Mussolini was arrested for allegedly instigating violence during the anti-war protests and imprisoned for several months. In 1912 he emerged as a folk hero, and he led the revolutionary faction of the PSI to success at the party's congress in July 1912. Taking editorial control of the party's paper, *Avanti!*, he opened it up to unconventional writers from the syndicalist tradition, thereby broadening the paper's appeal. He had declared in July 1914, as the diplomatic crisis over the murder of Archduke Ferdinand exploded, that the Italian proletariat would have nothing to do with a war that did not concern it, and as late as September he co-signed the PSI's antiwar manifesto. He announced that the working class would lose 'not a man, not a penny', and shed 'not one drop of blood' for this cause.[65]

Increasingly, however, Mussolini identified himself as a 'national' socialist – to put it another way, 'we are socialists, and from the national point of view, Italians'. By November, he was proposing a new form of socialism, one that recognized the legitimate claims of both nation and class. He was eventually expelled, and the subsequent highlights of his career are well known. But although the PSI remained pacifist, it did retain a substantial pro-war faction. Part of the reason for this was that, while the PSI was one of the strongly anti-militarist parties of the Second International, its commitment to Italian neutrality was underpinned by a revulsion against the Triple Alliance, in which Italy was bound to support the Central Powers. Many reformists, including those in the PSI, wanted an alliance with the Entente powers instead, because they were seen as being more progressive and democratic. Mussolini tried to push for this position in the party, but was condemned by the party's Directorate, removed from control of *Avanti!*, and expelled. Although Mussolini would work with others on the pro-war wing of the left in the campaign for Italian intervention, from early on he was already 'aligned with the national imperialists and Salandran conservative elites on an interrelated programme of territorial expansion and anti-socialism'. Later, in his arguments for 'democratic interventionism', he would invoke the memory of the Italian revolutionary nationalist Mazzini to argue that the defeat of Austria was a victory for freedom. 'Italy, the nation of the future . . . has liberated the peoples.'[66]

The voluptuous hallucination of a war for progress, civilization, democracy, a war to end all wars was, as we will see in Chapter 2, shared across the Atlantic. It could not have been more estranged from reality. The capitulation to chauvinism was not only disastrous for the 20 million who died as a result, both directly and indirectly. As Robert O. Paxton argues, World War I opened up 'wide cultural, social, and political opportunities' for fascism. It 'discredited optimistic and progressive views of the future', 'spawned armies of restless veterans', and 'generated social strains that exceeded the capacity of existing institutions – whether liberal or conservative – to resolve'.[67]

Communism, anti-fascism and anti-imperialism

The failure of socialist internationalism, Lenin had written, was a failure of a particular, opportunistic kind of socialism, and the Third International – the Comintern, as it came to be known – was above all an attempt to avert that catastrophe and re-establish internationalism as a principle of socialism.[68] The problem was that the post-war revolutions in Central Europe were all put down rapidly and, in

Germany, the SPD had taken control of the revolutionary situation, creating a new republic with strong welfare provisions and extending the franchise to women. It no longer possessed a colonial heritage to relate to, so this posed no problems. However, to retain power and contain the revolution, it hunted down the revolutionaries with the assistance of the ultra-right *Freikorps*, whose members would later become their sponsors' gravediggers. The Bolshevik revolution was the only one left standing, and following a prolonged Entente invasion, a cruel civil war and a calamitous famine, it was also a wreck. Conditions were far more ideal for dictatorship than workers' democracy, and soon the Comintern was being run by a dictatorial, privileged bureaucracy in Moscow which maniacally demonized its enemies, ruthlessly and often violently shut down opposition, and subordinated all loyal parties to its own interests. The effect was often catastrophic.

Take, for example, the Popular Front government in France. It was elected with an overwhelming majority in France in 1936, but survived for less than two years. It had been received with a wave of enthusiasm not only in France, but also in the colonies, where struggles for independence were percolating. Ho Chi Minh and Habib Bourguiba looked forward to a liberalization of the imperial structure. Yet the only substantial policy that the Popular Front promised for the colonies was to create a commission of inquiry into the circumstances of French North Africa and Indochina – sub-Saharan Africa did not receive a mention. Further, the bulk of the French Left advocated colonialism as a generous attempt to modernize, and extend republican values to, the subjugated. Pro-imperialist propaganda had been cranked up in the years preceding the Popular Front, reaching a peak with the Colonial Exhibition of 1931. The colonies were especially important to the French economy by 1936, since they took fully a third of all French exports – some industries found up to 80 per cent of their markets in the empire. The Popular Front government therefore sought to limit 'abuses' and humanize the colonies, which they saw as an indefinite preparation for self-government. The reforms proposed by the PCF were of little import, since they simply continued reforms that had already been underway. Marius Moutet, the minister for the colonies described a 'policy of humanism' that would pursue 'friendship between the races' without altering the system of white supremacy.[69]

With regard to French Indochina, Moutet advocated an 'altruistic colonization' to improve the economic condition (and buying power) of the masses. This was to ignore the fact that French Indochina was financed by three large state-controlled sources – namely opium,

gambling and alcohol – with consumption enforced by colonial officials (who even fixed monthly quotas for alcohol). Moutet did nothing
to break those monopolies, and instead sought to expand markets for
metropolitan industries. In Tunisia, there was early hope for change
when the reactionary Resident-General Peyrouton was replaced by the
more liberal Armand Guillon, who extended the Popular Front's
domestic reforms to the colony and restored civil rights. This was
rapidly eroded. The Popular Front explained that they could not free the
colonies since, if they did so, they would immediately fall to Mussolini
(Bourguiba, the leader of the liberal constitutionalist Neo-Destour
party, explained that there was little risk of this, since the nationalists
would readily form an alliance with France). When the Neo-Destour
struck in solidarity with their fellow North Africans under siege, the
French authorities did not hesitate to launch a crackdown.[70]

If the imperialism of the Socialists and Radicals was predictable, it
should have been straightforward for the PCF to oppose the colonies:
it was a Communist party, most of whose members were anti-colonial-
ists who had broken away from the SFIO in 1920 partially over that
very issue. They had campaigned in support of the modernizing anti-
colonial rebel Abd el-Krim during the 1920s Rif revolt in Morocco,
which was then under the joint protectorates of France and Spain, and
which France was attacking after the revolt had defeated the Spanish
armies, leading to an independent Rif republic that threatened France's
interests. It was a Communist party aligned with the Comintern, which
had in 1927 assisted in the formation of the League Against
Imperialism, with the involvement of such figures as Nehru. Its representative at the League was a Senegalese ex-serviceman named Lamine
Senghor, and, moreover, it had links with the Étoile Nord Africaine
organization, which was the first movement to demand full independence for Algeria. In fact, the record of the Communists was unique:
they alone had stood up against the tidal wave of chauvinism over the
Riffan revolt, sending a telegram to Krim pledging support, setting up
an Action Committee against the war, and leading a protest strike
involving (or so the party claimed) 900,000 workers, with the result
that their future leader Maurice Thorez was arrested and imprisoned.[71]
The party's unique stance won it the respect of French intellectuals and
artists, and when the 'Appel aux travailleurs intellectuels' was launched
in defence of 105 Communist militants who had been imprisoned as a
result of the repression, among the signatures was that of *Clarté*, a
surrealist group.

While the Socialists had even entered a plea in favour of the
bombing of Damascus by the Radical General Sarrail in the 1926

suppression of the Syrian revolt, it was Communist activists such as Paul Nizan who organized to expose the barbaric methods being used to crush an insurgency in Indochina inspired by the growing prominence of Chinese Communism. Nizan scorned those who complained about bad colonial administrators, but saw no crime in colonialism itself. As late as 1933, the pro-Communist journal *Commune* could proudly remind readers of the pro-Rif stance taken in the Moroccan war.[72]

However, the PCF's priorities had changed by 1936, and this was certainly not due to a change of line on behalf of the League. Indeed, when the League's Berlin office imposed Senghor as the party's representative to the founding conference in 1927 shortly before Senghor died the PCF leadership had considered this a crude imposition, which infringed on their primacy over the colonies. The PCF's attitude to Senghor reflected an already existing imperial patriotism, notwithstanding the brave stance over the Rif. By 1936, the PCF would rather attack any empire other than the French. Instead they confined themselves to attacking some of the racism and brutality of the colonies. So long as there was not a revolutionary movement in Algeria, they believed they could avoid having to call for independence.[73] Further, since the PCF was effectively subordinated to Moscow, it was bound by the Treaty of Mutual Assurance signed between France and Russia by foreign ministers Laval and Litvinov over a year before the Popular Front had been elected – thus the PCF was committed to defending the existing regime, and the empire was part of the package.[74]

One unintended consequence of the Popular Front's failure to liberate the colonies, or even substantially improve matters, was the disillusionment of two sympathizers then attending the Sorbonne, Michel Aflaq and Salah uh-Din Bitar. Both from Syria, then under a French mandate, they had hoped that Syria's independence would be achieved – but watched as instead the Syrian Communist Party became subordinate to the PCF, and then the French government. Suspecting that the Soviet Union was becoming a nationalist state and abandoning communism, they returned to Syria to agitate against French rule. They would go on to lay the intellectual and organizational bases for Baathism.[75] Another consequence of the pro-colonial attitude was particularly cruel. The same Spanish colonial forces that had led the 'Reconquest' of northern Morocco and collaborated with the French in defeating Abd el-Krim would lead the 'Reconquest' of Spain.[76] A Republican government had come to power in 1931, after a revolt against the dictatorship by the anarchist CNT union and the Socialists (PSOE). There were excellent reasons to doubt that the Socialists would take part in such an action, since they were impeccable gradualists, inspired in large part by the approach of the British Labour Party. Julián Besteiro, who had spent seven months in England during 1924 admiring the Fabians and Labour, had opposed the idea. In fact, King Alfonso's newly appointed ruler of the country, General Dámaso Berenguer, was pleased that the PSOE had no plans for active opposition to his regime under Besteiro, and a report from his director-general of security praised the PSOE leadership for keeping the rank and file out of political agitation. Besteiro was therefore obliged to resign from the presidency of the party when it decided to participate in the rebellion – although after some trepidation he did participate, and became speaker of the new Cortes (parliament).[77]

The parliament was dominated by the PSOE, radical Socialists and regional Republicans – the non-Republican right had only fifty-seven seats. But although their programme was relatively moderate, aimed at modernizing the military, extending rights to women (who had been 'double bound by patriarchy and poverty' as Shirley Mangini puts it), and introducing some labour reforms, there was an early effort, in August 1932, to overthrow the Republic by General José Sanjurjo, head of the Civil Guard, backed by southern aristocratic landowners. The 1933 elections brought a right-wing coalition to power, which engaged in an aggressive assault on the working class, dismantling reformist legislation where it could. In the same year, the Spanish Falange was formed, which mounted an increasingly vocal campaign against the Republic. The last straw for the embattled left was the attempt to introduce Gil Robles, a pro-fascist leader of the Catholic coalition, into the cabinet in October 1934. The call for a general strike produced a strong response only in the Asturias, and it was put down after three weeks by the Army of Africa, led by General Franco, and the Regulares Indigenas, an army of mercenaries recruited partly from the defeated rebels of the Rif. The relentless violence killed 1,000 and wounded a further 3,000. When the Popular Front slate won the elections in February 1936, defeating the National Front by a small margin, months of violence followed. The country was increasingly polarized, with leftist activists rushing to the Communist Party, and former supporters of rightist Catholic parties joining the Falangists.[78]

The military conspirators who sought to overthrow the Spanish Republic from 18 July 1936 were almost all schooled in their techniques through colonial combat. General Mola, the director of the conspiracy, had made his reputation commanding the Moorish Regulares. His instruction on the uprising was, 'He who is not with us is against us.' General Sanjurjo had served in the colonial wars in

Morocco, and was known as the 'Lion of the Rif'. The sixty-one-year-old General Gonzalo Quiepo de Llano y Serra was known for 'swashbuckling cavalry exploits' in Morocco. Franco, who had also developed his flair for military leadership in Morocco, was able to recruit thousands of troops there, and import the techniques of 'pacification' that he had picked up. Indeed, the putsch was to be launched from Spanish Morocco in the first place, and had it not been for airlifts donated by Hitler and Mussolini, the coup would no doubt have failed: the naval leadership agreed to speed their ships to Morocco once the military *pronunciamento* had been issued, but were thwarted by uprisings from the lower ranks.[79] One irony of the attempted military coup was that it stimulated precisely the revolution that it had warned was already afoot: once, a *pronunciamento* might have been enough to finish off a government for good, but now that the masses were used to being involved in political activity, they had citizens' militias prepared to fight back.

It was precisely the colonial policies of both French and Spanish forces against the Islamic liberation leader Abd el-Krim and his guerrilla forces that ensured that Morocco would become the source of fighters for the Francoists. Krim, who had united a tribal opposition to the colonial powers into an independent republic which declared itself an Islamic state, had managed to inflict several defeats on the colonialists before he was caught by French forces led by Marshall Pétain, and imprisoned. The Popular Front government in France did not care to release either him or the colonies, and the Popular Front in Spain did not fight for his release, even though he had pledged to fight against Franco: a great Muslim anti-imperialist fighter (whose successful tactics would inspire Ho Chi Minh and Che Guevara) had thus offered his services to the cause of anti-fascism, only to be rebuffed. And, while the putschists had warned the Moroccan caliph and grand vizier that the Republican government was likely to grant the country independence to undercut the base for the rebellion, the reality was quite the opposite. The government made no serious effort to stir up anticolonial feeling, and, from the moment Franco's forces launched the coup, the government was cautious to the point of lethargy about the response, refusing to arm the CNT and UGT, and advising citizens that 'this absurd venture' was going nowhere.[80]

Very soon, they discovered that their Popular Front allies in France were co-sponsoring a Non-Intervention Pact with Britain. The Soviet Union, which was both anxious to avoid making enemies of either France or Britain, and at the same time was increasingly concerned about the threat from the fascist movement in Europe, initially assented to the Pact, even though it was clear that neither Mussolini nor Hitler would feel themselves bound by it. Anthony Eden, the British foreign secretary, understood perfectly well that this was the case, but British policy at the time was to give a free hand to the fascist powers in acting on their antipathy to communism.[81] Once the Soviet Union decided that, on balance, its best interests were served by supporting the anti-fascists, it took every possible step to constrain the battle and to stop it from developing into a social revolution. Dolores Iaburruri, the brilliant Communist leader known popularly as 'La Pasionaria', publicly denied that a revolution was underway, and vigorously defended businessmen and small landowners at Moscow's behest. The arrival of Soviet arms, when every other state was shunning the Republic, meant that it could insist on the imposition of its policies and the exclusion of the anti-Stalinist left. There was to be no revolution during the war, but rather strict military discipline, firm political control of the army, and an ideology based on nationalism rather than revolution. The anarchists and the *trotskysant* POUM were suppressed, and many supporters were arrested. George Orwell wrote:

> I could understand their suppression of the POUM, but what were they arresting people for? For nothing, so far as I could discover. Apparently the suppression of the POUM had a retrospective effect; the POUM was now illegal and therefore one was breaking the law by having previously belonged to it.

Within months the revolutionary zeal had been sapped away, and by 1939 the war had effectively been won by Franco.[82]

It is not possible to say with any precision what the effect of freeing Morocco and allying with Krim might have been, but it would not be a wild claim that allegiance to the imperial idea is at least part of the explanation for why Spain would be lost for years to fascist rule, thereby supplying Vichy France with a strong southern ally and permitting Hitler to turn his sights on the East. The Spanish case thus stands as one of the more dramatic examples of complicity with imperialism helping to create a fascist blow-back. If the European social democrats proved ineffective in combating fascism, it was often for the same reasons that they were weak on imperialism: they accepted the moral authority of the state, preferred a top-down approach to political change, and were beholden to 'pragmatism' (roughly understood as co-substantial with gradualism and social compromise).[83]

In recent years, it has become commonplace in some circles to counterpose imperialism to fascism. The international relations scholar Fred Halliday, for example, asserted during the 1991 war on

Iraq that, given the choice between imperialism and fascism, he chose imperialism. Yet, as the foregoing would suggest, imperialism and fascism, far from being the neat opposition that such a perspective would imagine them to be, are in fact contiguous. The models for Nazi barbarism had been supplied not only by the bureaucratic institutions of European modernity – the workhouse, the prison, the barracks, the abatoir – but also crucially by European imperialism. Enzo Traverso explains: 'The notion of "living space" was not a Nazi invention. It was simply the German version of a commonplace of European culture at the time of imperialism'. It 'stemmed from a vision of the extra-European worlds as a space to be colonised by biologically superior groups'. Similarly, the ideological justification for racial extermination had been prepared by European Social Darwinism, and the process had been practised in various ways in Tasmania, Australia, New Zealand and the United States. L. Frank Baum, for example, reporting on the Indian Wars, had written:

> The whites, by law of conquest, by justice of civilization, are masters of the American continent and the best safety of the frontier settlements will be secured by the total annihilation of the few remaining Indians . . . better that they should die than live like the miserable wretches that they are.[84]

As Claudia Koonz points out, when the Nazis wanted to annul the legal protections of assimilated citizens, they appealed to analogies with American policy, hoping that Nazi racial codes would soon be as widely accepted as 'US immigration quotas, antimiscegenation laws, involuntary sterilisation programmes in twenty-eight states, and segregation in the Jim Crow south'. Adolf Hitler was himself full of admiration for Europe's colonial model – particularly the British role in India, which they had governed 'very well'. The Nazi *Drang nach Osten* was to repeat Britain's imperial successes:

> It should be possible for us to control this region to the East with two-hundred-and-fifty-thousand men plus a cadre of good administrators. Let's learn from the English, who, with two-hundred-and-fifty-thousand men in all, including fifty thousand soldiers, govern four-hundred-million Indians.[85]

Or again: 'What India was for England, the territories of Russia will be for us.' It was, for him as for the British, a matter of Aryan supremacy. He wrote in *Mein Kampf*,

The Aryan races – often in absurdly small numbers – overthrow alien nations, and favoured by the numbers of people of the lower grade, who are at their disposal to aid them, they proceed to develop, according to the special conditions for life in the acquired territories – fertility, climate, etc., the qualities of intellect and organisation which are dormant in them.[86]

National Socialism also shared important characteristics with Germany's own colonial past:

both called for a racial order based on racial reproduction as the foundation of the state; both sought, at least in part, to replace the classic nation-state with a racial state; both implied the dissolution of the bourgeois family through the complete subordination of sexuality to racial purity; and both entailed an expansionist drive to reproduce this racial order elsewhere.

And, of course, both involved genocide (in 1904, openly referred to as 'annihilation') in the pursuit of the race war. This connection was intuited by Hannah Arendt, who detected the basis for modern 'totalitarianism' in nineteenth-century imperialism. In fact, though most modern 'totalitarianism' theorists pay most attention to similarities in modes of rule between the USSR and Nazi Germany, the extension of the term to Stalinist Russia was almost subsidiary and – controversially, in the contemporary context – Arendt never included the original leadership of the Russian Revolution in that category. This is not often acknowledged by her imitators, and her book has been often reduced to the argument that Stalinism and Nazism bore substantial affinities as 'totalitarian' states.[87] The European imperialist connection has thus been largely occluded, in favour of the Asiatic, in homologous terms to the manner in which the revisionist historian Ernst Nolte argued during the 1980s that the Nazi genocide was in part a defensive reaction against a class genocide launched by the Soviet regime, thereby externalizing fascist violence as something originating in the East and spreading westwards.

The British turn to America

World War II had briefly reinvigorated Britain's imperial zeal and hardened its attitude to the colonies. Although the war effort relied on substantial contributions from the Dominions – India's contribution amounting to 2.25 million troops – the government's attitude continued to be that the colonies would be guided towards 'self-government' within 'the framework of the British Empire': there would be no timetables, and the Cabinet Office made it plain in 1943 that several generations would pass before some colonies became fit for self-government, particularly those with 'plural communities'. Had the British government had its way, in other words, it would still be chaperoning many peoples along the scenic route to self-government today. On the other hand, it was plain that Britain's powers were diminishing, and that it would need a powerful ally – and the United States was the only candidate.[88]

One of the enduring legacies of British colonialism was to be its rapid post-war defeat at the hands of its former allies, the Zionist movement. Palestinians had been resisting both the British and the Zionist movement since their arrival – a resistance that aimed at national liberation. The British had relied to a great extent on the Zionist movement in the crushing of the Arab revolt between 1936 and 1939. Jewish settlers were integrated into a Jewish supernumerary police and Special Night Squads, led by the British army officer Orde Wingate. The latter in particular acted as death squads, and became notorious for their brutality in the suppression of the Arab revolt, fully availing themselves of torture, beatings and summary executions. The British colonists prepared some of the legitimacy for a future Zionist state in its response to the uprising by advocating the partition of Palestine – but, most valuably, passed on a great deal of expertise in repression. Orde Wingate in particular is credited with helping form the military doctrine of the Jewish paramilitaries, and the future Israeli military leader Moshe Dayan was one of his star pupils. Tens of thousands of settlers benefited from the training, and a further 25,000 Haganah troops were trained by the British army during World War II.[89] The Haganah and other paramilitaries would form the core of the Israeli Defense Force, which would lead the subsequent conquest of Palestine by the Zionist movement and the ethnic cleansing of at least 700,000 Palestinians. This process was planned in advance, involved several massacres, and left hundreds of thousands of Palestinians living in camps under the Jordanian Hashemite police state, which had collaborated with the plans.[90] The West Bank and southern Lebanon eluded conquest at that point, partly because of worries that the purificatory feat could not be repeated there, although thirteen southern Lebanese villages were captured and mass executions carried out.[91]

These facts were not widely understood at the time. The mythologies produced by Israeli sources suggested that Zionists had faced down a mighty Arab army, determined to finish off what the Nazis had started, that the Palestinians had never existed as a group (they were nothing other than 'Jordanians'), and that their exodus from Palestine had been precipitated by orders from the Arab leadership.[92] So there might perhaps be an argument that the general indifference of European social democracy to the fate of Palestinians was the result of ignorance. However, there had already been a long-standing tradition of support for the colonization of Palestine by the Zionist movement in the British Labour movement. Ramsay MacDonald, for example, had been a consistent supporter of Zionism since the publication of his pamphlet, *A Socialist in Palestine*, in 1922. British Labour leaders such as Arthur Henderson had declared in favour of Zionism even before the Balfour declaration, and the party had had a significant role in getting the Zionist Marxist group Poalei Zion admitted to the Second International. In 1944 the Zionist leadership had already won the backing of the National Executive Committee of the British Labour Party, which made it part of its official programme to support the 'transfer' of Palestinians from Palestine to neighbouring countries (much to the embarrassment of Ben-Gurion and Chaim Weizmann, who were not admitting to such a goal at that point). It is hard to see this as reflecting anything other than colonialist contempt for non-European indigenes. As Herbert Morrison explained with some relish, the Zionist movement had 'proved to be first class colonisers, to have the real good, old empire qualities'. Thus, while the ethnic cleansing of Palestine was unfolding, the British, declaring themselves no longer responsible for law and order even where their troops were still stationed, turned over vital documents and data that helped in the depopulation of Palestine to the Zionist leadership. The Labour Party, both in parliament and at its grassroots, was thereafter strongly pro-Zionist, a consensus that would outlast even the 1967 war, only coming under sustained critique from its left wing in the 1980s as a result of the Israeli invasion of Lebanon.[93]

The Israeli leadership claimed to be trying to build a socialist state (a carefully constructed myth, as Ze'ev Sternhell has demonstrated),[94] and was soon backed by the Soviet Union. And since the United States rapidly formed a close relationship with Israel, support for the plucky Jewish state in the Levant was uncontroversial among most shades of social-democratic opinion. This hegemonic perspective would be scarcely challenged until the 1960s, and then only by some on the far left. For its part, the British Communist Party (CPGB) was extremely critical of the Labour government for not taking a pro-Zionist position immediately. This was a substantial change from its previous position, in which it had criticized Zionism for its reliance on British patronage, for its sectarianism (the Zionist trade union, the Histadrut, excluded

Arab members), and for the inevitable conflict with Arab aspirations towards self-determination – the Soviet Union's stance on the matter was, of course, not entirely unconnected to this volte-face.[95]

As a rule, European social-democratic parties did not pursue a foreign policy markedly different from that of the centre-right in the aftermath of the war. Some briefly pursued neutralism (Switzerland, Sweden, Finland, Austria, West Germany and Italy). Only in West Germany and Italy was this stance controversial, and both the PSI and the SPD had opted for Atlanticism by the end of the 1950s. The Labour Party adhered to a bipartisan consensus both on empire and on relations with the United States. Secretary of State James Byrnes commented on the transition to the Attlee administration during the Potsdam negotiations that 'Britain's stand on the issues . . . was not altered in the slightest, so far as we could discern'. In the wartime coalition, Labour had been part of the alliance with the United States, and proceeded to pursue nuclear weapons and the allotment of peacetime bases to America without any substantial discussion at all – in fact, the decision to press for the nuclear bomb was taken without parliament being consulted. Clement Attlee had told the cabinet during June 1943 that he had no intention of presiding over the dissolution of the Commonwealth, and insisted it would continue to carry its 'full weight in the post-war world with the US and the USSR'. In fact, the Labour Party did mount a substantial opposition on one foreign policy question, namely the invasion of Egypt in 1956 – but for different reasons, depending on which wing of the party was speaking: the leadership was opposed to any policy that could draw Britain into conflict with the United States.[96]

The United States government – eager to quell independent or pro-Soviet tendencies on the Left and antipathetic to British socialism – embarked on an ambitious programme of infiltration and co-optation. The CIA, in alliance with anti-Communist intellectuals and trade unionists, worked to promote the revisionist and right-wing elements in the labour movement, and split them from the Left where possible. The Atlanticist tendency in the Labour Party, today its dominant wing, was not invented by the Cold War – rather, its engagement in that period and its entanglement with American intelligence gave shape to already existing tendencies. If it was pro-Nato, generally favoured American subventions, and accepted anti-Communism as the only relevant basis for foreign policy, these were the corollaries of its pressing domestic commitment to refashioning the Labour Party as one of moderate welfare capitalism, rather than socialism. The one occasion upon which it broke with the United States over a substantial foreign policy issue was when Harold Wilson's government refused to send troops to Vietnam – in large part because of pressure from the Labour Left, on whom Wilson relied, and a sizeable anti-war movement led by the Vietnam Solidarity Campaign. However, he quietly supported the American policy and tried to make up for it by sustaining Britain's 'East of Suez' commitments, with forces in Malaysia and Singapore. Further, the Wilson administration did the US government a huge favour by forcibly removing the population from the island of Diego Garcia, in the British Indian Ocean Territory, and leasing it to the United States as a military base (bombing raids on both Afghanistan and Iraq would later be launched from this island).[97]

Algeria and the French Left

The French Communists did not join the Resistance until the Nazi invasion of Russia in 1941, but their performance once they did throw their weight behind it led to them being its largest single force by 1943, and in the immediate aftermath of Liberation their membership had increased from 338,127 in 1937 to 544,921. Communist parliamentary representation had increased from 78 seats during the Popular Front to 148 seats in October 1945. This had been achieved partly by the attenuation of their explicit Marxist commitments, and with the help of their emphasis on the patriotic element of the struggle. Yet, just as the PCF did not oppose the USSR's colonization of Eastern Europe, it was still only a nominal, occasional opponent of French colonialism. In fact, precisely as it had collaborated with the Socialists (SFIO) and Radicals in supporting the French Empire during the brief Popular Front government, its ministers would, in 1945, support the vicious repression of an uprising in the Algerian city of Sétif, followed by a political clampdown on all opposition. The course had been prepared by the Communists' 'national' stance during the Resistance. Florimond Bonte had told the Constituent Assembly in October 1944 that France 'is and ought to remain a great African power'. In July 1945, Etienne Fajon had argued that the interests of North Africans lay 'in the union with the French people'. So it was that when the rebellion struck, the 19 May 1945 edition of *L'Humanité* contained the absurd, frenzied call for punishment of 'the Hitlerite killers who took part in the events of May 8th and the pseudo-nationalist leaders who have tried to deceive the Muslim masses'. Because the French government closed down the commission of inquiry directed by General Tubert, there are no decisive figures on the numbers killed in the massacres. As is typical with colonial ventures, the name of every one of the 102 dead Europeans is known, but there is not even a rough total for the number of Algerians slaughtered, though it is estimated to be in the thousands. The same story would be repeated elsewhere: the Vietnamese were betrayed; Tunisia and Morocco had to wait until the threat of Algerian independence allowed them to claim some limited independence of their own in 1954; the Communists would barely even raise a protest when the French army and air forces assaulted Madagascar and massacred between 80,000 and 100,000 people in March 1947, in order to put down a national liberation movement that had begun as a *pacifist* struggle for freedom.[98]

The bulk of the French Left, including the Radicals and Socialists, directed the brutal suppression of the Algerian uprising that was launched in 1954, in the name of French republicanism. The PCF acquiesced, partly because of electoral considerations. As Daniele Joly points out, the large French community in Algeria (983,100 French citizens in 1954) were the only residents of Algeria permitted to vote. There were other pressures. The Communists had been excluded from the French government since 1947, and the increasing repression directed at them 'reached its height during the Pinay government when in 1952 after the Ridgway riot the Communist leader Jacques Duclos was arrested and absurdly accused of planning an insurrection'. The policy of the Cominform at that time was that affiliated parties should pursue a 'united front of patriots', so the PCF sought to placate its opponents. Moreover, the USSR had no interest in an independent Algeria since, were the power of France to be reduced, American influence would increase in inverse proportion; and, given the reformist strategy that the Communists had pursued since the 1930s, they were loathe to endanger a massive export market for French goods. In 1954 the three North African colonies of Algeria, Morocco and Tunisia alone accounted for a 96.22 billion–franc trading surplus – any blow against this relationship was an attack on the health of the system that the Communists now wish to manage, rather than revolutionize. The PCF, which had in 1939 denied the existence of an Algerian nation, therefore supported 'liberty' for Algeria, provided it was understood that this did not entail independence.[99]

On 1 November 1954, the Front de Libération Nationale (FLN) announced its existence with a communiqué calling for the 'restoration of the Algerian state, sovereign, democratic, and social, within the framework and principles of Islam'. François Mitterrand, then minister of the interior, declared in response: 'Algeria is France'. Unquestionably, the decision to take up armed combat was itself a response to the failures of the organized Left: Martin Evans's account, based on extensive interviews with participants, explains:

The year 1956 was a recurring watershed for interviewees. They explained how by the end of the year, confusion and uncertainty had disappeared. The voting of special powers by the PCF and SFIO; the call-up of reservists; the first rumours about torture: a clear set of political choices flowed from these events . . . For others subsequent events were needed to establish the same conclusions in their minds, and here a moment of further clarity was May 1958, with the overthrow of the Fourth Republic and the return of de Gaulle. Among the interviewees, there was a consensus that the reaction on the left was woefully inadequate. Instead of offering opposition, it just caved in, timidly accepting the new status quo.[100]

The French intellectual left was divided in its response to the war from the start. Albert Camus, an Algiers-born *pied-noir*, had been ejected from the PCF precisely on the grounds of his refusal to soft-pedal the party's previous commitment to Arab nationalism during the Popular Front era. But he went on to support the French repression of the Sétif rebellion in 1945, and opposed outright the demands for independence. He was for equal rights between French and Algerians, but considered the idea of Algerian nationhood a myth. His hopes were invested in the Socialist-led government, and he approved many of its actions, including press censorship. Camus did criticize some of the French government's methods, noting that, in the case of torture and collective repression, 'we are doing . . . what we reproached the Germans for doing'. But particular animus was reserved for the FLN and its terrorist tactics, and in a drastically misjudged statement that earned him obloquy for years to come, he told an Algerian student in Stockholm,

> I said and I repeat that it is necessary to do justice to Algerians and to give them a fully democratic regime . . . I can assure you, nevertheless, that you have comrades who live today because of actions that you know nothing about . . . I have always condemned terror. I must always condemn a terrorism which is exercised blindly, in the streets of Algiers for example, and which could one day strike at my mother or my daughter. I believe in justice, but I would defend my mother before justice.[101]

The imprisoned Algerian nationalist, Ahmed Taleb Ibrahimi, wrote a scathing open letter to Camus:

You, the man who condemns terrorism for fear that your own [family] will be victims of it, you who speak often in moving terms about your mother, do you know that some of ours have lost their entire families because of the searches [*ratissages*] of the French army, that others have seen their mother (yes, Camus, their mother!) humiliated by French soldiers, and in the most ignoble fashion?[102]

It was not only that Camus preferred his mother over justice, but that he had defended the French state's crackdown in doing so. Camus's old friend from the Resistance, Jean-Paul Sartre, took a somewhat different approach. Having spent some time on good terms with the PCF, Sartre was moving towards a more critical position by 1956. When Pierre Hervé was expelled from the PCF for some implied criticisms of the party in his book of that year, *La Révolution et les Fétiches*, Sartre's review of the affair accused the PCF of having failed to develop Marxism as an intellectual tool. Later, he would develop a thoroughgoing critique of Stalinism and, when Russian tanks crushed the Hungarian revolution, denounce the USSR's claim that what they were suppressing was a counter-revolution. The PCF, which had polled over a quarter of the vote in the January 1956 elections, was entering a period of profound crisis. It had insisted, after Khrushchev's revelations about Stalinist brutality, that any problems that existed in the USSR were a result of capitalist encirclement and Trotskyist sabotage. When Khrushchev's tanks invaded Hungary, the Party maintained that the revolution had been nothing but the ferment of the 'dregs of the fallen classes' assisted by 'fascists and former SS . . . returning to Hungary by the planeload'.[103]

In stark contrast to the position of Camus, Sartre launched an attack on colonialism as a system, condemning those who sought reforms for believing that there could be 'good colonists' – the 'purest of intentions', he maintained, would have led to the war. The liberation of Algerians *'and also that of France'* (italics in original) could only be achieved through 'the shattering of colonization'. The fruits of French colonization had been accumulated through the expropriation of the Algerian *fellahin*, and any moves towards assimilation and full political rights for the indigenes would necessarily result in 'the ending of colonialism'. The defence of colonialism 'infects us with racism' and 'obliges our young men to fight despite themselves and die for the Nazi principles that we fought against ten years ago; it even attempts to defend itself by arousing fascism here in France'. Finally, a swipe at the humanitarian colonists:

People who talk of the abandonment of Algeria are imbeciles. There is no abandoning what we have never owned. It is, quite the opposite, a question of our constructing with the Algerians new relations between a free France and a liberated Algeria.[104]

Later, he would champion the work of Frantz Fanon and write compellingly on the political thought of Patrice Lumumba.[105]

It is striking that even a right-wing opponent of pan-Arabism, leftism and Third Worldism such as Raymond Aron could declare himself in favour of independence in 1957, long before the Socialists or PCF. The Socialists, when De Gaulle's coup came, mounted no resistance – instead, they insisted on being the vanguard of the Fifth Republic, certain that the alternative was either Nazism or Communism (an 'anti-totalitarian' coup?). Laurent Casanova of the PCF politburo made contact with Francis Jeanson, a French philosopher and protégé of Sartre who had travelled to Algeria to work with the FLN two weeks after the coup. Jeanson was a delegate for the FLN in the meeting, and he insisted that the Communists support *independence*, and not merely peace. Although they promised to do so, it was only when de Gaulle eventually moved towards independence, and public opinion had turned dramatically against keeping Algeria as a French department, that the PCF altered its position. It finally gave full and unequivocal support to the FLN in 1960, at the same time as the USSR recognized the Gouvernement Provisoire de la République Algérienne, and one year after de Gaulle had called for independence. This intransigence may have sat well with the party's electoral strategy, which was to seek an alliance with more centrist parties, and with its appropriation of republicanism, and it was congruent with its distrust of Islam as 'essentially reactionary'; but it redounds to their enormous discredit in light of the brutality of the war waged by the French government and by terror networks organized under the rubric of the colonists' far-right organization, the Organisation Armée Secrète (OAS). The French military and police efforts alone killed upwards of 350,000 Algerians.[106]

Fabianism and decolonization

There is a long-standing myth in Anglocentric history that, almost alone among European states, Britain decolonized with minimal fuss and violence. This is how the sociologist Hendrik Spruyt puts it: 'The British government reconfigured its territorial framework without getting embroiled in colonial quagmires, save for incidental clashes such as in Kenya or Malaya'. Those incidental clashes happened to be extraordinarily bloody affairs, and in fact this reconfiguration took place only after a prolonged period in which nationalist and leftist challenges to the empire were savagely repressed. Malaya, for example, only achieved independence after a prolonged counterinsurgency war lasting from 1946 to 1957. This involved aerial bombardment as well as routine atrocities against civilians, with roughly half a million Chinese residents driven into concentration camps ('strategic hamlets' in a different language), mass deportations, and the use of defoliants, with up to 13,000 killed.[107]

In light of what we now know of the British Empire, it is remarkable how intensely apologists for the colonies on the Left shared the British government's avowed concerns, and how blind they were to its practices. The Fabians, while declaring 'full and happy consciousness of international unity', were nevertheless concerned about the prospect of leaving the colonized to their own 'primitive' devices. H.N. Brailsford remarked that Europeans had become 'settled and industrious colonists'. But who was bold enough to offer to the colonies 'a Beveridge plan'? Only socialists could be 'pioneers in showing how the primitive and colonial peoples can be integrated within the organised life of mankind'. Arthur Creech Jones, who was made colonial secretary in the immediate post-war Labour government, explained that the 'backward areas menace the rest of the world if they remain underdeveloped with low standards of living, with disease rampant and the people weak and ignorant'. He was to embark on a series of policies designed to boost productivity in the colonies, which the Labour-Left *Tribune* newspaper hailed as 'Fabianising the Empire'.[108]

Rita Hinden, a South African–born journalist who campaigned for colonial reform and supported Zionism, argued in 1959 that, while it would not be permissible for socialists to enjoy the fruits of empire, it would be better to accept the imperial 'heritage', 'with the determination to nurse and develop it for the advantage of its rightful owners till they themselves should have come of age'. Driving home the childhood metaphor, Hinden pointed to the precedent in 'Labour and the New Social Order', which spoke of Britain's obligations to the 'non-adult races'. Having thus recalled the familial metaphor, and relegated the colonized to the status of infants, Hinden proceeded: 'Anti-imperialism? Yes. But non-interventionism? No. We must intervene, but somehow it must be for the other man's good. We must be trustees, not imperialists.'[109] The language here is remarkably familiar: interventionism, but for the other chap's good; trusteeship rather than plunder (shades of the rhetoric that would be applied with respect to a US plan to take control of Middle East oilfields in 2003);[110] tutelage, rather than independence. As for the Fabians of 1900, and today's liberal interventionists, sovereignty for Third World nations was abridgeable if it interfered with 'rights' claimed by imperialist states.

Hinden noted that the natives were chafing at the bit: 'The more that was "done" for the colonial peoples, the further they advanced in wealth and welfare and knowledge, the less satisfied they have been to remain in tutelage, however benevolent.' The trouble was that in

> the plural societies; those colonies – particularly in East and Central Africa – where different races live side by side and refuse to mix, let alone coalesce into nationhood . . . [h]ardly any of the local population of whatever race, who can see further than the end of their noses, really wants the imperial power to recede while all those passions are on the boil. Someone is needed to keep the ring and to help forge a nation out of what is still no more than a collection of warring and suspicious 'tribes'.

It was a real dilemma: 'dare we withdraw from Kenya or Tanganyika or the Central African Federation, and so open the door to repetition of the South African story with its white minority domination?' The British government had itself raised the prospect of ethnic strife as a rationale for continuing the colonial relationship; yet this was at a time when in Kenya, for example, the British government was indeed enforcing white minority domination, having turned the country into a vast gulag embracing most of the population, and killing up to 100,000 people in their suppression of the Kikuyu.[111]

Finally, a new problem was raised, and a new solution proposed. Hinden directed readers to consider 'the Middle East crisis of 1956'. There, the empires had engaged in relations of trusteeship, and then the empire 'was in fact ended' with the resulting rule of 'petty princelings', in which

> oil companies intrigued and bribed; Big Power Politics played off one small state against another, encouraged their puppet regimes, seduced them with armaments. Was this so much better than the old imperialism? In some ways it might even have been worse . . . Imperialism, for all its faults, was a form of world order. *Pax Britannica* maintained some kind of peace and international security over large parts of the world. As country after country now throws off the imperial shackles, are they each to pursue their own self-assertive nationalisms unhindered? Are they each to be in a position to break international agreements,

to hold the world to ransom if geography or raw material assets favour them, to oppress their own minorities (or majorities) if they so wish, to arm and threaten their neighbours?[112]

The United Nations, it was hoped, would avoid this miserable outcome. The author would attend conferences of the Congress for Cultural Freedom along with Tony Crosland, Hugh Gaitskell and Daniel Bell, and would go on to become a supporter of the Vietnam War. Writing for the CIA's Cold War publication, *Encounter*, she sneered of Third World leaders that

> instead of being noble freedom-fighters, supported by the sympathy of all liberal-minded people abroad, they had at once to become politicians and administrators, caught up in a new power struggle which is an inevitable part of politics. And once they became politicians and administrators, they were open to all the seductions of power-intrigue, corruption, bribery, even thuggery.[113]

The Middle East crisis of 1956 might seem an odd example to raise in this context. What had in fact happened was that the nationalist officer corps that overthrew the pro-British monarchy in Egypt had decided to nationalize the Suez Canal: the occasion for this was provided by the decision of the US and UK to marginalize Nasser, in light of his refusal to allow Washington and London to determine key elements of his economic and foreign policy. The pressure exerted on him included the withdrawal of funding for the Aswan Dam, which Nasser decided to fund instead by nationalizing the Suez Canal.[114] However, in abrogating the Anglo-Egyptian Treaty negotiated with the monarchy in 1936, in which UK troops were permitted to remain in the canal zone, he left an enormous gap in the UK's position in the Middle East. Nasser was therefore punished with an invasion by Israel, followed by the UK and France, with the aim of toppling the Egyptian leader and restoring Anglo-French control of the Suez Canal Company. It failed partly because the US refused to support the plan, concerned as it was about the prospect of strengthening its colonial rivals. But Nasser had not threatened his neighbours or held the world to ransom: he had taken possession of a canal that was built through the vigorous extortion of the Egyptian treasury and the intense exploitation of Egyptian peasants in the form of corvée labour. An attack by Western powers precisely for the purpose of retaining colonial possessions and strategic advantage was thus interpreted as an outrageous affront by a 'petty princeling'. This was also the reaction of the Labour Party leadership and the Labour-supporting *Daily Mirror*. Nasser was – as all foes of the West must invariably be – a fascist, comparable with Hitler. The BBC described him simply as a 'barking dictator'.[115] This propaganda technique, only modestly refined, is still with us, except that there are some today who unreflectively reproduce these accents and assumptions of power, and offer them to us as a judicious critique of anti-imperialism.

Europe's colonialist and imperialist regimes did not simply obtain the support of some liberals and socialists because of Bad Ideas. Certainly, the colossal impact of white supremacy as a principle of planetary arrangement produced racist forms of knowledge that irradiated the metropolitan societies, reaching even into the most critical quarters. Yet there were also powerful material reasons for supporting the empire, particularly for those who accepted the basic legitimacy of the society and its institutions. For one thing, as we saw in the case of the SPD, there was the threat of repression from the state, although this would not have been sufficient had they not also accepted the legitimacy of the state. Secondly, there was the prospect that decolonization would drastically diminish the profitability of domestic industries, which was an unappealing prospect for those whose entire strategy for reform relied on a robust national economy. Thirdly, there were the exigencies of electoralism and coalition-building – sizeable imperial constituencies had been created through adept manipulation of patriotic symbols and regalia, and through military clubs and sodalities. Finally, there was the tawdry influence of the USSR, which subordinated loyal European Communist parties to its geopolitical manoeuvring, characterized at its lowest point by the shame and disgrace of the Molotov–Ribbentrop treaty, which saw what millions still believed to be a socialist state enter into a pact of aggression with Nazi expansionism.

The liberal and socialist supporters of empire accepted the moral authority of the polities in which they were active, and identified with their interests and priorities. As a result, they sleepwalked straight into the twin propellers of fascism and world war, and were duly dispersed. Not only did they overlook the evils of imperialism; they also either transferred its evils onto its victims (*they* are barbarous, uncivilized, fail to value human life, and so on), or energetically concocted prettifying patinas and rationalizations (altruistic colonialism, somehow for the other's benefit). Consistently denying the right (and even ability) of the indigenous to resist subjection, believing the worst about them and the best about the colonial overlords, they used their influence over 'hearts and minds' to neutralize liberal and leftist criticism of imperial forms of exploitation. As we shall discover, it was perhaps the United States government which first discovered how to fully exploit this particular mechanism.

2

CREATING AN IMPERIAL CONSTITUENCY

> Only in a world where irony was dead could an intellectual class enter war at the head of such illiberal cohorts in the avowed cause of world-liberalism and world-democracy.
>
> — *Randolph Bourne*[1]

> Those who view the history of North America as a narrative of genocide and slavery are, it seems to me, hopelessly stuck on this reactionary position. They can think of the Western expansion of the United States only in terms of plague blankets, bootleg booze and dead buffalo, never in terms of the medicine chest, the wheel and the railway. One need not be an automatic positivist about this. But it does happen to be the way that history is made, and to complain about it is as empty as complaint about climatic, geological or tectonic shift.
>
> — *Christopher Hitchens*[2]

America's exceptions and America's rule

Whatever may be said about Europe's empires, it is frequently averred that America is unique, that the masters of the New World ought to be assessed on independent criteria from those of the Old World. One contemporary account of American exceptionalism argues that Americans are distinguished by sharing a 'broad republican ideology', whose elements are subject to emphasis and marginalization according to specific objectives. This entails a commitment to democracy and egalitarianism within the confines of a 'free market', and an emphasis on constitutionalism and the separation of powers. 'With the monumental exception of slavery, society in America was more egalitarian than in Europe' throughout the nineteenth century: workers had been unionized as early as 1794; property restrictions on voting were eroding by the 1820s; by 1842, the right to strike had been recognized in Massachusetts; by 1860, the ten-hour day had been achieved. In these respects, then, the American wage-earner was in a superior position to his European counterpart, which thus partly explains the relative conservatism of the American working class and their lack of receptivity to socialist ideology.[3]

Discussing 'anti-Americanism', Christopher Hitchens argued in 2002 that

> racism and theological bigotry are 'anti-American' as nearly as possible by definition, since these things are condemned or outlawed – after a bit of a struggle, admittedly – in the amendments to the Constitution if not in the document itself.[4]

(Hitchens would later commend the American Revolution as the only one left standing,[5] and, having received American citizenship, he was able to address his audiences proudly, for the first time, as 'my fellow Americans'.)

America's domestic exceptionalism is said to radiate outwards into its imperial pursuits. Recall Michael Ignatieff's contention that America's domestic rights culture and its revolutionary legacy guided its foreign policy – which was very different from 'the ordinary narcissism and nationalism that all powerful states display'.[6] Claims to uniqueness are ubiquitous, however – one might add that they are usually both narcissistic and nationalistic. The question is not whether America is unique, but rather whether any valid distinctions that might be drawn authorize the glowing tributes made to America's commitment to liberty, human rights and liberalism, and why this doctrine should exert such a powerful appeal. The answers lie in the way in which a pro-imperial consensus was built in the United States.

White republic, elite democracy

The exceptionalists are surely correct in their assumption that America's overseas strategy is determined by its domestic structures. Crucial in the development of the American imperial idea was the tumultuous racial hierarchy, sometimes known by such euphemisms as the 'melting pot'. Although multiracial, multinational groups of workers had been crucial in the radicalization and success of the American Revolution,[7] and although many of the Revolution's participants and sympathizers were aware that slavery was inconsistent with their ideals, slavery would not be abolished until 1865, and full citizenship would not even be formally granted to African-Americans until 1965. Similarly, the revolt against Old Europe was followed by the annihilation by warfare of Native Americans. America's revolutionary egalitarianism had been fused with romantic nationalism, so that as the nineteenth century progressed, more and more Americans discovered the secret that their success lay not institutions, but in race and blood – a thought that would be elaborated by Barnum-esque race theorists for mass audiences. In some ways, American nationalism was *founded* on the principle of 'clearing' Indian Country and annexing it. Benjamin Franklin had warned the British as early as 1751 that a 'prince' who 'acquires new territory, if he finds it vacant, or removes the Natives to give his own People Room', should be considered the father of his own nation. As for the African slaves, Jefferson had come by the 1780s to suspect that they were inferior, a 'distinct race' which would never rise to the level of the whites.[8] This apparent paradox – of egalitarianism running alongside tyranny and racial extermination – is sometimes referred to as '*Herrenvolk* Democracy'.[9] The coincidence of the gradual abolition of impressments and indentured white labour with the continuation of black slavery; the erosion of property qualifications for voting coupled with the persistent refusal of citizenship for African-Americans; the democratization of the society for an expanding number of white males alongside repeated terror campaigns against America's racial minorities – this was the American analogue to Europe's continued practice of white supremacy in the colonies long after a series of revolutions had destroyed tyranny; and it was also the precedent and model for America's own overseas colonial adventures.

Slavery had always transcended the divide between domestic and foreign policy for the Americas. From 1500 to 1800, more Africans than Europeans arrived in the Americas, with up to 20 million Africans shipped against their will, and up to 100 million dying as a result of the trade.[10] It was both the main foreign policy, as it were, and the main labour-system. As David Brion Davis writes, 'from the very start, America's foreign policy presupposed the national government's commitment to protect and support the South's "peculiar institution,"' such as 'when the United States demanded either compensation or the return of the thousands of slaves who had been freed and taken off by the British during the War of Independence and then the War of 1812'. Similarly,

on November 7, 1841 . . . a slave named Madison Washington led an armed rebellion on an American coastal ship, the Creole, en route from Virginia to America's leading slave market, New Orleans. The victorious blacks steered the ship into the British port of Nassau, where slavery had been abolished seven years earlier. When the British authorities refused to return the blacks and validated their freedom, Secretary of State Daniel Webster sent an angry note to America's ambassador in England, even hinting war if the owners of the slaves were not compensated.[11]

In order to protect Southern slavery, both Britain and France had to be excluded from the Spanish territories of North America. The slave-holders feared that Britain, whose colonies could no longer compete with the rich slaveholding South, would trigger an emancipationist insurgency on the model of Haiti in Cuba, Florida, and the Gulf States. When Texas settlers engaged in combat with the recently inde-pendent state of Mexico, their chief concern was its prohibition against slavery, which was seen as a threat to their 'property'. Mexico in 1821 still embraced California, Nevada, Utah, Arizona, New Mexico, Texas and parts of Colorado and Wyoming, and was thus a key enemy for the expansionists. The Americans noted that Mexican independence had been achieved under the leadership of those of European 'stock', which prompted some deeper thought about 'race' and its various layers. The Spanish, it was decided, were 'Mediterranean', of lower European stock than Anglo-Saxons, and were at any rate beholden to a Catholicism that produced autocracy rather than the democracy and constitutional republic favoured by Anglo-Saxons. Further, they had been alarmingly willing to mix with the natives, thus degenerating their 'whiteness'. Mexicans were unworthy of a prize like California, and Latin Americans in general were ready for civilization or extermination. President Polk's campaign in favour of the annexation of Texas and California in 1844 made copious use of the language of 'the race', 'the march of civilization', 'the path of progress'. It was believed that the fact of American domi-nation would either 'regenerate . . . the people of Mexico' or gradually exterminate 'her weaker blood'. Republicanism and progress were thus fused with Anglo-Saxon and Protestant virtue. The contiguity of racism and the ideology of 'liberation' was exemplified by a New York poet, who put the following words into the mouth of a jubilant Mexican: 'The Saxons are coming, our freedom is nigh!'[12]

If global struggles had a bearing on America's domestic rifts, so domestic struggles over the Union and slavery intersected with hemi-spheric concerns. The slave South had seen the possibility of a better alliance with Brazil, particularly in light of the continuing pressure from London against slavery. Between 1600 and 1850 approximately 4.5 million slaves were sent to Brazil – ten times as many as went to North America – with the trade reaching an all-time peak in the 1840s. By 1820, Brazilian slaves numbered 2 million, approximately two-thirds of the population. As this illicit business increased in the 1840s, enslaved Africans were transported disproportionately on ships made and/or registered in the US, and flying the US flag. As time passed, increasingly these ships carried American crews and were financed by American capital. Technically the practice was illegal, but the ships continued to depart from Baltimore, New York, Providence, Boston, and Salem, and they refused to allow the Royal Navy to search them. This trend was one of the chief dynamics supporting the rise of Deep South nationalism, but the prospect of expansion into Brazil fired the imaginations of many US state and military personnel. Thus Matthew Fontaine Maury, US naval commander, hoped to seize the Amazon and consolidate a slave empire with Brazil, which would act as the 'safety valve of the Union'. Maury's designs on the Amazon were taken seriously enough to worry Brazil's Foreign Ministry, which received an unconvincing reassurance from US Secretary of State William Marcy.[13]

The gold rush in California involved thousands of Americans stopping off en route at Rio, which meant that they could catch a glimpse of the slave trade in action. A recent secretary of state to the US minister in Brazil, observing the process, was ecstatic about the prospects. He wrote to the infamous filibuster William Walker, who had recently taken over the Republic of Nicaragua and declared himself president, urging him to forget his current possession and help prevent 'the fairest portion of God's Creation rotting away in the hands of a decrepit race incapable of developing its resources'. In 1862, committee of the House of Representatives on 'Emancipation and Colonization' considered Maury's ideas. As early as 1858, a group of Republican leaders in border states and in the West introduced legislation to subsidize black colonization in Latin America; and during the Civil War Washington's ambassador to Brazil, a comrade of the southern slaver John C. Calhoun, sounded its foreign ministry out about the idea, with no success.[14]

Lincoln pressed hard for this policy, and instructed Congress to raise $600,000 for the purpose. Fearful of European recognition of the southern confederacy, he supposed that the proclamation of emancipation would galvanize international support, and was assured of the same by his ambassador in Madrid. At the same time, however, he wished to neutralize criticisms from the Democratic Party that his policy would lead to the 'Africanization of America'. In the effort to secure London's support, the US offered to send freed slaves to the British West Indies. The British accepted the idea in principle, but made it clear that they had no intention of accepting the elderly or infirm. They wanted only agricultural workers of 'pure' African stock, who would work under indenture for three years. Gradually, however, London came to oppose the whole idea, and planters in Caribbean islands to which they might be deported suspected a Washington scheme that would not be in their interests. The Civil War was almost internationalized when it seemed to the US that Brazil was being too protective of the Confederates, who were using Brazil's ports to attack.[15]

When the war was settled on the side of the Union and hundreds of thousands of slaves were freed as a consequence, former slaveholders spent decades trying to resuscitate the moral and intellectual basis for slavery. The basic defence of slavery had already been elaborated before the Civil War – for example by Matthew Estes in his 1846 polemic, 'A Defense of Negro Slavery As It Exists in the United States' – and it drew very much on the same ideological resources that sustained colonialism. The arguments were that the practice of slavery was mandated in the Old Testament; that it was a stage through which all races had to proceed en route to maturity; that it was for the benefit of the slave, who would learn habits of industry and the arts of civilization. The overthrow of slavery after the Civil War put racial conservatives on the defensive, and the arguments had to be regurgitated or refashioned. A former owner of slaves, writing under the pen name of 'Civis', claimed that slavery had 'brought absolute savages into contact with civilization and taught them to be skilled labourers'.[16]

Another former slaveholder, Colonel Robert Bingham, reasoned that 'the condition of the ante-bellum free negro among us' was 'worse than that of the slave'. He maintained that the very freedom which former slaves now enjoyed was precisely *because* of slavery: 'Under our treatment this savage was so developed in the arts of civilization in a little more than a century that he was deemed worthy by the people of the North to share with them in the citizenship of this great Republic'. Slavery had been liberation, courtesy of the white man: 'We are Teutons, God's kings of men. But every step towards the highest freedom was won in the best blood of our race.' The ancestors of America's rulers had, he noted, exterminated the Celt in England, and the 'Red man' in America, while excluding the 'Yellow man' – only the institution of slavery had protected 'the negro' from a similar fate. The abolition of slavery had thus brought great dangers to 'the negro' by loosening the shackles of civilization, encouraging drunkenness, low morals and assaults on white women. Therefore, 'the freed negro must face the race antagonism of the man of Anglo-Saxon blood, before which stronger races have fallen'.[17]

Perhaps the most stunning defence of slavery was offered by George Fitzhugh, who maintained that it was a bulwark against capitalist exploitation. Fitzhugh's reactionary anti-capitalism, inspired to a great extent by thinkers such as Carlyle and Maistre, held that slavery was a venerable pre-capitalist institution with bonds of social solidarity embedded in hierarchical relations. Capitalism, which he saw as coextensive with free labour, dissolved these bonds and gave rise to terrifying symptoms such as communism, socialism, and free love. By being property, the slave acquired a value to the owner that he lacked as a rented labourer. A slave would be looked after and kept in health, while a wage-labourer could expect only indifference to his general well-being, since he could easily be replaced.[18] Such were the humanitarian arguments for slavery.

When the war was settled on the side of the Union, and hundreds of thousands of slaves were freed as a consequence, two immediate results were the flight of slavers to Brazil, taking their slaves with them, and a dramatic increase in 'black-birding' (slave-trading) in the Pacific. The main targets of this practice were Melanesians and Polynesians, and their chief destinations were Australia and Fiji. In Queensland, American planters would provide the vanguard of the bonded labour system, and in Fiji they would introduce a local chapter of the Ku Klux Klan to maintain racial order with a very high hand. They were in many ways the pioneers who first shifted America's frontier out into the Pacific Ocean; and it was the labour system in Hawaii, run by white planters, that led to some of the first sparks of competition with post-Restoration Japan, whose rising star led the king of that country to import thousands of Japanese workers to the island chain.

Commodore Matthew Perry had already led the 'Black Ships' of the US navy to attack Japan, and force the country open to international trade in 1854. Secretary of State William Seward had been obsessed with Asia as a whole, but particularly with Japan, whose 'simple people' he thought should be made to respect the 'institutions of Christianity'. He was concerned about indigenous resistance to the Shogun, whose policy of acquiescence to Western powers produced enormous resentment. Lincoln's US minister to Japan, Robert H. Pruyn, visited the country in 1863 during a renewed international assault, and found that Western powers there were 'in the outposts of civilization. It is here as with our Indian tribes'. He recommended sending an international flotilla force to open the Straits of Shimonoseki. The victors had collected the spoils at the 1866 Convention, in which a system of tariffs advantageous to foreign powers was forced on Japan. The indigenous war against the shogunate in the two years that followed was thus partly a war of national resistance under the rubric of imperial restoration. The victory of forces under a fifteen-year-old emperor (who adopted the name 'Meiji', meaning 'enlightened rule') did not immediately challenge the framework of its treaty obligations. But the new regime did seek to revolutionize the country's relationship with external powers, and it could not have failed to notice that states with strong industries and armies were winning all sorts of prizes. The 1866 treaty, while enriching the West, sent money pouring out of Japan. Consequently, the income for a military build-up had to be accrued by taxation on rice and land – a policy that eventually caused the Satsuma rebellion in 1877, the same year as an enormous US general strike. The rebellion was destroyed, but the Japanese state had learned to avert domestic class conflict by deflecting internal tensions onto external enemies.[19]

The state that competed with America in the Pacific islands was thus a modernizing regime, intent on imitating the European powers the better to beat them at their own game. Japanese workers faced racial discrimination in Hawaii at the hands of the regnant Euro-American elite, while Japan became an ally of the Hawaiian royal family when white interests overthrew the royals with the imposition of the Bayonet Constitution of 1887. The trouble for the white planters was that labour was in short supply, black-birding was diminishing, and Europeans were not anxious to come. The Japanese labourers were given to militancy; and opening the islands to unlimited Chinese immigration as an alternative did not solve the problem. By the 1890s, Japanese labour on the islands was the most significant part of the workforce – a situation that induced the white elite to legally curtail Japanese labour and press for American annexation. By the time the US was conquering Cuba and the Philippines, the presence of a number of Japanese soldiers in Hawaii worried the planters. The contest for the islands was seen as a race war, which would decide whether the islands were an American colony or an Asiatic one. Furthermore, Japan's successful war against Russia in 1905 raised the hackles of US military leaders such as Alfred Thayer Mahan, who regarded America's Asiatic competitors as being more 'virulent' than the 'niggers' the US had such 'problems' with domestically. One race war thus shaded directly into another.[20]

The American Revolution's other victims were Native Americans, some of whom had fought alongside London. They were expected to make immediate, large cessions of land as a result of a peace treaty signed in Paris that they had had no part in. The racist denigration that accompanied this had been developed in the early colonist battles against the American Indians. Initially, they were rarely colour-coded by writers; and insofar as they were, they were the colour of the 'juyce of Mulberries' or 'Olive coloured of a sad French green'. They were understood as having been 'naturally white', but darkened by the climate. Only when relations between them and Europeans were characterized increasingly by military combat were the racial codes introduced. Indians were then lumped in legally with 'Negroes' and 'Mulattoes'. The leaders of the new white republic decided that, since a war with the Native Americans would be disastrous for the incipient republic, an initial boundary would be established that would shortly be expanded and pushed to the West.[21] Andrew Jackson, prosecuting the wars, appealed to Americans to abandon any sentimental attachment to the 'aborigines'. 'Humanity has often wept' over their fate, but their extermination

has never for a moment been arrested, and one by one many powerful tribes have disappeared from the earth . . . Nor is there anything in this which, on a comprehensive view of the general interests of the human race, is to be regretted.

At any rate, who could prefer a wilderness populated by 'a few thousand savages' to a cultured and prosperous Republic?[22]

Walter L. Williams has argued that the absorption of Indian Country was colonial in form, in the sense that Native Americans were subsumed under the rule of the United States without being granted citizenship. As Congress moved to contain and roll back its treaty engagements with Native Americans following the successful Mexican war and the Oregon settlement, the Supreme Court declared that Indians were not entitled to citizenship guaranteed under the Fourteenth Amendment. They were 'nationals' with obligations but without rights – precisely the same status that would be accorded Filipinos during America's occupation of the Philippines. The analogy was not lost on the conquerors of the Philippines, who frequently referred to the Filipinos as 'braves' as the resistance wore on. More traditional comparisons were also evoked, as when the war was referred to cheerfully as the 'nigger-fighting business'. One soldier exulted: 'I am in my glory when I can sight my gun on some dark skin and pull the trigger'. Michael Krenn writes that 'Americans in the Philippines routinely referred to the natives as " niggers"'.[23]

By 1890 the frontier was breaking up, a point noticed and emphasized by Frederick Jackson Turner, for whom its very existence was central to the unity of American culture and society – a thesis which had a great impact on Theodore Roosevelt. Richard Slotkin points out that the Myth of the Frontier, which has 'long outlived the material reality that produced it', is underpinned by the ideology of Social Darwinism and 'survival of the fittest'. This doctrine was shared by America's military leadership. Rear Admiral Stephen Luce held that 'war is one of the great agencies by which human progress is effected'. Once the US had won the Mexican War and the Oregon Settlement, what was known as 'Indian Country' was no longer the effective Western boundary – it now divided two parts of the United States from each other. The drive for living space in the West was encouraged by the United States government with the Homestead Act of 1862, which offered 65 hectares of land in the West to anyone over the age of twenty-one who would settle on it for five years and build a house. In seeking to create a modern agrarian capitalist economy in Indian Country, the Republicans were resisted by the southern states until they seceded, because such a plan threatened to undermine plantation slavery. Union Pacific and Kansas Pacific railroads began working their way westward from Omaha and Kansas City, to carry the homestead-ers to their new land. Indian Country's boundaries were being deliberately eroded, and there was no longer any distant place into which to corral the Native American population.[24] The logic of the frontier thesis was that a new American West must stretch overseas.

Aside from supporting the logic of elimination, the great expansion of the railroads underpinned the development of oppositional working-class movements. In the latter quarter of the nineteenth century, it had become clear that America's overland expansion had failed to produce domestic bliss. In addition to a civil war that had killed 600,000 Americans, America was in the grip of a bitter class war. For instance, strikes in 1877 were so violent and tenacious that the *St Louis Republic* described them as a 'labour revolution'. More than 3,000 railroad strikes took place between 1881 and 1885. So many strikes occurred in the 1880s that the period is known as the 'Great Upheaval'. The emergence of the Populist Party, an alliance between farmers and the Knights of Labor, was one of its manifestations. This growing insurgency worried American capitalists and provided the military leadership with the *raison d'être* for a large standing army and the heavy military investment that they had been seeking since the end of the Civil War and the closing of the Western frontier.[25]

As always, America's labour problems contained a powerful racial dynamic. The abolition of property qualifications for voting in the 1840s had enfranchised a growing Irish working class, which, in a struggle to acquire a share of political power, had relied on sheer numbers and machine politics to get its representatives elected. The suspicion of mainstream America was that 'Irish Catholic despotism' threatened its democratic order. The Progressive era would therefore be characterized by efforts to chip away at this system, although in fact machine politics was just as common in non-Irish neighbourhoods. But the Irish, like Italian and Slavic migrants, could gradually attain 'whiteness'. Chinese immigration was perceived as a much greater menace and was resisted with greater force. Thus, in the latter half of the nineteenth century, political elites and militias in California and the Pacific Northwest engaged in purges against thousands of Chinese American residents, and expropriated their property in a vicious wave of ethnic cleansing. The American government even attempted in 1893 to impose photo identity cards on Chinese workers. In 1854, California had passed a law in its state legislature making it illegal for Chinese Americans to testify against whites in a court of law, thus depriving them of the right to self-defence in a society where they were increasingly under siege. The Joint Special Congressional Committee to Investigate Chinese Immigration in 1877 worried about the 'safety of republican institutions' were Chinese Americans permitted to vote, particularly as they were 'inferior in mental and moral qualities'. State courts insisted that the Chinese, being of the 'Mongolian race', were not entitled to white liberties and citizenship rights. In 1882, the Chinese Exclusion Act was passed to prevent further immigration – one of the first victories for the nativist Right in the post-Reconstruction era. Subsequently a barrage of immigration barriers was passed in law, as Chinese and Japanese immigrants in particular were deemed inassimilable. Prominent 'race' scientists claimed that census evidence proved immigration was not increasing the population but replacing one 'stock' with another. The culmination of this was the 1924 Johnson–Reed Act, which restricted the entry of Japanese labour in particular. A cultural outpouring of hysterical literature devoted to the 'Yellow Peril' was the signature theme to this era.[26]

That this nativist reaction should have occurred when American eyes were sizing up China for plunder, while parts of Asia were being subjugated, and while Japanese competition was escalating, is simply one more aspect of the way in which the American racial order connected its domestic labour system with its overseas expansionism. Indeed, the ingratitude of the 'Chinks' was noted by John Hay, the author of 'Open Door Notes', in which he complained that, in appointing itself the protector of Chinese markets, America had rendered the Chinese a great service which they did not seem to recognize. American policy-makers had been stunned by the Boxer Rebellion in

1900, and had sent forces as part of the 'International Relief Expedition' to suppress the uprising, with tens of thousands of Chinese killed in the process. The ideological justifications by which the US repressed Asian immigration – namely those of scientific eugenics – would later be used to weed out the weaker elements in America's labour force, with forced sterilization and segregation for the 'morons' and the 'feeble-minded'. Building a master race, expunging the weaknesses that made people unfit for self-government, was an explicit priority particularly for Progressive politicians throughout the first half of the twentieth century. The eugenicists considered a variety of means by which they could eliminate weakness. Birth control through forced sterilization was one that was widely adopted and imposed as policy in twenty-eight states. The surreptitious euthanasia of newborns was another, carried out in Chicago hospitals. Gassing in lethal chambers completed the picture. And, as Edwin Black points out, many American eugenicists would prove only too anxious to cooperate with the German regime of the 1930s.[27]

Along with the intersection of race and class, America's gender ideology was vital to the elaboration of the new imperial doctrine. The stories that Americans told one another about conquest were coded in gendered terms, either by defining masculinity as robust, outgoing and adventurist, or using the tropes of femininity to 'domesticate' the imperial mission, converting barbarian savagery into a benign and providentially determined process of civilization.[28] These dynamics would be central to the convergence of imperialism with progressivism.

'A community of heroes': Roosevelt's New Nationalism

The fanciful notion expressed by many commentators after 9/11 that a state of war would restore structures of American solidarity (without fundamentally altering the social status quo) updates an older ideal, rooted in American nationalism. The first attempt to develop a fully imperialist state with a popular constituency in America was initiated by a coalition of military reformers and 'progressives' from the Protestant capitalist elite, such as Theodore Roosevelt, at the tail-end of the nineteenth century. Roosevelt and others proposed a 'new frontier' through which 'Americans would be impressed by their collective power' and would 'come to see themselves, as they had done in the Civil War, the Indian Wars, and in the colonization of new land, as a community of heroes engaged in a struggle upon which the future of humanity depended'. The military was depicted by the 'progressives' as a classless zone of national solidarity in the pursuit of a higher mission – a heroic idealization that clashed with the more realistic assessment of the military leadership that conquest meant conscription and authoritarian discipline. Moreover, one of the reasons given by military reformers for an expanded and professionalized army was the threat of domestic insurgency, and instances of working-class uprisings were cited to this purpose.[29]

Roosevelt was wary of some of the negative effects of capitalism, but was most mindful of the 'over-softness, in fact washiness and mushiness' of modern American society, and hoped it was possible to retain the 'barbarian virtues' of militarism. He hated nothing more than 'slothful ease', preferring a life of strife, challenge, and combat. 'As it is with the individual, so it is with the nation.' 'Thank God for the iron in the blood of our fathers,' he exclaimed, for by fighting and risking all, they had proved equal to the mighty days. America should not 'be content to rot by inches in ignoble ease within our borders, taking no interest in what goes on beyond them, sunk in a scrambling commercialism', Roosevelt averred, with the fate of China in mind. Rather, '[i]f we are to be a really great people, we must strive in good faith to play a great part in the world'. Had the US not fought and defeated Spain, 'we would have shown ourselves weaklings, unable to carry to successful completion the labors that great and high-spirited nations are eager to undertake'.[30]

The British colonist Charles Pearson, writing from Australia, had warned of a decline in the white race. Pearson's influence in Washington had been noted and welcomed by Roosevelt, and it was in part the reason for Roosevelt's urgent struggle for the revivification of American nationalism. The 'dark races are gaining on us', he worried, 'as they have already done in Haiti, and are doing throughout the West Indies and our Southern States'. Yet he was not as despondent as Pearson, to whom he wrote, with a reassurance that the 'inferior races' would never successfully challenge white domination. In the Southern States, he remarked, any insurgency would be put down 'absolutely mercilessly', while any 'Indian outbreak on the frontier' would result in 'something approaching a war of annihilation'. Roosevelt regarded the spread of the 'English-speaking peoples', which he believed was a triumph of the 'white race', with pride. The settlement of North America and the winning of the West, in particular, constituted a 'great epic feat in the history of our race', which 'by comparison utterly dwarfs all the European wars of the last two centuries'. However, the accomplishment was marred by 'the presence of the negro in our Southern States', a 'legacy from the time when we were ruled by a trans-oceanic aristocracy'. For Roosevelt, 'democracy' was advantageous because it 'saw the race foe, and kept out the dangerous alien'. [31]

His prospectus for a 'New Nationalism', described in a 1910 speech, was closely modelled on his experiences as an imperialist. He advocated a 'proper sense of proportion' in the 'relative estimates of capital and labor', a square deal for the working man, but no 'sordid and selfish materialism', and certainly no hand-outs for any lazy bums. Sustained parallels were made with the condition of the army, which was a model for how society ought to be in its administration, loyalty, zeal, and so on. The frontier wars, the Civil War, the American Revolution – all were instances in which Americans, he said, had fought for the general interest and not some narrow section of society. The New Nationalism would therefore be one in which the classes would remain, as would dividends and property, but they would be accompanied by a moral revival in which citizens would aspire to more than these things, and in which politics would not be divided by class warfare. The qualities, then, that Roosevelt most admired in battle were those he advocated in peace. Roosevelt's 1903 book celebrating his time with the Rough Riders, a national volunteer squad that he led into battle with the Spanish over America's claim to Cuba, devoted little time to the political motives for war; rather, it gushed with exhilaration about the discipline of the men, the fraternal bonds, their self-reliance and spirit of sacrifice, and their 'manliness'. Roosevelt idealized his comrade, Colonel Leonard Wood, a 'man of high ideals' with 'a keen sense of adventure', who devoutly longed for the opportunity to 'lead men into some kind of hazard'. He exalted recruits from various walks of life, 'in whose veins the blood stirred with the same impulse which once sent the Vikings over sea', and who required no commission, merely wishing to show that 'no work could be too hard, too disagreeable, or too dangerous for them to perform'. Their 'self-reliant spirit' was evident at the end of their battles, at which point, though deserving aid, they evinced a 'sullen, sturdy capacity for self-help'. [32]

Like most nationalisms, Roosevelt's was sentimental and camp. Its hypertrophic militarism and white supremacism were exemplified in his *Winning the West*, in which he mocked the view that 'these continents should be reserved for the use of scattered savage tribes, whose life was but a few degrees less meaningless, squalid and ferocious than that of the wild breasts with whom they held joint ownership'. If its raciological dimensions were apparent, this was deeply connected with its gendered nature: he repeatedly upbraided women who chose 'sterility' for threatening 'race suicide'. Roosevelt's masculinism, and his celebration of the barbarian virtues, were precisely calibrated to favour 'race' survival in various ways. The family, so often relied on as a metaphor for nationhood, is the site of 'racial' reproduction – biologically, culturally and symbolically. Roosevelt wished to see the family run according to certain 'old truths' pertaining to the woman's natural status as a mother and house-keeper. He urged mothers to raise children who would expect to have to succeed through struggle and adversity, but worried especially about women who chose to avoid childbirth, referring to 'sinister' trends in the diminution of families that pointed towards the prospect of 'extinction'. The familial metaphor could be taken further: America was a nation that had come of age, which had – from the 'hot and lusty youth' of Germanic and Anglo-Saxon nations – evolved the virtues of civilization.[33] The future of humanity was the white male, who alone was capable of disciplining the bestial and corrosive impulses of humanity, and who alone could order the world.

Anti-imperialism in the United States

The Spanish-American War of 1898 was the culmination of trends that had been in evidence throughout the preceding century. The acquisition of Cuba had long been nurtured as a goal by America's political elite. Jefferson was anxious to acquire Cuba, but believed that defending its independence against all the world except Spain would be almost as valuable. In 1854, Secretary of State William L. Marcy explained that obtaining the island would be 'of the highest importance as a precautionary measure of security'. The US had even tried to purchase Cuba several times, but to no avail. The Spanish, meanwhile, had experienced repeated uprisings which they had always managed to put down; and so, despite American interest, few stirred with the rumours of *Cuba Libre* in 1895. However, the Cuban freedom fighters were now better organized than they ever had been, and expanded their army across the whole island gradually, over eighteen months, reaching a peak of 50,000 soldiers. They obtained support from all classes and inflicted several defeats on the Spanish, who tried vainly to retain power by reforming their bloody statutes. They even granted a new autonomous government, which assumed power on 1 January 1898; but General Maximo Gomez was determined to lead the fight for full independence. The Spanish loyalists saw the reforms as tantamount to treason, and organized nationwide resistance. But all parties were agreed that Spanish rule was finished. US Assistant Secretary of State William Day averred that the Spanish government was proving 'unable to conquer the insurgents'.[34]

America was quick to fill the vacuum. Secretary of State Henry Clay announced that the Cuban population was 'incompetent at present . . . to maintain self-government'. McKinley's minister to Spain agreed that the population was not 'fit for self-government'. Once again, there were racial reasons for this: the blacks were too strong, and would certainly prevent 'effective good government'. Only the United States could 'secure and compel peace'. These in fact constituted the higher motives for invading, and for persisting with the venture into the Philippines. President McKinley, in a familiar vein, explained that he had been ordered by God to spread freedom. Regarding the Philippines, he was to 'take them all, educate the Filipinos, and uplift and civilise and Christianise them'. At any rate, when McKinley forwarded his 11 April 1898 message to Congress demanding authorization to 'secure a full and final termination of hostilities between the Government of Spain and the people of Cuba', there was no mention of independence. They approached the Cuban resistance leaders and negotiated an alliance – though they would not give Cuba recognition, they offered assurances that they were committed to Cuban independence and had no claim over the island.[35] Of course, having defeated the Spanish, the United States failed to grant independence. Rather, they occupied the island, imposed racial segregation, and eventually burdened the country with a brutal dictator named Batista and a mafia–capitalist class.

The peace treaty with Spain on 10 December 1898 ceded all Spanish territories to the US. The Filipinos, who had been fighting for independence, thus launched a guerrilla war against US troops. The response was a savage 'scorched earth' policy, with an infamous order to shoot everyone over the age of ten. A total of about 220,000 Filipinos died as a result of the war. The racist stereotypes bruited to legitimize the slaughter made the Filipinos out to be agents of 'savage anarchy', 'loot, pillage and rape'. Not only that, but they were 'children' (as Senator Beveridge explained), 'as incapable of self-government as college freshmen' (as Brigadier General Thomas Rosser explained). Quite apart from the noble civilizing mission, the Philippine archipelago was attractive to the US on account of its proximity to the immense, 'illimitable', Chinese markets, especially as America's domestic markets were 'not enough for our teeming industries'. Thus, the US was involved for the first time in a full-blown overseas colonial enterprise which, as contemporary observers noted, greatly resembled the British suppression of the Boers. In fact, as Britain was at that moment 'already the lord of the Orient', US colonial officials spent a lot of time circulating in the British colonial world, selectively adapting its methods and policies.[36]

American expansion had already faced substantial opposition – some of it from those who simply wanted to stick to the Monroe Doctrine and expand across the Americas. The Mexican War had generated widespread opposition both from anti-slavery Whigs and from pro-slavery racists such as John Calhoun, who opposed incorporating chunks of Mexico on racist grounds. The prolonged annexation of Hawaii, after the 1893 putsch by white businessmen and planters overthrew Queen Lalioukalani, a critic of white rule, produced a variety of arguments against from elaborate constitutional objections to Frederick Douglass's anti-racist critique (the *New York Times* bore the pragmatic critique: America should only annexe Hawaii if it intended to hold onto the Philippines). But the conquest and colonization of the Philippines produced the Anti-Imperialist League, a mass movement comprising among its supporters two former presidents; a dozen senators; several business leaders, including Andrew Carnegie; and Mark Twain. Uniting 'Bourbon Democrats' who favoured classical liberalism and strongly supported business interests with Republican Mugwumps, labour leaders such as Samuel Gompers, and left-liberals such as John Dewey, they appealed to the principle embraced in 'your Immortal Declaration of Independence' that 'governments derive their just powers from the consent of the governed'.[37] Mark Twain, who had initially supported American involvement in the Philippines as he had expected it to free the Filipinos, wrote:

> I thought we should act as their protector – not try to get them under our heel. . . . It was not to be a government according to our ideas, but a government that represented the feeling of the majority of the Filipinos, a government according to Filipino ideas.[38]

In this, he described both the evangelizing allure of an American imperialism claiming an egalitarian foundation, and the ways in which such doctrines could be reclaimed by the opponents of imperialism.

In the 1900 election, the Democrat, William Jennings Bryan, stood as the anti-imperialist candidate, and gained the support of the Anti-Imperialist League with little dissent. His statement upon receiving the nomination of his party was characteristic of the Progressive era, in that it made a point of defending private property while it censured the opposing party for having become the party of 'plutocracy' and the 'dollar'. But it also censured the US government for having defeated

Spanish imperialists only to deviate from 'American principles' and 'imitate European empires'. They could not complain if 'subject races' heeded the American example and demanded liberty, or death. Further, the colonization of the Philippines would require a standing army, which constituted both a financial burden and a threat to the republican form of government. In this, he anticipated some of the contemporary libertarian critiques of empire. Profoundly aware also of the power of racial-nationalist exceptionalism as an argument for colonialism, he tried to muster its virtues against colonialism to maintain America's pristine distance from Old Europe.[39]

Bryan lost the 1900 election to McKinley, who was succeeded by Roosevelt upon his assassination in 1901. But the League's impact had terrified the pro-imperialists. Whitelaw Reid, owner of the *New York Tribune*, complained in 1899 that it was time for America to abandon the 'absurd' clause in the Declaration of Independence that all just power derives from the consent of the governed – a contention that could as easily apply domestically as in the Philippines. The League, though it entered into decline, continued to decry expansionism. When US Marines and a legation guard arrived in Nicaragua in 1912 to begin an occupation that would last until 1925, the League denounced 'the growing tendency, in our country, to interfere forcibly in the affairs of our smaller and less powerful neighbors; and to assert a paternal over-lordship in their affairs' on behalf of 'investors'. The League was again decisive in opposition to the invasion and occupation of Haiti in 1915, in which up to 11,500 Haitians were killed. The invasion, ordered by Woodrow Wilson after the overthrow of President Guillaume Sam, had been in the making for some time, with plans for possible landing operations drawn up as early as July 1914. The State Department declared that the motive of the invasion was humanitarian, to prevent widespread bloodshed and anarchy; but Wilson privately argued that the United States had to occupy the country for the long term. 'Those who did not come to terms with the Americans', writes Hans Schmidt, were subjected to 'decimation by marine patrols', 'vicious hunt-and-kill tactics'. The troops were drawn chiefly from the Deep South, exacerbating the intense 'racial and ethnic contempt' with which Haitians were treated. The occupation was managed as a technocratic venture, mirroring the sway of Progressive doctrine in the United States, but in fact embodied 'all the progressive attributes of contem-porary Italian fascism'. The US began to restructure the country in its business interests: the Haitian military was reconstituted as the Gendarmerie, moulded in the image of the US Marine Corps, and brutally conscripted the local population into forced labour. The

League united with the Haitian opposition and derided 'the Wilsonian phrases with which United States thuggery disguises its deeds'. It demanded: 'What reason can be given for our imperial policy save the desire of the ruling class to plunder and invest?'[40] While the occupiers attested to paternalistic motives, and stressed the uncivilized nature of Haitian politics before the arrival of American forces, few voices of criticism were heard outside the League, apart from that of W. E. B. Du Bois and Jane Addams. As the US faced a war of resistance by insurgents known as *Cacos,* the Anti-Imperialist League worked to build solidarity with the insurgents. In 1920, James Weldon Johnson, then president of the NAACP, visited Haiti and wrote scathingly for the *Nation* of the occupation and the denigration of Haitian culture. The *Nation* carried an advertisement from the Haiti–Santo Domingo Independence Society denouncing the ongoing occupation in 1921, but by this point the focus of anti-imperialist activity was increasingly moving into the orbit of socialist and Communist opposition.[41]

Wilsonian imperialism and self-government

Woodrow Wilson, the paladin of 'liberal internationalism', is the recipient of both neoconservative and liberal esteem. 'Militant' Wilsonianism amounts, in Paul Berman's words, to an effort to 'get people to . . . invest their hopes in building a liberal society' – an 'extremely radical idea'. From this, one would gather that Wilsonianism is an effort of persuasion by setting a good example. Woodrow Wilson himself opined in 1917 that 'God planted in us the vision of liberty' and that 'we are chosen, and prominently chosen, to show the nations of the world how they shall walk in the paths of liberty'. According to David Rieff, it is not an imperialist doctrine; rather, the aim was 'to take temporary control over certain territories' and install a state that could manage its own affairs. Michael Ignatieff agrees: Wilson 'bequeathed to the [twentieth] century the idea of self-determination', a 'moral internationalism' whose obverse is 'isolationism'. If anything, Ignatieff finds Wilson's legacy excessively *anti*-imperialist. It has created imperialists with bad consciences and a messianic commitment to human rights, and a world in rotten condition.[42]

A Protestant intellectual of the 'Progressive' era and a retrograde racist of the Jim Crow one, Wilson was the first twentieth-century American president to articulate a doctrine of international intervention in order to create and defend a liberal world order. He is credited with having been instrumental in instilling 'militant interventionism' in American politics, particularly in the South, which has since registered the highest support for war both in its elected representatives and in opinion polls. In the argot of International Relations, Wilson has been branded an 'idealist', in contrast to the practitioners of *Realpolitik*. The extent of Wilson's moralizing fervour has been the topic of endless discussion. Clemenceau, presented with Wilson's 'Fourteen Points' for a post–World War I order, retorted: 'Wilson has Fourteen Points, but God had only Ten'. Freud even made it the topic of a post-mortem analysis of 'little Tommy Wilson', whom he describes as burdened throughout his life with an irresolvable conflict of desires over his father, an overpowering Reverend who 'lectured him incessantly, kissed him, hugged him, preached at him and dominated him as the representative of God on earth'. Little Tommy made an unconscious identification of himself as 'the Saviour of Mankind' – literally the son of God. This narcissistic conviction guided his political practice so that if 'by defeating Germany, he could dictate a permanent peace to the whole world, he would be a Prince of Peace indeed!'[43]

The ideational component can be overstated, however. Wilson's 1907 account of the American imperialist drive marked his acceptance of the role of economic interests and the need for violence to secure them:

> Since trade ignores national boundaries and the manufacturer insists on having the world as a market, the flag of his nation must follow him, and the doors of the nations which are closed against him must be battered down. Concessions obtained by financiers must be safeguarded by ministers of state, even if the sovereignty of unwilling nations be outraged in the process. Colonies must be obtained or planted, in order that no useful corner of the world may be overlooked or left unused.[44]

He urged that 'our interests must march forward, altruists though we are; other nations must see to it that they stand off, and do not seek to stay us'. Here, as elsewhere, moralism was an alibi for, not an alternative to, imperialism. For example, Wilson's insistence that he would teach Mexicans to 'elect good men' reflected both his liberal convictions and the commercial interests of the US in Mexico. The Monroe Doctrine, which expressed the United States' claim to hegemony in South America, was promulgated by the administration, in the words of Wilson's Secretary of State, Robert Lansing, with a view to 'its own interests' while 'the integrity of other American nations is an incident, not an end'. Besides, as Frank Ninkovich suggests, Wilson's 'idealism' had more to do with the non-empirical nature of its outlook than with moral judgement.[45]

Wilson's attitude to self-government is much more complicated than his plaudits from liberal interventionists would indicate. His racism, for example, was not merely an unfortunate blemish on an otherwise Progressive outlook. Wilson's entire view of government and world politics was pervaded by his perception of a natural racial hierarchy. As he explained in his essay, 'The State':

> In order to trace the lineage of the European and American governments which have constituted the order of social life for those stronger and nobler races which have made the most notable progress in civilisation, it is essential to know the political history of the Greeks, the Latins, the Teutons, and the Celts principally, if not only, and the original political habits and ideas of the Aryan and Semitic races alone.

However, 'Semitic institutions' must 'occupy only a secondary place in such enquiries. The main stocks of modern European forms of government are Aryan'. Neatly, Wilson demonstrates the connection between this racialized view of government and the religious and patriarchal one: the original source of 'magisterial authority' and government is a 'real or feigned blood relationship', for '"State" is "Family" writ large'. In fact, the state has the status of an 'Economic guardian', as well as a 'Spiritual god-parent' operating through education and the 'suppression of vice'. Those 'races' that had 'remained stationary' had been pervaded by the 'reckoning of kinship through mothers only' while the 'patriarchal family' was 'the original political unit' of the Aryan 'races'. Wilson's sympathy for the Ku Klux Klan was cited in D.W. Griffith's film, *Birth of a Nation*: 'The white men were roused by a mere instinct of self-preservation . . . until at last there had sprung into existence a great Ku Klux Klan, a veritable empire of the South, to protect the Southern country.' Having seen the film, he remarked: 'It is like writing history with lightning, and my only regret is that it is all so terribly true.'[46]

Wilson's support for imperialism was based in large part on his conviction that it would revive American domestic politics. He resented the rise of 'sectionalism', which was being driven by America's divergent patterns of regional growth. The various issues that Americans were faced with – foreign policy, migration, tariffs – were chiefly economic, so 'how shall we settle these questions except on the grounds of interest? Who is to reconcile our interests and extract what is national and liberal out of what is sectional and selfish?' He was particularly worried about the rise of socialism which, if 'individual initiative' was seen to fail, would replace the system with 'communal initiative'. The solution lay in the 'nationalization of the motive power of government'. Nationalism, like religion, relied upon the 'means of moralization' – indeed, patriotism was 'the duty of religious men'. Wilsonian patriotism would not be blind, but it would rely on coercion as well as morality: an 'apprehension arising out of our consciousness that we cannot determine the way in which others will regard our acts or deal with them'. Here, he had learned from the experience of 1898, which, he observed, had produced a sense of shared fate, apparently reversing the traditional American distrust of leadership. He expected the war to produce an alteration in political opinions so that people were no longer obsessed with 'the money question', a shift in the balance of government so that 'once more our presidents are our leaders', and a change in political science based on experimentation in annexed and occupied lands, which would reveal the natural origins of political institutions and 'yield us a sane philosophy of politics which shall forever put out of school the thin and sentimental theories of the disciples of Rousseau'. The New Nationalism would be set, not against economic interests, but against foreign powers.[47] This doctrine would prove crucial in the repression during America's entry into World War I, and the subsequent 'Red Scare'.

With respect to the 1898 war with Spain and the subsequent conquest of the Philippines, Wilson was guided throughout by his conviction that, if Filipinos were ever to have self-government, Americans would first have to prepare them for it. In his memorandum from 1 August 1898, 'What Ought We To Do?', Wilson maintained that the war need not be won in such a way as to please the jingoes. Rather, since the war was being fought 'without calculations, upon an impulse of humane indignation and pity', its settlement should be based on a 'moral obligation'. The Democrats, whom he would become involved with in 1904, were opposed to the colonies, but Wilson maintained that self-government was not a state that people are adequately prepared for without 'the long discipline which gives people self-possession, self-master, the habit of order', and so on. He argued in 1908 that 'we cannot give them self-government. Self-government is not a thing that can be "given" to any people, because it is a form of character and not a form of constitution.'[48] In the *Atlantic Monthly*, he wrote that America should rule the Philippines

> with a strong hand that will brook no resistance, and according to principles of right gathered from our own experience, not from theirs, which has never yet touched the vital matter that we

are concerned with . . . They are children and we are men in these deep matters of government and justice.⁴⁹

He later argued that the United States had a duty as 'trustees' to make arrangements for the Filipinos that would contribute to their prospects of later freedom, and would support a Senate bill in 1916 to grant autonomy to the Philippines with full independence following in 1921. However, both the imperialists and the Catholic hierarchy – who feared a loss of Church property in the event of independence – rallied to defeat the measure. Wilson's reasoning throughout had been guided by the same doctrine that would later come to be institutionalized in the system of League of Nations 'Mandates'. With regard to Wilson's appeal to the right of 'self-determination', Robert Lansing explained that it did not apply to 'races, peoples or communities whose state of barbarism or ignorance deprive them of the capacity to choose intelligently their political affiliations'. Wilson himself had explained that the principle of the 'consent of the governed' could hardly apply in the same way to 'politically undeveloped races, which have not yet learned the rudiments of order and self-control' as it did to Americans.⁵⁰ This was an outlook that would leave anti-colonial movements profoundly disappointed as World War I ended and the foundations of the Cold War were laid.

World War I and the first stirrings of the Cold War

Consistent with his white supremacism, Wilson was more willing to cede self-determination to those nations founded by 'Aryans' than those by 'Semites' and others. Wilson's 'Fourteen Points' included the demand for an independent Polish state, the removal of all non-Turkish territories from the Ottoman empire, and the 'adjustment of all colonial claims' according to the interests of the governed (in fact, most of Europe's remaining colonial powers expanded their holdings after Versailles). Rhetorically, Wilson's address was suffused with his characteristic pieties, but in terms of statecraft this was an instrument of *Realpolitik*, utilizing the language of national self-determination against the claims of Leninist internationalism. But it also inaugurated a radical new US strategy. The US turn to empire had coincided with what the geographer Neil Smith has described as a 'scalar shift' in US interests.⁵¹

By the time Lenin was upbraiding European social democracy for its collapse into chauvinism, Britain was already beginning to give way to American power. America's share of global production had risen from 23 to 38 per cent in the period 1870–1913. Between 1860 and 1870,

Britain had 54 per cent of its investments in Europe and the US, while by 1911–13 it had only 25 per cent of its investments in these continents. The City of London's predominance, already vitiated by protectionist policies implemented during the late-nineteenth-century crises, weakened further during World War I, and the centre of finance shifted to New York.[52] America's entry into the war therefore signalled its arrival as a global power. More than that, it furnished an opportunity for Woodrow Wilson to undertake a dramatic attempt to remake the global order in America's interests. For, while the United States had acquired some colonial interests beyond its formally annexed territories, it did not yet represent any competition for the European states in that regard. As the 'Open Door' doctrine had suggested, its main mode of domination would be the use of market relations backed up by force. A challenge to the European colonial system was being flagged up.

The US had been formally neutral until April 1917. It was, however, shipping supplies to the Allied powers, and a German attack on US trading ships provided the occasion for Wilson's declaration of war. From the beginning, Wilson's main concern was the shape of the peace that was to result from the war, and for the purpose of devising a US strategy he appointed to a secretive body called the Inquiry figures including the journalist Walter Lippmann and the geographer Isaiah Bowman. Gathering prodigious amounts of data and analysis, the Inquiry's first major success was to devise Wilson's 'Fourteen Points'. The Inquiry's work would be vital to the crafting of America's intervention in the Paris peace talks, its cartographical work providing the basis for the 'rectification of frontiers', as Wilson put it. The Soviet government's revelations about secret territorial treaties being drafted by the Entente powers was an embarrassment for those who maintained that the war was about national self-determination and making the world 'safe for democracy'. The 'Fourteen Points' thus sought to devise a post-war settlement of national territorial states across Europe, to address the 'menace' of Bolshevism and yet also to placate the Soviet leaders who technically remained allies. The imposition of new territorial states – particularly the carving out of an independent Poland from what had been Prussia – was framed in the terminology of 'national self-determination' (language co-opted from the Bolsheviks) and the consent of the governed. It would destroy the old order of autocratic rulers like the Hohenzollerns. But its main effects were to diminish an emerging power that had hitherto been a serious competitor with the United States, and produce a large buffer state separating Germany from Russian Bolshevism. In that respect, one of the first breaches of the 'Fourteen Points' was the violation of Russian integrity with coordinated deployment of US troops in support of White Army regiments from September 1918. The 'Fourteen Points' also sought to stipulate America's hegemony in Latin America, particularly as several Latin American states had exhibited pro-German attitudes, and were perceived as potential co-belligerents. The new order would be a liberal one, with American access to markets assured.[53]

Wilson's doctrine was extremely well received, and European state leaders were already under pressure from domestic constituencies, including the Left, to accept Wilsonian terms for peace. America's gospel also stimulated considerable interest among non-European peoples who were not necessarily intended to have self-determination. The same Committee on Public Information that distributed propaganda vigorously in the United States was also at work throughout Asia and Central and South America. Egyptian, Chinese and Korean nationalists, as well the Indian National Congress and the young Ho Chi Minh, all looked to the United States to fulfil what they believed were clear declarations in favour of self-determination. But the Wilson administration began carefully to refine its arguments about self-determination, so that ultimately the colonial powers retained their possessions. The essential attitude to self-determination was expressed when Wilson led the European nations in rejecting a clause calling for racial equality, since that would imply equal treatment for all nations. While some nationalist leaders had understood Wilson to be an opponent of the colonial order, such views 'hardly reflected the man himself', who 'thought that non-Europeans needed the trusteeship of more "civilised" powers'.[54] This imperialist disposition on the part of Wilson and American power was to hand the Bolsheviks one of the first victories of the early Cold War. While the US administration had worried that taking the rhetoric of self-determination seriously would stimulate something akin to Bolshevism,[55] nationalist movements that had sometimes flaunted their opposition to Bolshevism developed into communist movements. Pan-Asianist currents also developed to resist white supremacy – a situation that the increasingly aggressive Japanese power was adept at manipulating.[56]

Domestically, too, the democratic promises of the war were to culminate in a new wave of repression and the entrenchment of the old regime. Liberal intellectuals were enthused by America's involvement in the war, and it seemed that public opinion broadly agreed with them. This was a dramatic transformation, since Woodrow Wilson had been elected in 1916 on a platform of peace, but if there was a 'Spirit of 1914', it was expressed in the pages of American progressive publications, such as the *Independent*, the *Public*, and the *New Republic*, rather than in the teeming masses of the German public (see Chapter 1). For almost every progressive intellectual converted rapidly to the cause of war, seeing in it the prospect for a transformation of the American polity along liberal lines. Many of them had been Progressives of Rooseveltian ilk, committed to expansionism and racially arrogant; but the socialists and single-tax radicals who ended up supporting the war had largely been anti-imperialist. Randolph Bourne, one of the few left-wing intellectuals not to succumb to war fever, bemoaned the fact that the intellectuals were not merely complacently chauvinistic: they had persuaded themselves that they were behind the war, that they had 'effectively willed it' against 'the dim perceptions of the democratic masses'. Rational 'neither in his hindsight nor in his foresight', the American liberal intellectual was convinced that the mere 'force of ideas' had guided America into the war.[57]

One of the outstanding socialist intellectuals to support the war was John Spargo, who had migrated from Britain to the United States in 1901. He had brought with him a distinctive blend of Marxism, which he had acquired from his time in Henry Hyndman's Social Democratic Federation, and Wesleyan Methodism, which he had acquired as a boy in Cornwall. He also carried with him a number of prejudices that fitted in neatly with his new surroundings – especially those regarding the purity of 'races' and the evil of 'miscegenation'. He had gradually abandoned the idea of revolutionary socialism, and inclined increasingly towards evolutionary social democracy. He would welcome the publication of Eduard Bernstein's *Evolutionary Socialism*, and soon came to regard American Progressivism as the nation's equivalent to European social democracy – the basis for a gradual application of socialist tenets. In the period before World War I, he had become a combatant in the right wing of the Socialist Party, helping to win battles for the moderates against the influence of the Industrial Workers of the World, whose strategy he considered impatient and whose politics he described as reactionary. Although initially a foe of Woodrow Wilson, the latter's adoption of a number of key Socialist Party demands ensured that, by the 1916 election, Spargo could lead the right-wing Revisionists in an enthusiastic endorsement of a second term for Wilson.[58]

It was in the process of supporting American intervention into the World War, however, that Spargo first became a hard line anti-communist and, in his way, *the first neoconservative*. Initially opposed to American entry into the war, he nonetheless blamed Germany for it and hoped for its decisive defeat. He argued within the Socialist Party against demanding an arms embargo, since this would benefit the German side of the war, but did not initially ally with the pro-war socialists who argued for a 'Democratic Defense'. When the US entered the war, he subordinated whatever scepticism he retained about its goals to the need for victory. Like the leaders of the British Labour Party, whom he admired, he argued that a success for 'German militarism' would menace socialism and democracy, as well as civilization itself. Having failed to win the Socialist Party to his position, he resigned from its National Executive and left the party, regretting its 'pro-German policies and propaganda'.[59]

Spargo became a propagandist for the American government through the pro-war labour organization it sponsored, the American Alliance for Labor and Democracy (AALD), the first of a series of organizations that would unite organized labour with the American empire. He argued that war conditions would be conducive to increasing industrial and political democracy. From within the AALD, he formed the Social Democratic League, which Wilson sent on a speaking trip of Europe, to rouse support for the war among a devastated and increasingly restive population. In the aftermath of war, he abandoned the idea of a distinctly socialist organization – socialism would come, but not through any 'avowed and distinct Socialist movement'. Travelling to Italy on behalf of the Committee on Public Information (CPI), he allied with Benito Mussolini against the anti-war Left, and was especially impressed by the future dictator's anti-Bolshevism. Just as Mussolini's newspaper, *Il Popolo d'Italia*, had been the first in Italy to rally to the 'democratic' defence of the war that Spargo cleaved to, it would be the first to carry an article from Spargo on the Bolsheviks. Spargo would become a leading authority for the political Right, as well as for the pro-war anti-Bolshevik socialists, on the threat posed by Bolshevism to political and industrial democracy. Just as he had argued that the anarcho-syndicalism of the IWW was reactionary, and would in fact lead to bureaucratic authoritarianism, so he argued that the revolutionary socialists were, by eschewing the patient parliamentary road, liable to spawn a new authoritarian regime. But there was more to this than a critique of revolutionary socialism. It was also for him a matter of civilizational combat, in which the 'Western' civilization was the bearer of democratic and progressive values. Russia, as he saw it, needed saving from the 'Oriental yoke'. For Spargo, it became essential that the revolution be defeated in part because the Bolshevik victory would eventually place Russia in a nexus between the 'Teutons' of Germany and the 'semi-Oriental' Japanese monarchy. He was confident that the

'Slavonic' race of Russians was a natural ally of the West, but worried that Bolshevik rule would result in Siberia seeking an alliance with Japan against the Communists. Russia would end up being 'linked to the civilization of the East and become an important element in an orientation of power full of peril to all the democratic and progressive nations of the world'.[60]

Spargo argued that the Entente powers should support the Mensheviks and encourage a programme of social democracy to meet the grievances that had produced the Russian Revolution. And, as the socialist Left showed no sign of being receptive to this message, he turned his attention to cultivating liberals and conservatives, and particularly to goading the Wilson administration into a contest with the Bolshevik regime – Wilson was indeed prepared for this, but not to the extent that would have satisfied Spargo. Increasingly disposed to paranoia about Bolshevik manipulation of the labour movement, and 'intrigues' in America's back yard, Spargo moved steadily to the right, celebrating the 'free enterprise' system, supporting anti-Communist politicians such as Coolidge and Hoover, and harshly criticizing Roosevelt's 'New Deal'. He was opposed to any negotiations or diplomatic relations with the Russian regime, to the extent that he maintained relations with the then-fascist dictator Benito Mussolini in order to encourage him to de-recognize the Soviet Union. Though he declared a hatred of fascism, he supported Hitler and Mussolini in the Spanish Civil War, on the grounds that a victory for communism in Europe would be catastrophic. And when Stalin finally defeated the Left Opposition within Russia and produced a nationalist, heavily militarized regime, Spargo expressed relief that it was now 'only nominally Communist', and therefore much less dangerous. He would later blame Roosevelt's policy of diplomatic relations for the Nazi–Soviet Pact of 1939, the Nazi annexation of Poland, and the Russian war on Finland. In this extraordinary political transformation, Spargo pre-empted future anti-Communists by several decades. The transition from socialist, to anti-Communist liberal, to belligerent conservative was a template that future generations of American intellectuals would mimic, more or less faithfully.[61]

But the war fever spread much wider than the 'Revisionists' of social democracy. Even leading figures of the African-American Left were swept up in it. W.E.B. Du Bois supported the war on the grounds that it would transform American society, oblige the government to address racial injustice and result in an independent China, a self-governing India, an Egypt with representative institutions, and an Africa for Africans. Most mainstream black organizations, including the NAACP and the Tuskegee Institute, were initially supportive too (although, later, a racist pogrom in East St Louis, and the indifference of state authorities, produced a more critical attitude). This, of course, did not stop the Justice Department from launching a wide-ranging investigation into 'Pro-Germanism Among the Negroes', who were suspected in the press and at the highest levels of government of foreign affiliations. Daily 'revelations' poured out of the press of 'German Negro Plots', especially in the south, where it was alleged that the German government was trying to stimulate a black uprising. This arrant nonsense produced such a violent wave of repression against southern blacks that up to half a million of them had to emigrate to the north to escape. Wartime intelligence agencies as a rule treated black dissent as the work of foreign intrigue, and not the expression of legitimate social complaint.[62]

A relentless propaganda drive, stigmatizing socialist and pacifist opponents of the war as unpatriotic German stooges, was put into action. George Creel, an investigative journalist appointed to head the Wilson administration's United States Committee on Public Information, revealed the doctrine underlying the Committee's activities in his triumphant post-war memoirs, How We Advertised America (1920). One of the CPI's other luminaries was Edward Bernays, a nephew of Sigmund Freud, who would go on to become a pioneer of the propaganda industry (rebranded as 'public relations' after World War II). For Bernays, propaganda was a matter of the guidance of a largely unintelligent public by the 'intelligent few'.[63] The mission in this case was to exalt the 'gospel of Americanism'. Public opinion, Creel noted, was especially important for a democracy entering a war, particularly in a polity as polarized as the United States. What was required, therefore, was

> passionate belief in the justice of America's cause that should weld the people of the United States into one white-hot mass instinct with fraternity, devotion, courage, and deathless determination. The war-will, the will-to-win, of a democracy depends upon the degree to which each one of all the people of that democracy can concentrate and consecrate body and soul and spirit in the supreme effort of service and sacrifice.[64]

Parlaying Rooseveltian and Wilsonian rhetoric into a multi-layered propaganda operation, this frenzied nationalism was promulgated through a network of artists, social clubs, religious institutions, and the Boy Scouts of America. The Committee also maintained contact with immigrant groups to ensure they did not step out of line, and found their 'pathetic devotion to the professed ideals of America', despite the multiple persecutions they were subject to, nothing less than 'inspiring'. Up to 75,000 individuals were scattered throughout the country to proselytize and testify on behalf of Wilson's 'idealism', from church pulpits and, especially, in movie theatres.[65]

The liberal press did its best, demanding the abjuration of class conflict, which could 'cripple' the nation, beating the drum for 'unavoidable' war, calling for the suppression of those guilty of 'false preaching' and 'violent and incendiary rhetoric against the government' and urging the public to trust that Wilson had information that he could not divulge. Relentlessly, the Teutonic Threat was crammed into the American gullet: 'German militarism' was a 'danger that threatens the world'. Patriotism handily dispensed with the right to dissent: 'He who is not for the United States is against it,' the *Washington Post* declared.[66]

A prosecutorial atmosphere was thus maintained. Wilson himself had promised to treat acts of disloyalty with 'a firm hand of stern repression',[67] and he proved true to his word: a wave of investigations and arrests initiated by the Bureau of Investigation and directed at leftist organizations was accompanied by Congressional actions, including the Espionage and Sedition Acts, which made it illegal to interfere with the success of the military or use disloyal language, and was aimed at socialists such as Eugene Debs who were advocating resistance to the draft. This repression continued after the war.

The October Revolution spread a lively terror among America's ruling class, but also provided a new raison d'être for expansionism and repression. A post-war wave of working-class struggle stimulated another state crackdown, and the fact that it often involved radicalized migrant workers meant that state counterinsurgency operations could be described as national defence. The first 'Red Scare' was characteristic of the deliberately paranoid propaganda of American business. For, while it was the turmoil of a society recalibrating to a post-war situation, with inflation running at 15 per cent, that had produced a mass strike wave – 3,360 strikes in 1919 alone, involving 4,160,000 people, or almost a quarter of the workforce – the common line from American business was that 'the Bolshevist spirit' was ready to take control of industry. The grassroots conservatism expressed by the Seattle Minute Men (a group of veterans of the Spanish-American war who had formed to promote the continuation of war with Germany and were also important in repressing the 1919 Seattle General Strike) supplied one way to defend both capital and the national state. Business communities used Pinkerton strike-breakers and Minute Men to supply the Bureau of Investigation with false or exaggerated claims. They sponsored 'patriotic societies', which, though many in number, were poor in members. Unions in particular were charged with being pro-Bolshevist, and thus anti-American. And when the Justice Department launched its crusade against radicals, one of its favourite methods was deportation: 1,200 members of the anarchist-leaning Union of Russian Workers were deported. Thousands of suspect 'subversives' were arrested, and homes and offices were raided across thirty-three cities. Southern politicians claimed that blacks were being manipulated by subversives, just as they would claim again during the next 'Red Scare' and throughout the civil rights campaign.[68]

Though successful in thwarting the immediate threat from labour and the Left during the 1920s, the first 'Red Scare' did not completely finish off anti-imperialism, although it had been substantially weakened by the third decade of the twentieth century.

It is often asserted that the United States turned 'inwards' during the 1920s. In the sense that it abandoned the rhetoric of Wilsonian internationalism, this is true, although it continued to manage its colonies and client-states with ruthless violence. The political class concentrated instead on maintaining its existing colonial possessions and managing its domestic order. Thanks in part to the successes of Wilson-era Jim Crow policies, that order was fertile territory for the far right. The Reconstruction-era gains made by African-Americans had been decisively rolled back in the south through a contrived, wholesale shrinkage of the electorate by means of poll taxes, strict residency requirements, literacy rules, and so on – because voting by blacks would promote black education, freedom of movement and legal protections against labour exploitation, thus threatening the system of white supremacy. Indeed, the language used to convey this was frequently chilling: 'final settlement', 'elimination', 'acting to remove the negro as a factor'.[69] Violence was meted out, in both the north and the south, especially to blacks who appeared to have made some economic progress. Conservative craft unions refused to allow Asians and African-Americans in as members, and AFL leaders lent their weight to the 1924 National Origins Act.

Every new wave of immigration produced a surging torrent of racist hysteria. Lynching was frequent, and more violence had been done to Jews in America than in Germany – in fact, although it was not the main focus of the American far Right, it was something of a tradition for the Protestant elite. During the Civil War General Ulysses S. Grant, suspecting disloyalty, had ordered every Jew out of his military jurisdiction. Throughout the 1920s, Henry Ford raised a vocal anti-Semitic campaign, which received the support of the Ku Klux Klan. The Klan was a national organization with a strong base in the Protestant lower middle class, and organic connections with state power, especially in the south. Yet, when the Great Depression struck, America did not produce a mass fascist movement. The Klan was on the retreat, collapsing everywhere, wilting partly in response to the resistance of migrant groups themselves who, alongside white Americans, battled the Klansmen in the cities and urban centres.[70]

By the 1930s the American Left was resurgent, but was more concerned with settling its domestic battle with the ruling class, and with the fate of European workers at the hands of fascists, than with America's colonies. In fact, the *New Republic* could argue in 1931 that the Moros of the Philippines should 'put aside their Mohammedan traditions' and remember that they had been subjugated by a 'paternal invader in the name of humanity and justice for oppressed peoples. They should – but they won't – any more than the stubborn peoples of India will recognize the beneficence of British rule.' The *New Republic* was a mildly pro-Soviet publication at that point – a widely shared stance among much of the American liberal Left of the era. The combination of capitalist crisis, the rise of fascism, and later the fact that the USSR was the sole state supporting the Spanish Republic from 1936, produced enormous sympathy for the Soviet Union, despite the criticisms of a minority of Trotskyists and anti-Stalinists. The Abraham Lincoln Brigades, which organized Americans to fight fascism in Spain, was overwhelmingly composed of working-class radicals, who generally looked eastwards for a blueprint for a rational, socialist future. Self-consciously a 'people's army', it mobilized Chinese Americans, Native Americans, Filipinos, Puerto Ricans – victims of America's racial hierarchy domestically and overseas. For some African-Americans, fighting in Spain provided a first sense of real freedom. And most of those who returned would go on to fight for the Allies in World War II. This coalition, often with the African-American Left in the vanguard, was the basis for the Popular Front alliance during World War II.[71]

But countervailing pressures were already visible. The Molotov–Ribbentrop Pact alienated many sympathizers of the Soviet Union. The formation of an 'anti-totalitarian' pole on the Left, represented by figures such as Arthur Koestler, Reinhold Niebuhr, Walter Lippmann and Sidney Hook, can be attributed in large part to this, and to the show trials of leading Communists such as Bukharin, leading to the growing awareness of severe repression in the Soviet Union. Koestler's

Darkness at Noon, published in 1941, could not have been more timely in this respect. It presented a stark imaginative metaphor. Through the experiences of the old Bolshevik Rubashov – modelled on Trotsky, Bukharin and Radek – at the hands of the Stalinist state, a dream-work is set in motion in which Stalin becomes Hitler, and the Stalinist secret police become the Gestapo. It resonated with those on the Left who had been shocked by the Molotov–Ribbentrop Pact – a pact, as Max Shachtman pointed out, of aggression, in which the USSR invaded Finland while Nazi Germany helped itself to Poland. The novel also dramatized the growing hold of the concept of 'totalitarianism', whose utility to imperial ideology is perhaps illustrated by the praise showered on the book by Henry Luce's *Time* magazine, among others.[72]

Anti-fascism and the race war

Many Americans who fought in World War II were committed and courageous anti-fascists, but the attack on Pearl Harbor refuelled the hysteria over the 'Yellow Peril'. For, in stark contrast to what was supposed to be a war for democracy in Europe, the Pacific war was widely understood as a 'race war'. The Japanese empire had already managed to impress the white supremacists in Washington. Theodore Roosevelt, observing the victory against Russia in 1905, commented: 'what extraordinary soldiers those little Japs are!' The explanation favoured by American elites as to how the Japanese had won was that they – unlike the rest of the Orient – were willing to learn from the West. Yet, though they had defeated a ('slavic') white power, they would never be considered equals. The respect was sufficiently strong, however, that, when Roosevelt moved to curtail Japanese immigration in 1907, he negotiated a 'Gentleman's Agreement' with the regime, in which no laws would be passed if Japan ceased issuing passports to its workers to migrate to the United States. In 1919 the Japanese delegation to the Paris Peace Conference, inspired by Wilson's rhetoric, proposed a 'racial equality' motion; unfortunately, they had horribly misread the situation. Not only did Great Britain and Australia vigorously oppose the motion ('Slap the Japs' was the Australian prime minister's slogan), Wilson blocked it, even after it had passed relatively comfortably, on the grounds of 'too serious objections'. But Wilson was willing to concede to Japan Germany's former economic rights in Shantung, China.[73] Subsequently, of course, the 'Gentleman's Agreement' was dropped, and Japanese immigration legally blocked in 1924. The attack on Pearl Harbor, Hawaii, therefore bore an historical freight of racial conflict. World War II involved deliberate attacks on civilians on all sides and in all theatres, as a matter of policy; but the Pacific war had the added dimension of a perceived existential struggle between races.

The Japanese empire had conceded universal male suffrage from 1925, circumscribed by the Peace Preservation Law, outlawing those forces which contested the rights of private property. It was at war from 1931, with the seizure of Manchuria, imposing a version of the Monroe Doctrine on Southeast Asia. The rapid succession of devastating successes took hundreds of thousands of lives, particularly during the 'Rape of Nanking' in 1937, and imposed a cruel and predatorial system on its victims. It engaged in human experimentation with captured prisoners of war, particularly in the infamous Unit 731 which – under the direction of Shiro Ishii, who looked for all the world like a Japanese General Kitchener – froze its subjects to death, infected them with the plague and other diseases, and subjected them to vivisection. The prisoners were called *murata*, or 'logs of wood'. Native women were prostituted, and hundreds of thousands were killed across Southeast Asia – perhaps up to 15 million in China during World War II. Japan consciously sought to invert the racial hierarchy (rather than overthrow it), and encouraged its prison guards to treat European and American prisoners of war as subjugated and subhuman. The attack on Pearl Harbor, followed in less than a day by the attack on the British empire in Hong Kong, can be seen as part of that effort – a fact not lost on London, but actively suppressed because of its traumatic implications for white supremacy.[74]

After Pearl Harbor, the US government launched a war that sought both to annihilate civilian population centres, instilling the suitable sense of shock and awe, and to preserve the conservative Japanese elite for a post-war alliance (they were, after all, a plucky bunch). As the historian Richard Drayton points out, we prefer to ignore or forget crimes committed by the good guys – such as the rape of over 10,000 women by American troops in Europe during the war. Other crimes were either lauded as humane or generally forgotten. The worst were committed in the race war. Immediately following the bombing of Pearl Harbor, the Justice Department rounded up 1,393 German nationals, 264 Italians, and 2,192 Japanese. The United States government then overruled the military leadership, which insisted that the west coast of the Pacific was beyond Japanese reach, and used a putative threat to the US to initiate a pre-emptive war against Japanese-Americans. The trouble with the Orientals, it appeared, was their inscrutability: Attorney General Earl Warren told the House Select Committee chaired by California Congressman John Tolan that we believe that when we are dealing with the Caucasian race, we have methods that will test the loyalty of them . . . But when we deal with the Japanese, we are in an entirely different field and we cannot form any opinion that we believe to be sound.

General De Witt's 'Final Report: Japanese Evacuation from the West Coast' effaced any notion that the Japanese in question were Americans. In his testimony to the House Naval Affairs Subcommittee, he explained: 'A Jap's a Jap . . . There is no way to determine their loyalty . . . It makes no difference whether he is an American; theoretically, he is still Japanese and you can't change him.' Similarly, when Assistant Secretary of War John McCloy sent Colonel Karl Bendetsen to serve as a liaison officer to General De Witt in San Francisco, he concluded that rounding up Japanese-Americans was the 'safest course to follow' since 'you cannot tell which ones are loyal and which ones are not'. To some extent, they were even egged on by the British Foreign Office who, weeks after the surrender of Hong Kong, scolded the Americans for their laxity and briefed them on the 'lessons' of Pearl Harbor, including the claim that Japanese girls had been dating US marines, and that some of the attackers were Hawaiian and had attended US high schools. They were astonished that such a race-obsessed society had permitted an Asian-American hybrid community to develop.[75]

And so 120,000 Japanese-Americans, two thirds of whom were citizens, were driven out of their homes and deposited in concentration camps in the American heartland. One of the architects of the policy was Secretary of War Henry Stimson, who had been first Calvin Coolidge's special executive agent in Nicaragua, in which role he had negotiated the return of the Marine Corps to the country in 1927 to consolidate a pro-US regime; and then governor-general in the Philippines in 1928–9, where he had considered the natives unfit for self-government since, although they might evince 'hopeful progress under our supervision', they had a 'racial tendency toward backsliding'. Stimson was not only a man thoroughly acquainted with America's modes of imperial rule, but also a white supremacist. He told President Hoover in 1932 that 'I believe in assuming [the white man's burden]. I believe it would be better for the world, and better for us'. One of Stimson's colleagues was Assistant Secretary of War John McCloy, a Republican Ivy Leaguer who had a Harvard law degree and an extensive career on Wall Street. After the war he would enjoy a variety of positions, including president of the World Bank and US military governor and high commissioner for Germany. There he insisted on releasing all industrialists convicted of war crimes, including Alfried Krupp, whose company had used slave labour from the Nazi concentration camps and supplied the German army with tanks and cannons. He would go on to work for Chase Manhattan, chair the Ford Foundation, and participate in the Warren Commission. Visiting Japan in 1946 as assistant secretary of state, he deplored the moderate liberal reforms being pushed through by General MacArthur on the grounds that they would open up opportunities for the Left, and described the trials of war criminals as a 'fiasco' on the grounds that guilt was impossible to assess, since 'most Japanese look alike, in more ways than one'. Another key figure was Dillon S. Myer, a New Deal liberal, who would go on to receive the Medal of Merit, and would head the Bureau of Indian Affairs in the 1950s (after turning down the governorship of Puerto Rico), during which time he launched an attack on tribal rights and identities known as 'termination'. The camps, each consisting of a square mile surrounded by barbed wire fences and guarded by military police, were seen as too liberal by many, and Myer himself was convinced that at least half of their occupants had 'never had it so good'. The camp commissioners were seen as 'social workers', and a great emphasis was placed on 'Americanizing' the internees, especially since their cultures were considered unfit for democratic citizenship. After the war, the whole procedure was endorsed by the civil libertarian Alan Barth, who told *Washington Post* readers that it was a 'Job Well Done'.[76]

The overseas war was prosecuted with extreme ruthlessness, and was accompanied by a stream of propaganda brimming with every racist cliché in the American lexicon. Although it became important in the course of the war to avoid open assertions of white superiority, or anything too explicitly racist – even Canberra had to make a rhetorical retreat from its White Australia policy – Frank Capra and a host of scriptwriters were employed to produce films that would acquaint American audiences with the enemy in such a way that they would not resent mowing down a million or so of them. Scripts were turned down if they appeared to humanize or evoke 'too much sympathy for the Jap people'. Their homogeneity, obedience and fanaticism were insisted on. While propaganda on the European front mocked and derided Hitler and Mussolini, rather than Italians and Germans, propaganda for the Pacific war was thoroughly racialized. It was a war of good against evil, civilization against barbarism. Beneath the thin veil of civilization, every Japanese was a 'subhuman beast' who had to be beaten by the 'jungle rule of tooth and claw'. It was not considered out of order for the *New Yorker* to refer to the Japanese as 'yellow monkeys'. Admiral William Halsey rallied his men with the instruction, 'Kill Japs, kill Japs, kill more Japs'. Thus, although Roosevelt had repeatedly condemned Japanese attacks on civilians during its expansionist wars of the 1930s, the US military had been envisioning the torching of Japan's cities even before the attack on Pearl Harbor, and from March 1945 – when 16 square miles of Tokyo were destroyed by incendiary bombs, killing up to 100,000 people and making more than a million homeless – this tactic was effectively deployed.[77]

And then, there was annihilation. The current mainstream of scholarship on the dropping of the uranium bomb on Hiroshima and the plutonium bomb on Nagasaki concludes that it was an exercise in what Gar Alperovitz calls 'atomic diplomacy'. The Truman administration did not need to use that weapon in order to obtain a Japanese surrender, which was practically assured upon Russian entry into the Pacific war – and Stalin had already promised to join the war by 15 August 1945. Even a clarification of surrender terms would probably have yielded peace. This was advocated by practically the entire civilian and military leadership of the Anglo-American war effort. However, a number of key figures in the US administration who had knowledge of the development of S-1, the atomic bomb, hoped that it could be used to coerce Stalin into accepting American terms in Europe. Roosevelt had sought to limit Soviet intervention by securing an agreement to support the beleaguered Chiang Kai-shek, but the State–War–Navy Coordinating Committee (SWNCC – a predecessor to the National Security Council) wanted ways to avert any Soviet involvement if necessary, recommending exclusive American rule over Japan and economic reform in the interests of making it an American outpost.[78] When a successful test was finally carried out in Alamagordo, New Mexico, Truman discovered that he no longer needed the assistance of the USSR. Dropping the bomb was now preferable, not only because it would prevent the USSR from having a post-war claim in Southeast Asia, which the US planned to hegemonize, but also because of the beneficial effects it was likely to have on diplomacy with Russia in Europe. For these reasons, over 200,000 Japanese civilians lost their lives in two nuclear strikes.

But this picture – supported by intercepted communications between Japanese officials, the US Strategic Bombing Survey, a War Department study on the 'Use of Atomic Bomb on Japan' written in 1946, diplomatic records, the statements of significant military and civilian leaders, and the private journals of Harry Truman – did not become clear for some time. In fact, a significant effort was made right away to obscure both the true reasons for using nuclear weapons and the alternatives. In 1947, Henry Stimson, who as secretary of war had approved the bombings, composed a justificatory essay for *Harper's* magazine, 'The decision to use the atomic bomb'. And the reaction of the mainstream American Left and of the Communist Party (CPUSA), around which many liberals gravitated, did not suggest that there would be many problems with persuading people of the justice of the bombing. The CPUSA had been disgracefully complicit in the anti-Japanese witch-hunts launched by the US government. In early 1942, following Japan's bombing of Pearl Harbor on 7 December the previous year, the CPUSA expelled all of its Japanese members. And the party remained silent on the US government's policy of forced evacuation and incarceration of Japanese-Americans. At any rate, only 1.7 per cent of newspaper editorials disapproved of the attacks, and the left-leaning press, including the *Nation*, *New Republic*, and *PM*, were all supportive. The managing editor of *PM* even saw the destruction as an occasion for the promotion of democracy, slyly urging the US to take out Tokyo as well, so that the royal family would be eliminated and thus 'clear the bases for democracy after the war'. An opinion poll found that 13 per cent of the public favoured the complete annihilation of the Japanese people, while an advisor to the SWNCC proposed the 'almost total elimination of the Japanese as a race'.[79]

Parenthetically, we might note that one ugly offshoot of the Manhattan Project was the thirty-year programme of radiation experiments on 20,000 mostly unwitting Americans, lasting from 1944 to 1974. This included direct injections of uranium, polonium and plutonium into unsuspecting patients, as well as the testicular irradiation of prisoners and the intentional release of radiation into the atmosphere, with many dying as a result. Those targeted included not only the terminally ill, but also pregnant mothers, prisoners, and the residents of an institution for 'feeble-minded boys'. Although President Clinton's Advisory Committee on Human Radiation Experiments only examined the data up until 1974, the Committee noted that the experiments could still be occurring and that US laws still permitted the secret release of radiation into the atmosphere.[80]

The American empire arrived as the hegemonic world power in 1945 after an intensive period of expansion and competition, usually viewed through the lens of race. Racism did not stand, as one might expect, in strict opposition to egalitarian and humanist rhetoric. Rather, in the hands of imperialist politicians, each was suffused with the other. And this hybridic ideology was systematically deployed in wide-ranging, hectoring propaganda efforts from at least 1916 onwards. Yet many

Americans repeatedly appropriated and subverted the evangelizing discourses of statesmen to oppose empire, to challenge its racial hierarchy, and to fight fascism overseas, thereby providing a model of internationalism that would be repeated by solidarity activists in Central America during the 1980s, by pro-Palestinian activists since the turn of the millennium, and by human shields trying to stop the attack on Iraq in 2003. What made way for the emergence of a solid, hegemonic imperial constituency was the de-radicalization of the Left and its near-collapse under the bitter experience of McCarthyism and associated forms of repression. Once again, the USSR played a central role here: the betrayal of the early democratic promise of the Russian Revolution was crushing for many; and the repeated, bewildering changes in Moscow's party line were disconcerting for those who kept the faith. Socialism was thereby rendered a singularly unattractive proposition to most Americans, particularly given the relative stability of the post-war West. The stage was thus set for the spectacle of liberal intellectuals defending the patently indefensible in the name of 'anti-totalitarianism'.

3

NEOCONS AND APOSTATES

America's imperial constituency was decisively entrenched through Cold War anti-communism. Alienated from the Soviet Union, and increasingly from socialism as such, a number of left-wing intellectuals began to favour American hegemony. Together with liberal nationalists who owed more to Theodore Roosevelt than to Leon Trotsky, they articulated a new centre in American politics, with liberal social policies to attenuate the appeal of communism, authoritarian crackdowns to reduce the influence of radicals and their actual or alleged sympathizers at all levels of American society, and military adventurism to contain, and where possible roll back, the 'Soviet threat'. At least nominally committed to anti-racism, their support for American imperialism was presented as a necessary and urgent aspect of combat against 'totalitarianism', and as part of a slightly less urgent attack on colonialism. Kennedy's 'new frontier', binding social-democratic policies to aggressive American expansionism, was the zenith of this tendency. His administration contained many of the liberal intellectuals who had enthusiastically encouraged the anti-Communist crusade, and they helped devise policies such as the war on Vietnam, the Bay of Pigs invasion and the 'Alliance for Progress' in Latin America. Though post-war American administrations would repeatedly threaten atomic destruction and hot war with the Soviet Union, the Kennedy administration came closest to bringing these about.

A wave of insurgency, in both East and West, transformed this situation: as before, many young Europeans and Americans began to see those struggling against imperialism and colonialism as their brothers and sisters, and as partaking in a common struggle. The repression in the Warsaw Pact states helped to produce a 'New Left' with a more critical attitude to the Soviet Union and its satellites than the previous 'Popular Front' Left, while the movements for racial justice in America and growing labour militancy in the Western states punched holes in the Cold War consensus. It was this challenge that produced the neoconservative movement which, contrary to some depictions, was first and foremost a critical evaluation of liberalism, in light of its failure to withstand the assault of the new radicalism. The neoconservatives, though not all of left-wing backgrounds, did inherit a conceptual apparatus drawn from the Left, as well as a sociological sophistication that had been less evident in the Old Right. They helped not only to morally resuscitate imperialism, but also to provide an intellectual veneer for the rightist lurch of American administrations after the mid-1970s.

Anti-totalitarianism: ex-Communists for the CIA

The post-war 'antitotalitarian' Left was the culmination of the de-radicalization of a layer of socialist intellectuals and leaders and their subsequent integration into the imperial state. This movement found its voice in such journals as the *Partisan Review*, and the *New Leader*, and in authors like Arthur Koestler, Sidney Hook, Max Eastman, Irving Kristol, Melvin Lasky, and most notably Arthur Schlesinger Jr. Though attentive to the vicious and vulgarizing cadences of Stalinism, their own rhetoric was often shrill and their political choices dubious. The *New Leader* had been an organ of the Socialist Party, whose luminaries had included Bill Haywood, Max Eastman and Eugene Debs. In 1936 it came under the editorial control of Samuel Levitas, a Russian Menshevik émigré, who would go on to form close relations with the CIA, to the extent that he invited Allen Dulles to write a piece in 1949 advocating a commission of internal security to counter subversive organizations. The Socialist Party, meanwhile, slowly became aligned with the Democratic Party. Its leader Norman Thomas wrote to President Truman commending him for his tough stance over the Berlin Blockade.[1]

Both the *Partisan Review* and the *New Leader* would receive funding from the CIA, but it was the *New Leader* that was to take the most aggressive stances: violently opposed to Tito in Yugoslavia, outraged by the prospect of a working alliance between Italian Socialists and Communists, it eventually ended up supporting McCarthy. When Henry Wallace visited the UK, the *New Leader* sent a cable to Aneurin Bevan purporting to be from American liberals (but including the signature of Henry Luce and a Roman Catholic bishop), explaining that Wallace was only supported by

Communists, fellow-travellers and 'totalitarian liberals'. The language used by these publications frequently reflected that of paranoid red-baiting magazines such as *Counterattack*, which accused the Communists of being 'a Fifth Column, a Conspiracy'. Likewise, *Partisan Review* accused the *New Republic* and the *Nation* of representing a 'fifth column'.[2]

The organ most directly organized by the CIA was *Encounter*, a publication of the American Committee for Cultural Freedom (ACCF), the US branch of the CIA's global outfit, the Congress for Cultural Freedom (CCF). Irving Kristol was appointed its editor, and he ran it as a bluntly pro-American magazine. This reflected the balance of opinion among the American contributors, who were obsessed with socking it to the Communists, while Stephen Spender – the distinguished English literary editor – was concerned that there should be a serious attempt to complement this with a critical liberalism based on the goal of equality. A brief attempt to replace Kristol with Dwight MacDonald, an anti-Communist who was also critical of the United States, worried the ACCF leadership, who thought that Kristol was precisely the kind of anti-Communist that was needed. Sidney Hook threatened to resign and 'blow the Congress out of the water' if Kristol was deposed. The evidence is that many of the leading participants in the ACCF knew very well where their money came from: Diana Trilling recalled that Norman Thomas would call 'Allen' every time it went broke and plead for more funds. No one, she said, was in any doubt that 'Allen' was the head of the CIA.[3]

Anti-Communist liberals such as Arthur M. Schlesinger, Jr, Reinhold Niebuhr, Eleanor Roosevelt and Hubert Humphrey participated in the founding of Americans for Democratic Action (ADA), which broke with the 'popular front' liberalism of the previous era, denounced the 'totalitarian Left' and supported Truman's policies in Europe, such as support for the British-installed Greek monarch, and the Marshall Plan. They pressed for an active US foreign policy of containment of the Soviet Union – which, they argued, in language echoing that of NSC-68 and George Kennan's article on 'The Sources of Soviet Conduct',[4] was both militarily and politically expansionist, annexing Eastern Europe, and pervading the remaining democratic societies. Niebuhr argued that for anti-communism to succeed as a doctrine, it would not be sufficient to point to 'the crass corruption of the original dream of justice'. The cause would be won not by the comfortable, but through the solidarity of 'the insecure and impoverished'.

Arthur Schlesinger's chief contribution to the intellectual argument of the antitotalitarians was *The Vital Center*, a short and lightly footnoted review of liberalism's brief eclipse by communism, and a programme for its restoration. The 'tense, uncertain, adrift' Western man, the product of an era in which modern technology had stripped away the old feudal bonds and created an atomized man living in fear and quiet desperation, had been wooed by a totalitarian version of community and solidarity which disavowed man's inherent limitations and frailty. The bunkered authoritarianism of the Soviet Union was no accident, he insisted, anticipating what became a fixture of 'antitotalitarian' orthodoxy.[5] Lenin, he said, had 'laid the foundations' for 'Stalinist absolutism' through a putative revision of Marxism, by deifying the party and concentrating power in its hands. Even Trotsky was only 'the left-wing of the bureaucracy', who had suppressed the Kronstadt rebels and disparaged the sanctity of life.[6] This part of the argument, though occasionally ill-informed and incoherent,[7] bore a certain charm for those finally repudiating what was becoming a difficult and thankless struggle: Why try to sustain a non-Stalinist socialism when the whole enterprise had been tainted from the beginning? And Schlesinger outlined an alternative that sought to reclaim anti-racism for the political centre, denounced statist authoritarianism in America and appealed to its 'libertarian' tradition, and called for political and economic action to restore the 'balance' between 'individual and community'.[8]

Above all, Schlesinger's imperial liberalism was *manly*. He appealed to the legacy of Theodore Roosevelt and Andrew Jackson as model reformers who, unlike 'Doughface progressives', 'sentimentalists', 'utopians' and 'wailers' for whom liberalism was 'an outlet for private grievances and frustrations', were practical and administration-minded. American Communists, he said, were impaired individuals who derived 'social, intellectual, even sexual fulfilment' from the party, which they were unable to obtain by other means. The American ruling class had been emasculated by insecurity. Businessmen had everywhere become 'irresolute and hesitating', and it was for this reason that the British and French ruling classes had engaged in 'middle class cowardice' towards Nazism. By contrast, Schlesinger and the New Dealers could not suppress an 'invincible repugnance' as regards the cowardly 'Doughface', who escapes into Utopianism, and thence at any moment into the protective arms of totalitarian masters. This virile liberalism assumed its global responsibilities without sentimentality – Theodore Roosevelt was the hero of this story, for he 'was the first president to try to educate the nation to its worldwide terms of existence'. Thus Schlesinger commended the Truman Doctrine and its application in Greece, where the US army supported the pro-monarchists in the civil war, as an instance of necessary containment policy. At the same time, he argued for American commitment to a liberal world order, in which the US would back nationalist regimes as a necessary prophylactic against communism, but also try to encourage them to move in a democratic direction.[9]

When Truman issued Executive Order 9835, launching a wave of investigations against federal employees, the Cold War liberals had conflicting feelings. Schlesinger had endorsed loyalty investigations to root out Communists, but was opposed to more extreme Republican-inspired measures such as the Mundt–Nixon Bill, since they would simply play into the hands of the reds. The ADA, despite some criticisms, broadly supported it. When some in the American Committee for Cultural Freedom, the US affiliate of the CIA's Congress for Cultural Freedom, condemned McCarthyism, Sidney Hook insisted that the matter was not one for a 'cultural' committee. Max Eastman, the former ally of Leon Trotsky, aggressively denounced claims of a witch-hunt as a 'smear', claimed that the national executive were failing the 'struggle against infiltration by the enemies of freedom' and attacked the 'fuzzy liberals' who were 'giving the best help' to an enemy 'bent on destroying every freedom throughout the world'. The former Trotskyist novelist James T. Farrell argued that one should side with American power as the only realistic opponent to Stalinism: 'There is no fooling yourself about Stalinism. You either join it, support it, stay with it, or else it has only one statement to make to you: Death.'[10]

In this way, the Cold War liberals contributed to a red scare that was not only used to hound up to 20,000 people out of work (mainly militant trade unionists rather than Communist Party members), and impose loyalty oaths on workers across the country. Up to 80 per cent of states would impose loyalty oaths by 1953, and those that wished to wage open war on domestic radicalism would launch mini-HUACs which, by the early 1950s, reinforced the reigning order. The range of laws passed at the national and state level were broad in scope, and all passed on the premise advocated by liberal anti-Communists that the Communist movement was a 'conspiracy'. Communists were to be denied access to the ballot, to public employment, even outlawed in some cases, while Texas contemplated the death penalty for commu-nism. Deep South states used local versions of these repressive laws to defend the white power system and prevent unionization drives. Spurred on especially by the Korean War, this repression extended to the creation of national and local commissions involved in strike-breaking and investigating union leaders as much as in repressing actual Communists.[11]

The irony is that the Communist Party USA, which was to experience the rough end of the Smith Act[12] and state sedition laws, was already far down the road to 'Americanization'. Some of the leadership had already been convinced of the need for this as early as 1934. Earl Browder, a skilled 'popular front' builder and general secretary from 1932 to 1945, was the chief advocate of this policy. Under his leadership, the party had been supportive of Roosevelt's 'New Deal', covered for the appalling treatment of Japanese-Americans in World War II, opposed disruptive strikes and, in 1944, attempted to put some distance between the party and the USSR. Public criticism of Browder's stance from Jacques Duclos of the French Communist Party was perceived as an attack from Moscow, and Browder was replaced by the more old-guard pro-Russian leader, William Z. Foster, in 1945. Browder was expelled from the party the following year. But it was the old guard that was in the most precarious position when Khrushchev made his revelations about the Stalin era, and in particular during the Hungarian revolt. In 1956 the *Daily Worker* began to carry, for the first time, more critical views on Russian policy – much to the outrage of some; but the fact that many of the old cadres, and even many reform-minded members, defended the crushing of the Hungarian revolution, fearing a 'fascist' restoration, drove thousands out of the party. At the start of 1956, the party had 20,000 members. In the two years following their Twentieth Party Congress, two-thirds melted away. The CPUSA would soon find itself pursuing a revisionist line.[13]

The former revolutionaries among the Cold War liberal coalition had given in to what Irving Howe had previously mocked as 'Stalinophobia'[14] – a condition with which he himself would soon be afflicted. James Burnham and Max Shachtman had polemicized mercilessly against the men of letters who were turning not only against the Kremlin, but against the revolution itself. Burnham was not quite, as Christopher Hitchens claims, the first neoconservative (that honour belongs to John Spargo – see Chapter 2). However, he did make one of the most rapid conversions in history. He argued in *The Managerial Revolution* (1941) that Britain should go into imperial receivership and allow America to launch its world empire, a stance that would certainly have appalled both Trotsky and Shachtman. Isaac Deutscher wrote scathingly about the ex-Communists, but noted that the Stalinist regime had done enough to discredit and bring shame on socialism:

> There can be no greater tragedy than that of a great revolution's succumbing to the mailed fist that was to defend it from its

enemies. There can be no spectacle as disgusting as that of a post-revolutionary tyranny dressed up in the banners of liberty. The ex-Communist is morally as justified as was the ex-Jacobin in revealing and revolting against that spectacle.[15]

These ex-Communists made their own distinctive contribution to the terrible reaction that handicapped all meaningful left-wing politics, while inculcating irrational political attitudes into the mainstream. By 1954, at the point at which McCarthyism was entering terminal decline, no more than 5 per cent of Americans were prepared to express even a mildly favourable opinion of the Soviet Union, and only 27 per cent would allow a Communist the constitutional right to speak in public. Only 23 per cent of Americans believed that the West could live peacefully with the Russians, while 61 per cent held that a major war was inevitable.[16]

Decolonization, dictatorship and Cold War liberalism

The United States engaged itself on several fronts of open or surreptitious warfare and intervention in the post-war years: the Caribbean and Latin America, Africa, the Middle East, Southeast Asia, and Europe. Only the latter case, usually privileged in Cold War studies, did not involve direct confrontation with decolonization struggles. There would be much to say if space allowed about America's extensive involvement in European politics, often falsely depicted as struggles with the Soviet Union – for example, its manipulation of the 1948 Italian elections, its support for the right-wing pro-monarchy forces in the Greek Civil War, its support for Franco, and its extraordinarily aggressive policies that not only helped divide Europe and raise the Berlin Wall, but also ran the risk of igniting a new hot war.[17] However, Europe was not the main zone of US activity in the Cold War years, and the overriding focus on it is misleading. America's main engagements as an 'anti-Communist' force were in the Third World, particularly in decolonizing areas, and it was here that Cold War liberals were called upon either to devise policy as statesmen or to legitimize it as historians and commentators. A realistic engagement with America's attitude to decolonization must start from the fact that it remained a colonial power itself until 1946, when the Philippines were granted independence (the disadvantaged Moro south was not granted autonomy at the same time, leading to a long-standing conflict that is still raging). Arguably, the experience of successfully implanting client regimes in Cuba (1901) and Nicaragua (1937),[18] together with the negative experiences of attempts at direct rule, which were met by ongoing guerrilla resistance, forced the United States to adopt a new strategy to face the rising global arc of anti-colonial resistance. Secondly, one must take account of America's long-standing support for right-wing dictatorships as an alternative to genuine self-government, including those not directly fostered by its actions. As David Schmitz shows, such support had been axiomatic for decades before World War II.[19] Thirdly, even though it abandoned the idea of direct colonial control, the US government often found itself on the side of its old colonial rivals, and its efforts to control the pace and direction of decolonization involved it in a sequence of worldwide atrocities, reaching cataclysmic scales in Indochina. The preferred narrative of the US was summarized in 1953 by Assistant Secretary of State for Near Eastern, South Asian and African Affairs Henry Byroade, who explained that

> we believe in eventual self-determination for all peoples . . . There are regions where human beings are unable to cope with disease, famine, and other forces of nature. Premature independence for these peoples would not serve the interests of the United States nor the interests of the free world as a whole.[20]

In the Caribbean, a wave of leftist and labour insurgency immediately after World War II sought to unite the islands in a federation and free the remaining French and British colonies from tutelage. The area was geopolitically significant to Washington because of its riches (bauxite, sugar, bananas, oil) and its cheap labour, and because the islands formed an 'outer defence ring' around the US underbelly, were clustered near the eastern mouth of the Panama Canal, and formed the zone through which many of America's imports flowed. Moreover, the region was domestically significant because of labour migration and the impact of radicalization on America's own black population. Precisely as those struggling for independence were unwilling to accept segregation and racial subordination in the Caribbean islands, they were a direct challenge to the Jim Crow behemoth to the north. The African-American left, including W. E B. Du Bois and Paul Robeson, saw the significance of this and sought to develop links with the people of the West Indies.[21]

The US responded to the diminishing power of the old empires in the Caribbean by erecting a network of bases on the islands, and seeking to co-opt various anti-colonial leaders. However, it was the overthrow of the US-imposed Batista dictatorship in Cuba in 1959 that both accentuated the tendency towards radicalization and introduced a dangerous new era of international politics, when the incoming Kennedy administration decided to try to oust Fidel Castro. The Eisenhower administration, which had funded the Batista regime and supplied weapons to it to help suppress opposition, was immediately hostile to the new regime, and Kennedy's incoming Democrats, keen to be the better anti-Communists, undertook an aggressive war against the new regime. It started to train Cuban exiles in camps in Guatemala to invade and overthrow Castro as early as 1960, placed the tiny island in an economic stranglehold, and, in April 1961, sent the exiles off to invade from the south at Playa Giron. The invasion by what Robert Kennedy called 'rebels' was an immediate failure. Operation Mongoose, a policy of sabotage, attempted assassination and planned terror attacks, was promulgated. Castro was not a Communist when he began his revolutionary career, but as a result of his wholly reasonable hostility to the United States government and its attempts to sabotage his new government, he was inclined to seek the assistance of the Soviet Union. The Kennedy administration's policy, as Sheldon Stern has shown, was to a large extent responsible for the ensuing 'missile crisis'. The Soviet Union's leadership was convinced by Castro, believing he would be a good asset for them, and offered to provide a missile defence against the United States, believing that to be the only way to defend the Cuban government. The Kennedy administration responded by stimulating hysteria about the Communist threat, despite the fact that the United States not only had eight times as many rockets as the USSR, but had them positioned around the latter's perimeter, and aimed at its cities. The US engaged in a naval blockade around Cuba and prepared for all-out nuclear war, averted in the end only by a Soviet climb-down.[22] As becomes clear in the light of other interventions, the US regarded its nuclear advantage as decisive: the temptation to consider the use of atomic weapons when faced with a difficult enemy was powerful, and sometimes only narrowly averted. However, the fact that American leaders were prepared to place millions of American lives at risk in the business of manoeuvring against this particular enemy suggests both how irrational the postwar system was, and how maddening it was that someone had defied the Monroe Doctrine.

The 'Alliance for Progress' programme is often celebrated as an essentially liberal foreign policy – a programme of much-needed aid to Latin America that combined anti-communism with social justice. Such is Peter Beinart's argument, for example. The project was overseen by a liberal president who made a point of surrounding himself with advisers such as Schlesinger (although most of his advisers were not at all fresh faces). In fact, however, US policy towards Latin America was no less imperialist in 1961 than it had been in 1912, 1915, or 1937, when the Somozist dictatorship had been imposed on Nicaragua at the height of the so-called 'Good Neighbor' policy. The Eisenhower administration had already imposed a right-wing dictatorship on Guatemala, overthrowing its democratically elected social-democratic leadership, essentially to protect the profits of the United Fruit Company and the position of the local elite. That elite had relied upon 'feudal' labour and vagrancy laws, as well as on a massive concentration of land ownership, to keep the workforce in virtual slavery for much of the time. A post-war wave of revolt and reform began to enfranchise labour, and the 1950 elections delivered a victory to the left-wing Arbenz, who launched an ambitions programme of land reforms. US bombs imposed the anti-Communist Colonel Carlos Castillo Armas as president.[23]

Kennedy's instincts and preferences were conservative and focused on continuity. However, the obsession with Cuba and the spreading 'bacteria' of communism called for a vaccine. The 'Alliance for Progress' fitted into a number of coterminous policies designed to convey the image of a magnanimous and dynamic America, generous to a fault. Its declared goals were economic growth, structural transformation and democratization. Yet it was during the period of the 'Alliance for Progress' that the State Department, the Department of Defense, the CIA and the Green Berets were put to work building up the internal security apparatuses of Latin American states, producing the very death squad systems that would ravage Latin America in the 1970s and 1980s. In El Salvador, the two systems built up under Kennedy were the Agencia Nacional De Servicios Especiales (ANSESAL) and the Organisacion Democratica Nacionalista (ORDEN). The former coordinated security operations, while the latter acted as a rural militia, upholding a corrupt and autocratic social order that would explode into revolutionary ferment in the 1980s. Significantly, the lessons of this counterinsurgency would be applied in the United States as well. General William Yarborough, for example, instructed the Colombians in 1962 on the need to build up paramilitary units in order to engage in 'sabotage' and 'terrorist activities'. He would later lead the Green Berets in Vietnam and coordinate the FBI's notorious 'COINTELPRO' project – an effort to subvert and repress oppositional groups in America, which included assassinations. Under Lyndon B. Johnson, the rhetoric of liberal reform was largely dropped, and was replaced by a stress on the interests of private capital. It became, in the words of Senator T. P. Gore, 'a subsidy for American business and American exporters'. Johnson supported the first in a wave of counter-revolutionary coups that took place across Latin America, beginning in Brazil in 1964 and finishing with Argentina in 1976.[24]

The American strategy in the Middle East varied with circumstances. The perceptions of political and military leaders in the region were shaped by racist contempt, as well as by geopolitical strategy. When the US wanted to recognize Israel in 1948, and faced the opposition of Arab states, White House counsel Clark Clifford mocked the idea of America 'trembling before threats of a few nomadic desert tribes'. Palestine desk officer Robert McClintock warned against letting 'these fanatical and overwrought people' curtail American interests. George Kennan's wartime experience in Iraq had left him bilious about its people, whom he regarded as selfish and stupid and 'inclined to all manner of religious bigotry and fanaticism'. Dwight Eisenhower considered Arabs 'explosive and full of prejudices'. When the US invaded Lebanon in 1958 to defend a pro-American regime, Eisenhower reminded the National Security Council that 'the underlying Arab thinking' was rooted in 'violence, emotion, and ignorance'. John Foster Dulles considered the reformist Iranian Prime Minister Mossadegh 'a wily oriental'. US interests led it to take an anti-colonial position at times, despite the apprehensions of state leaders. For example, it initially gave the nod to Nasser's overthrow of the pro-British monarchy in Egypt, and opposed the invasion of the country by France, Britain and Israel. But for some time the US took great pains to defend the French Fourth Republic, over which it exerted considerable leverage in the post-war years, when it was faced with the Algerian uprising. Further, although it was not inclined to create American colonies, it did apply the client-state model several times. Together with British intelligence, the United States helped to overthrow the elected Mohammad Mossadegh in 1953. The *New York Times* recorded the exultant reaction of official liberalism:

> Underdeveloped countries with rich resources now have an object lesson in the heavy cost that must be paid by one of their number which goes berserk with fanatical nationalism. It is perhaps too much to hope that Iran's experience will prevent the rise of other Mossadeghs in other countries, but that experience may at least strengthen the hands of more reasonable and more far-seeing leaders.[25]

From Japan to Vietnam

America's engagement with Asia in the post-war world was relayed to ordinary Americans through humanitarian appeals, middlebrow Orientalist cultural output in the form of Hammerstein musicals, and advertising. These tended to depict the Orientals as children in need of good American parenting and schooling in the old imperialist fashion. In creating sentimental attachments, they also helped consolidate the Cold War consensus which rejected a narrative of conquest. Instead, American action was seen as both protecting and nurturing the needy infants. The reality was less august. The post-war construction of a favourable state-system in Southeast Asia following World War II faced several challenges, the most significant of which was the threat of anti-colonial revolt. Roosevelt, worried about this prospect, had contacted Anthony Eden about the possibility of placing Indochina under international control, rather than permitting France to repossess its colonial holdings.[26] But that idea, if it ever had any prospects, was dropped by the Truman administration. (One of Roosevelt's other forgotten policies was a scheme to crossbreed the Japanese with 'docile' Pacific islanders – compulsory eugenics would, he said, eradicate the 'primitive' brains and 'barbarism' of the enemy race.[27]) The first priority was to suppress the rise of leftist and nationalist movements in countries formerly occupied by Japan. For this purpose, the US postponed removal of Japanese army units from north China, Indochina and the East Indies. They instead joined the battle with Communists and assisted Dutch and French colonial administrations in efforts to prevent the emerging nationalist forces from consolidating themselves.[28]

In Japan itself, the policy was to break up the old structures that it was believed had promoted Japanese expansion, with the assistance of the traditional conservatives, and of a segment of the business elite who had sought a peaceful settlement as early as 1943. This initially involved a period of liberal reform modelled on the American 'New Deal', under the improbable direction of the conservative General Douglas MacArthur. As usual, this imperial liberalism was suffused with racism and self-interest. Truman saw the Japanese as 'vicious and cruel savages', who had deserved their fate at Hiroshima and Nagasaki, while MacArthur periodically announced 'new victories in taming and spiritually transforming a warrior race'. At the same time, when it became clear that the reforms could potentially strengthen Japan's labour and leftist movements, they were swiftly curtailed. MacArthur intervened several times in labour strikes, sending out verbal threats, banning where necessary, and at one point threatening the intervention of the occupation authorities if the government could not resolve the situation. Labour rights were dramatically rolled back in 1948 and 1949, and a new conservative hegemony was inaugurated with the foundation of the Democratic-Liberal party. George Kennan, whom Peter Beinart credits as a model Cold War liberal, must take much of the credit for the policy change around 1947. He had argued that the 'Asiatic peoples' would not accept liberalism, and so the US should cease speaking in terms of human rights and deal in 'straight power concepts'. He called the reform process destructive, and saw it as threatening the stability of a needed 'bulwark' against the Soviet Union.[29]

US policy in Southeast Asia was seen in some ways as continuous with its acquisition of hegemony in Europe. Paul Hoffman, a Marshall Plan administrator, explained in 1951: 'We have learned in Europe what to do in Asia, for under the Marshall Plan, we have developed the essential instruments of a successful policy in the arena of world politics.' But two epic wars, barbaric to the bitterest end, illustrated what scale of violence might be necessary to achieve the rule of acquiescent, seduced elites. The Korean War was the first of these, and it consolidated two trends – both the 'national security state' elaborated domestically, and the international attempt to manage decolonization through the use of client-regimes. Though the struggle against the Japanese colonial power had produced a powerful nationalist current, the peninsula was divided between the Soviet Union, which occupied everything down to the 38th Parallel, and the US, which occupied the southern half. The division happened to overlap with some important historical and social facts. The northern part of the peninsula had been marginalized for centuries, and its residents denied high office. Those living there had been stigmatized as violent, and both the Chosun dynasty and the Japanese had found the north-east extremely difficult to control. Mutual aid associations had been more prevalent in the north-east than elsewhere. Nevertheless, a roughly identical set of social problems afflicted both the north and the south – particularly the social and economic dislocations that had produced waves of peasant rebellion – and it was these that produced the civil war that would be internationalized in 1950.[30]

Unlike the USSR, the United States had a long imperialist history in Korea dating back to the mid-nineteenth century. The Soviet Union was admired by many Koreans, who thought that it presented a model of how, as Milovan Djilas put it, to 'skip over centuries of slavery and backwardness'. This prestige was seriously damaged by the indifference and brutality of the occupying Red Army and the early policy of rice confiscations to feed Soviet soldiers. But the model of 'communism' that developed in the north was not, at any rate, simply a 'revolution from abroad'. It was decisively shaped by indigenous factors and the reforms most closely associated with the new regime; land reforms, benefiting 70 per cent of households, were extremely popular. The historian Charles Armstrong concludes that a revolution would very probably have occurred regardless of the Soviet occupation. In the south of the country, which the US occupied, the policy was to thwart leftist insurgency by supporting Synghman Rhee, rightist groups, and elements of the colonial apparatus left behind by the Japanese. In the war's aftermath, 'people's committees' had developed across Korea, and these had formed links with workers, peasant unions (which had led the fight against Japanese colonialism in the 1930s) and student and youth movements. Though proclaiming neutrality in the domestic struggle, the US was in fact committed to undermining the KPR and backing the old order. Lieutenant General John R. Hodge, head of the occupying forces, noted that this policy was making the US extremely unpopular in the south, and that they were being blamed for the partition. By 1947, after a series of bloody atrocities and summary executions, the Left had been destroyed as a public force in the south of Korea, and it was driven to undertake a guerrilla war against the regime.[31]

Though Korea was not significant in itself for the US, it did fit into a broader strategy of managing Southeast Asia. When it saw that it could not exert control over the north, the US opted to pursue partition of the peninsula, pressuring the United Nations to hold separate elections for the south, which amounted to a virtual coup. It was clear that not only were the Soviets and Koreans to the north opposed to this policy, but so were the bulk of Koreans in the US-occupied south. The decision was rejected almost unanimously by the UN Commission as well. The head of the UN Commission, the chief delegate from India, withdrew his concerns about the elections after some straightforward blackmailing of India by the US State Department over Kashmir. After the 1948 elections, and the establishment of two separate governments in autumn of that year, political violence surged. US intelligence and UN studies indicated that the war that began was the latest link in a chain of insurrection that had begun in 1945. The main source of violence was internal struggle, however – the Yosu rebellion in late 1948 and a counter-guerrilla drive by the southern regime in late 1949 marked the peaks of violence, but there was also mass strike activity led by the South Korean Labour Party. The crushing of one rebellion in Cheju-do saw 30,000 people killed – about a tenth of the island's population. The Rhee government claimed that a wave of border attacks were being launched by the northern government, but did not acknowledge that a greater number had been initiated by the south. Domestic propaganda in the United States made Rhee out to be a rather handsome sort of Christian Democrat, rather than the brutal authoritarian he actually was. The CIA, meanwhile, considered him erratic and increasingly 'senile', which was not quite true either. If the US worried that it could not control its South Korean ally, Rhee was aware of this and used his leverage to considerable advantage. The Republic of Korea was receiving $100 million a year from the US by 1950 (a substantial sum when it is recalled that the entire national budget for the Republic of Korea in 1951 was $120 million).[32]

Rhee was hoping for a northern invasion, while Kim Il Sung hoped that the south would move first. Some of the worst fighting had already taken place, in August 1949, when northern forces attacked southern units occupying mountains north of the 38th parallel, an operation resulting in the complete routing of southern government forces. In an effort to reunite the peninsula, Sung repeatedly sought Stalin's support for a military intervention in the southern civil war on the side of the rebels. US troops had pulled out in 1949, and Stalin, although initially cautious, gave his assent after receiving intelligence indicating that the US would not defend the Rhee regime – although he stipulated that practical assistance would be slight.[33] Whatever intelligence Stalin had, the US was certainly not moving away from military solutions. In an effort to curtail Rhee's surging ambitions, the US had told him that they would only intervene if he was attacked unprovoked, but they were readying themselves for aggressive manoeuvring.

Operating under the assumptions of 'vital centre' liberalism, the US State Department's policy planning staff had produced a document, NSC-68, in early 1950. A portentous, not to say preposterous, document, it claimed, in language reflecting Kennan's earlier rhetoric, that America's 'free society' was 'mortally challenged' by the USSR, which was not only 'wholly irreconcilable' with American values but 'implacable in its purpose to destroy' the United States. Its proposals for an aggressive 'national security' policy were supported by administration liberals such as Dean Acheson and Paul Nitze. Kim Il Sung's intervention in July 1950, which had been expected by the US administration for some time, provided ample justification for the US to test out its new aggressive posture, especially since China had been 'lost' with no small amount of help from North Korean fighters.[34]

Dean Acheson, one of the empire-builders of the administration, pressed for immediate war, and obtained it, while the UN mainly ratified American decisions. Truman was 'going to let them have it'. He explained to a White House aide that 'Korea is the Greece of the Far East'. The UN mission in Korea (UNCOK) blamed the war entirely on the North Korean side, relying on American and South Korean sources, which Acheson found to be 'of invaluable assistance'. Although many in the administration favoured holding down military spending and maintaining a balanced budget, the war permitted the introduction of massive deficit spending to maintain a vast military arsenal. Military spending rose from $13.5 billion before the war to $52 billion afterwards, while the scope for state intervention to regulate labour relations and bolster production was expanded. Eisenhower, though he would later gain a reputation for military restraint, in fact supported this move at the time, and his post-war cuts to military expenditure were somewhat less dramatic in effect than they appear, since production stretch-outs kept billions of dollars in the pipeline, and in effect he repackaged policies already planned by Truman. The short-term economic benefits of military mobilization were substantial as well: while wages were held well below prices for many workers, war production raised the average income by 3 per cent per year after inflation, and by 1952 the GNP was rising by 5 per cent annually.[35]

The decision to intervene internationalized a civil war, but for Cold War liberals it was a straightforward case of Communist belligerence (despite the border not being internationally recognized). Almost fifty years after the war had ended, Schlesinger would still describe it in terms of the classical narrative: it was 'direct aggression' by the Communists, or Soviet 'satellite aggression'. And the anti-Communist consensus was now so watertight that few who wished to retain respectability were prepared to oppose this stance. Vaguely pacifist organizations such as the United World Federation announced that they backed the war, noting that it was supported by the UN and was therefore an 'international police action'. The Socialist Party's National Action Committee voted unanimously to support the war, and Norman Thomas, who was one of the few to oppose the bombings of Hiroshima and Nagasaki, warning of the 'horrified hatred of millions', nevertheless supported the war as a clear curtailment of aggression. The traditionally antiwar *Progressive* approved of the war and castigated 'true-blue pacifists' for lacking realism. The war was also supported by the *New Republic*, the *Nation*, and even Henry Wallace, who repudiated Communist support for his Progressive Party.[36]

Young socialists such as Michael Harrington were forced out of the Socialist Party because of their opposition to the war, and ended up joining Max Shachtman's Young Socialist League. Shachtman, who would become important in the development of neoconservatism, took a rather unusual position on the invasion of Korea. While he was unwilling to support the American war, he was far more horrified by the prospect of Stalinist forces winning power than by the conflict itself. He argued that socialists should not support the war, but allow capitalist democracies to hold back the Stalinists, convinced that this would make room for 'Third Camp' socialists of his own kind to emerge. He called for the transformation of the 'imperialist war into a democratic war' and, if the war-making powers committed themselves to ending relations with dictators like Syngman Rhee and abided by the principle of self-determination, he would support them. The only barrier was that, as the US did not have a labour government, he did not trust it; but he supported British troops in Korea, because Britain had a Labour government. Moreover, he refused to call for America to quit Korea, and opposed any negotiated settlement on the grounds that 'Labour and socialism CANNOT "peacefully coexist" with Stalinism in the same world'. Whatever the failings of imperialism, Shachtman had begun to see in it a shield against the successes of Stalinism.[37]

As noted earlier, the war ratcheted up patriotism and paranoia in equal measure, and contributed to the wave of repression not only against Communists, but against liberals who were broadly supportive of the anti-Communist crusade. The McCarran Act was passed, requiring the registration of Communist organizations with the Attorney General, while the Subversive Activities Control Board was appointed to investigate 'un-American' activities. Criticism of the administration tended to come from the Republican 'internationalists', who felt that the government underestimated the threat of communism, and who thus wanted a more vigorous policy, or from hard rightists like Senator McCarthy, who was charging that the government was packed with Communist infiltrators. General MacArthur's own call for the war to be extended was part of the reason for his dismissal in January 1951.[38] Dissent from the Left was restricted largely to Communists and 'fellow travellers' such as I.F. Stone, whose 1952 history was the first attempt to engage critically with what had happened.

The war for the south was easily won by 30 September 1950, and over 110,000 South Koreans had already been killed (the number of North Korean deaths is not known). Since the claim was that Kim Il Sung had transgressed an internationally inviolable boundary by crossing the 38th parallel, the driving of his forces north of that line should have completed 'containment' and ended the war. Yet the boundary seemed suddenly more permeable from the south. As South Korean units swept north, the US ambassador described the 38th parallel during the march to the north as an 'imaginary line' – which was as much to concede that the initial 'aggression' had not taken place. General MacArthur's forces followed the South Koreans, and swept all the way to the Manchurian border. It was now roll-back rather than containment. Kim Il Sung, who had been an effective guerrilla fighter against the Japanese occupiers, led his soldiers into the mountains and launched an unconventional war against the American-led occupiers. By the end of October 1950, it was clear that the occupation of the north involved destroying 'Communists and collaborators'. The South Korean forces, acting under the rubric of the UN, were carrying out atrocities, from mass arrests to 'truckloads' of murders of women, children and old men, while rightist cults from the south engaged in attempts at mass political indoctrination.[39]

But the crossing of the 38th parallel by US forces provoked the intervention of the People's Republic of China (PRC), which was anxious to protect its own territorial integrity. It inflicted a series of crushing defeats on the US and South Korean armies, and by late 1950 Washington was in a panic. Having dismissed threats of PRC intervention as 'blackmail', Truman now insisted that the US 'would not consider surrender to these murderous Chinese Communists', while Acheson deemed the PRC's intervention 'a fresh and unprovoked aggressive act'. Truman publicly threatened the use of the atomic bomb, a possibility that had been discussed and included in contingency plans. On the day Truman delivered this threat, Air Force General Stratemeyer sent an order to General Hoyt Vandenberg that the Strategic Air Command augment its capacities to include 'atomic capabilities'. MacArthur requested the use of atomic bombs on 24 December 1950, although this was not approved, and a similar request by his successor General Ridgway for the same in May 1951 was rebuffed. The main reason the weapons were not used was the disinclination of the USSR and PRC to escalate. Even when peace negotiations were underway, Truman fantasized about deadlines to total war against the PRC and USSR if they did not comply, with the possibility of nuclear annihilation.[40] Atomic diplomacy had worked so well before, after all.

Chemical weapons were also considered, but instead the US opted for an air war that levelled North Korea and slaughtered hundreds of thousands before it was finished. MacArthur ordered the creation of a wasteland between the war front and the Chinese border, destroying every 'installation, factory, city, and village' over thousands of square miles. Tonnes of incendiary bombs were dropped on Sinuiju, 'removing [it] from the map'. Hoeryong was hit with napalm. The US burned out the houses of peasant farmers, creating masses of refugees. When a reporter for the *New York Times* found inhabitants of a village burned by napalm, in the exact positions they had occupied when killed, Acheson wanted the censorship authorities notified about this 'sensationalized reporting'. An armistice was eventually reached in 1953, under the Eisenhower administration, but no peace treaty was signed. Up to 1.5 million people had been killed during the second phase of the war. 'Both Koreas,' historian Bruce Cummings writes, 'had watched as a virtual holocaust ravaged their country and turned the vibrant expectations of 1945 into a nightmare'.[41]

This holocaust, with the threat of weapons of mass destruction hovering over the proceedings, was mandated throughout by virulent liberal anti-communism. The latter doctrine arguably helped keep levels of support for the war higher than they otherwise might have been: the venture was initially supported by over 80 per cent of the American public, although that fell to well below 50 per cent in its later stages.[42] The Korean War would become known as the 'forgotten war', but political repression at home and the success of the warfare state kept it alive as a model – so much so that George W. Bush would identify the conflict as an example for Americans to look to in the 'war on terror'.

The failure to achieve complete victory in Korea – and the success of the Chinese Revolution, despite its obvious difficulties and flaws – left US planners increasingly anxious to prevent the success of the anti-colonial revolution in Vietnam. Ho Chi Minh, like most Communist leaders in South-East Asia, had come to Lenin through his treatment of the colonial question. But the success of the Communists in Vietnam rested on their ability to adapt Marxism to circumstances in which peasants, rather than the urban working class, were the main revolutionary base, while their main strategy was to form popular fronts against the French colonists. For a long time, their key strategy was one of mass mobilization rather than military mobilization, and their seizure of power in August 1945 was the result not of military prowess but of their ability to organize against the destructive impact of the Japanese–French war. Since the French had contributed to a food crisis by agreeing to supply the retreating Japanese with Vietnamese rice and other agricultural materials, the Viet Minh told the peasants to 'break open the rice stores to avert famine'. Having declared a general insurrection on 12 August against the French colonialists, the Viet Minh could lead millions of euphoric people into the streets of

Hanoi, Hue, Saigon and dozens of other cities, even though the party itself was still only 5,000-strong. On 2 September 1945, Ho Chi Minh declared an independent Democratic Republic of Vietnam, citing the American Declaration of Independence. With British and French armies to the south, the Viet Minh's best chance was to link its efforts to master the famine and lead a mass literacy campaign to the anti-French struggle. Though the French had taken control of the cities by 1947, two years later the CIA reported that the 'vast majority' of Vietnamese, including a good portion of anti-Communist Catholics, backed Ho Chi Minh.[43]

The United States was especially worried by the rise of the Viet Minh following the collapse of the Kuomintang in China in 1949. By 1954 the US had successfully helped its client-state in the Philippines defeat the Huk Rebellion – another leftist insurgency based in the peasantry – by sponsoring a combined counterinsurgency and land reform programme;[44] but the Chinese nationalists had proved no match for Mao's guerrillas. So the Truman administration sought increasingly to shape the post-war settlement in Vietnam, first by encouraging the French to promote an anti-Communist nationalist alternative to the Viet Minh. When the French selected Bao Dai, a long-time colonial collaborator, to run the country in 1948, the US thought it was a step in the right direction, and sent $3.6 billion in aid to the French military between 1950 and 1954. While the PRC and USSR gave diplomatic recognition to Minh's DRV, the US recognized the French puppet dictatorship. By the time Eisenhower came to power, the bulk of the cost of France's war was being shouldered by the US government. At the Geneva Conference of May 1954, the French arrived at a peace with the Viet Minh, and the country was divided at the 19th parallel. The US, worried by the prospect of the revolution spreading to the new southern state, refused to support the agreement and threatened the use of atomic weapons against the Viet Minh. Once again, this was not merely bluster: behind closed doors, their use had been seriously proposed by Admiral Arthur Redford, chair of the Joint Chiefs of Staff (JCS), although it was rejected at the time by the president and others on the JCS.[45]

As the French withdrew, the US expanded its interference, backing Ngo Dinh Diem as an anti-French, anti-Communist alternative to the Bao Dai regime. The Geneva Conference had resulted in an agreement to hold elections in July 1956, but the CIA told Washington that the Viet Minh would certainly win any elections south of the border, and a variety of pretexts were confected to delay them. To contain dissent and protect his regime, Diem built a large standing army and engaged in robust urban repression. In the period 1955–57 alone, 12,000 people were killed, and by 1961 there were roughly 150,000 political prisoners. However, even prior to the Geneva agreement, the Viet Minh had controlled up to 90 per cent of the south, and the fighters were if anything more militant than those in the north.

An aggressive liberal administration had taken power in the United States, which was committed to two geopolitical principles: the first was the 'domino theory', according to which the 'fall' of one country to communism would result in others rapidly following suit, which meant that no country could be permitted to choose communism for itself if this could be avoided; the second was 'credibility', which expressed the obsession of policy planners with the successful use of force, and the effect this should have on potential challengers. Especially after the catastrophic and potentially deadly interventions in Cuba, the American government decided that it was time to study the 'new concepts, the new tools' of counterinsurgency. They sent increasing numbers of military advisers to help Diem defeat the guerrillas – by late 1962, these had risen to 9,000 – and obliged the Diem dictatorship to launch a 'Strategic Hamlet Programme', forcing Vietnamese peasants into militarized compounds to deprive the guerrillas of a base. By 1962 there were 16,000 such compounds across South Vietnam.[46]

Many observers believed that the Kennedy administration's policy was irrational: allies, neutrals, and even Khrushchev warned that the Americans would in all probability lose against the Vietnamese guerrillas. The administration was certainly fanatical in construing the insurgency as part of a global offensive launched by Moscow and Beijing. And it is true that the Johnson administration, though it had every intention of continuing the war, came to bitterly regret the deranged optimism of its predecessors – and even as Defense Secretary Robert McNamara orchestrated escalation, he warned that there was no guarantee of success. Arguably, nothing short of outright genocide would have secured victory for the United States. However, as Jonathan Neale points out, the US government had every reason to be confident of its abilities. It had defeated the Huks, Arbenz, Mossadegh and Lumumba, all of whom had led popular movements. Intervention *should* have worked.[47] The projection of massive, unconscionable levels of violence was hardly new to the United States government. And the obsession with credibility possessed a kernel of rationality, since the successful application of force might have intimidated others sufficiently that the US would find enemies more pliable, while the consequences of failing to apply force credibly could potentially have redoubled themselves many times.

So Johnson, who had run as a 'dove', promising 'no wider war', constructed an event that would provide the trigger for all-out war: the Gulf of Tonkin incident, in which North Vietnamese forces were provoked into attacking the USS *Maddox*, a naval destroyer operating as a spy ship (a subsequent attack on the USS *Turner Joy* was fabricated). This enabled the administration to seek and obtain a resolution supporting escalation of the war. The administration, which was already bombing the south, immediately launched a bombing campaign against North Vietnam. Later, he reluctantly heeded advice and sent Marines to fight on the ground, beginning a build-up of troops that would soon reach 500,000. By 1965, Assistant Secretary of Defense John McNaughton wrote in a memorandum that 70 per cent of the US war aim was about simply avoiding humiliating defeat.[48]

In the same year, the American government won a huge strategic victory when, together with British intelligence, it helped General Suharto overthrow the democratically elected Sukarno government, in a military onslaught that killed up to one million people. The Indonesian Communist Party, with 3 million members, was the most sizeable Communist movement outside the Soviet-aligned bloc. Its disenfranchisement, along with that of the country's militant working class and peasantry, not only propped up the dominoes, but also provided a powerful right-wing ally to the US and a friendly business climate for American multinationals. The scale of violence demanded in the assault on Vietnam was to be even more intense, and the toll much greater: on a conservative estimate, a total of 3 million people died across Vietnam, Laos and Cambodia. Although atomic weapons were not used, as had been threatened, 8 million tonnes of explosives were, representing an explosive power corresponding to 640 Hiroshimas. The bulk of it was aimed at more or less defenceless peasants in South Vietnam (bombing the North was more risky, since one in forty planes was shot down), and at the end of the war there were 10 million bomb craters across the south, covering 100,000 hectares. At the same time, certain techniques of sophisticated torture and killing were refined during the conflict. Napalm was mixed with polystyrene to make it stick to human bodies, while white phosphorus was added to ensure that it burned even under water. The United States and its allies also sprayed defoliants that caused cancer and birth defects on a fifth of South Vietnam's jungles; 7 million South Vietnamese became refugees; almost all of North Vietnam's industry, bridges and transport system were destroyed; and 1.35 million South Vietnamese were wounded.[49]

Although US political culture remained profoundly racist, the use of racial metaphors was difficult in Vietnam, since the argument was that there were 'good' Vietnamese – despite the array of 'gooks', 'slant-eyes', 'dinks' and so on that were on the other side. Still, as it became clear that, short of genocide, the US could not terrorize the South Vietnamese into abandoning their loyalty to Ho Chi Minh, the US responded with the 'mere gook rule', especially after the My Lai massacre, in which US soldiers had burned, looted, raped and shot their way through a village. The rule maintained that if it was dead and it was Vietnamese, it was the enemy. As Gabriel Kolko points out, the 'body count' – whereby US soldiers were encouraged to keep tallies of the numbers of corpses they produced, with superior officers' careers depending on the results – was no mere bureaucratic eccentricity. It was a logical military strategy, given the imperative of defeating a highly popular insurgency, and a racist culture sanctioned the ensuing brutality. The term 'gook' was not invented during the Vietnam war. It had been used by Marines to describe Haitian rebels in 1920, Filipinos during the US occupation, Spanish-speaking Nicaraguans during the 1920s, Hawaiians as late as 1945, and Algerians during the French colonial wars. Its use augmented anti-Communist rhetoric during the Korean war, and became so widespread that General MacArthur had to prohibit it, since it brought America's commitment to democratic ideals into question. When it was deployed in Vietnam, it came with resonances of the Indian wars. Thus Robert Kaiser reported: 'The only good gook, it is said again and again on US bases throughout Vietnam, is a dead gook.'[50]

However, a prelude to the contemporary adaptation of racist doctrines in which 'race' is commuted through the tropes of 'modernity' and 'backwardness' was provided by Walt Whitman Rostow. He entered the Kennedy administration as a national security adviser with his development thesis, which held that if the US could stimulate 'bourgeois revolution' and defend capitalism, the economies of the southern hemisphere possessed the preconditions for 'take-off'. For the administration's purposes, Rostow's argument also asserted that the strategy of relying on civilian governments to bring modernity was wrong. The populations in question were culturally unprepared for modernity, and so the 'benevolent authoritarianism' of military rule would best accomplish the spread of 'Western' values. Hence, one US ambassador to South Vietnam explained that the mission was to 'bring this medieval country into the twentieth century'.[51] To bomb a country into the twentieth century was to turn it into a moonscape and incinerate and shred millions of people to death. To 'modernize' it, under this construction, was to destroy its infrastructure and try to maintain the population as the terrorized property of a highly personalized autocratic state.

The collapse of the liberal consensus

In the aftermath of World War II, a large number of the world's socialists were, as James Young puts it, living in 'totalitarian and colonial labyrinths'. These were to include the vanguard of the New Left, and many of its heroes. Paul Berman celebrates the fact that many contemporary liberal interventionists have a history in the New Left: Bernard Kouchner, José Ramos-Horta, Joschka Fischer, André Glucksmann and, implicitly, himself. One could add Christopher Hitchens, Adam Michnik and, to a much lesser extent, Bernard-Henri Lévy and Michael Ignatieff. They are all in some ways descendants of both 1956 and 1968, even if their descent has not yet ceased. The first stirrings of that movement were seen following the suppression of the Hungarian uprising, which drove many European and American Communists to abandon Stalinism and seek a means of renewing Marxism as critical thought. In the United States, far more important was the crisis of liberal nationalism. As one writer on 'Americanism' points out, war had figured centrally in the minds of Americans who wished to forge a liberal nation, from Theodore Roosevelt to Kennedy. Vietnam decisively severed that connection to the extent that, even today, liberals seeking to renew liberal nationalism by drawing upon the legacy of putatively liberal wars (the Civil War and World War II) find it difficult to reckon honestly with Vietnam.[52]

Gradually, despite initial enthusiasm especially among 'vital centre' liberals, intellectuals who had been part of the liberal foreign policy establishment began to distance themselves from Washington's policies. Liberal journals supportive of the Vietnam War had included *Foreign Affairs* and *Encounter*, while *Dissent* carried regular bulletins from Joseph Buttinger, who was a vociferous advocate of the Diem regime. Early criticism of the US intervention that did emerge was pragmatic, broadly accepting US goals. Norman Podhoretz's *Commentary*, which published David Halberstam's early critique of the official story, 'Getting the Story Straight on Vietnam', was nevertheless strongly supportive of the anti-Communist position as late as 1965. The *New Republic*, though it had broadly supported the venture, came to a critical position as the bombing of North Vietnam escalated. The *Nation*, whose early attacks on the policy had mainly focused on the use of Diem to achieve the stated goal of the intervention, later came to demand a negotiated withdrawal – the only major journal to do so.

The criticisms that were delivered by Cold War liberals tended to stop short of calling for withdrawal. Arthur Schlesinger's attack on the war, *Bitter Heritage*, challenged some of the assumptions of the war, such as the 'domino theory', and the claim that the war was a result of aggression by Mao – who, predictably, had been compared with Hitler by Eisenhower's secretary of state; but he insisted that the war was more a result of bureaucratic error and misperception than Machiavellian intrigue. His challenge was not to ends, but to means, and so: 'let us adapt the means we employ to the ends we seek'. The US, he said, should 'taper off' the bombing of North Vietnam as prudently as possible, leaving a substantial force in South Vietnam to impress upon the Viet Minh that there would not be a Communist government in the south, and negotiate on that basis. 'They must have no illusion about the prospect of an American withdrawal' since 'holding the line in South Vietnam is essential'.[53]

But such criticisms were already being overtaken by New Left scholars, who mounted an attack on the conventional Cold War narratives that had been guarded by the likes of Schlesinger and Rostow.[54] Breaking with the anti-Communist consensus, they maintained that if the people of Vietnam wanted a Communist government, they were entitled to have one. Their arguments connected with a growing radicalism among students in particular. The Students for a Democratic Society (SDS), which would have 100,000 members by the end of the 1960s, was the result of a break-away from the student wing of the increasingly right-wing and Shachtmanite-dominated organization, the League for Industrial Democracy. The SDS's Port Huron statement of 1962 took up some of the themes of the old Anti-Imperialist League, denouncing US efforts 'to build a "profitable" capitalist world' blind to most of humankind's needs. The students railed against the acceleration of 'man's opportunity for self-destruction', and looked to the 'counterimpulse to life and creation superbly manifest in many Asian, African and Latin American peoples', which stood in such 'embarrassing contrast' to 'American apathy and stalemate'.[55]

It is fitting that participants in the ensuing peace movement gained much of their ideological and tactical training as participants in the Civil Rights movement, through organizations such as the Congress of Racial Equality (CORE), which pursued non-violent civil disobedience. It would have been inconsistent to support the liberation of black people elsewhere but not to fight for the same in the United States, and the African-American Left had long understood the connections between the struggles for freedom in the US and overseas. CORE and the Student Non-violent Coordinating Committee (SNCC) engaged in 'Freedom Rides', punctuated by anti-segregation protests in which they placed themselves in physical danger. Black protesters would enter 'white only' areas, while white protesters occupied 'coloured only' zones. They were, upon arrival at many stops, clubbed by police and pelted with rocks by members of the public. The experiences fuelled their indictment of America as a corrupt, racist and elitist society, laid the basis for later alliances, and provided an array of tactics that, as Irving Kristol later bitterly reflected, could be used 'at the drop of a hat'. As well as developing a series of movements, pursuing causes ranging from women's liberation to peace campaigns, the 1960s radicals became acquainted with anti-Zionism and the Palestinian struggle for liberation. I. F. Stone produced the first substantial critique of Zionism for American audiences, while Maxime Rodinson elaborated a revisionist account of Israel's formation for Europeans. As Mark Kurlansky writes, the word 'Palestinian' first began to be heard in 1968, following the Arab–Israeli war in which Israel had thoroughly pounded opposing Arab armies, and as Palestinian organizations turned towards guerrilla struggle. Rightly seeing it as anti-colonial, many radical groups, including the SNCC, publicly supported the Palestinian struggle, although this view never became part of the mainstream of the antiwar movement. Similarly, when Tom Hayden and Staughton Lynd of the SDS, together with the left-wing academic Herbert Aptheker, travelled to North Vietnam during a pause in the bombing, and conveyed a favourable impression of the North Vietnamese leadership and its position to the American public, they went well beyond the mainstream antiwar position. But, however uncritical they were, they did contribute to the demystification of America's opponents, and to the erosion of a prolonged campaign of demonization.[56]

The peace movement embraced a total of up to 6 million Americans, with an estimated 25 million sympathizers. For much of the time, they represented a distinct minority. In 1964 and 1966, only 9 per cent of Americans wanted to pull out of Vietnam entirely. By 1968, that figure stood at 20 per cent; and by 1970, 33 per cent. Only in retrospect did the principled anti-imperialist opposition to the war obtain the support of most of the American public.[57] Nevertheless, many of those who would go on to become neoconservatives saw the 1960s movement coming, and perceived in it a real threat to the fundamentals of American society.

Neoconservatism and the spectre of Leon Trotsky

'Studying the neocons', John Micklethwait and Adrian Wooldridge write, 'is like studying the Bloomsbury group in Britain . . . Everyone seems to have been to school together, live next door to each other, belong to the same clubs, write papers together, or be related to each other.'[58] Jacob Heilbrunn, a former neoconservative himself, remarks on 'the web of connections that constitute the neoconservative world'. The effort to find out what family resemblances of the inbred characterize this twisted sodality usually arrives at some root ideological source, such as the thought of Leon Trotsky. 'That crowd, the neocon group, somewhere in their cortex is the name of Leon Trotsky. If I were to say "Kronstadt" to Trent Lott, I don't think I'd get a whole hell of a lot for my trouble', Christopher Hitchens explained to George Packer, a comrade in the Iraq adventure. 'But if I were to say "Kronstadt" to Paul Wolfowitz, I think he would more than know what I was talking about'. The idea of a profound continuity between neoconservatism and revolutionary socialism is justly rejected by neoconservatives. As Alan Wald points out, none of the current generation of neoconservatives close to the White House have a background on the far Left[59] (Paul Wolfowitz was reportedly aware of the arguments of the Shachtmanites, but was never actually part of that scene).[60] The charge is frequently made that neoconservatives are possessed by revolutionary hubris and neo-Jacobinism,[61] but the reality is that neoconservatism is counterrevolutionary and profoundly pessimistic – about the state of sex, welfare, the movies, race relations, the prospects for a peaceful planet, and so on.

Mark Gerson writes that, though the neoconservative position is liberal in inspiration, 'a part of the republican virtue tradition', 'there is not one political position that can be considered distinctly neoconservative'. Rather, there are a set of shared intellectual biases. The first is an acceptance of private interests tempered by a concern for a version of the common good; the second is an insistence on the futility of blueprints for social transformation, since these are considered to be blunt external impositions, whereas the neoconservatives regard social problems as resulting from human failure; the third is the belief that social institutions 'embody inherited wisdom garnered as a result of longevity', even where they appear to be irrational; fourth, the theologically-inspired belief that human beings are agents of good and evil ('children of light' and 'children of darkness' in Reinhold Niebuhr's terms), and that these agents do not operate on equal terms, since 'children of darkness' are more cunning and ruthless than 'children of light', which spaniel-eyed saps only see the good and decency in others;

finally, the belief that politics and economics are functions of culture, and any attempt to replace culture with political economy will fail (Norman Podhoretz hence argued that capitalism's longevity would be determined by its congruence with Judeo-Christian morality, not by the power of its productive forces).[62]

As well as engaging critically with Cold War liberalism, neoconservativism's cultural reading of social institutions restored aspects of colonialist ideology. Thus, Irving Kristol argued that, since political democracy required a rare and exquisite cultural apparatus, it was quite correct to support the war on Vietnam and right-wing dictatorship: 'South Vietnam, like South Korea, is barely capable of decent self-government under the very best of conditions'. As two centre-right critics of neoconservatism argue, today's neoconservatives share the following beliefs: a belief that the human condition is characterized by the polarity of good and evil (moral clarity); a belief that interstate relations are characterized by violence and the willingness to use it (standing up to evil); and a primary focus on the Middle East as the theatre for military activism (the Islamic threat). This may well be a *militant* creed, but it is about as revolutionary as Richard I. Further, the cultural values it esteems most are those associated with a certain mythopoeic rendering of the 1950s: a gentle era of childlike innocence before gay liberation and female assertiveness. Newt Gingrich argues that Americanism is best expressed in Norman Rockwell illustrations from 1955, while Irving Kristol and Gertrude Himmelfarb are endlessly disturbed by the moral laxity, permissiveness and emphasis on difference (as opposed to cohesion) that characterize society after the ruinous 1960s and 1970s. There had been, Gingrich maintains, a 'continuous civilization' from 1607 to 1965, based on 'commonly accepted legal and cultural principles' which the leftists, Black Panthers and feminists collectively assaulted.[63]

One problem with the logic of reducing neoconservatism to a sequel of Trotskyism is partly that it overstates the coherence of neoconservative tradition and doctrine. Invented as a term of opprobrium by Michael Harrington in 1973, it came to refer to intellectuals, some of them Jewish, who were considered to be on the Left in some sense, but were increasingly indistinguishable from the Right. It is easy to list examples of people who had at one time advocated a version of Trotskyism who then migrated to the neoconservative fold: Daniel Bell, Irving Kristol, Gertrude Himmelfarb, Seymour Martin Lipset, and Jeane Kirkpatrick are prominent examples. On the other hand, many had not been Trotskyists: for example, Daniel Patrick Moynihan, Henry Jackson, Joshua Muravchik, Norman Podhoretz,

Midge Decter, William Kristol and Paul Wolfowitz. And none of the former category were any kind of socialist by the time the Cold War began.[64] Inasmuch as there are discernable 'roots' to neoconservatism, many of its disciples can be said to have been Cold War liberals who had become terrified by the explosion of radicalism they were witnessing on campuses, in black neighbourhoods and in Third World countries. Even those who had been Trotskyists usually did not move directly to the right; typically, they were social democrats, then liberals, and then conservatives. The intellectual and broader political context for their transformations varied, too, as did the duration and intensity of their affiliations with Trotskyism.

This is not to say that there is no discernible continuity. Max Shachtman once noted that it was in the course of defending Leon Trotsky in the 1930s, and exposing the 'show trials' in the Soviet Union, that much of the anti-Stalinist Left received its education in the nature of communism. Trotsky's own critique, as well as those of many of his supporters, sometimes described the Soviet Union as 'totalitarian'. The term was also applied to the American war-state by many radicals. Although it had not yet accrued the variety of theoretical associations that it acquired during the Cold War, the term did convey the sense of the state exerting total control over the lives of its citizens. As Nicolas Guilhot writes, for the non-Communist Left this concept provided a means of commuting anti-fascism into anti-communism. It facilitated the alliance with the more liberal components of the American state, which saw the non-Communist Left as the best defence against the threat from the East. For this transubstantiation to occur, however, the former radicals had to abandon precisely what was distinctive about Leon Trotsky's anti-Stalinism, which was his commitment to revolutionary socialism.[65]

Since a number of the ex-Trotskyists who joined the neoconservative circuit had been associated with, or mentored by, Max Shachtman, it is not surprising that he should be frequently fingered as the *deus ex machina* of neoconservatism, even though he remained on the Left for approximately two decades after Burnham's transformation, and long after others had joined the Cold War liberal coalition. His trajectory is worth summarizing in this context. Shachtman had been an energetic recruit to the Communist Party, having won its attention in 1922. A wry, multilingual graduate of City College, New York, he seemed to thrive as an ascetic party worker, living on a $10 weekly stipend from headquarters. It was while in the Communist Party that he had become acquainted with Trotsky's indictment of Stalinism – the 'Criticism of the Draft Programme', which James Cannon had smuggled out of the

Sixth World Congress of the Comintern in 1928. Expelled from the Party alongside Cannon, Shachtman met Trotsky and vowed to fight his corner. Working initially through the Communist League of America (Opposition), co-founded with Cannon, they later merged with the American Workers' Party, led by A.J. Muste, and, having attempted a merger with the Socialist Party of America, reformed themselves as the Socialist Workers' Party. Shachtman was recalled as a rousing speaker – a mimic, a bawdy entertainer, 'a kibitzer'.[66] He was also scathing in debate. During a public confrontation with Earl Browder in 1950, Shachtman mercilessly dissected the Soviet Union's claim to be a socialist country with the expert help of *Pravda*, the Soviet bureaucracy's own paper of record, and finished by reminding Browder of how lucky he had been to be expelled:

> When I saw him standing there at the podium, I said to myself: Rajk was the general secretary of the Hungarian Communist Party, and was shot, or hanged, or garrotted. Kostov was the general secretary of the Bulgarian Communist Party. And when I thought of what happened to them, I thought of the former secretary of the American Communist Party, and I said to myself: There, there but for an accident of geography, stands a corpse![67]

Earl Browder reportedly turned white upon hearing this.[68]

Shachtman was also an innovative thinker and an expert in the arts of organizational fission and fusion. Having arrived at the conclusion that the USSR could not possibly be any kind of workers' state, degenerate or otherwise, he found himself at odds with both Trotsky and Cannon, and led a split that took 40 per cent of the membership of an already tiny party into a new organization. The immediate trigger of the controversy was that the USSR had negotiated a non-aggression pact with Hitler, and waged war on Finland. Trotsky, though he agreed that the bureaucracy was trying to expand its privileges, maintained that this was not imperialism in the conventional Marxist sense because the USSR was still a 'degenerated workers' state'. Shachtman maintained not only that the USSR was imperialist in its war, but that any trace of progress in it had long since vanished: it was a new form of class society, which he characterized as 'bureaucratic collectivism' – even more vicious and exploitative than capitalism. Against the de-radicalizing impact of the CPUSA, and the subordination of the labour movement to the government's war aims, Shachtman argued for a 'Third Camp', a socialist movement independent both of the Soviet Union and of Western capitalist states.[69] Shachtman, like Trotsky, had hoped that the war would see another wave of revolutionary struggle at its end, which would both destabilize the Stalinist system and weaken capitalism. As we now know, it did not quite turn out like that: capitalism, despite the precariousness of its European powers, was in rude condition in the post-war US, and the Stalinist regime added some 'people's democracies' to its holdings.

Partly as a consequence of this, Shachtman drifted slowly to the right from the late 1940s, supporting the right wing against Communists in the labour movement. His anomalous position on the Korean War was implicated in a broader shift in his theoretical outlook. Shachtman not only maintained that the USSR was a new and more brutal form of class society – 'bureaucratic or totalitarian collectivism', as he called it; he also insisted that Communist parties beyond Russia and the Eastern Bloc were incipient ruling classes, rather than allies in the socialist movement. National liberation movements which entered into any engagement with the Soviet Union received no support from Shachtman's Independent Socialists. When it came to the Vietnam War, however, they initially supported the Viet Minh as an authentic national liberation movement, as Shachtman had perceived that the new American empire would not allow the peoples of Asia to have real independence. However, the recognition of Ho Chi Minh's government by Moscow led the Shachtmanites to describe the Viet Minh as a 'power instrument of Stalinist imperialism'. Shachtman and his supporters worked to build up influence in the trade unions, particularly the United Auto Workers union (UAW), and in 1958 joined Norman Thomas's Socialist Party, where Shachtman disappointed many by accepting the right-wing swing of its leadership. By 1962, he was arguing that the main obstacle for the socialist movement was not reformism, but 'the illusions of Stalinism'.[70]

It is tempting to see Shachtman's growing support for the United States in the Cold War in terms of his thesis of 'bureaucratic collectivism', and the idea that Communist parties loyal to Moscow were germinal dictatorships. But his biographer, Peter Drucker, demurs:

I think the essential reason was an adaptation to the US trade union bureaucracy. He started by adapting to the leadership of the UAW under Walter Reuther, who was pro-Cold War, but mildly critical. Reuther criticised the Vietnam War in the early 1960s, but by that point, Shachtman had already moved behind George Meany of the AFL-CIO, who supported it – he allied with the big guns. It is difficult to separate opportunism from conviction in these cases, but it is probably a mixture of the two.

But if you look at the people who held to the 'bureaucratic collectivist' position, they held a range of contrasting views on the Vietnam War, from the most pro-war position of Max Shachtman to the relatively critical position of Michael Harrington, to principled anti-imperialists. The idea of Communist parties forming the nuclei of bureaucratic classes did have consequences in allowing people to rationalize support for imperialism, but it came later. In the 1950s, what still identified Shachtman's tendency was the 'Third Camp': neither Washington, nor Moscow. However, he dropped that position when he supported the Vietnam War, and because of that some would say he broke with his own tendency.[71]

Shachtman's slide to the right also involved a break with his strong anti-racist politics, expressed in his booklet *Race and Revolution*.[72] 'When he first became associated with the Democrats in the early 1960s,' Drucker explains,

he had the idea of the civil rights movement splitting the Democrats, and then they would form another organization with labour and the civil rights movement and the racists of the Democratic Party clearly excluded from that. But by the time of the 1964 Democratic convention in Atlantic City, that was dropped and Shachtman moved very much away from his own ideas, and the crucial thing became to support Lyndon B. Johnson. This was a key point when the movement started to go into disarray. A lot of the activists in the SNCC who had been very close to Shachtman saw it as a betrayal, not only by him, but by the white Left. It should be said that at this point, Shachtman and Harrington were on the same side. Shachtman's alliance with George Meany is also important in this context because Meany was charged by many with racism – with some justification, because he came from a background in building and plumbing unions, which were the most segregated in America. So, for Shachtman to align with him involved swallowing a great deal. For followers of Shachtman, it became very important to say that there may once have been deep, ingrained, structural racism, but there is no longer. Perhaps there is a certain convergence with the neoconservatives on this question. The neoconservatives as a group really do believe that it is possible for African-Americans and Latinos to achieve equality in the neoliberal settlement, and they are very proud of Colin Powell and Condoleezza Rice for this reason. This is something they share with right-wing social democrats.[73]

Another possible point of continuity is the issue of Israel. However, Israel was in no sense as important to the Shachtmanites as it has been to most neoconservatives. Zionism, Drucker argues,

> was never important for Shachtman, except inasmuch as Israel was a US ally. Israel was a factor in the split between Shachtman and Michael Harrington. Harrington and [Irving] Howe supported dialogue with the PLO and a two-state settlement, which Max Shachtman thought was far too soft. But at that point [Schachtman's position] was far more anti-PLO than pro-Israel. Any Third World national liberation movement was seen as the local representation of Stalinism.

When Lyndon Johnson escalated the Vietnam War in 1965, Shachtman firmly declared that the Viet Minh were the greater danger, with the apparent acquiescence of many of his colleagues. Even though he negotiated compromise positions within the Socialist Party, favouring negotiations, he and his followers still declared their opposition to withdrawal as late as 1970, prompting bitter recriminations with Socialists such as Michael Harrington and Irving Howe. Like the neoconservatives and the Cold War liberals, Shachtman was increasingly prepared to defend highly authoritarian regimes on the basis of their moral superiority to the 'totalitarian despotism' of communism. The 1970 statement claimed that the US was fostering democracy in South Vietnam, although it could adduce little evidence to support the claim. Shachtman's stance on Vietnam eventually placed him to the right not only of the Socialist Party, but also of most Democrats. And though the Shachtmanites argued that the project of socialists should be to realign the Democratic Party to the Left, they connived in the Socialist Party's denunciation of the 1972 candidacy of George McGovern for proposing a 'neo-isolationist and conservative' foreign policy. The party's newspaper carried an open letter from Sidney Hook calling Nixon 'the Lesser Evil'. Shachtman, while he detested the New Left and preferred Henry 'Scoop' Jackson in the Democratic primaries, did not approve. Michael Harrington, one of Shachtman's former protégés, resigned in disgust, accusing his former comrades of 'doing the work of Richard Nixon'. Irving Howe joined in the denunciation, arguing that McGovern's appeal to the antiwar constituency would revitalize the Democratic Party. Though Shachtman died on 4

November 1972, his followers were delighted by Nixon's success, believing that it would open up the conservative wing of the Democratic Party and the union leadership to them, as indeed it did.[74]

Shachtman himself never became a neoconservative; and if some of his supporters or associates did, it is important to note that many of them certainly did not. Hal Draper, for example, led a minority in opposition to this tendency. Much of the supposed Shachtmanite connection is inferred from those who were in the increasingly right-wing and strongly anti-Communist Socialist Party while Shachtman was a presence in it. However, Drucker points out:

> To say that people had a connection to Shachtman does not mean that they had a connection to historical Shachtmanism. What you had in the Socialist Party was a very strong Stalinophobic position, which had existed long before Shachtman became involved in the party. There is a clear lineage, I think, from that one wing of the Socialist Party to the neoconservatives. This was the right wing that split from the Socialist Party in 1936 to support Roosevelt, and a segment of them rejoined in 1957, while another segment came back in 1972 to join with the most right-wing elements in the Socialist Party to form the Social Democrats USA. By contrast, Shachtman joined the Socialist Party and then adapted to that. The people who have been influenced by Shachtman, such as Joshua Muravchik, were influenced by that tendency . . . If you go back to people like Jeane Kirkpatrick, she explains that she was a Humphrey Democrat, and I think that is essentially true. There were people in the Democratic Party who were very pro–Cold War liberals and some social democratic elements who supported them. The reasons why people make this connection to Trotskyism vary. I think that there are some mainstream US liberals, who want to say that all extremisms are the same, which strikes me as a shallow analysis. But there is also a powerful anti-Trotskyist element in the old Left, which originates in the 1930s when it was fashionable to say that every Trotskyist was pro-imperialist, and we may be seeing that in a mutated form. One of the things that liberal Democrats don't often mention, however, is that neoconservatism is one of the most genuinely bipartisan currents in US politics. They have done very well under both Republican and Democratic administrations.[75]

Similarly, Irving Kristol and Philip Selznick left the Shachtmanite Young People's Socialist League as early as 1940 on the grounds that

Marxism was inherently corrupted and ought not be the basis for socialist politics. They joined the Socialist Party and were, by the end of World War II, not altogether keen on socialism any more. The basis of their critique of it was a rejection of 'utopianism', not its transferral to another plane. They maintained that humans were not inherently worthy of self-government, and had to be held in check by the constraints of a liberal state. They learned from Cold War theologians like Reinhold Niebuhr that there were impulses towards evil in the human constitution, and that the role of coercion and domination in human affairs was 'irrepressible'.[76] Once again, it is not hubris, but a fundamental pessimism and a willingness to believe the worst about 'human nature' that characterizes the neoconservative intelligentsia.

The entire schema of neoconservatism as the heir of Trotskyism is chimerical, in fact: it operates through a metonymic substitution of imagery at the expense of detailed and often highly conjunctural Marxist analysis. For example, Trotsky's theory of 'Permanent Revolution' is often used as a metaphor for neoconservative imperialism. Michael Lind argues that 'the concept of the "global democratic revolution" has its origins in the Trotskyist Fourth International's vision of permanent revolution'.[77] How so? Trotsky's theory argued, against the intellectual tide of European social democracy at the time, that it was not necessarily the case that a socialist revolution should follow a period of capitalist development combined with liberal-democratic institutions. Rather, Trotsky maintained, in certain underdeveloped states (Russia), the bourgeoisie could not be counted on to implement land reforms and political democracy, and so the working class would have to take power. In order maintain power, however, it would be necessary for the revolution to spread to surrounding countries – otherwise it would not be able to withstand external pressures. This bears some resemblance to what happened in Russia, but it is a considerable stretch to see it as a description of current neoconservative policy towards the Middle East. It is possible to extract from it an abstract template for global transformation and give it a neoconservative twist – 'for democracy to survive, all dictatorships must fall'. But such a gesture takes the neoconservative claim to oppose dictatorship far more seriously than many neoconservatives appear to take it themselves; and it would be hard to distinguish it from the 'domino theory' of international relations promoted by the United States government during the Cold War.

It is true that Michael Ledeen and other neoconservatives speak of a global 'democratic revolution'. Ledeen wrote during the Clinton years that this 'revolution' was being 'betrayed'. But it is important to note the context. Ledeen has never been a Trotskyist. On the contrary, he spent time in the 1970s studying Italian fascism, concluding that it was a genuinely revolutionary movement. Some argue that his admiration for America's 'historic mission' of 'creative destruction' owes more to his reading of the Italian far Right than to American conservatism. But the tradition he draws on is distinctly American. For 'historic mission', read 'manifest destiny'; for 'creative destruction', substitute the social Darwinism that characterized the wars of expansion after the American revolution. The revolution referred to is explicitly one bearing 'the values of the American revolution, supported and advanced by American military power'. Ledeen meant to dispute the Left's claim to have a monopoly on the revolutionary tradition on the grounds that American society is inherently revolutionary.[78]

While neoconservatives have often rejected the association with Leon Trotsky, one influence they have been more willing to accept is that of Leo Strauss, who could hardly be more different. This hitherto obscure figure became the topic of heated debate in the aftermath of the invasion of Iraq in 2003 – particularly when the investigative journalist Seymour Hersh set about detailing the influence of Strauss's ideas. Strauss, Hersh argued, was an advocate of the 'noble lie', an elitist who felt that knowledge had to be concentrated among a select and knowing few. Everyone else, from the public right up to leading statesmen, could be lied to. Neoconservatives have sought both to embrace Leo Strauss and to defend him against charges of elitism. He was a 'firm believer' in American democracy, writes Max Boot. Francis Fukuyama dismisses the impact of his political opinions on his followers. Of course he had his political opinions, but these boiled down to a preference for liberal democracy over communism and fascism. The charge of elitism was 'nonsense, and in parts vicious nonsense', Peter Berkowitz told *Weekly Standard* readers.[79]

The neoconservative defence of Strauss is that he was uniquely attuned to the weaknesses of liberalism – its tendency towards relativism, which could degenerate either into totalitarian 'nihilism' of the Nazi or Soviet variety, or into a directionless, value-free permissiveness. Far from being an elitist, they say, he was a believer in excellence and civic virtue, very much in the republican tradition.[80] But such a defence is unsustainable. The liberal writer Stephen Holmes pointed out long before Strauss was the stuff of controversy that he was very close in his critique of liberalism to the far-right legal thinker Carl Schmitt, who exerted a great influence on him, as did Martin Heidegger. He abhorred the rationalist, universalist components of modern liberalism, defended the concept of mutually exclusive human communities, and espoused a belief in a natural hierarchy. Recently, a letter from Strauss dated to his time in exile was translated by Scott Horton, and it cast considerable light on Strauss's formative politics. Although he was critical of the Third Reich, from which he had to flee, he embraced the legitimacy of fascist and imperial principles:

> the fact that the new right-wing Germany does not tolerate us says nothing against the principles of the right. To the contrary: only from the principles of the right, that is from fascist, author-itarian and *imperial* principles, is it possible with seemliness, that is, without resort to the ludicrous and despicable appeal to the *droits imprescriptibles de l'homme* to protest against the shabby abomination.

Horton writes that, although there is evidence for Strauss's views changing, several of his key political concepts, such as his embrace of the figure of the 'philosopher–tyrant', advert to the endurance of such influences on the elder Strauss.[81] Leo Strauss's actual influence on policy has, arguably, been vastly overstated. But he was, in all the essentials of his thinking, much closer to the contemporary neo-conservative vision, in terms of both its role in the 'culture wars' and its imperialism, than was Lev Davidovich Bronstein.

Finally, it seems odd that a group so dedicated to resuscitating 'bourgeois' values and the interests of business against what they describe as a 'New Class' of intellectuals and public servants who resent the power of capital, should be in any way associated with the name of an anti-capitalist revolutionary. The conception of the 'New Class' originated in anti-Stalinist writings, such as those of Milovan Djilas;[82] but in the hands of neoconservatives it became the basis of opposition to the welfare state. Irving Kristol had argued that the capitalist class would have to develop a distinctive business ethic, and he offered to help, believing that intellectuals and the business commu-nity should form a bloc against radical criticism of America's inequality. He provided some of the basis for the moralization of cap-italism by arguing that it was in fact meritocratic – that human talents tended to distribute themselves along something like a 'bell curve', which reflected the inequitable distribution of wealth.[83]

One might want to suggest that those, such as Kristol, Gertrude Himmelfarb and Jeane Kirkpatrick, who made their nests from the 1970s onwards in such institutions as the American Enterprise Institute, the Wilson Centre and the Heritage Foundation, brought with them a history of sectarian argument, an understanding of methods of organization and communication, and an intimacy with the enemy that the Right traditionally lacked; but some of them were arguably just as schooled in CIA methods, deriving from their time spent as employees of the agency in the 1950s.[84] Further, by the 1970s, a new generation of right-wing liberals was emerging who had never had been Trotskyists at all. Typical of these was Joshua Muravchik, who had been a socialist but a strongly anti-Communist one, and who had watched in horror as liberals 'collapsed' in the face of the radical assault. Conserving, rather than revolutionizing, American society was their cause.

Imperialism, Israel and neoconservatism's 'Negro problem'

The neoconservatives were largely those who had been critical of the Vietnam War for pragmatic reasons rather than principled ones, and who objected to the incursions of radical critique. However, Irving Kristol – the 'godfather of neoconservatism' – had never really opposed the venture, although he foresaw its difficulties. He worried that the US would be unable to take up the burdens of empire, because that would require anti-egalitarian ideologies and landed ruling classes driven by imperial glory, while America lacked both of these. He noted that the Vietnam War was increasingly taking on the dimensions of an imperial war, and had a presentiment of endless 'dirty little wars' in the future that the US would have to find a way to fight. The most coherent opposition to the war, as he saw it, came from Walter Lippman who, he noted, was not concerned about what the Vietnamese wanted, and was not opposed to Johnson's intervention in the Dominican Republic. He had no respect for the antiwar movement, and delighted in announcing that 'the United States is not going to cease being an imperial power, no matter what happens in Vietnam, or elsewhere', because empires were appointed by historical conditions far greater than any electorate or movement.[85]

Many of those who had been critical about the war were anxious to deflect the growing consensus that it was not merely a mistake, but a crime. Precisely as Nathan Glazer had insisted that he could not help believing that the war was the 'result of a series of monumental errors', so Norman Podhoretz later worked to restore the anti-Communist narrative about the war, in which the NLF was a 'north Vietnamese proxy', and thus the 'war in Vietnam was a case of external aggression' (not by the US). Munich, for Podhoretz, was the better comparison: then, as in Vietnam, a 'totalitarian political force' was attempting to expand the area under its control. If American politicians had only made a fully moral, rather than tactical, case for the war, he lamented, they could have kept Americans on board. As it was, the US had never tried to 'raise feeling against' Ho Chi Minh, instead allowing him to be presented as a kindly old uncle. This ludicrous stream of falsehoods and miscues was produced for the purpose, as Podhoretz made clear, of undermining the view of Vietnam as 'the self-evident symbol of a policy that must never be followed again'.[86] Anxious not to allow a rational aversion to more of the same – known by the pseudo-medical coinage of 'Vietnam Syndrome' – to characterize American political culture, the neoconservatives subsequently worked to promote the most hawkish politicians with the most febrile imaginations about the Communist Threat possible.

Defending America's global supremacy also meant defending it from its domestic adversaries. Though genetically estranged from racist paleoconservatism, the neocons had a 'Negro Problem' from the start. Norman Podhoretz, who by then had a mountainous reputation as *Commentary*'s hard-man editor, explained to readers of that magazine what the problem involved as of 1963. He – and he felt sure the same was true of other whites who then still regarded themselves as liberals – retained a feeling of intense hatred towards black people. Since it was not unique to him, he supposed, the moves towards integration in the country were unlikely to address the problem. Putting his own racism down to his childhood experience of black people principally as competitors in a tough urban struggle, as underachievers, and as violent thugs, he acknowledged that his feelings were 'sick'. And he insisted that the only way to solve his 'Negro Problem', and everyone else's, would be if black people would 'disappear' as a separate minority, through 'miscegenation' rather than integration. Exemplary of Podhoretz's narcissism, this argument was also to become typical of the neoconservative attitude towards racism: that it was principally a matter of personal prejudice, to be dealt with through open testimonial (perhaps as he had hoped, a number of readers commended Podhoretz for his 'honesty').[87]

Recoiling from the demands made by black Americans, the neoconservatives also despised the internationalism of the *soixant-huitards*. A growing minority of Americans, many radicalized by the civil rights struggle, had come to see men and women struggling in Vietnam and Palestine as brothers and sisters. The ethnic cleansing and takeover of Palestine was gradually being understood as a continuation of European colonialism, and not morally superior because the Jews had themselves been the primary victims of Europe's most recent bout of extreme depravity. The SNCC charged Israel, 'this illegal state', with massacring and oppressing Arabs. H. Rap Brown explained that 'we are not anti-Jewish . . . We just don't think Zionist leaders in Israel have a right to that land.' This didn't stop Nathan Glazer arguing that anti-Semitism among black communities was widespread, despite studies from the era indicating that it was in fact much less widespread among blacks than among whites.[88]

In general, the neoconservatives found the New Left to be anti-Semitic, and those of Jewish background increasingly stressed their identity as the source of political action. Some had long been sympathetic to Israel. Arthur Koestler, though sensitive to the indignities and absurdities of the Soviet Union's increasingly demented bureaucratic elite and the viciousness of the Nazi regime, displayed alarming indifference when Palestinians suffered a lesser, but certainly comparable, form of repression and expropriation. For he was an ardent supporter of the Zionist cause in Palestine, cheering on the 'Jewish terrorists' when they campaigned against the British, and he fired off several letters, articles and pamphlets supporting the immediate partition of the country and an independent Jewish state. A European Jew who had spent much of the 1930s and 1940s being imprisoned by fascists, escaping before the Nazis began the Judeocide, and who had recently fallen out with Marxism, could easily find Zionism attractive. In fact, however, Koestler had been in favour of the Zionist colonization of Palestine since the early 1920s, and had befriended the Revisionist Zionist Vladimir Jabotinsky in 1924. Enraged by the violence of Palestinian revolts, he was for the conquest of the land by paramilitaries as early as 1925. No wonder that in his letters, he jokingly referred to himself as a 'colonial'.[89]

Nathan Glazer explained that the New Left were attacking every social role that Jews might fulfil: academic, financial, legal, and so on. But the neoconservatives also took issue with the claim that America was deeply racist: were this the case, they reasoned, Jews would not have been able to succeed so well. Further, though few of the neoconservatives were of a profoundly religious background, many would go on to criticize liberal Jews for being more loyal to their liberalism than to Judaism. Nothing in the Jewish religion mandated their advocacy of abortion rights, for instance, and secular humanism was inadequate to provide a moral structure. Norman Podhoretz maintained that the formative question of his politics would henceforth become 'Is it good for the Jews?' – a question that would exercise his *Commentary* magazine especially after the 1967 Arab–Israeli war. Later, Seymour Martin Lipset would argue that low support for Israel was more prevalent in poorer communities, and was associated with anti-Semitism 'especially among blacks'. Midge Decter would go on to attack liberalism as 'bad for the Jews . . . because it endorses quotas . . . and regards the PLO (as it once regarded the Viet Cong) as a worthy instrument of national self-chastisement'.[90]

The neoconservatives have been said to belong to an 'Israel Lobby', which is accused of warping US foreign policy and driving it in extreme directions. Stephen Walt and John Mearsheimer write that the reason formerly left-wing intellectuals drifted to the right was that their commitment to Israel left them frustrated with those who opposed military build-up and identified with Third World causes, while the anti-Communist Right seemed better able to protect Israel's interests. Now, with prominent positions in a network of think-tanks and institutions such as the American Enterprise Institute, the Centre for Security Policy, the Hudson Institute, and the Project for a New American Century, they press for policies that benefit Israel, while arguing that these are identical to those promoting US interests.[91] It is doubtful that this 'lobby' really determines US policy. It seems more likely, as Daniel Lazare points out, that Israel has become important to the American right for other reasons:

If 'Israel has earned the respect of the American people,' it is because the United States, devastated by its experience in Vietnam and humiliated by the embassy takeover in Tehran, watched with growing envy as Israel racked up stunning military victories in 1967 and 1973 and then sent specially outfitted jets streaking across the desert to bomb Iraq's Osirak reactor in 1981 (a feat the White House would dearly like to emulate in Iran). The Israel Defense Forces were everything that aggressive imperial elements in Washington wanted America's traumatized military to be. Hence, in their bipartisan struggle to overcome 'the Vietnam syndrome,' the Republicans and Democrats set about remodeling themselves as overseas branches of Israel's hawkish Likud Party. Groups like AIPAC did not grow of their own accord. Instead, the war party in Washington encouraged them to grow to help it win its battles on Capitol Hill.[92]

As far as the neoconservatives are concerned, moreover, most have defended American state interests wherever a potential conflict has emerged with the State of Israel. For example, many neoconservatives, including Jeane Kirkpatrick, Paul Wolfowitz and Richard Perle, organized through pressure groups such as the Balkan Action Committee for US intervention in the former Yugoslavia, while the Likudniks in Israel with whom they are closely aligned were adamantly opposed to US intervention in Kosovo. Israel was arming the Bosnian Serbs while the US was supporting the Bosniak army and facilitating the transport of Islamist fighters and weapons to help them. Israel is important to the neoconservatives precisely to the extent that its interests are seen as identical with those of American power. But it is US power, not Israeli power, that the neoconservatives exalt. The heroes of neoconservatism, Max Boot writes, are 'Theodore Roosevelt, Franklin Roosevelt, Harry Truman and Ronald Reagan' – empire-builders, in other words, who have 'successfully wielded power in the service of a higher purpose'.[93]

Some argue that what is distinctive about neoconservatism is a particular Jewish experience that has guided most neoconservatives – barring a few Catholics, such as Daniel Patrick Moynihan and Michael Novak. Such is the view of Murray Friedman, who argues that neoconservatism is a 'Jewish revolution'. Jacob Heilbrunn similarly argues that neoconservatism is characterized less by a specific ideology – whether Trotskyism or Zionism – than by a 'mindset' shaped by the 'Jewish immigrant experience, by the Holocaust, and by the twentieth-century struggle against totalitarianism'.[94] This is an account very much from the inside – Heilbrunn is himself a former neoconservative and the child of a Holocaust survivor. Yet it raises more questions than it answers. Leave aside those who are or have been prominent neoconservatives and are not Jewish – not only Moynihan and Novak, but also Jeane Kirkpatrick, William Bennett, James Woolsey, James Burnham, Rev. Richard Neuhaus, Linda Chavez, Thomas Donnelly, Francis Fukuyama, and John Bolton. It is clearly the case that, for many Jewish neoconservatives, their Jewish identity mattered; but there are surely a variety of ways of experiencing life as a Jewish immigrant in the United States, and many more ways of relating to that experience. The berating of secular and radical Jews by Jewish neoconservatives at least suggests this.

For the neoconservatives, as for previous ranks of messianic American imperialists, the global order came to intersect with the domestic racial hierarchy to alarming effect. The PLO and black militancy threatened, respectively, the state they increasingly supported, and their class privileges. Diana Trilling complained about the Columbia uprising, in which black radicals angry at the university's attempt to evacuate residents of the housing they owned in Harlem protested and occupied alongside white students, who were angry at the university's links with the Defense Department. She was particularly frightened of black militants because, for them, 'the authority of the white world is an illegitimate authority'.[95] Irving Kristol famously pronounced himself sick to death of welfare mothers, while neoconservatives in general opposed measures such as affirmative action, arguing that societies were naturally characterized by certain ethnic and religious alliances and that this – not structural discrimination – was the real source of racism.[96]

'Reverse discrimination' rapidly became a habitual cavil of the neoconservatives, and implied that racial inequality was in some sense *meritocratic*. It also recoded the vulgar and explicit racism of the Old Right in the language of free-market ideology: since the market was now a zone of meritocratic competition, interfering with its operations with affirmative action was unfair to white workers (rather than being, as one would have thought, a pathetic excuse for reparations). The 'colour-blindness' of neoconservative ideology is in fact purblindness: it whitewashes everything, up to and including the neoconservative defence of social inequality.

Of course, if the system *was* meritocratic, then the explanation for violent uprisings, as in Watts, Los Angeles, had to lie elsewhere than in the racial hierarchy itself. Moynihan, a liberal who would soon become the toast of neoconservatives, had the answer: weakness in the black family caused the problem, particularly on account of absentee fathers and overbearing mothers dependent on welfare. This argument was greeted with considerable fanfare in the media. Essentially, Moynihan argued, large parts of the black population had ceased to practise American values (patriarchal families, lifelong marriage, and, as a corollary, heterosexual relations). Their behaviours differed from the American norm, creating a cultural degeneracy that disabled black men from being able to communicate with their peers. The superior access, then, of white people to wealth and opportunity was construed as an artefact of their superior value-system. Far from being intelligible as aspects of the American system, problems in black communities were a 'tangle of pathology' which was perpetuated without 'any assistance from the white world'. The solution was twofold: black men needed to be employed more, and they needed to be taught to be 'real men' by those used to administering white male supremacy, in the military. Military service was a 'desperately needed change: a world away from women, a world run by strong men of unquestioned authority', and so on.[97] This was an old, and not very stirring, anthem. Precisely as they were doing overseas, tough white men – Rough Riders in fact – would educate the benighted races about self-discipline and self-government at home, with the full range of kinetic force at their disposal.

Moynihan soon found himself on the receiving end of much criticism, including from CORE activist William Ryan, who described his report as 'Blaming the Victim'. Few liberals defended him, and many considered him a bigot. 'My God, I was not a racist, I was not a bigot', he protested. But he noticed that he received more pleasant reviews in William F. Buckley's *National Review* (which had spent much of the preceding period defending segregation), and soon found himself proposing a liberal–conservative bloc to defend American society from the radical assault of 'rich college fucks' with their 'mindless assault on the civic and social order' and their 'nihilist terrorism'. Moynihan defended himself publicly, partly by accusing the liberal critics of a 'curious condescension' which sought to defend and explain away 'anything, however outrageous, which Negroes, individually or collectively, might do'. Nixon found Moynihan's views congenial enough to appoint him his assistant for urban affairs, in which role he advocated abolishing Aid to Families with Dependent Children, instead proposing a negative income tax plan which could guarantee a minimum income at a lower cost. But it was his brief service at the United Nations in 1971 that would introduce him to what he considered to be the 'anti-Americanism' of the Third World. Influenced by 'British socialist opinion' (Fabianism), they had a 'suspicion of, almost a bias against, economic development'. Against complaints of US imperialism and exploitation, he insisted that the poverty of Third World nations was 'of their own making and no one else's'.[98]

When appointed US ambassador to the UN by Henry Kissinger in 1975, Moynihan spent his time castigating Third World states, and noted that it was 'no accident' that a 'racist murderer' such as Idi Amin was head of the Organisation of African Unity – it was indeed not an accident, as the role was rotated between member states. He was especially assertive in defence of Israel against the claim that Zionism was a form of racism, and maintained that democratic 'values' were everywhere under attack by 'totalitarianism'. Since Israel was a democracy (at least for those with full citizenship rights), any attempt to undermine the legitimacy of Israel was a means to revoke its existence, and thus to threaten any small democracy by similar means. A UN resolution could mean de-recognition, he later noted, citing the example of Rhodesia.[99]

It hardly mattered to Moynihan that Israel would become more democratic by abandoning Zionism, in the same sense that Rhodesia would be more democratic by abandoning white rule. He became the neoconservative favourite as candidate for president. Midge Decter recalled that 'He was our horse', until Ronald Reagan became the 'Cold War Democrat' of choice. In fact, it would be interesting to consider what policies he might have recommended in the global battle against 'totalitarianism'.[100] One of the policies he was party to as ambassador to the UN was the US-sponsored invasion of East Timor, which went ahead despite a Security Council resolution against it. Moynihan, noting that the result had been the massacre of 10 per cent of the population – almost the same proportion of casualties experienced by the Soviet Union during World War II – recalled that '[t]he Department of State desired that the United Nations prove utterly ineffective in whatever measures it undertook. This task was given to me, and I carried it forward with no inconsiderable success.' The frustration of an anti-colonial struggle, with the murderous consequences mentioned, was once more explained in terms of the anti-Communist imperative, namely by blocking a party (the Fretilin) that was 'totally' backed by China. Anti-totalitarianism at this point appeared to consist of helping bring about massacre to thwart a leftist insurgency.[101] One of Moynihan's final triumphs was to attack the Carter administration – a centre-right government reviled by the neoconservatives as a 'New Left' administration (largely because the neocons were excluded from major posts). He was particularly scathing over its acceptance that the racist regime in Rhodesia – which US policy-makers had tacitly supported since 1965 – would be replaced by black-majority rule, with 'Marxist guerrillas' in the government, on the grounds that they were 'armed by the Soviets'.[102]

Moynihan's report on 'The Negro Family' was typical of the way neoconservatives would argue about America's racial order and its intersection with empire. Linda Chavez later argued, in *Out of the Barrio*, that Mexican- and Cuban-Americans were following a classical trajectory of US migrant groups, working their way up the social ladder, obtaining 'mainstream' (white) status. However, Puerto Rico, annexed by the US in 1898 as a commonwealth without state rights, was the source of an exception. Puerto Rico had been a showcase of US tutelage during the Cold War, supposedly illustrating the rewards of democracy and prosperity that such a relationship provided. Migration to the United States was encouraged during the 1950s and 1960s, but Puerto Ricans did rather poorly out of the transaction. Chavez's argument was that the source of their poor fortune was their failure to pull themselves up by their bootstraps, due to an unwillingness to adapt to America's changing labour market – not because of inadequate family values, but because of altogether too solid family bonds, which made them reluctant to leave children in the hands of day care centres. Instead, propped up by welfare, they simply stayed put, and their families disintegrated. Linda Chavez may or may not have been aware that pathologizing the family had been one of the key forms of imperial ideology in Puerto Rico ever since it was annexed, including the stigmatization of sexual 'deviancy' and the introduction of eugenics onto the island in the 1920s and 1930s. But, logically, if her claim that welfare had a disintegrative effect on Puerto Rican families in the US mainland was correct, then the same ought to have applied to families in Puerto Rico, where welfare was also available, and where families were acknowledged to be strong.[103]

As the neoconservatives worked to defend the patriarchal principle and family values from feminist assault, and to defend white 'mainstream' America from the perils of 'multiculturalism', they reflected, whether they knew it or not, the oldest obsessions of the American empire. As in earlier periods, the survival of each race, and of the nation as such, depended on strenuous self-help, strong families headed by patriarchs, and the willingness to deploy violence on a global level. Self-government was a state of culture before it was a political state, and some peoples were simply unfit for it. The neoconservatives are thus aptly named 'Wilsonians', but not in the sense usually intended. It is fitting that they provided the shock troops arguing for, and frequently organizing, America's aggressive attempt to recapture Nicaragua during the 1980s, after the American-imposed Somoza dynasty fell. In the name of an increasingly shrill anti-communism, the neoconservatives were reinventing the moral case for imperialism.

Moynihan broke with the neoconservatives over Reaganomics, which he considered a dangerous fraud, and later wrote that they 'wished for a military posture approaching mobilization; they would create or invent whatever crises were required to bring this about'. The neoconservatives did not have to create any crises, but they were able, through a variety of successive bodies, such as the Coalition for a Democratic Majority – and then the Committee on the Present Danger and the Committee for the Free World – to shape the consensus in the political class on key issues, and to provide a vague sense of intellectual coherence to paranoid Reaganite propaganda that would otherwise simply resemble a sequence of poll-guided hot-button issues. Midge Decter argued, for example, that the USSR was driving the wars in El Salvador and Nicaragua as part of a hemispheric intervention. The Committee on the Present Danger produced relentless propaganda claiming that the US was drastically underestimating Soviet military capacities, and required an urgent build-up.[104] But a sense of danger was not sufficient on its own. The neoconservatives would prove to be particularly valuable to the Reagan administration for packaging foreign policy in the terms of 'human rights' (of which more in the Conclusion). And if imitation was the sincerest form of flattery, they were soon to receive an elaborate compliment from a new genre of French 'anti-totalitarianism'.

4

A COURAGEOUS RETREAT

[*Cruelty and Silence*] was a cry for elevating cruelty, violence, and abuse over any other consideration.
— *Kanan Makiya*[1]

What do extremist ideologies like the communism or Nazism of yesteryear and the Islamism of today have in common? . . . The root element is the attitude that anything goes, particularly when with regard to ordinary people.
— *André Glucksmann*[2]

The late 1970s produced a new 'antitotalitarian' movement, this time with its locus on the Left Bank in Paris. It too contained a large number of ex-leftists, but was endorsed by many who had never been on the Left. It reproduced many of the clichés of 1950s anti-communism, although ironically its most volubly expressed claim was to novelty. If it rejected domestic radicalism, it also contained a critique of 'Third Worldism', and a reassertion of Eurocentrism. At the same time, a number of other former socialists were engaging with the difficulties in various Third World conflicts and, gradually, reaching the conclusion that the rehabilitation of imperialism would be no bad thing. The war on Iraq, the first one launched by America after the 1989 revolutions in the East, was the occasion for several former critics of imperialism to throw their weight behind Pax Americana. The Soviet Union had been, even to many of its critics, a key reference point, and its sudden absence exerted a tremendously disorienting effect. And the protracted conflict in the disintegrating Yugoslav federation resulted in many calling for a more aggressive US policy. The last quarter of the twentieth century was characterized by a retreat from hopeful political engagement, a retreat from anti-imperialism with its concomitant insistence on the agency of the peoples of the Third World. Most spectacular of all, however, was the retreat from analysis: vacuous moralizing was offered as profundity, and pious platitudes were presented as the courageous insistence on fully encountering the awfulness of the world, and as a dogged refusal to subordinate facts to ideology. In this way, a collapse into glib ideologies elaborated by Cold War apologists for America became the basis for rehabilitating imperial ideology as humanitarianism.

The new 'anti-totalitarianism': working for the intellectual counterrevolution

The critique of Stalinism was by no means new, and *The Gulag Archipelago* contained no revelations. The New Left had almost unanimously held the Soviet Union to be a part of the problem, either because it was depraved, or because it was decrepit, or both. Solzhenitsyn's text rapidly became a much-hyped reference point for socialists moving to the right; but, as Michael Scott Christofferson writes, 'the vast majority of French intellectuals of the non-Communist Left were already acutely aware of the failures of Soviet socialism'. Although much of the French Left, fearing a fascist reflux, defended the Communists during the period in which they were increasingly ostracized, the Algerian war of independence and the Hungarian Revolution produced a more critical engagement. There had been at any rate a revival of libertarian and democratic ideals during Liberation's hangover, and a sustained effort was made to reconcile these with revolutionary principles. In February 1948, left-wing intellectuals had founded the Rassemblement démocratique révolutionnaire (RDR) as a coalition of the non-Communist Left, but it had collapsed by late 1949 on account of divisions over American power. Further efforts at developing a new Left committed to neutrality in the Cold War, anti-colonialism, and political and economic democracy, also floundered for the time being. The testimony of Victor Kravchenko – a former Soviet official who had defected and was associated with the CIA – confirmed the existence of concentration camps in the Soviet Union in 1947, and produced a debate among French progressives. Although the episode was marred by Kravchenko's stridency and his association with American propaganda efforts, even fellow-travelling intellectuals such as Merleau-Ponty and Sartre accepted that the concentration camps did exist and were not, as the PCF tried to claim, merely re-educational work camps.[3]

So, as early as 1950, and certainly by 1956, most of the non-Communist Left was apprised of the internal repression in the USSR – and certainly the Trotskyist Left had been arguing that the revolution had been betrayed since the 1930s. Still, *The Gulag Archipelago* provided the occasion for confession and conversion, and a host of former Maoist revolutionaries would later end up adopting hard-line anti-Communist positions, and rejecting in particular the Third Worldism that had characterized much of the French Left. These included such luminaries as Bernard-Henri Lévy, André Glucksmann, Bernard Kouchner, Alain Finkielkraut and Pascal Bruckner. Bernard-Henri Lévy was never a Maoist militant, but he had been close to Louis Althusser, one of the chief theoreticians of a particular strand of *normalien* Maoism before May 1968. BHL had not been closely involved in the May 1968 uprising (although he claims it as a key moment for him, he was actually engaged in an affair at the time); but his first book, a journalistic account of the Bangladesh War, was written from a Marxist perspective. However, Lévy was so mortified by Solzhenitsyn's exposé that he was moved to disparage his former Marxist commitments.[4]

Or was he? While some have cast doubt on Lévy's seriousness as a Marxist,[5] as late as 1975 Lévy was still defending the Soviet Union and the Eastern Bloc against dissidents, and against Solzhenitsyn in particular. As the French Communist Party (PCF) went on the offensive against the Soviet novelist and his defenders, Lévy assured readers that Solzhenitsyn was 'not a great writer' but rather a 'mythomaniac', a 'showbizman' and a 'gaffeur' (meaning 'blundering idiot'). He dismissed 'the few clowns who arrive with us periodically, nineteenth-century novelists mislaid in the twentieth century, the Solzhenitsyn type. . .' Regarding the dissidents, he maintained that they were hardly models of progressive thought themselves, and were 'even sometimes of perfectly reactionary cloth'. All their testimony showed was that the USSR was 'a country like any other', 'neither completely rosy nor completely black'. His preferred authority on the Soviet Union was Francis Cohen, whose chief distinction was that he had been the Moscow correspondent for the PCF's newspaper *L'Humanité*. It is possibly that Lévy's defence of the Soviet Union at this time was partly due to the influence of Louis Althusser who, while a critic of Stalinism, did not share the nostalgia for Tsarism that Solzhenitsyn exhibited.[6] Another reason was the strength of the PCF and its weight in the organized Left.

By summer 1975, Lévy had concluded that the Soviet Union was not quite like any other state after all. The cause of its tyrannical nature lay in an 'original sin', not any corruption, 'and the sin is Marx'. *The Gulag Archipelago* was 'the finally blinding proof that terror in the USSR is everywhere'. Not only did it discredit the USSR, it proved that 'terror is nothing more than the inside lining of sacrosanct socialism' – although at this point Lévy did not deny the possibility of socialism outside the USSR.[7] By the time he came to write *La barbarie à visage humain*, in 1977, he was convinced that the problem was not merely with the USSR, and not even only with overt Marxism, but with the whole paradigm of revolutionary thought issuing forth from May 1968 which, whether it knew it or not, was Marxist.

Lévy's method was as straightforward as his prose was convoluted: the Marxist conception of power involves a Master, or oppressor, a 'lucid and diabolical anticonfessor' who manipulates through ideology a 'population of sleepwalkers'. Were this population to be awoken, and apprised of the ruses of capital and the modes of their exploitation, they would rebel. This paradigm was, he maintained, the reigning wisdom even among the anti-Marxists of the New Left. 'There is a hidden impulse toward power, probably absolute power, whenever someone brandishes the slogan of total "liberation"'. The book affirmed a fundamental historical pessimism: progress was impossible, and every attempt at accomplishing it was a religious gesture, the 'faith' of 'militants' (Lévy's book is replete with such metaphors – the litany of the Left, shepherds and flocks, prophets and devils. 'Totalitarianism is confession without God, the inquisition plus the negation of the individual' – and so on and on, straining for effect in that fashion, based on nothing more than the insipid anti-Communist metaphor of *The God That Failed*). Far from being one of many responses to profound social iniquity, Marxism was 'fanaticism', a 'ghostly "prophecy"', and paradoxically a form of 'counterrevolutionary thought' dedicated to sustaining a given 'end of history'. The frustration of the attempt to radically transform social conditions would necessarily lead to repression, and ultimately to the gulag. Written on the eve of the municipal election victory of the Union of the Left, uniting the Socialists and the PCF, Lévy explained that it was intended as a warning shot: the French Left was on the slippery slope to totalitarianism. And so: 'There remains only the duty to protest against Marxism' in all of its forms.[8]

André Glucksmann had been, as noted in Chapter 3, both a Stalinist and a Maoist in his radical years. In 1956 he had been opposed both to the French 'pacification' of Algeria, and to the Soviet 'pacification' of Hungary. He had been a member of the violent Maoist group, *Gauche prolétarienne*, before that movement collapsed in the mid 1970s. In *Les Maître penseurs*, Glucksmann laid out the programmatic basis for his eschewal of Marxism: the master thinkers, including Hegel, Fichte, Nietzsche and Marx, had systematically legitimized the dominative strategies of the modern state. The gulag was a result not only of 'the logical application of Marxism',[9] but also of languages that 'enable one to master everything', admitting nothing outside themselves. Glucksmann's self-congratulatory retelling has it that

I began with concrete and timely criticism of the French Communist Party and the Soviet Union in the 1960s. Then I proceeded to a more extended critique of totalitarian thinking, in order not to be ensnared in a kind of intra-Marxist opposition – anti-Soviet but pro-Chinese, for example, or anti-Chinese but pro-Castro, and if not some form of sacred socialism, then the dear Third World . . . The next step was to fit this basic Marxist structure into a more general scheme, which I tracked to German philosophical thinking of the nineteenth century – a totalitarian-oriented world view which could be expressed in rightist as well as leftist ideologies.[10]

This is not quite accurate. Glucksmann, at this point, was still an opponent of the concept of 'totalitarianism'. The standard presentation, he said, had 'let the "non-totalitarian" regimes off the hook', ignoring the 'kinship' and 'filiation' which linked the 'harsh methods of domination employed in both the West and in the East'. He remembered that the British had developed concentration camps against the Boers before the Boers had thought of using them against black South Africans, and recalled enough of his anti–Vietnam War activity to point out the totalitarian resonances of the campaigns against 'the Indians', 'the Vietnamese, the South Americans . . . or the inhabitants of Dresden, Hiroshima or Nagasaki'. The 'critique of totalitarianism shows a tiresome tendency to boil down always to a critique of totalitarianism *elsewhere*'.[11]

This conception of a logical progress from anti-Stalinist critique to straightforward anti-communism is not simply a piece of self-serving revisionism by Glucksmann, however. It is a claim repeated by Julian Bourg in his account of the impact of May 1968 on French thought. As he puts it, 'The Marxist tradition ironically provided the resources for overcoming Marxism . . . the passage from anti-Stalinism to anti-Marxism completed a logic.' However, Bourg adds some heavy qualification to this somewhat glib observation. In the context of the death of Mao, the catastrophic rule of the Khmer Rouge in Cambodia, the crises on the European Left, and the declining fortunes of the French Left, Bourg maintains that Solzhenitsyn's text provided an orientation for those already prepared to escape Marxism. The idea that anti-Stalinist Marxism is logically already anti-Communist is in fact one that supporters of the Soviet Union have always been prepared to brandish. Thus, Dolores Ibárruri ('La Pasionaria') argued during the Spanish Civil War that the attacks on the *trotskysant* POUM were justified because the Trotskyists were counter-revolutionaries.[12]

However, while it is true that the Maoists had a critique of the Soviet Union and of the politically timid PCF, they were of course completely uncritical of an equally authoritarian regime in China, which was regarded as the vanguard of anti-imperialist revolt. Indeed, as one internal document of the Maoist group Gauche Prolétarienne argued, 'All error goes back to an incorrect interpretation of Mao.'[13] The cultish extolment of Mao as the philosopher and strategist of anti-imperialism did in many cases morph into a victimological approach to the Third World (the widely publicized fate of the Vietnamese Boat People providing a decisive moment for the 'new philosophers' and their co-ideologues). Equally, the 'anti-authoritarian' dynamic in the May 1968 generation could be re-interpreted as a critique of everything from the gulag to nationalization. It is, however, hard to see this as a strictly logical and coherent progression.

At any rate, Glucksmann's 1977 thesis bears some resemblances to classical 'totalitarianism' theory, and Glucksmann was increasingly content to use the label. It is also, as Alain Badiou (once a Maoist confederate himself) argues, a profoundly pessimistic doctrine. The thrust of Glucksmann's argument is that every 'collective will to the Good creates Evil'. There can be no positive politics, nothing too radically transformative, only a liberal–conservative consensus created by an awareness of Evil, and the need to resist it. Glucksmann would go on to warn that the Union of the Left shared a programme with the 'master thinkers'. Its left-Keynesian reform package, which was typical of the era, was seen as an attempt at maximizing state power. In an even more sinister fashion, the nationalization programme was, Glucksmann claimed, aimed at 'the Jewish side of the "private sector" . . . not privilege or exploitation'.[14]

Lévy and Glucksmann, known as the 'New Philosophers', became the stars of a new media product,[15] and were followed by a raft of penitent Maoists and ex-Marxists. One of the means by which Lévy exerted his influence was as editor at the prestigious *germanopratin* publishing house, Grasset, where he could publish his friends among the *nouveaux philosophes*, notably Glucksmann. This crowd were quick to draw accusations of anti-Semitism, and critics were treated as germinal totalitarians. 'You proceed like the police!', Lévy told a critic. The *nouveaux philosophes* had been treated to 'small Moscow trials', while an 'unavowed totalitarianism' was brewing. Glucksmann worked himself up to splenetic issue at a talk by Julia Kristeva, at which Kristeva proclaimed Soviet dissidence as a model for Western intellectuals. When Kristeva declined to say who she would vote for, Glucksmann screamed from the floor: 'We have finally got there!

Control of party cards, of loyalty to the party. Here's why we already need to be dissenting in France . . . the gulag has already begun.' On that shrill note – which confirmed the *nouveaux philosophes* in their self-aggrandizing identification with the figure of the 'dissident', despite the fact that the context provided far more rewards than dangers to those claiming it – Paris entrenched itself, in Perry Anderson's phrase, as 'the capital of European intellectual reaction'.[16]

This performance was received with some fanfare in the Anglo-American press. *Time* magazine, introducing the 'new philosophers' to its readership, borrowed the title of Jean-Marie Benoist's 1970 book, declaring: 'Marx Is Dead'. The *Washington Post* enthused about the 'gorgeous', 'olive-toned and prominently boned' Bernard-Henri Lévy. The *Economist* hailed 'Those magnificent Marx-haters'. Ronald Reagan even paid tribute to 'the so-called new philosophers in France' in his address to the UK parliament on promoting democracy, cherishing their 'rejection of the arbitrary power of the state, [their] refusal to subordinate the rights of the individual to the superstate, [their] realization that collectivism stifles all the best human impulses'.[17]

As Kristin Ross has argued, there was more in this movement than simply a rejection of any form of emancipatory politics beyond the confines of liberal democracy: it was also a reassertion of Eurocentrism against the Third Worldist sympathies that had helped to stimulate leftist revolt in the West at a time of relative economic stability. The ex-*gauchiste*, Pascal Bruckner, ridiculed Frantz Fanon's 'plea to "go beyond" Europe . . . It is impossible to "go beyond" democracy. If the peoples of the Third World are to become themselves, they must become more Western.' Naturally, with this came a plea to abandon Western 'guilt', as if anti-imperialist critique was simply a form of self-flagellation. In his 1982 book *Tears of the White Man*, Bruckner affirmed: 'Europe is our destiny, our lot. More than ever, we develop as individuals through the respect of its borders, its traditions, and its territorial integrity.' Bernard-Henri Lévy argued that the 'turning towards the Third World' that French intellectuals experienced during the Algerian war involved intense 'hatred of Europe', something which could be divined by one's support for the Black Panthers, for example. Israel, by contrast, had embodied 'democracy and European values' from its inception.[18] Ironies abound here: it could conceivably be argued that destroying a population, driving it from its territory by means of massacres, and engaging in continuous expansionist aggression in the name of creating an ethno-nationalist state is a fundamentally European value (one could call it '*Herrenvolk* democracy'); and there may indeed be something about the Black

Panthers that grates against 'European values'. But this hardly commends the 'values' that Lévy exhorts us to treasure.

In an age of officially 'socialist' states proliferating across the world, following national liberation struggles, anti-communism could shade quite easily into anti–Third Worldism, as in Maurice Clavel's 1976 evocation of the 'yellow peril': 'with the elimination of the Cultural Revolution figures and the ongoing Sino-Soviet reconciliation, a billion robots are already resting their weight on the Elbe. Those two billion eyes blinking, or rather not blinking . . .' Kristin Ross writes that the 'accession to political subjectivity of "the wretched of the earth"' had disrupted the master-narrative of the Cold War, in which liberalism was the sole appropriate alternative to the Soviet Union, and thus had to be revised.[19]

One form of revisionism was to behave as if the committed anti-colonial and anti-imperialist dimensions of the movement had never existed: thus, Bernard Kouchner, the current foreign minister of France, reduces his Maoist days to a period of 'navel-gazing' puerility. Only after his radicalism was aborted did he discover 'the Third World' (even though he had himself travelled to Cuba in 1960 to interview Che Guevara). Another was to excise the agency of the Third World itself, as during the colonial epoch, subordinating it instead to a rights discourse. Kouchner is after all a pioneer in the business of 'humanitarian intervention', as a co-founder of Médecins Sans Frontières (MSF), formed in 1971 from a fusion between the Groupe d'Intervention Médicale et Chirurgicale en Urgence, and the Secours Médical Français. The organization was to extend the ethic of solidarity into the business of humanitarian aid. However, Kouchner left MSF in 1979 to form a break-away organization called Médecins Du Monde. The occasion for this was a campaign to help rescue the 'Boat People' – a flood of refugees fleeing repression in Indochina – called 'A Boat for Vietnam'. This boat would bring doctors to offer treatment to the sick or wounded, and a number of journalists to bear witness. If some considered this approach excessively media-driven, it was only the accentuation of an already existing trend. Médecins Du Monde later developed the doctrine of the 'right to inter-vene', a doctrine which was outlined in 1987 by Kouchner and his associate Mario Betatti in front of the Socialist President Mitterrand and the conservative Prime Minister Chirac, thus gaining bipartisan support for it. To the argument that victims had a right to humanitarian assistance was added the stipulation that the state had an obligation to help provide it. With Kouchner in the cabinet from 1988 to 1993 – first as minister for humanitarian action, then as minister for health and humanitarian action – the consensus was sealed.[20]

Death squads as democracy-promotion

With impressive expedition, the language of 'anti-totalitarianism' and human rights was consistently activated on behalf of the United States government and its chief foreign policy priorities. The sweep of Third World insurgency reached its peak in 1979, with the overthrow of the Shah of Iran and the success of the Sandinistas against the Somozist dictatorship in Nicaragua – both regimes that had been imposed by the United States. The USSR, meanwhile, invaded Afghanistan following the overthrow of the pro-Soviet PDPA administration. Reagan's rugged nationalism made him the perfect avatar of a new wave of American aggression. To thwart the Iranian Revolution, his administration encouraged, funded and armed Saddam's invasion of Iran – as did several other European powers and the Soviet Union. To thwart the upsurge in Central America, the CIA sponsored a series of death squads: in Nicaragua, the 'Contra' army was set up to wage a merciless war against civil society, with the help of Argentinian fascist elements and the far-right fanatics of the World Anti-Communist League, money from drugs sold in south-central Los Angeles,[21] and information on the whereabouts of medical clinics, educational facilities and other 'soft targets' supplied by US intelligence. Meanwhile, since the USSR had been lured into Brzezinski's 'Afghan trap', billions of dollars were set to work creating a transnational network of *mujahideen*, ensuring that the Soviet Union would be bogged down in a war that ultimately emptied its coffers and contributed to its later implosion.

Bernard-Henri Lévy had by the mid 1980s become very close to the moderate wing of the French Socialist Party, and particularly to François Mitterrand, who had flattered and nurtured him from the 1970s onwards. The neoliberal turn by the Mitterrand administration in 1983, the rupture with the PCF, and the launching of a vacuous and apolitical campaign against racism (SOS Racisme) with strong informal links to the Socialist Party had given Lévy an entry point into court at the Élysée Palace. But he also did his bit for the struggle internationally when he was appointed to the support committee for an organization named Resistance International which described itself as an anti-Communist alliance of exiles. Alongside him were the centre-right French philosopher Raymond Aron, Simon Wiesenthal, and a select group of leaders of the Nicaraguan Contra army, including Edgar Chamorro and Eden Pastora. The organization, aside from the predictable belabouring of Cuba and the Soviet Union, devoted itself to assisting *mujahideen* fighters in Afghanistan, and lobbying on behalf of the Contras. In 1985, after scrutiny of the Contras and revelations about CIA activities in Nicaragua had caused Congress to withhold funding, Resistance International sent a thirteen-member committee to beg Congress to release $14 million of funds to the Contras, spending over $54,000 pursuing the campaign and a further $27,000 on a full-page advertisement in the *New York Times*, signed by a number of ex-Maoist converts. A petition on behalf of the Contras also appeared in *Le Monde*, with Lévy's signature. One of the organization's founders, a Soviet exile named Vladimir Bukovski, would later lead a pro-Contra outfit named Prodemca, funded by the National Endowment for Democracy.[22]

On the face of it, Lévy's activism on behalf of the Contras starkly contradicted his opposition to terror and to autocratic states (they were, after all, seeking to restore the dictatorship). This is one survivor's account of the Contras' actions when they attacked workers on the cooperative farms founded by the Sandinistas:

> Rosa had her breasts cut off. Then they cut into her chest and took out her heart. The men had their arms broken, their testicles cut off, and their eyes poked out. They were killed by slitting their throats, and pulling the tongue out through the slit.[23]

This was not uncommon testimony. Former Contras Edgar Chamorro and Arturo Cruz agreed that 'damnable atrocities', including 'civilian murders, mutilations, tortures and rapes', had been committed as part of a 'premeditated policy to terrorize non-combatants'. When asked by Philippe Cohen why he had signed the petition, BHL's embarrassment can be gauged by his response: namely that he had done so without really paying attention.[24] It would be too much, clearly, to expect Lévy and his votaries to challenge such acts in Central America, any more than they would oppose the United States now that it was supporting the Khmer Rouge in Cambodia – despite the fact that the 'new philosophers' had made so much of their opposition to the Khmers in the late 1970s.

Persisting with the anathematic style developed in the late 1970s, Lévy berated the Left's sympathy for Palestinians, complaining that it was anti-Semitic:

> Now leftists are saying, 'We love the Palestinians because they are the most persecuted people on the planet today. And who is responsible for that? Not just Israel and Begin and Sharon but all Jews and Judaism itself.'[25]

No evidence for this assertion was offered, and it would be pointless to expect any: such ecumenical denunciations are not raised as hypotheses for debate. André Glucksmann took this one step further, earning himself some praise in the American press for equating the putative 'anti-Americanism' of the European Left with anti-Semitism, on the grounds that structurally analogous forces – a secret, nebulous presence, subversive violence, and disintegrative propensities – were held to be at work.[26] By precisely the same rationale, of course, some might be tempted to accuse Glucksmann's anti-communism of also being 'objectively' anti-Semitic.

Glucksmann also wrote gallantly in defence of weapons of mass destruction, insisting on the efficacy of the nuclear deterrent at a time when Reagan's proposed 'Star Wars' system was under attack from anti-nuclear campaigners. When the French government resumed its imperial role with an intervention in Chad in 1983, both he and Bernard Kouchner rallied in support. In the same period, the relief organization originally founded by Kouchner, *Médecins Sans Frontières*, raised controversy in 1986 when it appeared to abandon its policy of neutrality by attacking the Ethiopian government, while its work with Nicaraguan 'refugees' in Honduras (the site of training for Contra death squads) raised complaints from its Belgian branch, which felt that the headquarters in Paris was moving rightwards. What particularly raised suspicion, however, was the foundation of a subsidiary organization, *Liberté Sans Frontières*, which aimed to counter 'left-wing Third Worldism'. On its board were French rightists such as Jean-François Revel and Jean-Claude Casanova. Although it subsequently declared itself to be 'non-ideological',[27] the *mot juste* would have been 'depoliticized': it was the gesture of extricating their priorities from the political field that allowed them to become hegemonic.

This depoliticization was an important component of neoconservative strategy in the United States as well. As Nicolas Guilhot points out, a crucial part of the neoconservative discourse focused on 'human rights'. This may seem counterintuitive at first. Many neoconservatives argued in the 1980s in support of authoritarian dictatorships and death squads on the grounds that they were superior to their 'totalitarian' Communist opponents. Jeane Kirkpatrick, the neoconservative intellectual who would go on to be appointed by the Reagan administration to the post of ambassador to the United Nations, wrote an article entitled 'Dictatorship and Double Standards' arguing that there could be no 'moral equivalence' between the authoritarian dictatorships supported by Washington and the totalitarian designs of

Moscow. In a later article, entitled 'The Hobbes Problem', she argued that, though the 'traditional death squads' that Reagan was supporting in El Salvador might be repugnant to most Americans, they were rooted in the Salvadoran political culture and were the only force capable of turning brute violence into legitimate and effective authority. With respect to right-wing militias in El Salvador, the neoconservative columnist William Safire argued that support for a 'military junta' that 'kills the opposition' was necessary in light of the 'aggressive totalitarian alternative' represented by the peasant and workers' movements resisting the junta. Similarly, neoconservatives in Reagan's cabinet considered Pinochet's dictatorship admirable because, as George Shultz put it, he 'was a friend of the United States and a bulwark against communism'.[28]

It was precisely this logic of 'lesser-evilism' that had animated the neoconservative shift in the first place, that had galvanized the 'nouveaux philosophes', and that would later encourage many former left-wingers to support an American attack on Yugoslavia in the 1990s. But there is no necessary sense in which such a logic is incompatible with appeals to human rights. In fact, the Reagan administration went to great efforts to re-describe its El Salvador policy in terms of human rights. Even as it applied the lessons of 'counterinsurgency' from Vietnam – raising Salvadoran troop strength from 3,000 to 50,000 – and provided a centralized intelligence and reconnaissance system based in Honduras and Panama to enable sweeping paramilitary attacks on the insurgent population and bombing from the air, it was argued that this was part of a humanitarian strategy. The US explained that it was opposed to the violent fascists of the ARENA party, who ran the government and represented the country's ruling elite – Reagan's ambassador to El Salvador, Robert White, reported that the general outlook of the ruling party was that there should be a 'cleansing' of between 300,000 and 500,000 people. In fact, the US backed a third force, the Christian Democratic Party, led by José Napoleón Duarte (who had in fact praised the counterinsurgency operations); but Duarte was unable to challenge the ruling elite, and was not allowed to negotiate with the rebels. A 1991 Department of Defense study confirmed that the rebellion had been contained thanks not to an American 'human rights' policy, but to the 'lavish brutality' of the death squads they supported.[29]

But it would be mistaken to assume that the Reagan administration considered 'human rights' simply a public relations pitch to mobilize support for its Central American campaign. In fact, the administration promulgated a new kind of organization, the National Endowment for

Democracy (NED), whose mandate was to engage in 'democracy promotion'. The neoconservative ideologues were critically important in framing the discourse around this, just as the Cold War liberals had colluded with the more 'liberal' wing of the state (the CIA and the State Department) to package policies and help mobilize important constituencies such as the labour movement. The Congress for Cultural Freedom had dissolved, and its successor, the International Association for Cultural Freedom, was wound up in 1977. The NED provided a new base for many of the neoconservatives, such as the former Shachtmanite Carl Gershman, who is currently president of the organization, but also for Joshua Muravchik, Seymour Martin Lipset, Albert Shanker and Tom Kahn, all of whom had been through one of Max Shachtman's organizations during his anti-communist phase. It was not just that neoconservatives were using their background on the Left to package arguments convincingly for left and liberal audiences in a way that the old Right might have found difficult. What was new was that they could market this as a form of *expertise*, with members of the Research Council deemed 'democracy experts'. The organization places a heavy emphasis on academic research, and produces a journal that – while not properly peer-reviewed – has all the appearance of being scholarly. The discourse of human rights and democracy was thus professionalized, and – although the Board of Directors has included such powerful figures as Henry Kissinger, Paul Wolfowitz and Madeleine Albright – offered as a neutral exercise. The regular run of US interference into other countries, including Nicaragua, was repackaged as professional assistance to beleaguered democrats.[30]

Paul Berman's Contra-temps

The counterinsurgency in Central America became the occasion for a miniature controversy in the United States, when an article on Nicaragua written for *Mother Jones* magazine by Paul Berman – who at that point still claimed to support the Sandinista revolution – was blocked for publication by the editor Michael Moore, on the grounds that it was inaccurate. Berman is a journalist with a dilatory style, heavy on description and declarative statements. Compared with the terse, argumentative modes of Christopher Hitchens or Noam Chomsky, for example, Berman is coffee-table material. Educated in the anarchist critique of Leninism,[31] and profoundly influenced by Sidney Hook, he is also steeped in the history of the Left, or at least a sentimental version of it. In the article in question, the first part of which was eventually published in the February 1986 issue, Berman had spoken to a number of witnesses, including an American diplomat doing intelligence work, who insisted that Nicaraguans were living under an oppression every bit as cruel as some of the states in Eastern Europe (or, he might have added, in Central America), and that many of them longed for an American invasion.[32] He concluded by referring to the Sandinistas as 'Leninists', and accused them of harsh repression and human rights abuses. The owner of the publication appeared to agree with Berman, and Moore was presently sacked (for other reasons, it was insisted) – but not before some sharp words had been exchanged. Moore explained the reason for withdrawing the article:

> Reagan could easily hold it up, saying, 'See, even *Mother Jones* agrees with me.' The article was flatly wrong and the worst kind of patronizing bullshit. You would scarcely know from it that the United States had been at war with Nicaragua for the last five years.[33]

Berman had another explanation: 'I think there is a conflict between the modern democratic left and a few Neanderthal remnants of the 30s, and the Neanderthals are afraid of an open public debate about political values.'[34] The trouble with Berman's account was that he had indeed mimicked the claims made by the Reagan administration – it was an article of faith in the White House that the FSLN government was a 'Marxist–Leninist' tyranny, as he himself had noted in his article. Further, his construction conflicted with the known facts at the time. The Sandinistas, though they included Leninists among them, were a broad coalition. The FSLN had certainly been inspired, when it was formed in 1961, by the Cuban example. But it was also inspired by the liberal anti-imperialist, Augusto Sandino, who had been murdered shortly after agreeing a truce with the US Marine Corps and the Guardia Nacional that it had created. It had endorsed political pluralism, nonalignment, and a mixed economy. And this was the coalition that, in 1979, had overthrown the American-imposed Somozist dictatorship despite repression that had cost between 40,000 and 50,000 lives, or almost 2 per cent of the population. Its immediate opponents were the business community: as the Association of the American Chambers of Commerce in Latin America put it in 1982, 'There is no future . . . unless the Sandinistas are thrown out'. Yet the nationalization programmes of the Sandinista government were comparatively modest, with only 30 per cent of GDP accounted for by the state sector in 1989. Nor were they especially repressive, even under conditions of war: there had been extended emergency periods, in which civil rights were suspended; but civil rights for most were respected much of the time. Indeed, the Sandinistas' human rights record was not only superior to that of their immediate predecessors and their American-sponsored neighbours, such as El Salvador and Guatemala, it was also a colossal improvement on that of their Contra rivals who, trained by Washington in bases in Honduras, raped and tortured their way through Nicaragua. The Sandinistas had decisively won a 1984 election, with almost 70 per cent of the vote, despite the terror campaign that Washington had launched and threats of reprisals against voters by the Contras,[35] and could therefore justifiably claim full democratic legitimacy.

Berman would go on to support the opponents of the Sandinistas in the 1990 election. The vote took place after a sustained wave of violence that had claimed up to 50,000 lives and initiated a period of intense economic warfare which had sent the country into freefall. Nevertheless, Berman maintained that Nicaraguans had voted in a free election for the candidate they wanted: Violeta Chamorro and her right-wing National Opposition Union (UNO) coalition were better agents of progressive change than the Sandinistas, although he acknowledged that they were led by 'a holdover from the bad old days of oligarchical rule'. (He did not acknowledge that the UNO was itself a creation of the American government, which united a disparate group of opponents into a well-oiled, well-funded political machine to complement the armed siege, through such organizations as the National Endowment for Democracy.) Of the Sandinista reign, he still insisted that they were 'deep down Cuban-style Marxist–Leninists', though he grudgingly conceded that 'tyranny in Nicaragua never reached a totalitarian level'.[36] He later explained that

> the Sandinistas were running a version of a Leninist revolution and [had] created a thorough system of top-down oppression which descended all the way into the workplace and the cooper-atives and the home and the neighbourhood and the school . . . I had stumbled onto a Central American Kronstadt.[37]

Insisting that the Sandinistas had lost a free election fair and square in 1990, he saw this as proving his point that they had made themselves unpopular through their 'tyranny':

> When George Bush took over the White House in early 1989 . . . the United States backed away from the Contra cause. The Sandinistas appeared to have won – and in that circumstance, they decided to hold a free election . . . The Bush administration

made it clear that a freely elected Sandinista government would not find an enemy in the White House. But when election day arrived . . . the Nicaraguans astounded the world by voting, in a clear majority, for the main civic opponent of the Sandinistas.[38]

One can but be struck by the number of falsehoods and omissions that mar this brief passage. Firstly, the elections of 1990 had been mandated by the constitution passed in 1987, before the Costa Rican president Oscar Arias had brokered a Sandinista-initiated peace deal; the first free election had been held in 1984, while the war was raging. Secondly, the Bush administration did not in fact back away from the 'Contra cause', since the administration funnelled $49.75 million worth of 'non-lethal' aid to the Contras, as well as $9 million to the UNO opposition – equivalent to $2 billion worth of intervention by a foreign power in a US election at the time, and proportionately five times the amount George Bush had spent on his own election campaign. When Violeta Chamorro visited the White House in November 1989, the US promised to maintain the blockade unless Chamorro won. In August 1989, the month that campaigning began, the Contras redeployed 8,000 troops into Nicaragua after a funding boost from Washington, becoming in effect the armed wing of the UNO, and carrying out a violent campaign of intimidation: no fewer than fifty FSLN candidates were assassinated. The Contras also distributed thousands of UNO leaflets. Years of conflict had left 50,000 casualties and $12 billion of damage in a society of 3.5 million people and an annual GNP of $2 billion – the equivalent figures for the US would have been 5 million casualties and $25 trillion in financial losses. The people of Nicaragua were being given a clear choice – between accepting defeat and voting for continued war – by an administration that had only recently invaded Panama. In a poll after the 1990 election, 75.6 per cent of Nicaraguans agreed that, if the Sandinistas had won, the war would never have ended – a view endorsed by 91.8 per cent of those who had voted for UNO.[39]

Berman argued that the real origin of the Contras was in legitimate peasant rebellion against Sandinista expropriations and 'fondness for a single-party state' (curiously, the Contras had been unmoved by the genuinely single-party state, if not single-family state, that had preceded the revolution). For Berman, the Contras were a legitimate movement against 'Marxist–Leninist tyranny' until they were co-opted by the CIA. This characterization is difficult to square with the fact that, of eight leaders of the first Contra group identified by the CIA, seven were graduates of the School of the Americas rather than rebellious peasants.[40]

The central focus of Berman's article, however, was the murder of Ben Linder, an American who had travelled to Nicaragua to help build a hydroelectric plant and ended up dead at the hands of the government's local auxiliaries. Berman purported to have interviewed the man (named 'Williams') who was behind the murder of Linder, and to have demonstrated that the attack was 'nothing more' than a response by Contras to a rumour about Cubans in the vicinity. The Contras, far from engaging in a brutal face-to-face execution of Linder and his Nicaraguan friends, had shot from several yards away in panic. This was a significant conclusion, since it relieved both the Contras and their American paymasters of responsibility for the murder of an American citizen.

Berman's account was challenged by two lawyers from the Center for Constitutional Rights who were working on the Linder case, Michael Ratner and Beth Stephens. They pointed out that Berman's witness was unreliable. 'Williams' was sixteen at the time of the attack, and claimed not to have even been present at the murder scene. Berman had claimed that the case for a point-blank assassination was based on the word of 'a couple of Nicaraguan doctors' who 'credited that possibility', and on a 'blurry photograph'. He had not mentioned the report by New York's chief medical examiner, Dr Michael Baden, who interviewed the doctor behind the original autopsy and examined the bullet, concluding that it had been fired into Ben Linder's temple from less than an inch away. Further, other Contras had testified that Linder's murder was deliberate and premeditated:

> Fermin Cardenas Olivas, alias 'Cain,' was head of operations for the regional command for the Cua-Bocay area, and knew of the plan in advance. He told our investigator that 'it was a directed attack from the Strategic Command . . . [Enrique Bermudez and others] . . . made the decision to kill Linder . . . a gringo 'gusano'. Linder's killer was then given a 'reward' of 2,500 Leimpiras.[41]

Berman responded that it was 'of no importance' whether the killing had taken place up close or not. But if the murder was a face-to-face execution, it cannot have been the action of jittery Contras firing at those they believed to be Cuban agents. This would thus falsify his entire thesis. By this point, Berman's blinkered anti-communism had led to him to some staggering misrepresentations and failures of judgement, culminating in his covering for Washington's potential guilt at a crime scene. It had also left him a defender of 'liberal interventionism'.[42]

From class to cruelty: Kanan Makiya's regime architecture

Among the neophyte critics of 'Third Worldism' was Kanan Makiya, a former Trotskyist who was profoundly disaffected with the cause in the wake of the Lebanese civil war, the Iranian Revolution, and the Iran–Iraq War. As he explains things, the categories of Marxism proved inadequate to explain the rise of religious and sectarian conflict in the Middle East. Unfortunately, like many converts, he tends to explain away his political disaffection by caricaturing and condescending to his formerly held views. Hence, he claims to have invested the Palestinians with a 'halo' (which was shed on account of their role on the Lebanese civil war), and believed that Israel was 'the font of all evil' until he met an Israeli who opposed Zionism – as though he had not previously known that such people existed. Later he implied that he had in fact known of anti-Zionist Israelis, when he told George Packer that he had expected Israelis who opposed Zionism to link up with the oppressed Arab masses and throw off the yoke of imperialism. He also remarked that he had experienced a 'seismic shift' in his consciousness when he realized he could 'no longer blame it on the United States'.[43] Given his own confused and cartoonish rendering of his previously held views, it is unlikely that Makiya is faithfully describing the political milieu from which he emerged.

Makiya thus discovered liberalism, writing to a colleague in 1984: 'Could it be possible that a Marx today in the Middle East political context is far less of a revolutionary than, say, a Voltaire?' He was particularly influenced by Judith Shklar's 'liberalism of fear'.[44] This liberalism, as Shklar puts it, involves 'putting cruelty first', hating it above all forms of human conduct and thus finding 'nothing to excuse or forgive acts of cruelty' – not religion, not the Revolution, not the nation, not even the exigencies of war. Shklar draws out the implications of this stance: a tendency towards misanthropy, given the sheer 'density of evil' in the world; a preference for 'negative egalitarianism', since some limit must be placed on unequal relations, given that principles of inequality generate cruelty; the assumption that equality is less important to solving the problem than 'modesty'; a 'conservatism of universal disgust', in which changes in beliefs or social institutions are considered unlikely to constrain human cruelty, since 'the alternatives are no better'; and finally, the separation of morality from politics, since politics can be just, and bind populations together, but can never effect a moral revolution without being tyrannical.[45]

As Michael Walzer has noted, this appears to be an entirely negative form of liberalism, offering a bulwark against the intrusions of high-handed officialdom, but whose positive content – alluded to only obliquely – is a defence of 'a particular regime and culture, individual autonomy, and the social space within which free men and women enact their plans'. It defends a 'highly specific American liberalism', a 'socio-historical construction' that is in no way merely given. Corey Robin has subjected this liberalism to a thoroughgoing critique, challenging the idea that fear can be the foundation of a political argument. It tends in fact to be the basis for an anti-politics, a 'humanitarianism' which is almost as militant as that of more radical liberals of previous generations, but which stops short of advocating a political vision. This strand of liberalism advocates an assemblage of adversarial governmental institutions and a strong civil society as means of minimizing the scope for political terror, and thus becomes a defensive strategy against the worst of aspects of human behaviour rather than a coherent programme in itself. Robin argues that the 'liberalism of fear' fundamentally misunderstands the nature of political fear: it is true that such fear is often inculcated by tyrannical states, which usually have the greatest resources for doing so, but political fear is also disbursed through the institutions of civil society and individual initiative that liberals often hold to be the antidote to state tyranny – notably during America's periodic anti-Communist or racist crackdowns. By contrast, mass movements and national states have often been important sources of pressure for fuller realization of the very ideals that liberalism – particularly American liberalism – espouses, namely freedom and equality. This suggests that the sources of political fear are located elsewhere, in the concentrations of political and economic power that are as prevalent in liberal polities as in illiberal ones. The 'liberalism of fear' therefore omits some of the key sources of political fear, and renounces some of the means by which it can be countered.[46]

Makiya's most celebrated book, *The Republic of Fear*, written through the late 1980s, bears the marks of the author thinking his way out of Marxism and into 'anti-utopian liberalism'.[47] Thus, he energetically opposed the legacy of revolutionary anti-colonialism, with its emphasis on violent liberation. It was preferable to cultivate 'feeling through description', because the problem was precisely that 'violence has turned into an end in itself'. 'The bodies', he said, 'have not stopped accumulating in Iraq. The stench of slaughter grows daily.' Intellectuals would have to reckon with the fact that 'the central problem is or was violence'. Rejecting any emphasis on imperialism, he insisted on the West's 'diminishing ability' to 'influence local events in the modern period'. Much of the book is therefore concerned with cultivating the audience's feeling through description – of the pervasiveness of the secret police; the brutality of the security institutions; the global reach of intelligence organizations subordinated to the *mukhabarat* (party intelligence); the anti-Semitism of intelligence leaders (leading Jewish Communists, alleged 'spies' and Zionist 'agents' are a particular source of Baathist ire); and the nurturing of political paranoia by the regime (the Revolution has 'eyes' which 'unmask' its enemies and search out the 'concealed resources' of imperialism in the country). Baathism's victims 'no longer have to do anything to become suspects'.[48]

Occasionally, Makiya nods towards the socioeconomic bases of the regime (the reliance on oil revenues and its relationship to 'statification'), but he makes it quite clear that this is not his chief interest. His is a work largely of evocation, with Kafka and Cold War 'antitotalitarians' as key references. The political fear that Baathists wield is sustained by spectacle – the public rally, the show trial, the unearthing of conspiracies, hangings, corpse displays, and the confession. Behind it looms the daily grind of sudden disappearances (and sometimes reappearances), in which a great pretence is made of going on as normal. Networks of informers corrode and destroy all forms of social solidarity, making resistance difficult, while political activity, narrowed to the range of party work, becomes degrading. Makiya emphasizes the supererogatory nature of the cruelty, above all, and its function in proving (and thus augmenting) the power of the state. Torture, he insists, is not simply a matter of social control – it is a technology for refashioning subjects deemed incomplete or morally deviant in the reigning ideology.[49]

Makiya proceeds to a denunciation of 'Third Worldism' – or at least his eccentric understanding of it – and of pan-Arabism in particular. Baathism thus derives its parochialism and mythologizing from 'Arab and Islamic traditions' bolstered with 'a host of concepts borrowed from the Left'. Even the Baath's supposedly modernizing measures, such as the integration of women into the labour force and the diminution of the patriarchal family, are 'particularist', reflecting the Baath party's unique usurpation of various political and cultural traditions. Nevertheless, there are external models for Baath conduct, such as the Stalinist regime, and its use of developmentalist arguments to justify political authoritarianism. And here Makiya makes an explicit break with his Trotskyist background – the critiques that Leon Trotsky and Isaac Deutscher aimed at Stalinism are faulted precisely for focusing on the social and structural conditions that enabled it to come about. These factors are called upon to explain so much that their profundity is diminished, according to Makiya. But the logic of explaining

authoritarian government as a consequence of harsh material conditions and the need for development, he maintains, is impeccable as an
expression of Baathist ideology. And so, 'Stalinism is the "original"
Third Worldism that Baathism as well as other post–World War II
nationalisms sought to emulate.' The pan-Arabist roots of Baathism
are thus explored, with an eye to its roots in European romanticism, its
appropriation of Islam as the 'Spirit' of the Arab body, its anti-
materialism, its mythologies, and the anti-democratic thrust of
Baathist guru Michel Aflaq's conception of society.[50]

In focusing on ideological roots as the determinant of political
action, and on the resulting contraction of individual liberty, the atomization of society, and the substitution of party and leader for
traditional social hierarchies, *The Republic of Fear* is written squarely
in the tradition of 'totalitarianism' studies. Not much that was in the
book in the way of analysis was new when it was published. Had the
author spent any time examining the socioeconomic basis of the
regime, he might have been better placed to point out the resources for
change from within. The comparison with Stalinism has its merits, at
least, since Saddam Hussein was himself an admirer of the Russian
dictator, but one of the criticisms of the 'totalitarianism' thesis applies
fully here: whereas Stalin consolidated his regime after the near-
destruction of the old propertied elite and the creation of a new
bureaucratic layer, Saddam's dictatorship was effected without
generalized expropriation. In fact, the extensive public sector built up
by the Baath regime both consolidated previous changes made by the
Free Officers and the Nasserists, and created conditions for an entrepreneurial elite (a 'bourgeoisie of contractors') to emerge. Agrarian
reforms, in breaking up the tributary structure, created a class of petty
commercial producers (whereas Stalin notoriously annihilated the
kulaks).[51] These points are important, because the illusion that political fear and repression in Iraq could be reduced to the question of the
violent state, which a liberal constitutionalist settlement might
overcome, was important in Makiya's later designs for the post-
invasion transformation of Iraq. There is little discussion of dissenting
trends other than the Iraqi Communist Party; and some assessment of
the Shia Islamist currents would have provided a clue about some of
the actors likely to be best organized in a post-Baath Iraq.[52] Moreover, the
account is marred by an unnecessarily apologetic portrait of British
rule in Iraq.[53] Nonetheless, the fact that it was a well-documented and
caustic attack on a grotesque regime in the Middle East, drawing on
Anglo-American liberalism for its argument, would have ensured it a
reasonable reception among the Western intelligentsia, even had Iraq

not invaded Kuwait without written permission from the Pentagon. But the war did gain it an unexpected popular audience, and Makiya became something of a media star. Thus began his trajectory from a 'liberalism of fear' to an imperialism of prodigious naivety.

Meet the 'new Hitler'

The end of the Cold War called for a new strategy for the White House that could take maximal advantage of its new dominance. A review of national security policy conducted in 1989, when George Bush Sr took control of the White House, articulated the following prescription:

> In cases where the U.S. confronts much weaker enemies, our challenge will be not simply to defeat them, but to defeat them decisively and rapidly . . . For small countries hostile to us, bleeding our forces in protracted or indecisive conflict or embarrassing us by inflicting damage on some conspicuous element of our forces may be victory enough, and could undercut political support for U.S. efforts against them.[54]

So, when, on 2 August 1990, the Iraqi army under the command of Ali Hassan al-Majid invaded Kuwait (soon to be re-baptized the 19th province of Iraq), the United States government, within the space of five days, launched Operation Defensive Shield – a massive mobilization of troops to Saudi Arabia. There are a number of reasons for Saddam Hussein's adventurism. By 1990, he was colossally in debt to Saudi Arabia (to the tune of approximately $40 billion) and the OECD states in general, having borrowed most of the money to fund the war on Iran. He was coming under increasing criticism from the United States government, and felt their friendship might be coming to an end. At the same time, the Soviet Union was collapsing, so neither he nor his allies could rely on its support. With a large military machine at his disposal, he was also anxious to impress himself on history. He could draw on traditional Iraqi nationalist claims that Kuwait was rightfully a province of Iraq, partitioned off by the British for its own interests. And the Iraqi ruler was also adept at manipulating legitimate Arab concern about US foreign policy and Israel's treatment of the Palestinians.[55]

It was asserted, by contrast, that America's involvement was intended solely to defend Saudi Arabia from an attack by Iraq. George Bush Sr explained that he intended to exhaust all possible means to resolve the crisis peacefully. However, as Zbigniew Brzezinski – Bush's national security adviser at the time – explains, the president had already decided on the use of war by mid August, and worked hard to evade efforts to negotiate Hussein's withdrawal while building a propaganda effort to persuade the public of the case for military action.[56] (Repeated peace negotiations in fact took place, offering real settlements that could have avoided war.)[57] It took some time to persuade the American public to support the case for military intervention,[58] but when support did come, liberals played their part in making it a palatable war. The propaganda effort entailed the use of one of the world's largest public relations firms, Hill & Knowlton, to spread lies about babies being ripped from incubators in Kuwait.[59] But it also made copious use of Hitler analogies and references to nuclear weapons programmes[60] – both themes that were repeated by liberal cheerleaders.

Many of those who were later to exalt humanitarian interventionism started their journey with this war: lifelong opponents of US imperialism prepared themselves emotionally and intellectually not only to accept but to demand US intervention. After all, it seemed fairly simple. Saddam Hussein had invaded Kuwait when, although it was ruled by a tyrannical and exploitative monarchical elite, it was nevertheless experiencing a civil society opposition for the first time.[61] Not only was Hussein guilty of aggression, but he had checked a potentially democratic movement at its birth. So Fred Halliday, a Marxist international relations scholar who had been influenced by Bill Warren's arguments against anti-imperialism, and who had supported the Soviet occupation of Afghanistan,[62] was quick to describe Baathism as 'a contemporary variant of the European fascism of the 1930s' with substantial similarities to German Nazism. Throwing his weight behind the war, Halliday would complain of abuse at the hands of former colleagues, and lobbed a bit back in return: the Left had 'helped fascism come to power' in the 1930s and was now engaged in a similar game. He claimed that it was not true that Bush had wanted a war since August, and that a peaceful resolution had been possible at least until December, and was only thwarted by the intransigence of the Iraqi regime. It was 'solipsistic in the extreme' to concentrate on US imperialism as the decisive question in this case, for, in 'a choice between imperialism and fascism, I choose imperialism'.[63]

The main task of the Left, as Halliday saw it, should be to 'promote, not non-intervention, but a positive Western response to Iraqi opposition appeals for help'. He was later joined by Norman Geras, a Marxist political theorist previously affiliated to the Trotskyist Fourth International. The 'third world', they said, 'are appealing for another, equally active, US policy . . . The opposition to imperialism is not non-intervention, but, rather, action in support of democratic change'.

They derided 'talk of sanctions or negotiations' as 'the stuff of dreams. Saddam would no more have left Kuwait peacefully than he will give up power peacefully'. Halliday's colleagues were unimpressed. Robin Blackburn replied that the Left had united with Iraqi and Kuwaiti oppositionists against the war, and so Halliday's charge of complicity with Saddam was unsustainable. Further, he wondered, if powerful imperial states should be trusted with the task of liberating those under attack by foreign powers, why had Halliday not called for the Warsaw Pact states to wage war on behalf of the Viet Minh?[64]

Kanan Makiya's book was propelled into the bestseller lists, and he now found himself being interviewed on American news stations. *The Republic of Fear* was immediately the cited authority for newspapers,[65] and for practically everyone who argued in favour of the war. Publishers saw a chance for a cash-in, and Judith Miller of the *New York Times*, who would make her name purveying falsehoods during the second Gulf War, was sent by Random House to rewrite the book with Makiya to make it more accessible to the general reader. Makiya apparently found her so unpleasant that he declined to work with her. Miller instead co-authored a book with Laurie Mylroie, who had suddenly decided that supporting Saddam Hussein was no longer the excellent policy that she had thought it to be only a couple of years before. But Makiya was very quickly promoted to the leading ranks of supporters of the war. He warned of Saddam's 'Dr Strangelove scenarios involving poison gas or nuclear and biological weapons', and advised that there was no point in relying on an internal Iraqi opposition, since it did not exist (a claim rendered ludicrous by the post-war rebellions). Calling for the full occupation of Iraq and the deposal of the Baath regime, he explained – in a way that has become depressingly familiar – that 'Schwarzkopf and his army will be welcomed with open arms by the people of Iraq'. Makiya was rapidly disappointed when the war ended with Hussein still in power, the Kuwaiti regime restored, and the suppression of the Shia revolt (enabled by the United States). Concluding that the US was too timid, and that it needed to be goaded into becoming the saviour of Iraq, he joined the exile organization, the Iraqi National Congress (the CIA front which was to excel itself in the production of pre-war propaganda in 2002–3), and authored a document entitled 'Charter 91', modelled on the Eastern European dissidents' organization, Charter 77. He became friends with Ahmed Chalabi at a meeting in Salahuddin, Northern Iraqi, in October 1992, apparently being 'drawn to his mind'. When the CIA, angered by the failure of INC attempts to depose Hussein, dropped their clients, Makiya and friends turned to Republican PR man Francis Brooke, and they quickly ingratiated themselves with Richard Perle, Dick Cheney and the Halliburton crowd, the American Enterprise Institute, and pro-Israeli lobbyists.[66]

Michael Ignatieff, the one-time anti–Vietnam War activist who had long since become a compunctious liberal, also censured the West for its timidity. Its 'unseemly democratic dissension' gave heart to Saddam. Sanctions, too, were for wets: 'The dictator is a military man: the West must speak his language.' There had been a 'power vacuum in the Gulf since the British left twenty years ago', and it was time to fill it and at long last 'guarantee stable strategic protection for [the West's] Gulf oil supplies'. At the same time, the Left was accused of 'conspiracy theories' for claiming that the war was about oil. Paul Berman agreed: it was a war against fascism, and the Left was 'fighting the last war'. Unlike the Vietnamese Communists, Saddam really was 'vigorously on the march', and resembled 'dynamic, expanding Fascism, 1930s-style'. Hans Magnus Enzensberger, Michael Lerner, Daniel Cohn-Bendit, and several descendants of the New Left found themselves approving of American military action – a fact that cheered Berman in his 1996 account of the New Left's trajectory, *A Tale of Two Utopias*.[67]

Naturally, the 'new philosophers' supported the war and accepted the propaganda surrounding it. Bernard-Henri Lévy was so angered with SOS Racisme's hostility to the war that he resigned from its board. André Glucksmann, elaborating on his argument for nuclear deterrence, would later claim that

> today we must make the transition from the old bipolar dissuasion to a more generalized deterrence . . . That idea is not exclusively tied to the reality of nuclear weapons. And in my opinion the UN action against Iraq was an initial expression of what I call generalized deterrence. Why can it be regarded as so paradigmatic? Simply because a Saddam Hussein in unhindered possession of huge oil reserves and weapons of mass destruction constituted a threat of world war – in the name of the religious 'liberation' of Jerusalem, on top of it all.[68]

One outstanding critic of the Iraq war from the Left was Christopher Hitchens. The cynicism of America's various 'tilts' in the Gulf region did not dispose him well to the claim that it was now a force for humanitarianism and international order: a 'Metternich of Arabia' followed by a 'freemasonry' of 'shady oilmen' was the more likely reality. America's furtive realpolitik had encouraged Saddam in his worst days, and backed the Iranian regime at the same time in order to maintain a 'balance'. Hitchens pointed out that America's 'signals' to the Iraqi regime through April Glaspie had encouraged Hussein to believe that he would be welcome to Kuwait (Glaspie later claimed that they had not expected him to take *all* of Kuwait), and suggested that a 'tilt' towards the Saudi regime, with a protective 'net of bases and garrisons' thrown over it, could have its own destabilizing potential. US policy was undermining democratic and secular forces, which would necessitate further wars. Hitchens would have none of the Churchillian rhetoric either: 'beware always of the Munich/Churchill rhetoric, as of the ignorant opportunists who make use of it'. About liberals who 'pronounced themselves co-belligerents', preferring 'imperialism to fascism', he suggested: 'Now with a ruined Iraq and a strengthened Saddam – not to mention a strengthened Al-Saud and Al-Sabah – we no longer have to choose between imperialism and fascism'.[69] Writing of atrocities committed against fleeing Iraqi troops, he looked forward to 'the editions of Sesame Street and other special programming in place of cartoon fare in which American children will have the turkey shoot explained to them'. The new world order, as Bush had dubbed it, inaugurated a period of

> direct engagement and permanent physical presence. Moments like this are traditionally marked by some condign lesson being meted out to the locals. The fantastic, exemplary bloodletting that took place after the ostensible issue of the conflict had been decided was in that tradition. I can hardly wait for the parades.[70]

Little was he to know that, slightly over a decade later, he would be cheerleading them, with a bumper display of Churchillian bluster, and plenty of the false consolations, euphemisms and evasions of which he had once been so contemptuous.

The collapse of the Soviet Union and the fall of Yugoslavia

One of the main foci of US foreign policy in the 1990s was the management of the political and economic evolution of the former Soviet Union and Warsaw Pact states. 'Shock therapy' was the all-round remedy: privatize, deregulate, break up economic union in the Comecon zone. Jeffrey Sachs, Washington's man in Moscow, insisted that the constituent states of the former Soviet Union and Warsaw Pact should refuse any 'third way'. The result as measured by the OECD was a dramatic collapse within months of shock therapy's introduction. In Russia, incomes fell by 40 per cent within six months. In

Poland, they plunged by 33.6 per cent between 1990 and 1992; and in the same period incomes in Czechoslovakia and Hungary dipped by 21.5 and 14 per cent respectively. Joseph Stiglitz writes, 'In 1989, only 2 per cent of those living in Russia were in poverty. By late 1998, that number had soared to 23.8 per cent, using the $2 a day standard.' Of the policies that led to this situation, 'What was important were the monetary targets, the budget deficits, and the pace of privatization . . . Almost everything else was secondary'. Privatizations were rushed, close friends of President Yeltsin became fabulously wealthy, and in many cases there was not even a tax system in place to collect revenues. By 1994, workers in 35,000 enterprises were not being paid at all, while the average delay in the payment of wages was three months.[71]

The political vectors of these policies were often those who had led the anti-Stalinist Left during the struggles of 1968 and afterwards. Jacek Kuron, for instance, one of the founders of the Polish Workers' Defence Committee in 1976, was minister for social welfare after 1989, and helped introduce many of these measures, arguing that he would like to be a left-wing leader in an advanced capitalism – but since there was no capitalism, it would have to be built first.[72] (Typically of Kuron, he actually apologized for this much later, saying that he was 'responsible for the new order in this country and I have to say, "I am sorry, I fucked it up".')[73] In the West, socialist critical analysis did not experience the dramatic revival that some had anticipated with the loss of the embarrassing Stalinist relic. Peter Gowan, a writer on international relations, recalls how former colleagues on the Left began to defect in different ways.

> I think each person has his or her own specific path to the 'Euston Left'. As far as Fred Halliday was concerned, the collapse of the Soviet Bloc was crucial. He had never had a political affiliation to far left groups, he didn't take that sort of thing seriously. He was much more interested in the resources that the Soviet Union provided – *there* was a political force! I think he had invested a lot in the Soviet Union at the emotional and intellectual level, so he looked for positive spin-offs from the powerful remaining sources. When these resources were evidently disappearing, Fred put a question-mark over absolutely everything in world politics.[74]

For others, such as the former *New Left Review* editorial board members Branka Magaš and Quintin Hoare, it was the collapse of Yugoslavia that induced a political shift:

With Branka and Quintin, it was all about Yugoslavia. Branka had a kind of *deus ex machina* that was going to solve the Yugoslav problem, and that was the Yugoslav working class. When that God didn't appear by April 1991, when Branka went to visit Zagreb, she flipped over to Croatian nationalism. I mean, she simply backed secession. The turn was very sudden, but it was prefigured in her earlier unsustainable commitment to a pristine Yugoslavist working class as a *deus ex machina* for Yugoslavist democracy.[75]

The rapidity with which much of the Left collapsed, and neoliberal economic ideas were adopted by parties of the Centre-Left, was soon matched by a widespread enthusiasm for the projection of military force. The proximate cause was the disintegration of Yugoslavia. While a great deal of the commentary on the former Yugoslavia focuses on internal political struggles in the Yugoslav federation (usually in a partisan and melodramatic fashion), Susan Woodward's in-depth analysis for the Brookings Institution has the merit of discussing changes in the global situation – especially the IMF-led attempt to restructure the world economy during the 1970s. Yugoslavia had responded to the global recession from the mid 1970s and the accompanying spiral in oil prices by borrowing vast sums of money. Austerity measures and privatization were imposed in order to obtain IMF loans. Unemployment across the federation had reached almost 17 per cent by 1988, with some of the highest levels in Kosovo and the lowest in Slovenia and Croatia. The economy repeatedly contracted throughout the 1980s, before a tremendous slump after 1989. Growth fell to −15 per cent by 1991. The IMF's solution to these problems was initially to centralize the banking system and create a properly national economy, with free internal movement of labour, capital and goods. The IMF also demanded majority rather than consensus decision-making at the National Bank. The effort to centralize was resisted above all by those republics which had become wealthiest within the federation, as it threatened substantially to reduce their means of control. Slovenia and Croatia also resented their contributions to the federal budget, which were redistributed to the poorer south – even though Slovenia in particular benefited from captive markets across Yugoslavia.[76]

Coterminous with this horrendous economic collapse was an upsurge in nationalism of various kinds. Some of its roots lay in the constitutional changes introduced by Tito in 1974, which had reduced Serbia's powers with respect to its two provinces Vojvodina and

Kosovo. In Kosovo itself, where the Albanian majority had grievances over its subordinate status in the federation, a nationalist intelligentsia was developing. Serbian nationalist intellectuals began to challenge Tito's settlement as a form of discrimination against Serbia.[77] As protests and strikes gathered, a contest emerged between leaders of the Yugoslav federation and its constituents over how the transition to private capital would be managed, and how power would be distributed in its aftermath.

Much Western commentary has focused either on the revivification of 'ancient hatreds' or the demagogy of Slobodan Milošević. Catherine Samary, of the Dauphine University, Paris, and the author of *Yugoslavia Dismembered*, argues that these accounts are misleading:

It was a socioeconomic political struggle resulting from both international and internal conditions. Internally, from the crisis of the Titoist regime, the single-party state transformed from the Seventies into a confederal state with increasing local powers. Nationalism was used by those people in power, both communists and the new forces, to redefine the state's power in order to effectively manage the transformations in social-property relations . . . There were not 'good' and 'bad' nationalisms, but an uneven relationship of forces and the fear for all minorities to be in the 'wrong state'. The struggle was about power and privatization, and the dominant powers were those who were able to impose their own solutions on the others. In fact there were three dominant powers – Croatia, Slovenia and Serbia, like in the first Yugoslavia as opposed to the Titoist one. Croatia and Slovenia could impose their own concept of self-determination and secession (while Bosnian and Macedonian leaders tried to convince them without success to maintain a flexible Yugoslavia). The Serbian power could use its position in the central institutions, and a combination of Serb nationalism and a kind of Yugoslavism. The kind of Yugoslavia that Slobodan Milošević proposed was a Greater Serbian Yugoslavia, in the sense that it opposed any kind of egalitarian relationship between different nationalities, putting forward the logic of Serbian majority, both in the provinces and at the federal level, against any further confederal Yugoslavia. For that purpose he would use Serbian minorities. But they were not only Milošević's 'tools' because as minorities they could be locally threatened, especially in Croatia. Milošević was not a real or systematic defender of those minorities. He was trying to get the broadest part of Yugoslavia on his side and relied on the Yugoslav National Army. Since the army was trying to defend its privileges in the Yugoslav federation and with Titoist Yugoslav traditions, he appealed partially to Yugoslavism. But when the choice for independence had been made in Croatia and Slovenia, the main tactic for Milošević was to try to have an agreement with the Croatian power on the division of Bosnia, behind the back of Serbian minorities.

Interacting with those competing for hegemony in Yugoslavia were the external powers.

The European and American powers were not in complete agreement about what should happen until 1991, when Croatia and Slovenia declared independence. Until then, the IMF and the US preferred transformation at the federal level because they feared Balkan instability, and they would prefer a strong liberal Yugoslav state able to impose market discipline and privatization [to] uncontrolled national explosions. They supported the last federal government of Ante Marković. He tried to work for the liberal transformation at the pan-Yugoslav level with the support of dominant foreign governments, to repay Yugoslavia's debts, to manage the conflict and introduce the first laws making radical changes in ownership. It failed not because of inter-communal hatred, but because the three dominant powers among the republics wanted privatization and integration in the world order at the level and under the control of their own powers, and because a Yugoslav liberal orientation was not able to propose social protections for workers.[78]

Much of the Left responded to the disintegration of Yugoslavia by romanticizing, or at the very least championing, one of the constituent nations or would-be nations – first Croatia, then Bosnia-Herzegovina, and then Kosovo. In doing so, they ended up demanding intervention on their behalf by European or American power. They consistently demonized Slobodan Milošević as a 'fascist' or its equivalent, which was a false and unnecessary embellishment when he was merely a bureaucratic thug; but they were slower to recognize the flaws of Tudjman or Izetbegović. Many ended up, in fact, supporting the very logic of nationalism that was generating the problems in the first place, while at the same time engaging in a reductionist argument, a moralistic fairytale, which overlooked the fundamentals. Having so rendered the problem, often as a deeply personal encounter with 'fascism' and those 'resisting' it, and having no intention of founding an International Brigade or even an Abraham Lincoln one, they embraced the logic of humanitarian intervention. And that logic prepared the ground for the Iraq debacle.

The eclipse of one of the main historical referents for the Left, even the anti-Stalinist Left, meant that a defensive position of supporting American or European power against aspects of the global order deemed even more barbaric was extremely attractive for some. And, whatever criticisms one could make of Izetbegović, the Bosnian side *seemed* far more attractive than its opponents – an appearance that was enhanced by the efforts of the public relations firm, Ruder Finn. James Harff, one of the company's agents, explained that one of his proudest achievements had been to get significant Jewish opinion in the United States to oppose the Serbs and regard them as Nazis – which he noted was a tough sell, given the anti-Semitism of Tudjman and Izetbegović's 'Islamic Declaration'.[79]

However, the claim that the war could be reduced to Serbian (and sometimes Croatian) aggression and Bosnian innocence was patently false. The depiction of the Bosnian government as an embattled anti-fascist movement was at odds with the reality of its sectarian politics. And the eulogies to the Bosnian leadership and the demands for Western intervention facilitated the re-emergence of discredited imperial ideologies, with all their devastating effects.

A number of those on the Left who had opposed the first Iraq war found themselves rallying to Croatia's side in the Yugoslav war. Ken Livingstone, for example, who was then Labour MP for Brent East, lined up behind Croatian independence, and called for force to be used against the Serbs. Former Labour leader Michael Foot pleaded for a British humanitarian intervention, and David Blunkett MP claimed that the situation was 'verging on genocide'. The left-wing journalist and historian Branka Magaš insisted that there had been 'few signs of systematic persecution' of the Serb minority by the Croat regime, and called as early as July 1991 for the intervention of EC powers to 'put an end to the aggression of Serbia and its allies'. The French 'anti-totalitarians' were also quick to take Croatia's side. André Glucksmann accused the French government of appeasement for not defending Croatia, only recoiling from the comparison with Munich because Hitler had had a substantially more powerful army than the Serb regime. Alain Finkielkraut (or Finkielcroat, as he became known by some) had become such a staunch defender of Croatia that he praised its non-intervention in Bosnia as late as September 1992. In fact the Croatian leadership had already announced its intentions in Bosnia more than two years before. By the time Finkielkraut was praising the regime, Tudjman's Croatian Democratic Union (HDZ) was in control of the Bosnian branch, and its members were perpetrating war crimes. For Finkielkraut, the conflict was a straightforward clash between the late-twentieth-century homologues of Nazis and Jews. He went to great lengths to cover up for the atrocities of the Croatian regime, vitriolically condemning the US-sponsored trial process in the International Criminal Tribunal for the former Yugoslavia (ICTY) when it sought to arrest leading Croatian military figures. Although he manifested an awareness of the atrocities perpetrated by the Tudjman regime – and the anti-Semitism of Tudjman himself – Finkielkraut would not yield in his support for them because, so he maintained, the Serbs were perpetrating 'Guernica'. The re-construction of the disintegration of Yugoslavia as a repeat of World War II left no other role for the Serbs to play than that of Nazis.[80]

The fascist metaphors were highly unfortunate, for it was in Croatia that the media began to explore forms of nationalism that had lain dormant since 1945. Right-wing Croatian nationalists appropriated the symbolism of the Ustashe, the fascist paramilitaries of World War II. The Catholic Church in Croatia sought to rehabilitate Archbishop Stepinac, who had been charged as a traitor for collaborating with the Nazis. Aside from the general sense of resentment that Croatian nationalists shared about the submergence of Croat nationhood in the federation, there was a specific grievance dating back to the purge of nationalists from the ranks of the Croatian Communist Party in 1971–2. Franjo Tudjman had made himself the leader of this nationalist movement in the 1980s with a number of books defending the Croatian record in World War II, and the HDZ was to receive substantial support from the diasporic community. Tudjman promised in his campaigning literature to claim parts of Bosnia-Herzegovina. Tudjmanism, in its presentation and thrust, was a mirror-image of Milošević''s so-called 'anti-bureaucratic revolution' – an elite operation offered as a grassroots insurgency, with the added drama of fascist symbolism. Thus, Tudjman launched a campaign of national reconciliation with the Ustashe, and when the HDZ won the Croatian multiparty elections in 1990, streets and squares across Croatia were renamed after individuals linked with fascism. At the first public rally of the HDZ, on 25 February 1990, Tudjman had said: 'The NDH [Independent State of Croatia under

Hitler] was not simply a quisling creation and a fascist crime; it was also an expression of the historic aspirations of the Croatian people'. Accentuating the ethnonationalist contours of the future Croatian state, the government included in its new Citizenship Laws the right of ethnic Croats living outside the country to apply for citizenship, so that a huge number of Croats living in Bosnia could vote in Croatia's elections, while nonethnic Croats who wished to apply for or prove citizenship had to demonstrate residency for a full five years.[81]

Arguably, some of those puffing Croatian democracy and independence were not to know that Tudjman had already been plotting the partition of Bosnia with Milošević'. Perhaps not all were apprised of the overtly racist nature of the Croatian government. But given Tudjman's open declarations, including his public claim to a large part of Bosnia in 1990, there was every reason for people to be aware of what was really at stake. Michael Ignatieff, who professed no love for Croatia, nevertheless insisted on self-determination on the grounds that the federation was deceased and only an independent state would guarantee Croats safety. Further, such a policy would require French and British troops to back it up. By exactly the same rationale, Serbs in Croatia had a right to secede, since they had been under direct threat – indeed, direct fire – before a single Yugoslav National Army tank had shown up in Krajina; but there was no international outrage on behalf of the autonomous Serb Republic. On the other hand, as Ignatieff put it elsewhere: 'One of empathy's pleasures is to forget one's moral inconsistencies'. Christopher Hitchens, who had never been taken in by Croatian nationalism, was persuaded that both Serbia and Croatia were led by 'fascist parties' seeking to impose mono-religious and mono-racial states following the carve-up of Bosnia – an exaggeration in both cases. At any rate, he was a partisan of Bosnia, which he maintained represented the multicultural ideal that Yugoslavia had once stood for, and denounced the Clinton administration for not taking up its cause.[82]

There was no getting away from the fact that the disintegration of Yugoslavia was taking place in Europe. It was a source of additional outrage that the wars were taking place 'only two hours by plane from Paris', as Pascal Bruckner put it, or 'two hours from Brussels' as Michael Ignatieff noted.[83] The emergence of a classical war on the European continent for the first time since 1945 seemed to leave people helpless in the face of World War II metaphors. Almost every side in the war characterized the other as in some sense 'fascist' (although

Tudjman was more likely to cast his opponent as Bolshevistic), but the Bosnian leadership used this charge most effectively. So, when Bosnia was under siege in mid 1992, its president, Alija Izetbegović, was visited by Bernard-Henri Lévy. Izetbegović told him: 'We are another Warsaw ghetto; we shall die to the last person. You must know we shall die to the last person.'[84] Lévy had first been turned on to the issue of the war in Yugoslavia by a journalist at Radio-France International, named Stanko Cerović. BHL had been about to accept an invitation to speak to the pro-Milošević Union of Serbian writers when Cerović persuaded him to get in touch with the Serbian opposition movement. Cerović has written:

> Evidently, I was right to plead for the support for the Serb democrats. In addition, I thought that carnage could still be avoided and that a man who had access to the media could contribute to that. But the most formidable error that I made during all the Yugoslav wars is undoubtedly to have put BHL on the Bosnian track.[85]

It was the issue of Bosnia that would lead to Lévy's first serious rupture with François Mitterrand and the Socialist Party. Initially, as Lévy called for the West to help Bosnia arm by altering the terms of the UN arms embargo on the whole of Yugoslavia to exclude Bosnia, Mitterrand seemed to be on side. When Mitterrand made a surprise visit to Sarajevo on 27 and 28 June 1992, Lévy wrote of how Mitterrand was promising that the West could not always 'tie the hands' of the Bosnians, and that the 'international community' was 'not unfavourable [to] the principle of lifting the embargo on the weapons bound for Bosnia'. But, at a speech to a dinner organized by the Socialist-aligned anti-racist group, SOS Racisme, on 25 January 1993, Mitterrand assured BHL and all present that 'France will never make war on Serbia'.

BHL's disappointment was compounded by the fact that he had defended Mitterrand from the attacks of André Glucksmann and Romain Goupil, who called him a 'Serbophile'. He bitterly denounced Mitterrand, taking the opportunity supplied by revelations that the French president had once worked for the Vichy government to declare: 'Mitterrand and Vichy. Add me to that pack? No. I had no desire. Bosnia was enough for me.' BHL subsequently joined in street demonstrations in Paris against the arrival of Milošević in the city, which he saw as a sign of French complicity, although in fact his presence had been requested for highly secretive discussions with UN negotiators

David Owen and Cyrus Vance. For Lévy, however, negotiations were a sell-out. In the paradigm of an 'anti-fascist' struggle, with its simplistic dichotomy of fascistic Serbs and democratic Bosnians, only resistance or collaboration existed as options. So he engaged in a number of ventures to force a change of policy, such as organizing a secret trip to Bosnia with the Socialist politician Roland Dumas and the minister for humanitarian action, Bernard Kouchner, with the intention of conducting negotiations between the Bosnian leadership and a French minister who did not support Mitterrand's policy of negotiations.[86]

Later, in the spring of 1994, Lévy began to consider the prospect of standing a list of candidates in the European elections. Initially hesitant, he worried whether it was not a form of mere gesture politics, whether it would really help Izetbegović, and whether it would not divide the interventionists from those in France whom they wanted to make links with. Nevertheless, he gave the list his backing for a while. Curiously, however, just when it seemed at its strongest, with the Sarajevo list registering 12 per cent in the polls, BHL quite cavalierly walked away from the venture. Part of the reason was that his list threatened to squeeze the centrist list of the Socialist Michel Rocard, who was then opposed to Mitterrand.[87] Philippe Cohen notes:

> It is a sign of BHL's nose for a transformative turn of events. It was a very idealistic, emotive issue on which to mobilise people: 'Never Again'. He convinced Mitterrand that intervening in Sarajevo would gain him popularity in a 'New Left'. He formed a list for the elections, and some of the early polls gave it as much as 14 per cent support. However, Michel Rocard invited him to a meeting, and offered to take on all his demands, at which point BHL dropped the list like a hot potato. Had he not pulled out, the list might well have polled between 5 or 6 per cent.[88]

And despite the heated diatribes against Mitterrand and his government's policy in Yugoslavia, Lévy had no difficulty in accepting largesse from the administration. First, in the middle of the argument over Bosnia in July 1993, he accepted without any quarrel a nomination from Mitterrand and his prime minister to the Board of Trustees for the television station *Arte*. Similarly, in 1995 Mitterrand conferred the legion of honour medal on Lévy's father, at BHL's request, as if there had never been the slightest disagreement.[89] Differences of such apparent principle need not obstruct the usual business of patronage.

If the cynosures of anti-fascism were ubiquitous, urgent claims that genocide was afoot were the logical corollary. Michael Ignatieff predicted 'genocide' in Bosnia long before the words 'Srebrenica massacre' were recorded in a news item – but then much of the news media began reporting 'death camps' and the apparatus of genocide in mid 1992. The Bosnian government published a list of what it described as fifty-seven 'concentration camps'. To make the implication absolutely clear, a journalist even mistakenly described concentration camps as 'a Nazi invention'. ITN broadcast some notorious footage of an emaciated Fikret Ali at the Trnopolje camp, which two British newspapers described as 'Belsen 1992', and one German newspaper branded 'a new Auschwitz'. Philip Knightley, an expert on war reporting, studied the footage and concluded that if Ali was starving, he was an exception: most of the other prisoners were not dangerously thin. The camp was not any kind of 'death camp'. He also drew attention to the fact that the Croat and Muslim forces in Bosnia were also running detention camps, but these did not draw the same headlines. Izetbegović later confessed to having confected Serb death camps in order to precipitate bombing raids.[90]

So, some having already blundered into supporting the nationalist enterprise in Croatia, many liberals and leftists subsequently joined Christopher Hitchens in transforming Izetbegović into an object of extolment and flattery. They joined what they considered an anti-fascist crusade, and demanded that the arms blockade, which had not been applied very effectively to Serbia and Croatia, be lifted for Bosnia. And this was the minimal demand. Far better, they thought, to send in a naval fleet and launch air-strikes: 'Save Sarajevo, Mr Major', pleaded the *Guardian* in May 1992, with a detailed exposition of the military steps that could accomplish the task in a mere twenty-four hours. Given that the issue was framed with cliché before anyone had even given it much thought, it is unsurprising that the Croatian nationalist regime had become the first repository of 'anti-fascist' credentials. It was somewhat easier in Bosnia, since the explicit appeal of the Izetbegović regime was that it was *against* fascism, rather than for national reconciliation with it. And Bosnia was itself one of the most urbanized and ethnically mixed republics in Yugoslavia, with less than 10 per cent of its population living in homogenous municipalities.[91]

However, the heroic idealization of Izetbegović's Party of Democratic Action (SDA) is also unsustainable. Philip Corwin, the UN's chief political officer in Sarajevo during the summer of 1995, threw cold water on the fantasy of the Bosnian leadership as an embattled anti-fascist brigade. All three sides in the conflict, he explained, were 'gangsters wearing coats and ties'. Corwin described how, following the Dayton settlement, thousands of Serbs were vindictively 'cleansed' from areas of Bosnia by state police forces.[92] Corwin was relentlessly critical of the media depiction of the events, in which the Nato bombing of Serb positions in 1995 supposedly brought an end to the war, and therefore should have happened sooner alongside a lifting of the arms embargo for plucky little Bosnia.[93] 'By taking the side of the Bosnian government, they actually undermined the peace process'.[94]

Some of those arguing for the superiority of the SDA's secessionism insisted that it was defending a multicultural ideal against the intolerant and violent nationalisms promulgated from Belgrade and Zagreb. If pan-Yugoslav solidarity was no longer good enough for Yugoslavia, it might still hold in Bosnia, and so to defend Bosnian secession was to oppose partition.[95] Catherine Samary argues that such a position relies on an overly rosy view of Bosnia:

> Up until 1991, Izetbegović (with Gligorov in Macedonia) tried to find a Yugoslav compromise. And in Bosnia the three parties representing growing nationalist forces promised to rule together in order to win popular support at the first elections. There was the possibility of inter-communal coexistence. But new logics were emerging with the aim of territorial regroupment. In the context of disintegration, and of attempted agreements between Milošević and Tudjman, there were also military and paramilitary forces in Bosnia under Croatian nationalists, as well as under Serb nationalists. On the Muslim side, there was also heterogeneity. Among the population, especially in an industrial area like Tuzla, there existed a rather large secularist current favourable to a multi-ethnic Yugoslavia or Bosnia. Muslim leaders themselves (even those who built the SDA led by Izetbegović) were divided and splits occurred (some preferred an alliance with Belgrade in a Yugoslav project, others a kind of Bosnian nationalism, others a more religious orientation with variants). So, you could find a kind of Bosniak nationalism which would consider Serbs and Croatians to be in occupation. There was also a kind of Islamism that Izetbegović could represent at certain moments, where Bosnia as such was not the issue, but re-establishing an Islamic horizon was the aim – although this was a minority. I don't place Izetbegović on the same level as Milošević and Tudjman. But he could not offer a consistent resistance to Serbian and Croatian nationalism because he presented himself as a Muslim leader, not as the Bosnian president; and he hesitated between different kinds of alliances.

It is true that, when the Yugoslav National Army withdrew from Bosnia in May 1992 at the request of the UN Security Council, some of those who stayed behind to defend Bosnia-Herzegovina were Serbs and Croats. And initially it looked as if the problem was simply one of Serb aggression, enabling a fragile alliance between Bosnian and Croat 'democrats' to last until 1993. However, the SDA, like the Croatian Defence Council (HVO) and Serbian Democratic Party (SDS), pushed in negotiations for the partition of Bosnia. Izetbegović was not the 'fundamentalist' he is sometimes described as. Catherine Samary points out that Izetbegović

> could not have a simple Islamic orientation, because he had to have different tools. He looked to the Islamic states, to the US and the EU. Of those, he explicitly stated that it was more important to have the support of the US and the EU.

Nevertheless, he was certainly committed to some form of 'Islamic' government, a prospect that did not appeal to the non-Muslim majority of Bosnia (hence the logic of partition). Izetbegović's 'Islamic Declaration' was originally written in 1970, and could be written off if it had not been reproduced during the 1990 elections. And while the Croatian and Serbian nationalist forces were gathering weapons and paramilitaries in preparation, the SDA had formed its own military wing in summer 1991, and was purchasing illegal weapons from Slovenia by autumn.[96] Put bluntly, the SDA was one of the nationalist parties seeking to use secession and military conflict to amplify its own power, not the guardian of the remnants of the Yugoslav dream.

The Bosnian leadership was also an American client: its rejection of the Vance–Owen peace plan, for example, was encouraged by a US administration that had decided to back Bosnian secession after losing the battle to prevent German recognition of Croatia. The Clinton administration, eager to extend US influence over the process, took up the cause of 'the Muslims' – the SDA, in other words – frustrating the only viable peace plan at the time, and instead undertook a process of intensive military escalation, threatening the use of air strikes, for example. Although neither Milošević nor Tudjman wanted an independent Bosnia, they had been prepared to compromise and accept a cantonization agreement in Lisbon in 1991. But Izetbegović was unhappy with this, and was encouraged by the US ambassador to Yugoslavia, Warren Zimmerman, to refuse the deal. The deal was not without serious flaws, as it presumed partition along ethnic lines; but the subsequent Vance–Owen plan departed from this assumption, and was still rejected by the Clinton administration. The Bosnian government was permitted to break the arms blockade (contrary to the perception at the time) and to draw in an international army of thousands of jihadists, many of them conveyed to the battle zone in US helicopters. Those present included one of the alleged 9/11 plotters, Khalid Sheikh Mohammed.[97] (This raises the question, for those who still laud the Bosnian cause but are now possessed by blood-curdling thoughts of 'Islamic imperialism': At what point did violent Wahhabism become a bad thing?) The Bosnian Muslim army went on to commit atrocities comparable in savagery with those of the other parties.

Interventionists were confident throughout the 1990s that genocide was being perpetrated by the Serbs against Bosnian Muslims. One account explained that 'fact-finding organizations have definitely found that genocide has occurred and have laid all the blame for it on the Serbs'.[98] The total number of deaths was estimated at up to 330,000, and the majority of these deemed to be Muslim victims of Serb aggression.[99] This analysis has not withstood the test of time. One of the most recent death tolls compiled by the US-sponsored International Criminal Tribunal for the former Yugoslavia reveals that approximately 102,622 civilians and soldiers were killed, comprising 55,261 civilians and 47,360 soldiers. The minimum figure for all war-related deaths was 67,530, with 45,980 of these being Muslims, 12,642 Serbs, and 5,629 Croats. Edward Herman and David Peterson point out that, of the total estimate for civilian deaths, approximately 16,700 were attributed to those living in Serb-controlled areas – not an insignificant number in itself. A later report by the Sarajevo-based Research and Documentation Centre suggested that of a total of 97,207 people had been confirmed dead, of whom 57,523 were soldiers and 39,684 civilians. Of both military and civilian deaths, the great majority – approximately 31,000 and 33,000, respectively – were Bosnian Muslims.[100] Given the balance of power among the combatants, and the viciousness with which the war was fought, these figures are unsurprising. In the conduct of the war, very real atrocities by Serb paramilitaries – such as the 'Tigers' of Željko Ražnatović, known as 'Arkan' – were brought to light. But the misleading reportage of 'death camps' and the Nazi allegories had the effect of overpowering analytical thought with emotionally potent oversimplification.

The atrocities committed by the Bosnian and Croatian armies were rarely reported with equal or even comparable vigour. Croatia's ethnic cleansing of up to 200,000 Serbs during Operation Storm (an operation described as 'the liberation of Krajina' by one author) combined a military take-over with repeated massacres of unarmed civilians. Yet it achieved nothing like the prominence of Serb atrocities. In 2006, it was reported by BBC Monitoring Europe that sixty-three mass graves had been found in the Republika Srpska, containing the remains of 3,251 presumed Serb civilians, indicating a large number of massacres committed by Bosniak forces. This story, like others of its kind, has hardly been touched. Other stories barely examined include what might be described as 'false flag' operations, such as the massacre of Bosnian Muslims at the Markale market in 1994, which helped precipitate the Nato bombing of Serb positions. Many UN officials believed that the shelling had come from the Bosnian army, and Unprofor accused Bosnian government forces of 'firing to provoke the Serbs, and of using hospitals and public buildings as cover for such fire'.[101]

Although Bosnian Muslim leaders, up to and including Izetbegovic´, came under investigation for involvement in the killings of innocent Serb and Croat civilians in ethnic cleansing, and in atrocities such as ritual beheading, very little attention was paid to them at the time that the war was going on.[102] Operation 'Krivaja 95', the Bosnian Serb plan to seize Srebrenica, designed after an attack on the nearby Serb village of Visnjica, on 26 June 1995, culminated in a massacre of up to 8,000 Muslim males.[103] It was one of the worst atrocities of the war. Designed to ethnically cleanse the territory and capture it decisively for the Republika Srpska, the operation is now considered by the US-sponsored ICTY and the International Court of Justice as the only instance of 'genocide' that can be shown to have occurred. Serbia, however, was cleared of involvement in the massacre.[104] Some scholarly opinion has cast doubt on the verdict of genocide,[105] and it could be argued that the purpose of the judicial process was less to establish the facts of the case than to determine a politically convenient verdict. Yet, whatever label one applies, it was clearly a grave atrocity. The massacre resulted from the ruthless strategy of Serb paramilitaries who, in seizing a territory, surrounded it, sealed it off, evicted the women and children, and kept the men to be either killed, or thrown in detention camps, or used for forced labour.[106]

However, the treatment of Srebrenica in the Western press highlights its capacity for selective attention. In the run-up to that atrocity, a wave of terror, including rape, by Bosnian Muslim forces in surrounding areas had terrorized and killed hundreds of civilians, with thousands of men of military age slain. Few have discussed these atrocities. Though the zone was supposed to be demilitarized, Bosnian soldiers, who outnumbered Serbs in the area, carried out regular 'sabotage' operations. This sequence of provocations in no way attenuates the responsibility of the Bosnian Serb paramilitaries who carried out the 1995 massacre, but it does suggest that the unique focus on Serb aggression, characterized by the cynosures of Holocaust memory since 1991, had the effect of diminishing and apologizing for the crimes of the war's other participants. And while Izetbegović was deified, Milošević received no credit for taking risks with his support by urging the Serbs in Krajina and the Republika Srpska to accept various deals to end the conflict. He urged the Croatian Serbs to agree to a ceasefire in November 1991 and to the Vance plan in January 1992, and he pushed the Bosnian Serbs to accept the Vance–Owen plan in the Spring of 1993.[107]

After a brief spell of US bombings of Serb positions, and the recapture of substantial Serb-claimed territories by joint Croat–Muslim forces, negotiations resumed. The Dayton Peace accords of November 1995 validated the claims of the nationalist parties and promulgated partition – the very solution that interventionists had hoped to avoid. The agreement formally recognized Republika Srpska, and allowed for elections that, predictably, mandated ethnic nationalist politicians, and therefore consolidated the settlement preferred by the nationalists under the quasi-colonial rule of the Office of the High Representative of the United Nations. As David Chandler points out, the protectorate has been 'faking it' in terms of democratic credentials ever since. The settlement not only empowered entities with no accountability to the population of Bosnia, but also continually deferred the day when Bosnians would have full sovereignty. In fact, the main source of legitimacy for the UN's ongoing and increasingly hands-on management of the Bosnian polity is precisely its claim to be inculcating democratic habits and forms.[108] The assisted death of Yugoslavia, and the subsequent creation of ethnically homogenous partitioned zones, stands in an ignoble imperial tradition of divide and rule. And liberals, by converting this appalling process into a romantic melodrama; by aesthetically packaging it for Western audiences relatively well informed about Nazi crimes but generally uninformed about colonial and imperial ones; by carefully grooming heroes and transmogrifying Serbs into a fungible racial horde; by obscuring the war's actual content as well as its causes; and especially by appealing to egalitarian and anti-racist discourses that would not have had as much credibility coming from the Major administration or from Bush and Clinton, provided the perfect alibis.

Finale: one last protectorate

The Spring 1999 war by Nato against Serbia, purportedly to save Kosovo from a wave of 'ethnic cleansing' by the Serbian military, led liberal 'interventionists' to the summit of war fever. The leaders of the main Nato states that carried out the attacks argued that it was a war against 'systematic efforts at genocide' (Clinton), a 'hideous racial genocide' (Blair).[109] For the first time in years, liberals could derive libidinal satisfaction from a heavily moralized episode of violent destruction, and squeal for much more of the same. The *New York Times*'s Thomas Friedman openly called for war crimes:

> Let's at least have a real air war . . . It should be lights out in Belgrade: Every power grid, water pipe, bridge, road, and war-related factory has to be targeted. Like it or not, we are at war with the Serbian nation (the Serbs certainly think so), and the stakes have to be very clear: Every week you ravage Kosovo is another decade we will [set] your country back by pulverizing you. You want 1950? We can do 1950. You want 1389? We can do 1389 too.[110]

The *Guardian* was so fanatically pro-war that its jingoistic rival, the *Sun*, took the opportunity to remind its editors gloatingly of the tragic side of combat. The liberal columnist Jonathan Freedland complained that the Left had become 'champions of moral indifference' by opposing the intervention. Once again, it was an anti-fascist war: 'It became one thing or the other: either the West could try to halt the greatest campaign of barbarism in Europe since 1945 – or it could do nothing.' And the Serbs were held to bear collective responsibility (thereby rendering themselves worthy of collective punishment, perhaps): 'Just as the US scholar Daniel Goldhagen has shown how it was impossible for ordinary Germans to be ignorant of the Final Solution, so today's Serbs can hardly claim to be in the dark.' Two weeks later, Goldhagen wrote for the same newspaper that 'Serbia's deeds are, in their essence, different from those of Nazi Germany only in scale. Milošević is not Hitler, but he is a genocidal killer who has caused the mass murder of many tens of thousands of people.' Not only were Serbs categorically implicated in 'genocide', the RTS television station was doing its bit whipping up 'genocidal passions'.[111] (This claim was made on the day after Nato's attack on the television station, carried out in the full knowledge that the building was occupied by civilians.)

New York liberals, too, were all for the aggression – including David Rieff, Susan Sontag, Tony Judt and Paul Berman. If anything, the difficulty was that Nato was not proposing to go even further and stage a ground invasion. Susan Sontag wearily charged European leftists opposed to the venture with 'anti-Americanism', and demonized 'the Serbs' *in toto* as Nazis involved in 'genocide', insisting:

'There is radical evil in the world, which is why there are just wars. And this is a just war.'[112]

Michael Ignatieff, with his characteristic combination of ebullience and lachrymosity, regretted only the belatedness of the invasion, complaining that nations which are relatively immune from the effects of war were so 'unwilling to run them'. Wondering at the 'biblical scale' of Serbia's repression of the Kosovars, 'the most meticulous deportation of a civilian population since the Second World War', he asked: 'How was it that after eight years of repeating that we wanted to banish ethnic cleansing from Europe, we could wake up to a whole nation expelled before our eyes?' This is how 'Empire Lite' works, according to Ignatieff: benevolent, but somnambulant and occasionally blundering. It requires an active lack of imagination to construe matters in this way; an alarmingly incurious mind. It is reasonably well known by now that the worst of the refugee crisis *followed* the bombing, and that ethnic cleansing was the *result*, rather than the cause of Nato's attack.[113] Washington no more dozed through the expulsion than Slobodan Milošević did. However, what is more conspicuous is the consistency of Ignatieff's complaint of Western *in*action. Routinely employed to comment on war zones with Western troops and Western bombs and Western diplomacy all working assiduously away, he consistently finds that Washington is somehow a slacker in the imperialism business.

Christopher Hitchens was less consistent than perhaps he would like to admit. While he was later to deploy the now familiar line that 'if the counsel of the peaceniks had been followed' something dreadful would have happened, he was initially less sanguine about the American strikes. On ethnic cleansing by Serb forces, he said that 'the cleansing interval . . . was both provoked and provided by the threat of air attacks on other parts of Yugoslavia'. About the responsibility of the warmongers for the fate of Kosovars, he added:

> The 'line of the day' among administration spokesmen, confronted by the masses of destitute and terrified refugees and solid reports of the mass execution of civilians, [was] to say that 'we expected this to happen.' . . . If they want to avoid being indicted for war crimes themselves, these 'spokesmen' had better promise us they were lying when they said that.[114]

It was, he feared, another imperial carve-up, and he said so repeatedly. Later, he proceeded as if he had never said any of this, or at least never really thought it. Hitchens was now arguing that the American state could be a moral agent in world affairs. He referred the Left to the 1994 US intervention in Haiti as an instance of military action taken against the preferences of the right-wing and 'the generals', which the Left should support.[115] To the extent that his growing enthusiasm for American overseas intervention conflicted with his critical attitude towards American politics and society, the latter tended to be attenuated. By 2001 he was reminiscing with *Reason* magazine about his admiration for Margaret Thatcher, and confessing that the idea of socialism was finished as far as he was concerned.[116]

But Hitchens would have done better to stick to his guns. The Nato attack drastically worsened the situation of Kosovars – and needlessly so, since Western leaders had thwarted a peaceful compromise that would have saved Kosovars from death and expulsion, not to mention preventing quite a few Serbs from being murdered. The pre-war negotiations leading up to the war were evidently intended to fail. A State Department official boasted that Nato 'deliberately set the bar higher than the Serbs could accept'. George Kenney, a former State Department Yugoslavia desk officer, reporting the comment, described the process as being equivalent to the Gulf of Tonkin incident, which had been used to justify escalation in Vietnam. The post-war attacks on Serbs were not only predictable; they were actually made more likely by the decision of Nato to insist that the KLA accept as their leader Agim Çeku – a major war criminal during Operation Storm who had helped ethnically cleanse at least 200,000 Serbs from Croatia. The occupation itself proved to be calamitous for the Serbs who were subsequently the victims of ethnic cleansing at the hands of the KLA (for which the ICTY later, somewhat hypocritically, charged Kosovar leaders), and subsequently subjected to repeated attack; for the Roma who were also ethnically cleansed by the KLA (being classic targets of racism); and for Kosovars who eventually demanded an end to 'colonial' UN rule, just as Iraq was descending into chaos in late 2003. And the man who headed the United Nations Mission in Kosovo for its first two years? Mr Humanitarian Intervention himself, Bernard Kouchner.[117]

It was frequently heard from liberal supporters of the war that it could not have been motivated by anything other than humanitarian outrage because, after all, Kosovo had no oil. This makes some strange assumptions about the nature of geopolitics and what might be classified as an interest. Did those protesting against the use of death squads in Nicaragua think they were defending the country's coffee supplies? The record was set straight on US interests by David Benjamin, a member of the US National Security Council under Clinton, when he rebuked George W. Bush for his insufficient understanding of American interests in the Balkans:

> Mr Bush showed a misunderstanding of a major strategic achievement of the Clinton administration . . . In particular [he] missed the intrinsic connections between enlargement and the conflict in the Balkans . . . Nato enlargement advanced US interests in dealing with one of the country's foremost strategic challenges: coping with a post-communist Russia whose trajectory remains in question.[118]

It was Daniel Pearl and Robert Block of the *Wall Street Journal* who conclusively debunked the claims made before and during the war that 'genocide' had been underway. Clinton had raised the Genocide Convention to galvanize UN support for the action. A statement demanding action to prevent 'genocide' was signed by Physicians for Human Rights, Minnesota Advocates for Human Rights, Refugees International, the International Crisis Group, Network Bosnia, the Coalition for International Justice, the Institute for the Study of Genocide, the Network of East-West Women, Freedom House, and the Balkan Action Council. David Rieff maintained that, by this point, human rights organizations had become the most ardent interventionists: no wonder that, during the takeover of Afghanistan, Colin Powell told a gathering of relief officials that they were part of America's 'combat team'.[119] Investigating the extensive efforts to exhume bodies by UN authorities (the US does do body-counts when it suits them), Pearl and Block noted that the campaign had certainly become one of ethnic cleansing, but was never genocide:

> British and American officials still maintain that 10,000 or more ethnic-Albanian civilians died at Serb hands during the fighting in Kosovo . . . But the number of bodies discovered so far is much lower – 2,108 as of November, and not all of them necessarily war-crimes victims.

They pointed out that much of the misinformation came from activists in Nato's de facto invasion force, the KLA. Even more important, however, was the complicity of human rights organizations in the propaganda. As it became clear that Nato's bombing campaign was exacting a growing civilian cost, the State Department issued the rights groups with proposed survey forms for interviewing fleeing refugees, with the aim of producing renewed 'genocide' hysteria. 'Genocide to come', the headlines once more affirmed.[120]

The UN-run Supreme Court in Kosovo eventually decided that no genocide had ever been undertaken in Kosovo. Some, such as the popular liberal author Samantha Power, have defended the Clinton administration for its 'genocide' claims. Power, writing in 2003, was at pains to give readers the impression that a comparatively low body-count did not mean that over 11,000 bodies were not buried. Claiming falsely that 'some 4,000 buried bodies had been found' in just over 100 of the sites to be checked (in fact, as Power goes on to clarify, the figure announced was 4,000 bodies or parts; and as she does not say, these were not necessarily all war crimes victims or all Albanians), she maintained that the 'UN tribunal has received reports that some 11,334 Albanians are buried in 529 sites in Kosovo alone'. The UN tribunal in question is the ICTY, which refused to investigate Nato war crimes during the bombing of Yugoslavia. It is true that it announced that it had received reports of bodies totalling 11,334 in 1999;[121] but Power was writing long after that figure had proved erroneous. Moreover, Power does not make clear, as Pearl and Block did, that many of those reports were disinformation provided by the KLA.

In one intriguing post-bellum episode, the UK House of Commons Foreign Affairs Committee, while dismissing the idea that there had been a Serb campaign of genocide in Kosovo, nevertheless insisted that the true issue was that Milošević's campaign would have continued for years had there been no intervention, thereby creating further deaths and more instability than the bombing. As David Chandler notes, this provides excellent post facto cover for literally any outcome that you can imagine – except, perhaps, the death of every single Kosovan.[122]

When there were calls for a cessation or pause in the bombing of Afghanistan, on the grounds that the interruption in the food supply could cause 100,000 deaths, countless 'humanitarian' reasons were presented for the refusal to do so, including the prospect of the Taliban marauding triumphantly around the country, killing many more people than the bombers could. If 100,000 deaths as a result of Western action would not have invalidated the humanitarian reasoning for war, then nothing could. Vociferously declared intentions matter as much, or more, for many commentators than the consequences of an action. Peregrine Worsthorne insists that 'the noble intentions should produce noble results, but if that – for reasons beyond our control – proves impossible, then it is at least something to be proud of to have had the noble intentions'. Similarly, Jonathan Freedland had suggested of the Kosovo war that not to intervene would have made us 'bystanders to evil'. Often, the salient aspect of a humanitarian engagement is what it means for 'us', not for its purported beneficiaries.[123]

This is well understood by those in power. The UK Ministry of Defence issued a report entitled 'The Future Strategic Context for Defence'. Under the section entitled 'Public Support for Military Action', the MoD acknowledged in its coy way the importance of propaganda and public empathy. 'We need to be aware', it said, 'of the ways in which public attitudes might shape and constrain military activity', and particularly attentive to the ways in which

> increasing emotional attachment to the outside world, fuelled by immediate and graphic media coverage, and a public desire to see the UK act as a force for good, is likely to lead to public support, and possibly public demand, for operations prompted by humanitarian motives.

Since 'public support will be vital to the conduct of military interventions', 'effective communication strategies to promote wider understanding of the rationale behind the conduct of operations will be vital if we are to avoid constraints which compromise our ability to achieve military objectives'.[124]

Perhaps the British military leadership even underestimated the willingness of intellectuals and commentators to fabulate on their behalf: who would have imagined that when the Serbs overthrew Milošević[125] – thus demonstrating, as many had said all along, that the people of Yugoslavia were not mere cattle, and could depose their own rulers – the revolt would be credited to Nato, as it frequently was? But, of course, the liberal interventionists of this era displayed a remarkable capacity for self-deception. They demanded recognition for Croatia, and an end to Serb expansionism: they obtained recognition and got both Serb and Croat expansionism. They said 'no partition', and demanded an American intervention: America intervened, and they were rewarded with partition. They deplored sectarianism and demanded support for the Bosnian leadership: they ended up with support for the Bosnian leadership and sectarianism to boot. They railed against ethnic cleansing, and demanded Nato bomb Serbia: Nato bombed Serbia, and there were two rounds of ethnic cleansing.

Ignatieff and the clash of civilizations

It is symptomatic of this era that Michael Ignatieff made his name, to some extent, during the Balkan wars. 'The key language of our age,' he maintained in *Blood and Belonging*, 'is ethnic nationalism'. At this stage, in light of the conflict in Yugoslavia, he maintained that no nationalism was self-evidently correct, that all forms were 'contestable' – but that Western forms of nationalism, with the exception of Germany, happened to merit a greater claim to sociological realism by insisting on civic rather than ethnic forms of cohesion. All forms of nationalism are 'supremely sentimental. Kitsch is the natural aesthetic of an ethnic "cleanser" . . . The latent purpose of such sentimentality is to imply that one is in the grip of a love greater than reason, stronger than the will, a love akin to fate and destiny'. However, 'if nationalism is persuasive because it warrants violence, it is also persuasive because it offers protection from violence'. Belonging, understanding the tacit codes of one's neighbours, is both a motive for oppressing others and a means of protection from oppression. How to escape the furnace of mutually reinforcing nationalisms? For Ignatieff, the greatest hope was in the emergence of a renewed cosmopolitan capitalism with diminished state sovereignty, since 'a global market has been limiting the sovereignty and freedom of manoeuvre of nation-states at least since Adam Smith first constructed the theory of the phenomenon at the outset of the age of nationalism'.[126] The problem was that, unlike in the past, the global hegemon had not decided to manage a global imperium – it defended its own national interests, and left 'large sections of Africa, Eastern Europe, Soviet Asia, Latin America and the Near East' to their own pitiful devices:

> Not surprisingly, their nation-states are collapsing, as in Somalia and in many other nations of Africa. In crucial zones of the world, once heavily policed by empire – notably the Balkans – populations find themselves without an imperial arbiter to appeal to. Small wonder, then, that, unrestrained by stronger hands, they have set upon each other for that final settling of scores so long deferred by the presence of empire.[127]

Of course, the classic example of the collapsing state, with no imperial guarantor, was Bosnia. Where states cannot impose order, one witnesses ethnic conflict: Ignatieff's other frightful example of the failure of cosmopolitanism was the Los Angeles riots which, far from being a revolt against the naked racism of the LAPD, were, apparently, in fact a form of 'ethnic warfare', which is always latent, and only barely suppressed by a powerful nation-state.[128] This, suffice to say, estimates humanity pretty cheaply: if human beings are given to raging violence justified by irrational particularism where they are not contained by a powerful state, or empire, little wonder that the human costs of empire appear to matter so little to Ignatieff.[129]

Similar arguments would be aired in *The Warrior's Honour*, which purported to oppose the Huntington thesis about a 'clash of civilizations'. Ignatieff set out 'to find out what mixture of moral solidarity and hubris led Western nations to embark on this brief adventure in putting the world to rights', and also what caused the crises that 'Western nations' were responding to. Replete with second-hand po-mo clichés (with an emphasis on stories rather than truth claims, narratives rather than historical exegeses, fictions rather than principles, the brevity of the televisual gaze, ambivalence rather than moral certainty, and so on), Ignatieff's excursion into the Balkan wars is intellectually undemanding. As far as the 'brief adventure' in humanitarianism is concerned, according to Ignatieff it is the artefact of an historical aperture after the Cold War and the rise of television – the former removing the old colonial apparatus and 'ideological struggle' so that 'what is left is a narrative of compassion', and the latter engaging human sympathy for brief exhortative spells. But television has to have material to work with, and so Ignatieff concludes that 'consciences were formed to respond as they do' during the unique historical circumstances that inculcated the 'myth of human equality'. The thesis regarding the origin of intra-state combat is that ethnic nationalism is a form of narcissism that authorizes the devaluation of human life excluded from the range of ethnic consideration. Ethnic nationalism, like most forms of identity, is mythical; but the myth becomes animating when states fail, populations are endangered, and the only people who will protect them is 'my own people'.[130] This is circular reasoning: the argument for the importance of particularism is that particularism becomes important – there is no explanation of why one form of identity is able to thrive against others.

It so happens that Ignatieff's thesis does not contradict Huntington's as much as he thinks it does. It also contains elements of Kaplan's thesis about anarchy resulting from state failure, but essentially it posits the following: a (European/Western) 'We', and a (Balkan/Oriental) 'They'; an historically produced value of universalism for 'us', and an historically constituted value of particularism for 'them'; truth for 'us', and repression for 'them'.[131] Granted that Ignatieff sees nothing 'fundamental' about these categories, they are nevertheless profound in his conception, being rooted in millennia of historical and religious experience, and capable of having a deep impact on the present.

This, at the very least, bears close resemblances to Huntington: perhaps the main difference is that, while Huntington evinces some limited respect for other cultures, Ignatieff displays none at all. The *only* sense in which history is permitted to impact significantly on the present in Ignatieff's reading is through the vector of culture. There is no room for political economy, and diplomacy is only a factor where it can be reduced to heroic Western efforts to upset the plans of despots. International intervention is something that happens in response to the barbarian emergency, rather than being a key contributor to the problem. The putative violent narcissism of the Balkan/ Oriental Other thus not only mandates extraordinary international violence on the part of European/Western nations: it also resuscitates colonial condescension in the mould of a liberal discourse of multi-cultural 'tolerance'.

Empire Lite, a slender travelogue and adventure tale, followed up on these insights with a call for humanitarian imperialism. Taking a whirlwind imperial tour around the garrisons of Bosnia, Kosovo and Afghanistan, described as 'frontier zones', Ignatieff celebrated the fact that revenge had been 'visited on the barbarians' and that more was to come, especially in light of a 'monstrous cult of martyrdom through violence' that was spreading through 'the Arab and Muslim worlds'. He rejoiced that the 'humanitarian empire' was 'the new face of an old figure: the democratic free world, the Christian West'. There was no need, he maintained, to worry about hidden agendas, since 'humanitarian action is not unmasked if it is shown to be the instrument of imperial power'. Once again, empire was fine, provided it did more than simply reproduce itself; provided it was somehow in the other fellow's interest; provided it prepared the barbarians for authentic self-government.

One of Ignatieff's heroes in this respect is Bernard Kouchner, the imperial governor of Kosovo. Kouchner's role was to negotiate a peaceful, lasting settlement between Kosovan Serbs and Albanians, but he had little luck: the Kosovans engaged in a 'conspiracy of silence' to perpetuate inter-communal violence. Kouchner, we are reminded, is a doctor – Kosovo is his patient (and thus preferably silent, and submissive). He claims, falsely, that Nato's intervention in spring 1999 halted Milošević in the middle of an ethnic cleansing drive, but finds the occupiers in the 'embarrassing' position of being unable to stop Kosovan Albanians from ethnically cleansing Serbs, and 'petty feuding among the Kosovar princelings' continued. 'Inter-ethnic violence' was, sadly, 'dampening' 'Western imperial ardour'. He persists with false-hood, claiming that, despite 'revisionist claims to the contrary',

Western claims of 10,000 Kosovar Albanians murdered by the Serbian army between March and May 1999 would be 'proved right'.[132] The mission was legitimate and humanitarian, even if the humanitarianism was an afterthought to the pursuit by imperial states of their own interests. The real trouble was that liberal imperialists so intensely want to do good, and to be loved as well, and yet are unwilling to take up the 'burdens of a permanent empire' – the burdens so providentially allocated to the white man.[133]

Not that Ignatieff looks favourably on ancient superstitions about white supremacy. The latter was, he says, a form of 'narcissism' that was ultimately empire's 'nemesis'. The trouble is that the remedy – self-determination – has been tried and has failed. Instead of equal and self-governing nation-states, the 'age of empire' was 'succeeded' by 'an age of ethnic cleansing and state failure'. Thus, empire is necessary to reconstitute the 'global order of stable nation-states', necessarily led by that country that the historian Gerald Horne has justly called the 'world heavyweight champion of white supremacy'.[134] To put it another way, Ignatieff dislikes the theory, but advocates the practice. Like Mill, Ignatieff is not a biological racist and does not favour excessively *arrogant* imperialism. However, for all the tolerant, inclusive inflection of his writing, he is committed to Western/European supremacy; is extraordinarily blasé about the use of violent coercion on its behalf; demonstrates incredible bad faith about its motives and their likely impact; and – as will be obvious in the discussion of Iraq in the Conclusion – can mobilize his theory of cultural 'narcissism' and state breakdown to cover for any imperial mess, and salve any troubled conscience.

.

The accommodation of formerly left-wing intellectuals to capitalism involved an energetic depoliticization of the issues. With politics reduced to human rights, and the insistence that these were best safeguarded through the reassertion of 'European values', crises could be extracted from the dense lattice of geopolitical and political–economic considerations to be depicted as stark morality tales. Urgency was the consistent theme: the gulag was around the corner; the genocide was coming; fascism was on the march only two hours away from Paris, or Brussels; Saddam was on a global Hitlerite mission, and might be developing nuclear weapons. With the contraction of available time came the reduction of analysis to moralism, and the narrowing of options: only war, immediate war, could work against the evildoers. The politics of good and evil (radical evil, no less) were no longer the preserve of Christian fundamentalists or neoconservatives. And thus liberals found themselves berating governments for being altogether too soft, too slow to kill, too merciful by far. They found themselves so strongly in agreement with a strand of neoconservative ideology that many of them would later simply give up the pretence of being either liberals or in any sense on the Left, and join their rightist confederates in calling for an expansion of American military power. All, of course, one is given to understand, for the good of its victims.

CONCLUSION: THE APOTHEOSIS OF HUMANITARIAN BARBARISM

The white man preaches, doses, vaccinates, assassinates and (from himself) receives absolution. With his psalms, his speeches, his guarantees of liberty, equality and fraternity, he seeks to drown the noise of his machine guns. It is no good objecting that these periods of rapine are only a necessary phase and pave the way, in the words of the time-honored formula, 'for an era of prosperity founded on a close and intelligent collaboration between the natives and the metropolis!' It is no good trying to palliate collective outrage and butchery by jury in the new colonies by inviting us to consider the old, and the peace and prosperity they have so long enjoyed.
– '*Murderous Humanitarianism*', *Surrealist Group of France, 1932*

'Americans believe that their country's role is that it supports democracy,' *Guardian* journalist Gary Younge told me.

That belief trumps all experience. All past experience is treated as subsidiary and aberrant. I don't think this is necessarily a result of the Cold War, except inasmuch as that confirmed America's historic role. It is rooted historically in colonialism, and the sense in the colonial countries of the historic role of the civilizing influence.

If this holds for Americans in general, it is particularly true of many liberal commentators, including those who were surprised by the pro-war stances taken by colleagues over Iraq. If we act as if there has been no history of centuries of white supremacy and racism, no colonial hauteur, no liberal collusion with a machinery of violent domination, then the conduct of liberals and former leftists during the 'war on terror' does indeed seem bizarre, outlandish, an affront. It is this pretence that I have sought to undermine here. Imperialism is not a distant relic, but a living reality, and the moralization of the means of violence has been the task of liberal and progressive intellectuals since they first competed with clerics for moral authority. The liberal façade is important for the empire, because those claiming to draw on leftist traditions are not, like their militarist friends on the right, sullied by having espoused principles of inequality for decades. Liberals and socialists can claim without embarrassment to support the empire because of their profound internationalism, because of their egalitarian commitments, because they hate fascism, and because they favour gender equality. A look at what they have helped to rationalize and humanize, and the means they have used to do so, suggests that the colonial habits of thinking have not left us. To cast some light also on the prominent personalities arguing in favour of war, I have sought the views of friends, colleagues, former associates and comrades, as well as of commentators sensitive to these questions.

Humanitarian intervention in an age of genocide?

The decade of 'humanitarian intervention' provided the ideological reflexes for justifying the war on Iraq. As Stephen Holmes writes,

> Having supported unilateralist intervention outside the UN framework during the 1990s, liberals and progressives are simply unable to make a credible case against Bush today . . . By denouncing the United States primarily for standing by when atrocity abroad occurs, these well-meaning liberals have helped repopularise the idea of America as a potentially benign imperial power.[1]

The doctrine of humanitarian intervention 'was absolutely new,' says Rony Brauman, former president of Médecins Sans Frontières.

> It became much easier to raise human rights as an issue. Previously, accusations in human rights terms had no consequences, or at least did not entail any military consequences. There were examples where human rights were cited in military intervention, but it was very local. It was not taken as part of a larger framework. Through the 1980s, it never came up as an issue. But as early as 1991, after the first Gulf War, it came up as an issue for the first time.[2]

Why was the 1990s the decade of 'humanitarian intervention'? One might think, listening to some commentators, that this decade was a high-water mark of unmatched genocidal outrage, characterized by

Western neglect and indifference. The bulk of Samantha Power's *A Problem From Hell*, for example, is concerned with conflicts of the 1990s, such as those in Bosnia, Rwanda and Kosovo. Though it was received by figures as diverse as David Hare and Niall Ferguson as a profound condemnation of Western policy, it actually pays no attention at all to the worst crimes of Western states,[3] some of which easily bested those that Power focuses on. Similarly, recalling the failure of the United States to ratify the Genocide Convention until 1986, Michael Ignatieff quickly explains that this 'doesn't mean that the United States fails to comply; no one has complained that the United States is currently guilty of genocide'.[4] This really depends on what one means by 'currently', of course: during the period that the United States was not a signatory to the Convention, it was certainly accused of complicity in genocide in Guatemala and East Timor; and its atrocities in Indochina were certainly closer to genocide than anything that happened in the former Yugoslavia. Moreover, while genocide was a consistent theme of the 1990s, it is not often recalled that the United States has been accused of such crimes, as a result of its leadership of the sanctions drive against Iraq, by two former administrators of the UN's 'oil-for-food' programme. And Ignatieff quite conspicuously overlooks the fact that one of the main reasons for the United States' failure to adopt the genocide conventions when they were internationally ratified in 1951 was the fear that they might be used against the United States in relation to its treatment of African-Americans because of the racist lynchings and repression in the Deep South.[5]

The assumption that the US military will have the answer to genocidal violence wherever it is occurring cannot work without this historical forgetting. Alex de Waal and Bridget Conley-Zilkic, of the Committee on Conscience at the US Holocaust Memorial Museum, have argued that this assumption is based on a narrative of 'liberation' dating from World War II, in which a predictable and inexorable genocide awaits external intervention. This narrative allows 'for only two endings: a completed genocide and a foreign military intervention'. But there are many ways in which genocidal violence is brought to an end or prevented before it begins: among them are successful resistance by the would-be targets; the weakness of the agents of genocide; fractures in the power bloc pursuing genocidal policies; and successful negotiations. As de Waal and Conley-Zilkic point out, in only a few limited cases has international intervention had any meaningful effect in thwarting genocide, among which we can count the Indian intervention in Bangladesh's liberation struggle against Pakistan, the Vietnamese invasion of Cambodia in 1979, and, of course, the Allied defeat of the Nazis. The rarity of such outcomes, and the special circumstances in which they emerged, call into question the utility of 'humanitarian intervention' as the ultimate genocide-prevention strategy.[6]

Nevertheless, an entire genre of literature has emerged on this interventionist theme, and this has helped to consolidate a consensus that has united liberals with a segment of the neoconservative Right, stemming back to the arguments that Bosnia ought to have been the occasion of early and overwhelming Western military intervention. The neoconservative campaign over Bosnia, organized forcefully through the Balkan Action Committee – the latest in an array of institutions designed to promote US interventionism, and a precursor to the Committee to Liberate Iraq – had not always been consistent with liberal humanitarianism. For example, Paul Wolfowitz, as a supporter of the Committee, criticized the Clinton administration for wasting time on interventions of no strategic importance, such as in Haiti, where the administration placed Jean-Bertrand Aristide in power in exchange for an understanding that he would accept the programme of his defeated opponent in the 1991 election.[7] In fact, while Wolfowitz can count among his admirers as a humanitarian and democrat such figures as Christopher Hitchens, Nick Cohen and the Labour MP Anne Clwyd, it is worth noting in passing that his career included extensive support for the Indonesian dictator General Suharto; and while he is sometimes credited with pushing for democracy in the Philippines, this change of policy was actually precipitated by a general uprising against the regime, which the Reagan administration saw as a threat to its military bases. Wolfowitz pleaded with the Marcos regime to reform before it was overthrown. While he used the language of democracy, he pressed hard to stop Congress from shutting off military aid to the dictatorship.[8] But the rhetoric of the humanitarian interventionists, together with the general indifference to Western crimes, proved to be congruent with the neoconservative moralization of the American empire.

In terms of scale, ongoing crimes carried out or supported by Western states throughout the 1990s (in Haiti from 1991 to 1993; Angola and Somalia from 1992 to 1994; in southern Turkey during the mid-to-late 1990s; in Algeria from 1992 to 1999; and in Colombia and East Timor at the turn of the millennium) were certainly comparable with many of the atrocities singled out as genocide in the former Yugoslavia, although they were also much smaller than the cataclysms of previous decades. In general, despite the grave peaks of atrocity in places such as Rwanda, global violence actually underwent a significant drop in the 1990s from a peak in the mid-to-late 1980s. Rather than being a response to a fresh refulgence of global violence, it seems far more plausible that the emergence of humanitarian interventionism reflected the conservative intellectual climate and the rehabilitation of imperialism throughout the 1990s. It is true that, in some crisis situations, the means for an internal solution seem scant, and this partially explains the appeal of 'humanitarian intervention'. But the claim of a right of such interventions is to insist on an asymmetrical right: it is a claim advanced by strong states against weak states. Given the obvious potential for massive abuse of such a right, even if one supposed that strong states were the appropriate instrument for curtailing humanitarian catastrophes, it is surely necessary to insist on strict limitations and standards by which any such claim might be judged. Stephen Rosskamm Shalom suggests four such conditions: 1) demonstration of credible concern about the humanitarian situation; 2) proof that force is a last resort; 3) a commitment to the minimum necessary use of violence; 4) a reasonable expectation that such use of force will minimize suffering. Questions of agency and history are paramount here. If the interventionist state in question is responsible for repeated atrocities, it is unlikely that it can be relied upon to be an auxiliary to what Alex de Waal calls 'the humanitarian international'.[9]

It could reasonably be objected that this would rule out support for practically every military intervention Western states have ever carried out; but if so, it is not at all to be lamented, given the catastrophic consequences of the carte blanche that the humanitarian interventionists have frequently allowed to those states, often to their later regret. There is a temptation to say that, given a sufficiently catastrophic situation, these stipulations ought to carry less weight. This is to say that humanitarians ought to be more willing to take risks with the lives of others by urging intervention, whatever the motives of imperial states. Precise calculations of cost and benefit are not necessarily always available, it could be argued. Sometimes, the interests of powerful states might coincide with those of oppressed groups. Let us concede that this is at least a possibility: that the strategy of one military power, even one guilty of the worst crimes, can lead to a reprieve for a threatened population. But, if we are really concerned about the fate of oppressed groups, we also have to concentrate on the other possibility: that even given the best motives, the intervention of powerful states can exacerbate the baleful conditions they were supposed to eliminate – and the burden of history suggests that we are never dealing with the best motives or even very creditable ones.

In fact, while most humanitarian interventionists cite genocide as the unanswerable, self-evident cause for intervention (and this means military intervention), they appear to have forgotten that war is itself the primary context in which genocide occurs. The sociologist Martin Shaw points out that there are inherent tendencies towards degeneration in the conduct of war, so that the category of 'civilian' is displaced and ultimately eradicated, especially where population groups are seen to shelter the enemy, or indeed are the enemy.[10] This is true not only where racial categories are explicitly applied: the degeneration of war has been visible in most long-term US engagements; and if Vietnam is the clearest possible example to date, Iraq could easily be catching up. Not only does war shade into genocide; it creates the conditions for it. This is a point one might think would be self-evident to, say, the pro-war commentator William Shawcross, whose *Sideshow* – which concerned the US bombing of Cambodia and its effects – described a classic instance of a war co-producing genocide.[11] So even – *especially* – in urgent crisis situations, the questions of agency, context, motive and history matter immensely. The strongest bias ought to be against encouraging the leaders of Western states to project international violence. And perhaps, in addition to exhibiting basic humility and recognizing that people often have resources and strategies of their own for coping with genocidal assault,[12] humanitarians ought to take responsibility for their actions. That means relying on their own solidarity efforts, rather than on the strategies of unaccountable state bodies.

It is also important to recognize that the history of imperialism yields endless examples of 'humanitarian' feeling commingling with racist contempt and murderous rage. After the attack on the Twin Towers, humanitarian claims for imperialism fused with violent fantasies of vengeance and civilizational combat. Gilbert Achcar writes of the 'narcissistic compassion' evident after the World Trade Center attacks. This compassion for 'people like us' was not only prevalent in the United States, but also in Europe, where *Le Monde*, for example, declared that 'We Are All Americans Now', while the EU declared a continent-wide day of mourning.[13] The satisfaction of killing people blamed for the attacks, which for many US troops and for much American public opinion actually includes Iraqis, was also suffused with moral outrage on behalf of the oppressed. The women of Afghanistan, no less than the Kurds and Shiites of Iraq, were to be the beneficiaries of America's expansive retort to 'al-Qaeda'. The consequences of these ventures, I will argue, bear out the claim that even the worst cases can be made all the more catastrophic by imperial violence. By contrast, the history of anti-imperialism itself shows that the melancholia of former humanitarian interventionists – particularly their sense that if the empire cannot be entrusted as a force for good, then we are stuck with a violent and despotic world – is unwarranted. Anti-colonial solidarity campaigns, it is often forgotten, are themselves a form of intervention: the state-centred prejudice which does not, for example, consider the campaign against South African apartheid a form of intervention, is misleading. In Britain, of course, this campaign originated in the anti-colonial movement. Internationalism and interventionism are terms, like humanitarianism and democracy, that have been captured for ends that are parochial and narrow, and harnessed to means that make a mockery of them. But there is no reason for us to accept this misappropriation. If young Americans like Rachel Corrie working in solidarity alongside Palestinians do not constitute an example of humanitarian intervention, then the phrase lacks all meaning.

Afghanistan

The claims of those who had argued that a dramatic humanitarian relief would be one beneficial side-effect of the occupation of Afghanistan were not to be borne out. Warning signs had been copious. The UNHCR had warned: 'We are facing a humanitarian crisis of epic proportions in Afghanistan with 7.5 million short of food and at risk of starvation.' The response of the United States to that crisis had been to demand the 'elimination of truck convoys that provide much of the food and other supplies to Afghanistan's civilian population'. Whatever else could be said about such a decision, it was not taken with the interests of those 7.5 million civilians at heart. Although that catastrophe was avoided, up to 10,000 civilians died as an immediate result of the bombing. One report for the *Guardian* in 2002 estimated that up to 49,000 could have died as an indirect result of the war.[14]

Many supporters of the war cited the return of refugees to Afghanistan as evidence of liberation – yet, at the height of the Taliban's authority, in 1998, the UNHCR was helping 107,000 refugees to return to Afghanistan. Further, a large number of those refugees who returned after 2001 were being forced back by the British and neighbouring states, despite their extreme reluctance to return. Kate Allen of Amnesty International wrote that 'with two thirds of the country unstable and covered in up to 10 million unexploded bombs and landmines', Afghanistan was not a safe country for those being forced to return. Infant and maternal mortality soared. In 2005, 20 per cent of Afghan children died before their fifth birthday, and one in seven died before their first birthday. The following year, one in four children died before the age of five. A 2007 Save the Children Fund report found that, once again, a full quarter of Afghanistan's children died under the age of five, in 70 per cent of cases due to preventable or treatable diseases, while 40 per cent of children were malnourished. The report calculated that 370,000 children were dying per year in Afghanistan.[15]

While direct civilian casualties were usually treated by military spokesmen and a pliant media as accidental, these were rooted in US military strategy. Chief Warrant Officer Dave Diaz, heading Special Forces A-Team, frankly advised his troops:

> Yes, it is a civilian village, mud hut, like everything else in this country. But don't say that. Say it's a military compound. It's a built-up area, barracks, command and control. Just like with the convoys: If it really was a convoy with civilian vehicles they were using for transport, we would just say hey, military convoy, troop transport.[16]

In fact, America's rules of engagement deliberately permitted the killing of civilians in Afghanistan. Marc Garlasco, the Pentagon's expert in high-profile targets, explained that 'if you hit 30 as the anticipated number of civilians killed, the airstrike had to go to Rumsfeld or Bush personally to sign off', but otherwise no one need ever be told.[17]

Since the overthrow of the Taliban, a government has been installed comprising war criminals such as General Abdul Rashid Dostum. A network of bribed warlords, as well as violent crooks like Jamil Jumbish, 'implicated in murder, torture, intimidation, bribery and interfering with investigations into misconduct by officers directly under his control', help hold Afghanistan together for the occupiers, while repeated and bloody war crimes have been inflicted on the civilian population by US forces. The condition of women in Afghanistan does not quite match the glowing pre-war rhetoric: stonings; child marriage; high levels of physical, mental and sexual violence all continue. From their base in Kabul, the occupiers have run a series of torture prisons, while extending courtesies to Uzbekistan – a dictatorship across the border every bit as vicious as the Taliban. As the crimes mounted, the Bush administration attempted to kill or substantially dilute the 1996 War Crimes Act, in order to reduce the prospect of US personnel being prosecuted. Little attention was paid by the supporters of the occupation to the atrocities or the attempt to legally facilitate further atrocities. Donald Rumsfeld remarked that Afghanistan was 'a breathtaking accomplishment' and 'a successful model of what could happen to Iraq'.[18]

Iraq: a brave face on things

We all recall the promises. Kanan Makiya suggested that Iraqis would greet the occupiers with 'sweets and flowers'. Christopher Hitchens was persuaded that 'a massive landing will bring food, medicine and laptop computers to a surging crowd of thankful and relieved Iraqis and Kurds' (he chose to call the introduction to his book on the matter, *The Long Short War*, 'Twenty-twenty foresight'). Democracy would flourish, and the New Iraq would set an example to others in the region. In fact, it was never at all clear that democracy was a priority in the US plans for Iraq. The State Department explained in a pre-war document: 'The towel heads can't hack it; the only way to achieve stability in the country is to install another strongman drawn from Saddam's Sunni minority.' Plans drawn up in late 2002 indicated that a long-term period of military rule was planned, perhaps under General Tommy Franks. As the US conquered Iraq, a turf war ensued between the Pentagon and the State Department over who would govern and in what fashion. It was eventually decided that retired general Jay Garner would run Iraq, and shortly thereafter Paul Bremer presided over a 'shock therapy' programme modelled on that imposed on the former Soviet Union and Yugoslavia.[19] American politicians would soon recommend the partition of Iraq on the basis that this had 'worked' in Yugoslavia. And the American government itself encouraged such ideas by using its clients in Iraq to push a sectarian constitution (with 'shock therapy' provisions included), which most Iraqis never read. Though they were able, through communalist politics, to obtain a vote for the constitution, it transpired that Iraqis had never supported any of its important provisions:

> Contrary to the impression purveyed by the media, federalism is opposed by a clear majority of Iraqis – by a majority of Sunnis and a majority of Shiites alike. According to a July 2005 survey conducted by the International Republican Institute, a US government-funded entity tasked to build the machinery of pro-free market Iraqi political parties, 69 per cent of Iraqis from across the country want the constitution to establish 'a strong central government' and only 22 per cent want it to give 'significant powers to regional governments'. Even in Shiite-majority areas in the south, only 25 per cent want federalism while 66 per cent reject it.[20]

This is typical of how things have been done in Iraq. America has no substantial support there, relying on the sectarian religious parties (and the ever-fond Kurdish leadership) to deliver the acquiescence it needs. In a patrimonial state, privileges and powers are divided among various pro-American interests. Having provided the conditions for the sectarian meltdown of Iraq alongside the ruinous counterinsurgency campaign, the American political class would go on to vote for a bill supporting the federal partition of Iraq – a policy which, if implemented, was sure to accelerate the ethnic cleansing already in process, and which was opposed by the vast majority of Iraqis. In fact, it was even opposed by the pro-US leadership of Iraq. The policy, its main sponsor Senator Biden explained, was inspired by the example of Bosnia.[21] When Biden heard of the Iraqi leadership's opposition to the plans, he retorted in stout colonial fashion: 'I don't know who the hell they think they are. We have a right. We've expended our blood and treasure in order to back their commitment to their constitution. That's the deal.'[22]

By 2004 at the latest, it was becoming clear that the invasion was not only a failure on the terms of its original sale – locating WMD, primarily – but actually a growing catastrophe on almost every index. The *Lancet*'s first peer-reviewed survey, in October 2004, studying excess deaths resulting from the war had shown that the occupation was worse than the combined effect of Saddam Hussein and sanctions – 100,000 worse, and growing. The second set of statistics, released in 2006, showed that the rate of death, especially violent death, had increased dramatically, and that the overall figure for excess death was approximately 655,000, 600,000 of which were violent deaths. Not only were the figures devastating in themselves, but the trend they spoke of was terrifying: the death rate was *doubling* each year. This trend seemed to be confirmed in September 2007, when research by the polling organization ORB found that 16 per cent of Iraqi households had experienced a violent death – a figure, they said, that corresponded to 1.2 million violent deaths since 2003. Despite some half-hearted efforts to discredit the *Lancet*'s statistics, it later emerged that the UK Ministry of Defence's senior scientist had advised the British government that the science behind the statistics could not be faulted.[23]

Many were shocked at the scale of the violence disclosed by these reports. It had barely registered in media reports, and then generally only if it could be attributed to insurgents; but a number of reports emerged to provide the background for this colossal loss of life. Following revelations about US planners considering a 'Salvador

Option',[24] in which the kinds of terror and atrocities visited on El Salvador by US-backed death squads might now be unleashed in Iraq, it emerged that the Special Police Corps (SPC), an Iraqi paramilitary outfit created and maintained by the US military's General David Petraeus,[25] were behind a large number of death-squad killings. The function of the SPC appears to be similar to that of the military structures created in several Latin American and Caribbean countries by the United States before and during the Cold War: ruthless counterinsurgency.[26] Though US soldiers are routinely noted for their experience of working with the SPC, and General Petraeus has applauded them, they have been accused by the UN of the filthiest crimes: torture, mutilation, and murder. The SPC is largely recruited from Saddam's former Republican Guard units and the Badr Corps, a Shiite sectarian militia.[27] In fact, the commandos are so brazen about their killings that that they are reported to have contacted Baghdad morgue, after having murdered someone and dumped the body, to demand the return of the metal handcuffs on the grounds that they are too expensive to replace. Reports of a 'secret' air war, with high levels of explosives being dropped on civilian areas, confirmed the estimate in the *Lancet*'s report that a large number of people were dying from regular aerial assault.[28]

And then, of course there were the set-piece assaults by the United States on cities and towns in Iraq. Fallujah was the worst of these, and emblematic of the entire occupation. Although it had been one of the most peaceful cities in the early months of the occupation, the first violent scenes broke out when, on 28 April 2003, US forces shot at a peaceful demonstration against the American decision to occupy a local school. Not only were people shot at for protesting, with twenty killed; shots were also fired at those trying to recover the bodies, and ambulance crews came under fire. Protests continued, and became more militant. Some 30 km away, prisoners were being subjected to torture at Abu Ghraib, and this became a critical factor in the development of local unrest. The killing and mutilation of US contractors in Fallujah on 31 March 2004 produced an outcry, and from then on the US treated the city as off-limits to reporters. It initiated an attempt to capture the city in April 2004, known as Operation Vigilant Resolve, during which it killed 600 Iraqis; but it ended up retreating as crowds of Fallujans demonstrated in victory.

From then on, the US subjected the city to repeated raids and assaults and, in November 2004, launched its most fearsome assault yet, known as Operation Phantom Fury. In the prelude to the attack, the US bombed the city to force those inhabitants who could to flee, and then sealed it off to prevent those remaining from escaping. War crimes such as the bombing of one hospital and the military take-over of another were openly reported, but less well reported were the beatings carried out on doctors and the attacks on ambulances. It later emerged that the US had used white phosphorus, a chemical that burns the flesh and melts right down to the bone. NGO estimates maintained that between 4,000 and 6,000 were killed in the assault, and that 36,000 houses, 9,000 shops, 65 mosques and 60 schools were demolished. And although the operation had been justified by the need to evict an 'al-Qaeda' cell said to be operating in the city, the leaders of the resistance there were found to be local. As the 350,000 dispossessed refugees were filtered back into the city, subjected to bio-metric scanning and prepared for forced labour, they still had to hear that it was all for their own good.[29]

Although the torture of prisoners at Abu Ghraib was widely reported – if not well reported – the continuation of this practice was barely mentioned. In a prison complex known as Camp Mercury on the outskirts of Fallujah, prisoners continued to be detained and subjected to brutal torture, known to soldiers as 'fucking' them. The ACLU gained sworn testimony that soldiers regularly 'beat the fuck out of' detainees. Later, US soldiers would go on record as saying that the deliberate and often random murder of Iraqis was a habitual occurrence, often legitimized with racist rhetoric about 'hajis'.[30]

In mid 2007 an extensively researched report by thirty NGOs for the Global Policy Forum described various aspects of the war on Iraq, but particularly the modus operandi of the occupiers when it came to assailing major towns and cities.[31] The report found that, when the US wished to subdue a main population centre in Iraq, its main techniques were as follows: 1) *encircle and close off the city*, as in Fallujah and Tal Afar, where they built an eight-foot-high wall around the entire city before pulverizing it. Colonel Nathan Sassaman described the approach quite bluntly in the early months of the occupation: 'With a heavy dose of fear and violence, and a lot of money for projects, I think we can convince these people that we are here to help them'; 2) *forcefully evacuate those who remain*, as in Fallujah and Ramadi; 3) *cut off food, water and electricity*, as in Fallujah, Tal Afar and Samarra; 4) *confine reporters and block media coverage*, with the sys-tematic exclusion of all non-embedded reporters during such assaults; 5) *conduct intense bombardment*, usually targeting the infrastructure; 6) *conduct a massive urban assault, using sniper fire, and put survivors through violent searches*; 7) *attack hospitals, ambulances and other medical facilities*. The defiling of cities and towns throughout Iraq could do little but cause massive deaths, injuries, refugee flows, chaos and, ultimately, violent resistance.

Abandoning the fight

As a result of the horrifying escalation, there came to be a number of apostates on the liberal imperialist wing as the war went on. By the time the second survey from Johns Hopkins University on Iraqi mortality was released in 2006, for example, Norman Geras explained that, had he been able to foresee such results, he 'would have withheld support for the war without giving my voice to the opposition to it' – a curious position, given that Geras devoted much of his writing in the 1990s to denouncing the evil of standing by passively in the face of catastrophe. Geras had by that point undertaken a different project, anyway. Alongside *Observer* columnist Nick Cohen and a raft of former far leftists, he drafted the 'Euston Manifesto'.[32] This was widely interpreted as an attempt to galvanize flagging support for the Iraq war, and though the organizers protest that this is not the case, the requirement that signatories commit themselves to the view that the invasion constituted a 'liberation' for Iraqis surely allowed no other conclusion.

The Manifesto was received with much hostile fire, and some bemusement. 'The one thing I found curious about the Euston Manifesto', Gary Younge said,

> was how disorganic it was. Usually such initiatives are introduced in order to bring legitimacy to a marginalized idea. People thrash out an agenda in a pub because there is nowhere else for them to do it. What the Euston people were doing was trying to provide intellectual ballast for a government project. They could just as easily have held their meeting at Downing Street or in parliament. Weirder still they had decided to tie their principle to a sinking ship – namely Iraq.[33]

Producing few ripples beyond the United Kingdom (a number of American commentators I spoke to had no idea what it was), the effort was even casually dismissed by the cautious 'patriotic' liberal Todd Gitlin, who declared: 'I recognize a shoddy piece of intellectual patchwork when I see one'.[34]

However shoddy the Manifesto may be, it did provide a focus for organizing a small, disarticulated group of disgruntled liberals – intellectuals committed to social democracy at home and humanitarian imperialism overseas. Their activities often overlap with those of other groups, like Engage, an internet claque composed of intellectuals supportive of Israel, and the neoconservative Henry Jackson Foundation, a British alliance including military figures, Labour and Tory MPs, and elements of the commentariat. Several signatories to the Euston Manifesto are also members of the Henry Jackson society, and the Eustonians have often coordinated their campaigns with the Jacksonites. At the Labour Party conference in 2007, a fringe meeting on 'winning the battle of hearts and minds against Islamism' was organized by both groups. It is the opposition to 'Islamism' that has particularly won the hearts of neoconservatives. Thus Michael Gove, columnist and Conservative MP, welcomed the 'anti-Islamist intelligentsia' that was challenging 'left-liberal appeasement'.[35]

The Euston group's activities also extend to defending Israel from the predations of the pro-Palestinian Left. When several British trade unions responded to a call from Palestinian trade unionists for a boycott of Israeli institutions by launching a debate on the tactic, the Eustonians coordinated with Engage to campaign against any such moves. In fact, when the lecturers' union, the UCU, voted overwhelmingly to proceed with a national debate on a boycott, it stimulated an immediate round of condemnations, including from the union's own head, and was followed by a campaign that involved legal threats from various quarters, including the American pro-Israel polemicist Alan Dershowitz. Over 450 pro-Israel academics weighed in – especially in the United States. After a prolonged fight, the UCU leadership announced that, on the basis of legal advice it had received, it was abandoning even holding the debate.[36]

A number of the Eustonians are not only pro-war and pro-Israel, but openly pro-Bush. One signatory, Gisela Stuart MP, risked the wrath of fellow parliamentarians by declaring before the November 2004 presidential election that a Kerry victory would produce 'victory celebrations among those who want to destroy liberal democracies'. Another declared that Kerry was an 'obscurantist reactionary' because of his belated and very mild criticisms of the war on Iraq.[37] Of course, not all of the signatories would agree with such a position, but most appear to be supporters of the war on Iraq, and the 'war on terror' more generally. As increasing numbers of pro-war liberals decide that they can no longer defend their support for the invasion of Iraq, the Euston group provides a counter-pressure against the shift to the Left that the antiwar movement has produced. It invites antiwar liberals to sign up to its principles and its denunciation of the larger part of the Left. The group enables a form of networking among co-ideologues. They can sustain their confidence and ideas in an unfriendly political atmosphere, and reinforce one another's arguments. These are not the CIA socialists of the Cold War – they're of a slightly lower stamp than that – but they are at least analogous.

However, for many former interventionists the enterprise of liberal imperialism is utterly tainted. David Rieff, who had made a reputation as a liberal interventionist in the Balkans, was finished with the whole enterprise by the time it arrived in Iraq. He explained that 'I realized I was seeing the rebirth of imperialism with human rights as its moral warrant'. Although Rieff still continues to bash the hard Left and Noam Chomsky (a signal that he remains 'responsible', perhaps), his critique of the humanitarian interventionism he once espoused is sometimes damning. Though he remains convinced that some interventions in the 1990s were necessary, he is no longer the same polemicist who called for 'one, two, three, many Kosovos', a 'new liberal imperialism'. Critical of the liberal–reactionary coalition on Darfur, he derides the simple moralism of the language used (particularly the racist bromides about 'Arabs killing black Africans'), and insists that the invocation of 'genocide' to describe massacres not only dilutes the term (if every massacre is a genocide, then every intrastate war is a genocide – indeed, one could justifiably accuse the US of committing genocide in Iraq), but is morally calamitous in that it produces action which may not be apt. He has been scathing about humanitarian and lobby organizations that have sought to simplify the conflict in Sudan, the better to mobilize calls for intervention.[38]

Inspired by Rieff's arguments, Rony Brauman takes an equally critical approach to the hubris of 'humanitarian' arguments for war. Brauman had supported humanitarian interventions in Rwanda and Bosnia, in the latter case on other than humanitarian grounds.

> I was a supporter of military intervention for two reasons – as a European and as an antitotalitarian. As Europeans, we had to show that it was forbidden to establish any programme based on the combination of race and force. In the situation after the fall of the Berlin Wall, new political forces were emerging, and so a signal had to be sent. I insist this is about Europe – it is not a universalist claim, it is not humanitarian. Humanitarian discourse had a certain role because it was invoked when UNPROFOR was sent in, but this was a smoke-screen. There was no protection involved. It was a humanitarian alibi.

Brauman is particularly scathing about an approach that mixes the humanitarian approach embodied by organizations such as MSF with the human rights discourse invoked to support war – in other words an approach that treats war as an extension of humanitarian operations. This approach

> is one that can set fire to a situation. Darfur was a very good example of this. The human rights NGOs said there was a mass campaign of rapes, and atrocities including genocidal war. The whole thing was depicted as like Central Europe under the Nazi regime. That was the permanent intellectual background. Now, I will not defend Khartoum – but the situation was not as human rights groups depicted it.

This is a key problem with the contemporary 'humanitarian interventionists'. 'Bernard Kouchner [a former president of MSF, and current French foreign secretary] is an example of this dangerous mixture of the humanitarian approach with the human rights discourse.' Brauman insists that, although the references to Nazi Germany are ubiquitous, they are 'instrumental'.

> We have to take into account that it is a very easy argument to say 'Nazi' and 'genocide' – then the curtain falls, you have to act, there is no time to reflect, and all thought is discredited. This is why I don't think of the new philosophers as philosophers. Philosophers are supposed to reflect. They may be new, but they are not philosophers!

Indeed, as Kristin Ross points out, urgency is a particularly valuable currency for the *nouveau philosophes*. Or, as Bernard-Henri Lévy puts it, 'Urgency today is a genre in itself.'[39] Brauman argues that the interventionists all too often see war as a panacea, and much of this perspective originates in outdated imperial attitudes.

> I think the main thing is about keeping in mind the people you intend to help – how far do you think it is your role to liberate mankind? If you think Burmese or Iraqis are just passive people enduring dictatorship, this makes sense, but it is a very old liberal way of seeing things. I rely on people liberating themselves and building their own history. This takes us back to the civilizing mission, because this was serious, the Left was pro-colonial.

Often it was the Right who opposed wars on narrow, economistic grounds.[40]

Some North American liberals who had supported the war were coming to accept a similar critique of humanitarian hubris. By early 2007, the formerly pro-war liberal Peter Beinart concluded in a despairing passage that

> We can't be the country those Iraqis wanted us to be. We lack the wisdom and the virtue to remake the world through preventive war. That's why a liberal international order, like a liberal domestic one, restrains the use of force – because it assumes that no nation is governed by angels, including our own. And it's why liberals must be anti-utopian, because the United States cannot be a benign power and a messianic one at the same time.[41]

Michael Ignatieff finally abandoned his support for the war in 2007, although, like Michael Walzer, like Schlesinger, like the Fabians, like most of his predecessors, he insisted that ending the war would have worse consequences than continuing it:

> Staying and leaving each have huge costs. One thing is clear: The costs of staying will be borne by Americans, while the cost of leaving will be mostly borne by Iraqis. That in itself suggests how American leaders are likely to decide the question.

In fact, Ignatieff shows no sign of understanding why he went wrong. He says that he 'let emotion carry me past the hard questions, like: Can Kurds, Sunnis and Shiites hold together in peace what Saddam Hussein held together by terror?' This strongly implies that Iraqis have proved themselves to be incapable of self-government, and so should be ruled through terror – a conclusion that Wilson would have understood, and certainly one that is congruent with the argument of neoconservatives that self-government is a precious cultural state that may not be available to everyone. Almost 90 per cent of the apology was not about Iraq, in fact. Rather, it was an extended, self-serving rumination on the nature of politics and the political career (namely, his political career – the one that suffered a setback when he failed to win the vote for the leadership of the Canadian Liberal Party, largely on account of his support for the Iraq war). He even hinted that he might not be entirely sincere about anything he says: 'Nothing is personal in politics, because politics is theater. It is part of the job to pretend to have emotions that you do not actually feel.' But nevertheless, he claimed to be 'worthy of trust' because he has not had a 'charmed life' like the American president, and is a man of sorrow 'acquainted with grief, as the prophet Isaiah says'. (Isaiah did indeed say this (53:3) – about the Messiah: What exactly is Ignatieff trying to tell us?) And, whatever his criticisms of the Iraq misadventure, Ignatieff remained one of the few Liberal allies of the Canadian conservative government over the prolonged mission in Afghanistan.[42]

Johann Hari, a British liberal commentator, had been enthusiastically pro-war. Not only did he think America could bring democracy to Iraq; he was also convinced that a few bombs dropped on North Korea would not go amiss.[43] Hari still accepts most of the arguments advanced by the belligerati, but finds the basic fault in their shortsightedness about neoconservatism:

> I think the unfortunate thing about so many of the pro-war Left is that they have degenerated into caricatures. They recognized the crucial importance of Islamic fundamentalism and the fact that it is an analogue to fascism. That was a correct insight. However, then you have to be careful not to support something that makes it worse. You might support people you disagree with as part of an alliance against fascism, but then you still have to say where you disagree with them. Not so with people like Christopher Hitchens or Nick Cohen: they go far further than is necessary by acting as if explanation of the circumstances that produce fundamentalism is itself the act of an apologist. Baathism is analogous to fascism as well, which is another reading that the pro-war Left got right. So, by all means be with the anti-fascist power, whoever that happens to be. However, these insights are negated by the reliance on neoconservatism as the force to carry out that fight. And quite often these commentators slipped into coyly or openly supporting neoconservatism.

Was this the only reason why the war on Iraq failed?

> What went wrong in Iraq is a combination of things. It should have been obvious from the beginning – it should have been to me, but it wasn't – that the neoconservatives didn't mean what they said. And one obvious problem right away was the economic programme they tried to impose. I interviewed Joseph Stiglitz, and he said it's as if they looked at what happened in the former

Soviet Union and thought 'great idea'. Any country you impose that on is going to go up. If you had 70 per cent unemployment in Britain today, there'd probably be a guerrilla war happening here.[44]

It is true that the US developed some its techniques of state-building and economic restructuring during its interventions into the former Yugoslavia, as well as Russia and the Eastern Bloc. But there still seems to be something odd about Hari's argument, which raises the comparison between Islamic fundamentalism, Baathism and fascism. It is clear enough why people see similarities between these phenomena, even if these are imprecise. It is not clear how far the analogy can be stretched: to take the side of the 'anti-fascist' power in the 1930s is a very different thing to taking the side of the United States as it invades Iraq. Yet this is an extremely commonplace argument. Vivek Chibber, a sociologist and expert in imperial history, says:

Of course Islamic fundamentalism is totalitarian, but the United States ruling class is obviously not worried about it as a threat, otherwise they would not be undertaking policies guaranteed to increase its incidence. What they're worried about is popular nationalism.

Chibber argues that the vocal stirrings of the 'pro-war Left' after 2001 were really nothing new.

What happened through the 1970s and 1980s was a brief lull in imperial ideology in the intelligentsia. It became *verboten* to openly call for military aggression. Slowly after 1989, such support for aggression increasingly came out in the open. Previously this had been the norm, but that was interrupted by Vietnam and the New Left had real effects because militarists are much more embattled now than they were before.

The current tendency, he claims, has its origins in the dilemma of the American intelligentsia: 'It has no base in an organized Left. There is no national organizational affiliation, so [intellectuals] gravitate toward centres of power.' And their advocacy will continue to be important:

The position advocated by Niall Ferguson espousing a formal empire with colonies was a non-starter for US policymakers. That's not on the cards, even without the debacle in Iraq. What is going to be around is open advocacy for US imperialism along the lines advocated by Walzer et al. American culture is genuinely liberal, so it is hard to get support for openly militaristic or fascistic policies.[45]

Liza Featherstone of the *Nation* argues that the function of the pro-war liberals is to

> legitimize war among the intellectual set. Iraq had been the obsession of a small number of very right-wing people, and liberal support did give it more legitimacy than it would have had. It relieved pressure on the Democrats to dissent and removed it from the realm of a fruitcake right-wing obsession.

Although much of the impetus behind support for the invasion of Iraq originates in liberal opinion over the former Yugoslavia,

> in some ways it is a dynamic of former leftists, not liberals. Someone like Hitchens, for example, is animated by his 'revolutionary zeal'. There is also an absolutely strong tradition of labour unions supporting imperialism. For example, the Solidarity Center was involved in fighting the Soviet Union and so on.[46]

Imperial feminism was 'very important', although

> most feminist groups were stalwartly opposed to the war on Iraq. There were some prominent figures like Phyllis Chesler, a very important feminist author who had become more and more right-wing, and eventually ended up supporting the Bush administration in Iraq. But while some feminists were ambivalent on Afghanistan, most were very strongly opposed to the invasion of Iraq. Laura Bush basically used feminism, but was pretty rapidly discredited by feminists, which was easy because the Bush administration had de-funded family planning clinics and abortions, and diverted funds to missionaries.[47]

Indeed, despite the attempt to invest the war on Afghanistan with a feminist flavour, the administration had not only reinforced traditional patriarchy in Afghanistan but had helped construct a new one in Iraq. It is indeed strange to consider US Marines as the bearers of women's liberation. However, as Zillah Eisenstein points out, to some extent the successes of women in America and their access to a greater variety of roles has permitted the use of 'sexual decoys': that is, there may well be women in the military, and some of them will end up helping out with the torture at Abu Ghraib, but this only serves to mask what remains a deeply masculinist enterprise.[48]

Where the pro-war intellectuals did not retreat, they slipped into denial. To this day, Kanan Makiya maintains that Chalabi is the right man to lead Iraq: 'He's the most likely of all those capable of leading Iraq to go in a democratic direction'. He told *The American Prospect* in May 2007: 'Of course I still support the war . . . How can I not? I don't know an Iraqi who doesn't.' This confirmed what many must have suspected all along – Kanan Makiya does not know many Iraqis. If hundreds of thousands of deaths, torture chambers, rapes, casual murders, 4 million refugees and a vicious sectarian war co-sponsored by the occupying forces could not dissuade Kanan Makiya from believing in the justice of the war, nothing could. He had invested too much, in any case, having been recruited by the State Department to participate in the Future of Iraq Project, which devised plans for a post-war Mesopotamia. Together with a few confederates, such as Salem Chalabi (Ahmed's nephew), he had practically taken over the writing of the report, with the aim of producing a transition 'from totalitarianism to democracy'. The aim, it seems, was to empower Ahmed Chalabi, Iraq's 'one democrat' according to Makiya. Initially, Makiya complained that Ahmed was being sidelined, and worried for a brief while that the administration would either back off from the war, or would stop short of full democracy. However, having met President Bush, Condoleezza Rice and Dick Cheney on 19 January 2003, he emerged 'deeply reassured'. However disappointed he is, Makiya proclaims that the 'ideas were fundamentally all there and sound'. The blame rests, if anywhere, on Iraqis and on exile politicians who demonstrated insufficient 'character'.[49]

Makiya's position is a perfectly logical one for him to take. His campaign to help the American government implant a liberal state in Iraq made sense if the sole source of repression and political fear was simply the concentration of power in the hands of a ruthless party machine. This perspective also made the de-Baathification policy comprehensible.[50] And, after all, since the US introduced pluralist political institutions with competition, a number of newspapers with opposing points of view, and even elections, then Iraq ought to be a success. Unless one is prepared to subscribe to a racist view that Iraqis are incapable of self-government, which is a step Makiya is not prepared to take, then either the sociological analysis underpinning the support for liberal imperialism was wrong, or there must have been a series of catastrophic errors. It seems in fact that Makiya's 'anti-totalitarian' account of tyranny in Iraq misconstrued the nature of the dictatorship, obscuring its sociological base. His faith in the American government was misplaced, and his rejection of the critique of imperialism, meant that he was unable to understand why Iraqis would resist the occupation. Meanwhile his newly acquired political liberalism gave him no reason to expect that civil society institutions, political competition and an adversarial separation of powers could become vectors for the promulgation of a new form of terror.

Makiya thus bears some responsibility for helping to frame, intellectually and organizationally, the Bush administration's destruction of Iraq. Unsurprisingly, it is a responsibility that he has declined to accept. Nevertheless, the spectacle of some liberals trying to blame their support for the war on Makiya was hardly more edifying. George Packer's book, *The Assassin's Gate*, is an extended eulogy for Makiya, and an attempt to show that Packer's own support for the war originated from his romance with the Iraqi Solzhenitsyn – as he is so often dubbed – and his vision for a beautiful, liberal Iraq. Peter Beinart, for whom Cold War liberalism could not be resuscitated fast enough, finally imploded into self-pitying despair. He had supported the war on Iraq, he said, 'because Kanan Makiya did'.[51]

Still, let us accept that Makiya was an inspiration for many who were already ideologically disposed to support 'humanitarian' wars. What explains his enduring faith in the redeeming power of American might? Gilbert Achcar, one of Makiya's former friends and comrades, says the following:

> There are really two views about Kanan. One of them is that he is a careerist, and the other, my own view, is that he tended always to be politically naive. These assessments are not incompatible, of course. One can find a certain degree of careerism in his attitude: not the appeal of money – he comes from a wealthy family – but rather the appeal of prestige, social and intellectual status, access to the *New York Times* and *Washington Post*, etc.

Indeed, the book that made Makiya an 'Iraqi Solzhenitsyn' had the enormous good fortune of roughly coinciding with a war on Iraq.

> *Republic of Fear* put a view that was very much influenced by anti-totalitarian literature. The basic historical information is reasonably accurate, and the Iraqi Baathist regime was certainly one of the most ruthless and terrible, a quasi-fascistic regime, but

Makiya's view overstated the case, displaying the same flaws that usually characterize anti-totalitarian ideology. The book didn't make much noise initially, when it came out in 1989, but was hugely promoted after the invasion of Kuwait in August 1990. Makiya was projected to celebrity status, invited to television debates, and I think he enjoyed that role. He got support from Kuwaiti sources. After that, he became associated with Chalabi and the Iraqi National Congress, moved to the States and got a position at Brandeis. When he moved to America, this only increased his sense of his own importance. But I tend to think that he sincerely believed most of the views he put forward later, in the run-up to the US invasion of Iraq in 2003. He was naive enough to believe in Chalabi, who is a Machiavellian crook, and he helped provide respectability and intellectual cover. Chalabi has used him. Washington planners had no clue about Iraq: with the help of Makiya, Chalabi got them to believe that it would be a remake of post-1945 Germany. The disillusionment was bitter – and tragic for the Iraqi people. I think Makiya himself is now bitterly disappointed. His recent statements reflect an acknowledgment of defeat.

If some blamed Makiya for their errors, others were quick to eschew responsibility for their decisions. Paul Berman mused that 'it's extremely hard to judge what the people in the administration really do think. On what points are they sincere? On what points are they hypocritical? They haven't allowed us to be able to tell.'[52] True enough, politicians occasionally allow misapprehensions about their actual intentions – but surely it cannot be so difficult to make an assessment, even if purely provisional, about how seriously one can take them? For instance, many of the administration's leading figures were active in destroying Central America in the 1980s, a fact that Berman presumably acknowledges. One or two of them were involved in assisting Saddam Hussein's war on Iran in the same decade. Wolfowitz, sometimes construed as a 'sincere' democrat, spent much of the 1990s covering up for the Indonesian dictatorship, as we have already noted. The Bush administration had already given an indication of how much it prized democracy when it supported a rightist coup in Venezuela. Its closest allies included torturers and murderers, such as Islam Karimov of Uzbekistan. Still, Berman chose to believe, and trust. In Spring 2007, he still insisted: 'Bush and his administration did sincerely desire to achieve a democratic outcome in Iraq'.[53]

Christopher Hitchens, faced with the *Lancet*'s first set of statistics on excess mortality in Iraq in 2004, described them as 'politicised hack-work', a 'crazed' fabrication, whose conclusions had been 'conclusively and absolutely shown to be false'. When presented with the results of the second *Lancet* survey in 2006, Hitchens abandoned Lysenkoism for sophistry: now, the devastating results were merely proof of how evil the enemy was. This bizarre abdication of basic intellectual honesty was perhaps a logical necessity, given the vindictiveness of Hitchens's apostasy, and the increasing stridency and swaying bellicosity of his rhetoric as the war on Iraq had begun. As liberation was being exposed as a hollow lie, Hitchens derided the antiwar Left for depriving itself of the 'pleasure and privilege' of 'seeing the faces and hearing the voices of Iraqis and Kurds who had undergone the once in a lifetime experience of human liberation'. Today, Hitchens declares himself 'coarsened and sickened by the degeneration of the struggle', which he compares to the Spanish Civil War.[54]

I spoke to a number of people who had known Hitchens, or could be counted as sympathetic. There is general agreement that two episodes in the 1990s – the war in Bosnia and the impeachment of Bill Clinton – pushed Hitchens to the right, but most also agree that Hitchens is idiosyncratic. 'Hitchens is different', the urban theorist Mike Davis told me, 'he's a unique case. Historically people break from the far Left and end up on the far Right. Christopher Hitchens isn't like that; he continues to attack many of the idols of the Right, including God himself.' Alex Callinicos, who knew Hitchens at Balliol when his sobriquet was 'Hypocritchens' on account of his tendency to march with the socialists and dine with the rich, agrees: 'What strikes me is the effort he makes to be consistent. If you wanted to find a well-known columnist who would go on the radio today and defend Leon Trotsky, he's the one who would do it.'

Hitchens has sometimes been accused of careerism. Upward class mobility does indeed seem to be important to him. He once related to Ian Parker of the *New Yorker* an argument he had overheard between his parents, in which his mother exclaimed: 'If there is going to be a ruling class in this country, then Christopher is going to be in it.'[55] But there are easier ways to make a living than by defending a Russian revolutionary and publicly enjoying the death of Jerry Falwell. Mike Davis suggests that Hitchens is animated by a variety of conflicting drives:

> I knew Hitchens briefly in the 1990s. He was a charming and big-hearted guy. He had a tendency to develop profound emotional attachments to Third World groups, particularly the Cypriots and the Kurds, and I think that eventually blinded him to the reality of American wars. He has created this 'contrarian' niche but is its

only true inhabitant: he supported Wolfowitz and the neoconservatives in the invasion of Iraq, but on the other hand maintains his fierce critique of Nixon and Kissinger and their responsibility for genocide in Southeast Asia. Whereas all the other pro-war liberal forces gravitated around the belief that a realistic Left has to cling to the centre-right mainstream, Hitchens is an unpredictable maverick. On some days, he sounds like an editorial in the *Weekly Standard*; on others, he's recalling his collaboration with the *New Left Review* with genuine nostalgia. The problem, of course, is that the Left once adored Christopher for his brilliant better angel, while the neocons only like him as self-caricature: the eloquent British drunk. I suppose he reminds me of Dylan Thomas a little. He certainly shares Thomas's perverse delight in baiting angry audiences and head-butting his critics.

'Hitchens is drawn to dynamism', Adam Shatz suggested,

> to the forces that are actually reshaping the world. I suspect that to him the radical Left increasingly looked like a group of outsiders, losers, and he was tired of the association. It was a short step to embracing revolutionary neoconservatism, which had energy and power on its side.

Sasha Abramsky, author and colleague of Hitchens from his days at the *Nation*, considers his appeal: 'There's almost something Churchillian about him. He was always very articulate and very good at thinking on his feet, but it's his image as the Bad Boy Brit that makes him exotic to American audiences.' As far as his political transformation is concerned,

> there was probably a gradual recalibration after 1989, especially when it came to Bosnia, where the criticism of the United States was its abnegation of its international responsibilities. But there really was a schism over Clinton, and I guess that a lot of it is personal bitterness, because Christopher was utterly ostracized, and the diatribes against him were often really nasty. He was unapologetic in his distaste for Clinton, but it was sometimes very weird – he identified real flaws, but was more hateful to him than he is to Bush.

Hitchens's resistance to cliché and kitsch has its limits, however. He has gravitated towards the neoconservatives, features frequently on right-wing talk-shows, and is regularly seen with David Horowitz. In his trajectory, he shares much with those neoconservatives for whom the 'culture wars' are less important than American power overseas. And even his attempted efforts at consistency do not always place him on the Left. For example, he was an ardent supporter of Thatcher's war with Argentina over the latter's repossession of the Falkland Islands, a tiny outpost of Britain's empire. The Malvinas conflict produced an extraordinary recrudescence of imperial feeling in Britain, and was in fact widely supported on the Left.

Hitchens, who had been on the far Left since the late 1960s, had already disagreed with his comrades in the Socialist Workers' Party over support for the far Left in the Portuguese revolution. 'He did criticize me for talking about a "dictatorship of the proletariat",' Alex Callinicos recalls. 'I think at that point he had become a left-wing social democrat. It was moving to the United States, I think – the belly of the beast as it were – that shifted him to the left again.' He had left the Party for good by the time he gave his approbation to the Falklands War – on the grounds that General Galtieri was a fascist whose regime would be weakened by defeat.

One-time colleague Alexander Cockburn is convinced that Hitchens always had an affinity for empire:

> Hitchens was on a trajectory toward this for quite a long time. He has always had this crude Marxist stageist view of history, and he now applies this to Iraq – so the 'Islamofascists' have to give way to secular, historically progressive forces that the US supposedly represents.

With only a hint of the lack of generosity of spirit that has often characterized Hitchens himself, Cockburn urges that he be left behind:

> People seem to have an obsession about him – you know, 'the Hitch'. I don't get it, it's almost like a sex thing. He's not a very good writer. If you've read him, you know he has a couple of tricks that he always uses. He's not that funny either. Increasingly he's a very boorish personality – but there was always an element of that in private.

One other topic on which Hitchens has indeed always been consistent is his hostility to religion. His anti-theistic polemic, *God Is Not Great*, features many of the same themes, and sometimes the same one-liners, that appeared in his 1980s writing on the topic, not to mention his brisk overturning of Mother Teresa's saintly reputation in *The Missionary Position*. His hostility to Islam can be dated to the fatwa against his friend Salman Rushdie. The current anti-theism now bears new freight, however. It has become the means by which Hitchens interprets the 'war on terror' in its favour. It is a war, as he sees it, with a degenerate version of a religion that he regards as corrupted in its very origins. Maintaining this approach requires considerable self-discipline and practised purblindness. Hitchens has been known to boast that he knew he was an atheist at the age of nine, but Corey Robin argues that Hitchens's strident commentary represents a slide in the quality of his argument.

> When you compare what he used to write in the 1980s with what he writes today, the language has become degraded. Hitchens maintains that you have to be against religion if you are in favour of reason, as if rational cogitation were not a part of religion. How can you understand the survival of a religion over thousands of years without there being arguments and debate, grounded in some form of reason? How is a jurisprudence based in religion, of which there are many, supposed to develop through that period without substantial elaboration? No collective human experience works like this and a millennium is a very long time.[56]

But the reality is worse than that. When Hitchens endorses the neoconservative Mark Steyn's paranoid ruminations on the rate at which Muslims are giving birth, he does not simply engage in an oversimplified and essentialist reading of Islam, or blame religion for Bush's policies. At this point, he begins to portray the Muslim population itself as an enemy. So, when young Muslims rioted in protest against police brutality in France, Hitchens offered the following verdict: 'If you think that the intifada in France is about housing, go and try covering the story wearing a yarmulke.'[57] The stereotype of French Muslims being particularly anti-Semitic (or even *fascistic*, according to some) would be an important factor in converting a number of France's pro-war intellectuals to full-blown *sarkozysme*.

The French 'anti-totalitarians' turn to Le petit Nicolas

The 1990s was a golden decade for the French ex-*gauchistes*. It was an era in which the death of left–right distinctions was widely rumoured, and yet one in which the 'totalitarian' threat managed to assume new guises. The discourse of 'human rights' had assumed a new prominence. Most of these figures continued to be associated with the

Socialist Party, however. But now, apparently furious with old Socialist and Gaullist establishment leaders for having half-heartedly opposed the war on Iraq, a number of the former leftists decided throw in their lot with Nicolas Sarkozy's hard-right presidential campaign in 2007.

One of the key issues was the perceived eclipse of pro-Israeli sentiment in French politics. Sarkozy successfully captured a disgruntled layer of supporters of Israel, including many of the pro-war intellectuals. This alignment has its origins in global dynamics, but also in developments distinctive to France. Dominique Vidal, a journalist at *Le Monde diplomatique*, explained some of the historical background:

> French policy before 1948 was very hesitant toward the Palestinian question. Most of the French leaders – with the exception of Zionists – were afraid that helping Israel could lead to huge problems in the 'French' North Africa. So, Paris was one of the last capitals to vote for partition, under blackmail from the United States – if you want the Marshall Plan, you must support the partition of Palestine. Yet, from the 1950s to 1967, France was the biggest ally of Israel, for a number of reasons. Vichy had taken a very active part in the genocide of Jews. The Jews were not arrested and deported by the Germans, but by the French police or *Milice*. Seventy-five thousand (of 330,000) were deported, 3,000 came back. So, there was guilt. The second reason is that France after World War II had big problems in Tunisia, Morocco and above all Algeria. They thought that the Algerian rebellion was strong in part because Nasser was supporting it, so they saw supporting Israel as one way to fight it. Subsequently, there was the Suez Crisis, in which the French, British and Israeli armies tried in 1956 to invade Egypt. During that time, the French government went so far as to give Israel the technology for the A-bomb and then the H-bomb. And French opinion was 95 per cent pro-Israel. Even the PCF has been pro-Israel in 1945–49 because the Soviet Union was.
>
> Then, in 1967, Israel launched the Six Day War and defeated its Arab opponents. De Gaulle, who was absolutely against this war, radically changed French policy. He held a press conference in November 1967, in which he not only condemned the war, but also the occupation of the West Bank and Gaza Strip. It was an incredibly lucid critique. He described clearly how Israel would start to encounter national resistance, which it would call terrorism. And until Chirac, all French presidents followed the Gaullist

view, which favoured Israel's right to exist in pre-1967 borders, but also a state for the Palestinians. Pompidou, Giscard d'Estaing, Mitterrand and Chirac all supported the two-state solution. Chirac went so far as to take in 2003 the leadership of the 'peace camp' against the US intervention in Iraq. However, after the murder of Rafik Hariri in Lebanon, there was the beginning of a change in the Chirac position. Now Sarkozy is much more openly shifting toward a pro-Israel position. But, after 1967, public opinion had progressively changed. It changed in 1973 because of the oil shock, and again in 1982 because of the massacres at the Sabra and Shatila refugee camps. With the beginning of the first Palestinian intifada at the end of 1987, opinion had largely changed, so that by the 1990s public opinion consistently favoured a Palestinian state with Jerusalem as the capital, and the return of refugees.

Although the campaigns to suppress pro-Palestinian opinion in the US are well known, the ferocity of similar campaigns in Europe are not. In the UK, one might mention the case of Nasser Amin, a student at the School of Oriental and African Studies (SOAS), who was vilified as an antisemite for supporting the Palestinians' right to resist the occupation. His name was dragged through the mud not only in the press, which subjected SOAS to a campaign of harassment, but also in parliament, where an MP raised the prospect of Amin being tried under laws against incitement to racial hatred, under which one can be jailed for up to seven years.[58] In France, however, there was a much noisier set of controversies, and actual court cases did result. Dominique Vidal takes up the story:

> The long-term evolution of public opinion is the starting point of the problem for the friends of Israel. For them, the fact that a huge majority of French people wants a Palestinian state alongside Israel is totally unacceptable. And after the failure of Camp David and the so-called 'generous offer', and Arafat's refusal, we had a sustained campaign – by those such as Alain Finkielkraut and Bernard-Henri Lévy – against not only the Palestinian point of view, but also international law, and to stigmatize all those who favoured Palestinian rights. The violence of the second intifada was used as an argument in this campaign, but it did not affect public opinion massively. The pro-Israeli publications, such as *L'Arche*, became more and more nervous, especially since the military re-conquest of the West Bank by Sharon in 2002. In that

operation, everything was destroyed – hospitals, housing, and so on. There was a terrible battle in the Jenin refugee camp. There, it was clear once again: if you disagreed with Israel's policy, you were an antisemite. There was a sort of intellectual terrorism and there were quite literally organized trials for journalists. For example, Daniel Mermet, one of the most widely broadcast journalists over the last fifteen years, produced a report on Palestine in which he did the same thing as he had done for Chechnya, Tibet and so on, and he was described an antisemite. There was an attempt to indict him for this, by Lawyers Without Borders, the International League against Racism and Anti-Semitism, and the Union of Jewish Students in France. The court agreed with Mermet that his criticisms of Israeli policy were 'unrelated to any racial considerations'. And there was another attempt to indict him for incitement to racial hatred over a programme which he produced in 1998, which in fact helped secure the conviction of Hans Münch, a Nazi doctor at Auschwitz. Mermet won both cases.

A second example is one of the best-known intellectuals in France, Edgar Morin. He is a sociologist whose first well-known research in the 1960s was about anti-Semitism in the city of Orléans. Even he was accused of anti-Semitism and taken to court because of an article in *Le Monde* stating that the occupation of Palestine was a cancer. The judge said no way was this anti-Semitism. There was an appeal, however, and the second time he was convicted! He had to fight another appeal to be acquitted. Seeing that even Edgar Morin can be accused, people started to become afraid. While public opinion did not change radically, what has changed has been the approach of a lot of intellectuals and media. For example, since Hamas was elected in Palestine, there are few voices calling for negotiation. In the years since Camp David, 1,000 Israelis have been killed, mainly soldiers; 5,000 Palestinians have been killed, mainly civilians. And with the election of Hamas, a boycott was imposed – in a situation where almost three-quarters of Palestinians already live on less than $2 a day. No one talked about this.

When the Israeli film-maker Eyal Sivan made the documentary 'Road 181', following the theoretical Israeli–Palestinian border envisaged in 1947 by the UN, Alain Finkielkraut said that film displayed 'Jewish anti-Semitism' and Sivan's 'hatred toward the Jews', that Sivan envisaged 'killing them, liquidating them, making them disappear'. There was not a word in the documentary that could have been considered anti-Semitic. Sivan took Finkielkraut to court for libel, and lost. He appealed, and in the second trial, Bernard-Henri Lévy testified on behalf of Finkielkraut. There were two testimonies for Sivan, one of which was provided by myself. The judgment of the second trial was that that Alain Finkielkraut was guilty of racial defamation, whereas the plaintiff had complained only about simple defamation. Therefore his appeal was refused. Not one newspaper, radio station or television programme quoted the judgment except to note that Finkielkraut had won.

All this intellectual terrorism was very effective. More experienced journalists have thicker skins, but young reporters without much knowledge were particularly afraid of experiencing any problems. How can you explain that Finkielkraut has described 2002 as 'a Kristallyear' without creating a public scandal? I had to make a radio broadcast stating that either Finkielkraut's calculator is broken, or he is lying – during the Kristallnacht (9 November 1938), 180 synagogues were destroyed, 7,500 Jewish stores were rampaged, 90 Jews were killed and 20,000 to 30,000 Jews were deported. That happened in one night. You multiply that by 365 days, and ask yourself if 2002 was really a 'Kristallyear'![59]

If Sarkozy's pro-Israel stance was important for some, also decisive was his abrasive stance on the *banlieue* riots of Autumn 2005. Pascal Bruckner, who wields his grudge against 'Third Worldism' as forcefully today as he did thirty years ago, wrote of the events:

If a significant fascist party existed in France, it is among these young Arab and North African children of immigrants – the so-called *black-blanc-beurs* – that it would recruit for its storm troopers. Confronted with such brutality, too many members of the press and the intelligentsia have chosen to play an ambiguous role. They engage in reflexive 'Third Worldism,' justify the riots as a reaction against French colonialism, and display a pernicious fascination with the violence of the lumpenproletariat and contempt for an open society.[60]

One wonders whether it has escaped Bruckner that there is actually a significant fascist party in France, led by a certain Jean-Marie Le Pen; that it had attained a fifth of the popular vote only three years previously; and that its members are as white as Bruckner himself.

Nevertheless, he was in excellent company. Alain Finkielkraut described the riots as an 'anti-republican pogrom', and bewailed the concessions that the French state had made to French Arabs:

> Now they teach colonial history as an exclusively negative history. We don't teach anymore that the colonial project also sought to educate, to bring civilization to the savages. They only talk about it as an attempt at exploitation, domination and plunder.[61]

Both Bruckner and Finkielkraut went on to praise Sarkozy during the 2007 election. André Glucksmann, who had supported Bernard Kouchner as the Socialist Party presidential candidate, threw his weight behind Sarkozy in light of the latter's foreign policy stance. Bernard Kouchner, who had supported Royal in the election, was offered the position of minister of foreign and European affairs by the Sarkozy administration and jumped at it, thus earning his expulsion from the Socialist Party.[62] Not even a little chastened by the evident failure of his time as colonial governor of Kosovo, he was immediately on the pulpit, proselytizing for war preparations against Iran.[63] Since then he has directed French troops to intervene in Chad, to defend the besieged pro-French government of Idriss Déby, whom he describes as 'an elected and legitimate president', despite the fact that none of Déby's election wins have been deemed free or fair by observers: the opposition had boycotted the most recent election amid allegations of vote-rigging, resulting in a turnout estimated at only 10 per cent.[64]

While Sarkozy shared nothing with the Left, his pro-American and pro-Israeli stances did sufficiently overlap with those of the French 'antitotalitatarians', whose claim to being on the Left had long since become a mere fetish. And his pledge to 'liquidate' the legacy of May 1968 must have pleased those who had been doing their best to destroy it for several decades. In fact, Sarkozy accused the *soixant-huitards* of having undermined 'morality, authority, work and national identity'.[65] Such rhetoric was often accompanied by appeals to the Left and invocations of great figures such as Jaurès. Indeed, the strange neoliberal coalition that Sarkozy has assembled brings together figures originating both from the far Left and also the far Right. Alain Madelin, who became a leading figure in Sarkozy's UMP, and was also one of the most enthusiastic supporters of the invasion of Iraq, had been a member of the far-right group *Occident* during the 1960s. The same is true of leading UMP politician Patrick Devedjian, who was one of Sarkozy's closest advisors during his campaign. Serge Halimi, a journalist who observed Sarkozy's campaign, says that Sarkozy's rhetoric about May '68 has been overplayed.

> Many of those supposedly identified with May '68 are either behind Sarkozy or are close to Sarkozy . . . [Their rhetoric] appeals to the conservative voters because they associate it with the media image of children not obeying their parents, and classrooms being unruly. But we all know that May '68 was about more than this. It was the largest social movement, the largest wave of strikes we have had in our history. This is not the May '68 that Sarkozy is talking about. He is in a sense using the media image of May '68, as being just a student movement for free love and so on.

A large part of Sarkozy's appeal for the former *soixant-huitards* is his pro-American stance.

> Sarkozy is a lot more pro-American, I would say even pro-Bush, and pro-Israel, and pro-right-wing Israeli, than any of his predecessors. He loves money – not in a personal way, but he thinks, and his minister of the economy agrees, that we [French] have some sort of Catholic complex toward money. What he loves about America is that you can make money and show it off . . . His campaign used all the techniques of the American Right. You know, the theme of decline and the need for neoliberal reform, the anti-intellectual tendency, the opposition between the poor and those who are even poorer – you are paying taxes to pay for welfare spongers. All those themes, Sarkozy took from Reagan and Bush.

Halimi points out that one of the few pro-war Socialists not to defect to the Sarkozy camp was BHL, who instead was deeply involved in Ségolène Royal's campaign. This was not, he maintains, for ideological reasons.

> If you read his recent book,[66] which I think I am the only person in France to have actually done, it argues basically that the Left should support free-market capitalism. Very consonant with what Sarkozy wants to do. He also argues that those on the Left who do not want to embrace capitalism are antisemites. He says this explicitly about people like [the late sociologist] Pierre Bourdieu and [the late philosopher] Jacques Derrida. There is a

kind of personal critique of Sarkozy, but in ideological terms he is certainly shifting the discourse to the right in the same way that Sarkozy has done. But while Sarkozy has done it in the conservative camp, Lévy wants to do it in the Socialist camp. Before, BHL was a media phenomenon – now, he is more and more a political phenomenon. He has an effect.[67]

One is thus driven to wonder whether Philippe Cohen's satirical invocation of the BHL 2012 presidential committee might not soon come to look like prophecy.[68]

Resistance: evildoers, one more time

I have argued that 'lesser-evilism' guides much liberal imperialist ideology. Michael Ignatieff himself made the point in his book, *The Lesser Evil*, in which he argued that liberals can acknowledge that American violence is an evil, that torture is an evil, that the suspension of the law is an evil, but nevertheless defend these practices under certain circumstances.[69] Indeed, such a logic is integral to liberal 'anti-totalitarianism': Stalinism was the greater evil that mandated a coalition with the CIA, support for loyalty oaths, the muting of serious political criticism, and enthusiastic support for American aggression. On the face of it, the logic is childishly simple to comprehend. Every evil that one endorses is the 'lesser evil'. But there is an underlying account of twentieth-century politics and a theory of political action buttressing this claim, always invoked but rarely explained in serviceable terms. The vocabulary of totalitarianism has never been far away when liberals (and neoconservatives) talk about foreign policy.

The polysemic nature of the term 'totalitarianism' has been remarked upon, but not resolved. Anson Rabinbach argues that

> Totalitarianism is a protean word, available and useful in new and ever-changing political constellations . . . the polyvalent associations of totalitarianism created dilemmas for the anti-communist left of the cold war era, especially when they found themselves thrown together with right-wing anti-Communists. The same dilemmas bedevil today's left and liberal antitotalitarians.[70]

As a result of the problems of definition which plagued discussions of the term, few writing in the late 1960s would have expected the revival of totalitarianism theory. Many historians remain critical of the theory especially because of the differences it obscures between fascist regimes and Stalinist states, and the seemingly arbitrary distinctions it makes between 'totalitarian' fascism and 'traditional, authoritarian' fascism.[71] Enzo Traverso suggests that totalitarianism is essentially 'a category based on the recognition of formal analogies between regimes whose historical origins, social contents, ideological bases and political objectives are deeply different and essentially incompatible'.[72]

If, for some (Hannah Arendt, Simone Weil), totalitarianism is historically rooted in imperialism, for others (Friedrich Hayek) it is a result of collectivism, and for still others (Jacob Talmon, François Furet) it is a result of the eighteenth-century revolutions and their construction of the idea of an abstract 'man' who can have 'rights'. The latter might agree with the rightist critic of the French revolution, Joseph Marie de Maistre: 'In my life, I have seen French, Italians, Russians, etc.; I know very well, thanks to Montesquieu, that there may be Persians; but as for man, I hold that I have never met one in my entire life.' Others have argued that de Maistre, a supporter of state terror, prefigured the 'totalitarian' terror of the twentieth century. Some liberals argue that totalitarian regimes are those which destroy the constitutional state and political pluralism (Zbigniew Brzezinski, Carl Friedrich), while the conservative theorist Eric Voegelin argues that it is a result of secularization, which produces political forms that mimic religion. There are also Marxist versions of 'totalitarianism' theory. Max Shachtman's critique of the 'totalitarian collectivism' that he saw in the Soviet Union was shared in some respects by Cornelius Castoriadis and Claude Lefort, for example. These would echo the idea that totalitarianism is a specific form of class rule, rather than an inevitable outcome of the attempt to overthrow class societies.[73]

The aporiae of 'totalitarian' theory notwithstanding, however, the concept was given a new lease of life by the eclipse of the New Left, the rise of the neoconservatives and French anti-totalitarians, and the final demise of the Soviet Union. Therefore, when it came to Iraq,

> several respected former dissidents and heroes of the global left such as Vaclav Havel, Adam Michnik, André Glucksmann, and José Ramos-Horta supported the war on liberal-humanitarian grounds, invoking the imperative of resisting totalitarianism.[74]

For most liberal anti-totalitarians, human rights and the eighteenth-century revolutions are the antidote to totalitarianism. Thus, the founders of the Euston Manifesto intend to echo the 'great rallying calls of the democratic revolutions of the 18th century'.[75] Part of the Eustonians' critique of the Left is that they do not know a threat to that revolutionary tradition when they see one. Some of their number have argued that the Left, far from being too fanatical about abstract rights, is overly dismissive of them.[76] Some of the signatories to the Manifesto explained that the Left needs to realize that 'radical Islamism' is 'the third major form of totalitarian ideology of the last century'. Joschka Fischer has also spoken of a 'third totalitarianism'. It is an idea shared by many liberal pro-war intellectuals, although it is not absolutely clear what is included in this category. When Rabinbach endorses Adam Michnik's snide claim that antiwar protesters did not take the threat of al-Qaeda seriously enough, he appears to endorse the logic according to which Baathism and al-Qaeda are somehow, at root, the same.[77]

Paul Berman, as we have seen, considers Baathism a component of the Muslim branch of totalitarianism, which includes al-Qaeda. In this vein, Berman provides in *Terror and Liberalism* the basis for his endorsement of war against Iraq. Following the Iraqi invasion of Kuwait in August 1990, the situation 'had the look of Europe in 1939'. Iraq was an expansionist power, led by a 'terrifying' man. He had a 'weird hatred' of Israel, although its border was hundreds of miles away (Berman may not have learned, as Iraq did in 1981, that Israel has an air force capable of travelling that distance and dropping munitions). Berman wanted to support a 'war for democracy', and his main criticism of the Bush administration was its 'Nixonian' justification for the venture. Similarly, his main criticism of the 'Saddam is a Hitler' line was that Bush was insufficiently serious about the charge. The apparent success of the war was, Berman argues, a tragedy. Like World War I, it was a pseudo-settlement, and as such it contained the seeds of the next war. Saddam, so Berman maintains, was chastened by the first war, but not for long. The UN inspectors discovered Saddam's weapons production to be 'greater than previously imagined'. And so, Saddam weathered 'pin-prick' attacks from the United States (Berman does not mention the sanctions regime), 'grew stronger' and 'threw the inspectors out' (straightforwardly untrue).[78] America's lack of resolve encouraged Saddam and allowed Middle Eastern fanatics to think it was weak. Thus, from the failure to overthrow Saddam came attacks on embassies and the hijacking of airlines.[79]

This highly improbable narrative introduces what would prove to be an influential summary of contemporary liberal 'anti-totalitarianism'. In Berman's account, totalitarianism is an 'irrationalist cult of death and murder'. Thus, discussing a short list of colonial crimes, he asserts, but fails to argue, that these crimes – such as Belgian atrocities in the Congo – were 'insane', and proved that a nihilistic reflux against liberal modernity was taking place. Such is the 'totalitarian' virus. It is violence for its own sake, nihilism and – curiously – fanaticism too. Not just imperialism, but also the mass movements of the twentieth century that Berman pulls together under the rubric of 'totalitarianism', are 'death-obsessed', 'apocalyptic', and 'millenarian'. Bolshevism and fascism, though apparent opposites, are said to be alike in this respect at least. And 'Muslim totalitarianism', with its pedigree descending from Hassan al-Banna and Sayyid Qutb, is the presently regnant form of this totalitarian menace. The least that can be said about this argument is that the similarities it describes between the movements it seeks to conjoin are extremely vague, and the unifying theme vaguer still. Further, its claims outstrip the evidence or sustained exposition that Berman is competent to provide – presumably, this is why a great deal of it is given to impressionistic rumination and bald assertions that are counterintuitive where they are not simply false.[80]

Implicit in Berman's account is a model of rationality that appears frequently in the writings of the pro-war liberals. Thus, when Paul Berman complains of a 'rationalist naïveté' in which 'everything that happens is rationally explicable', he gives us to understand that 'totalitarian' movements, and contemporary Islamist movements in particular, are not merely morally repugnant, but irrational. Similarly, he upbraids Noam Chomsky for his rationalism, insisting that 'no single logic rules the world'. Berman insists that 'totalitarianism' is not 'about' anything – there is no 'why', and those who try to detect a rational core in it end up as its apologists.[81] As well as insulting the intelligence of his readers – who presumably were not expected to recall Berman earnestly explaining the rational kernel of grievance that motivated the Contra death squads – this supposes that rationality is neatly separable from ideology and desire. An alternative way of looking at this would be to say that cognitive biases (racism, for example), material interests (the need to terrorize in order to maintain control, or the need to resist subjugation) and desires (to contribute to the freeing of a nation, or to the making of a tyranny) themselves have an impact on the balance of risks and benefits: they co-determine what is rational.

Totalitarianism theory often insists on the central importance of irrationalism. This is not without its problems: clearly, the Soviet Union, for all the irrationality it exhibited in its worst periods, related to the Enlightenment and rationalism in a very different way to fascism. The official ideology of the Soviet Union was a dogmatic and scholastic version of Marxism, which revolutionized the Enlightenment rather than rejecting it. Further, the relationship of explicitly irrationalist fascist movements to enlightenment and rationality is more complicated than simple rejection.[82] However, Berman goes further, and insists that such movements are not merely irrationalist at the ideological level, but irrational at *every* level. He also implies that to try to distinguish any rationality in motive or strategy is ultimately apologetic. This is a rather crude handling of the issue: after all, rational analysis is what provides the basis of critical enquiry, and to eschew it is potentially disarming. It is also a quite unnecessary step, since moral disapproval does not rely on a charge of insanity. In fact, the usual result of such a charge is to relieve the agent of responsibility for their actions, and reduce the cause for resentment – which could itself be considered apologetic. One result of ruling out inquiry in this fashion is to thwart any analysis that might find US foreign policy to be at fault, and to threaten those who do find such fault with the stigma of being apologists for fascism. And this is manifestly the intended objective.

The *Observer* columnist and Euston Manifesto co-founder Nick Cohen, who professes to being profoundly influenced by Berman, avers in a similar style that

> the famines Stalin, Mao and the Ethiopian colonels unleashed, Pol Pot's extermination of anyone who could read or write, or Hitler's annihilation of the Jews, gypsies, gays and Slavs, Saddam's regime of torture and genocide and the Islamist cult of death aren't rationally explicable . . . It is more profitable to look at persecution fantasies, group loyalty, the strongman's will to power and the feeble personality's willingness to obey.[83]

This is strange reasoning indeed. Cohen insists that 'totalitarian' movements are not rationally explicable, yet he still attempts to outline a set of explanatory possibilities (albeit ones that exculpate Western states). He does not elaborate on those suspiciously slight generalities, perhaps because he cannot. One advantage of this Mysterion approach to political analysis is that, by declaring in advance the impossibility of rational explanation, one does not have to aim very high in whatever explanation one attempts.

Not everyone accepts this prohibition on thinking about 'root causes'. On 21 September 2007, General Sir Richard Dannatt, head of the British army, addressed the International Institute for Strategic Studies. Of the Iraqis who were resisting the occupation, he said:

> The militants (and I use the word deliberately because not all are insurgents, or terrorists, or criminals; they are a mixture of them all) are well armed – certainly with outside help, and probably

from Iran. By motivation, essentially, and with the exception of the Al Qaeda in Iraq element who have endeavoured to exploit the situation for their own ends, our opponents are Iraqi Nationalists, and are most concerned with their own needs – jobs, money, security – and the majority are not bad people.

Of the insurgents in Afghanistan, he added:

There is a lazy tendency for them all to be lumped under the term 'Taliban', but it is not as simple as that. Yes, there is a hard core of Islamist extremists of varied ethnic and national origin, but the great majority of the people we are engaged against are those who are fighting with the Taliban for financial, social and tribal reasons. So we must beware of tarring them all with the same brush, as I am sure that one day we will need to deal with and eventually reconcile the elected Government with the majority of these people.[84]

This was the first time a senior military figure involved in the occupations of both Iraq and Afghanistan had made these points so starkly. In fact, it has been particularly important to the occupiers of Iraq to dehumanize the widespread and expanding armed resistance to the occupation. As Diana Francis writes, the sanitization of Western violence with false consolations and euphemisms (indiscriminately destructive bombs are called 'daisy cutters', for instance) is complemented by the reduction of the enemy to ciphers of evil. Western soldiers have biographies and grieving relatives and mentions in the news when they die: Iraqis and Afghans who are killed by the occupiers tend not to have even a face, never mind a life history. Not only does this obscure reality; it constitutes a primary moral justification for the use of force.[85]

The Taliban, in 2001 a discredited and marginal political force in Afghanistan, began in 2006 to make a come-back in the south of the country. Lieutenant-General David Richards explained: 'We need to realize we could actually fail here.' Contributing to this was the failure of the occupation to resemble the promised emancipation, the mass starvation, and the ongoing and intensifying attacks by the occupiers on civilians. Hints were issued that the developing insurgency must include elements other than the Taliban, and the old colonial metaphors were reached for. The Senlis Council reported in 2006 on the main insurgent areas of Afghanistan, and found that one reason why growing numbers of people were taking up military resistance was that poor farmers were being targeted by the occupiers' destruction of the opium crop, while rich farmers were being left alone. In 2007 the

UN reported a 30 per cent rise in suicide attacks in the country, but noted that the vast bulk were directed against occupying forces or their Afghan auxiliaries rather than against civilians, and that the attackers were 'motivated by a variety of grievances such as foreign occupation, anger over civilian casualties and humiliation'.[86] General Dannatt's comments on the nature of the resistance were therefore a realistic statement on the current situation.

To avoid facing this reality, commentators usually reduce Afghanistan's problems to the Taliban's intense guerrilla war and the strategy of suicide attacks (although in fact the only available statistics show that most of deaths are caused by the occupiers). As the NGO workers Chris Johnson and Jolyon Leslie point out, the Taliban have been demonized out of all proportion. Their repression, brutal as it was, should not have been understood as simply an emanation of their own peculiar, reactionary ideology. It was rooted in the common social practices of the most conservative elements of society in Afghanistan, which fused with the conditions of war, and then civil war, to produce a militant war on 'sin' and 'vice' (with well-known and savage punishments, such as stonings and amputations). It is these elements that the US has recruited to the new regime. Nasreen Ghufran noted in May 2001 that the Taliban's claim was that it needed time to develop the correct environment for girls and women to be educated and to work: it saw its model, ironically, as the Islamic Republic of Iran.[87] Nevertheless, women's struggles were able to exert some impact. As Jeanette O'Malley wrote in 2000,

> In early June, supreme leader Mullah Omar issued an edict allowing for the expansion of mosque schools for young boys and girls. The mosque schools are apparently little more than a substitute acceptable to clerics and hard-line officials for state-run schools, as they offer the same curriculum.

NGO groups working in Afghanistan were able to set up a school for girls by simply telling local Taliban officials that it was a mosque. The Department for the Promotion of Virtue and the Prevention of Vice continues to operate. Reports last year that it would 'return' after a resolution passed by Karzai's cabinet in 2006 were misleading: the department, although now synonymous with Taliban terror, had actually originated under the US-recognized Rabbani regime, and continued under Karzai's regime in various forms. The Vice and Virtue squads continued to operate in Kabul, warlords like Ismail Khan imposed the old regime, and Karzai's 'Accountability Department' took over many of the other department's roles. It is therefore entirely consistent for the US now to seek to re-engage with the Taliban. It emerged in October 2007 that the US was allowing its Afghan clients to pursue negotiations with the Taliban leadership, with the aim of bringing them into the government: the logic presumably being that, if there is a growing popular movement, it is better to have the well-armed Taliban fighters on the side of the government's counterinsurgency efforts.[88]

There are some telling contrasts when it comes to the reception of resistance to a Western occupation regime, however brutal. For example, when Saddam Hussein was raping, killing, imprisoning and torturing Iraqis, military resistance was deemed entirely legitimate. And not all of the war's supporters are unwilling to countenance legitimate violence against US troops. Christopher Hitchens once conceded that 'the Sudanese government, repellent though it is' would have been entitled to a 'retaliatory strike, provided that it was against a military target', for the bombing of the Shifa pharmaceutical complex in 1998. In recognizing a right that would never be fulfilled, Hitchens at least strove for moral consistency – but when crimes abound in Iraq, and military targets present themselves to Iraqis abundantly, he draws a line, as it were, in the sand: 'Where it is not augmented by depraved Bin Ladenist imports, the leadership and structure of the Iraqi "insurgency" is formed from the elements of an already fallen regime, extensively discredited and detested in its own country and universally condemned.'[89] Norman Geras takes a similar line on the 'murderous "insurgency"', as does Jeff Weintraub of *Dissent*, who describes the resistance as an attempt 'to restore fascist dictatorship (or an Islamist replacement)'. The preamble to the Euston Manifesto derides support for the 'gangs of jihadist and Baathist thugs of the Iraqi so-called resistance'. Some antiwar commentators have repeated these claims. Katha Pollitt, writing for the *Nation*, characterized the resistance as 'theocrats, ethnic nationalists, die-hard Baathists, jihadis, kidnappers, beheaders and thugs'.[90]

This portrayal – a montage assiduously constructed by US military propagandists – ignores the bulk of what actually takes place in Iraq. There are restorationist elements in the resistance, and there is also a Salafist wing. But there is also a civil war dynamic unfolding in Iraq, encouraged by the sectarian policies of the occupiers. In particular, the US has incorporated sectarian militias into the post-Baath state, and encouraged its allies to promote a sectarian constitution. They have also used Shiite and Kurdish death squads to attack their rivals. But the findings of the US Department of Defense, of the CIA, of the

Multi-National Forces in Iraq, and of independent think-tanks, indicate that the bulk of the resistance is neither Baathist, nor Salafist; nor, on the whole, does it target civilians. The resistance is dominated by local, decentralized, disarticulated groups who overwhelmingly attack military and not civilian targets. At the time of writing, the most recent statistics available from the US Department of Defense suggested that, by April 2007, of over 1,000 weekly attacks, almost 800 had been directed at US troops, while approximately 200 had been directed at Iraqi security forces, and less than 100 had targeted civilians. This had been the case, described in repeated studies, since the occupation began. Indeed, it is widely reported that the mainstream of the movement has been fighting the Salafist elements whose actions have hindered, rather than helped, the effort to evict the occupiers, and has sought to defend Shiites from resistance attacks. This is perhaps one reason why support for the resistance among Iraqis has been growing, so that fully 61 per cent of Iraqis now support attacks on troops. It may have been a recognition of this growing sentiment that led Iyad Allawi, as he was being appointed by the occupiers in 2004, to admit that the resistance attacks were legitimate.[91] However, in amplifying the role of Zarqawi and people like him, pro-war commentators may have become unwitting vectors for a propaganda campaign mounted by the US military. Documents reproduced in the *Washington Post* in early 2006 discussed an American psychological operation aimed at demonizing the armed resistance as foreign fighters and 'al-Qaeda'. Tactics discussed included: 'Eliminate Popular Support for a Potentially Sympathetic Insurgency; Deny Ability of Insurgency to "Take Root" Among the People', and 'Villainize Zarqawi/leverage xenophobic response'.[92]

There are, of course, certain groups who are easy to demonize because they are in fact ruthless, vicious thugs. Michael Ignatieff did not court controversy when he described the 9/11 attackers as 'evil people'. Similarly, Christopher Hitchens was not writing in the mode of a contrarian when he described Saddam Hussein as 'evil'. As contemptuous as many people were of Bush's puerile ranting about an 'axis of evil', itself a successor to Reagan's 'Evil Empire', the notion of evil as an active and animating force is one with considerable currency. Hitchens, defending Bush's language, described evil as 'an X-factor' which one processes and assimilates without being able to fully analyze it; it was 'the surplus value of the psychopathic – an irrational delight in flouting every customary norm of civilization'.[93] Kanan Makiya agrees:

Evil is something that, when you see it, when you know it, it's intimate. It's almost sensual. That is why people who have been tortured know it by instinct. They don't need to be told what it is, and they may have a very hard time putting it into words.[94]

This didactic impressionism does not become any clearer when the authors are more specific. In the same conversation, Makiya is moved to comment on another kind of evil: the banal kind. A videotape depicting Osama bin Laden laughing with his confederates shows 'a totally ordinary social conversation, perhaps around cups of coffee and teas and pastry . . . But what they're talking about is the death and destruction of 3,500 people, and they're praising it and so on.' This is 'exactly like Eichmann sitting behind his desk'.[95] On the one hand, evil is banal, and on the other, it is something so obscure that it cannot be registered except through instinct or intuition. One might suggest that, by the same token, Makiya's insights are simultaneously banal and obscure. Paul Berman proffered another possible interpretation:

Evil is an absence. In the skyline now, there is an empty space where the twin towers used to be. I gaze out my study window, where I am used to seeing the towers, and I can hardly believe what I see. I see nothing. Smoke and sky. It is the symbol of absolute evil.[96]

This is an aesthetic reaction, if not a downright aestheticization of catastrophe; but perhaps it takes us closer to understanding the point of the recursion, and the infantilization of discourse. We are being invited to see certain phenomena as not entirely intelligible, not completely of this world, partaking instead of a mysterious realm that hints at the satanic.

What these authors have in common, then, is a tendency to pathologize social conflict, to reduce some of its worst aspects to an 'evil' that is always externalized. This is a theological, or demonological, conception of politics. Though these shibboleths were cultivated and nurtured by the French 'anti-totalitarians', they constitute an old and worn technique of imperial ideology: recall that the opponents of the British empire were 'fanatics' and 'barbarous'. The explanations for their actions tended to be cultural, racial and theological, obscuring the social and political reasons for violence. And this also informs much of the argument for 'humanitarian' warfare in other parts of the world, particularly in Africa. Predictably, for example, explanation of the fate of Darfur is reduced to 'Islamism' and 'totalitarianism' in the hands of the pro-war liberals.[97] There may or may not be a war in Sudan – as things stand, peacekeepers are more likely to be involved in conflict with rebel groups than with the Sudanese government; but it is almost certain that, if there is, that fact will have nothing to do with Islamism. The fact is that the government is Islamist, but then so is much of the opposition. In fact, the Justice and Equality Movement has a better claim to Islamic piety than the Bashir government, which is why the war against the rebels, launched with bitter vindictiveness and including genocidal violence in 2004, did not adduce Islamism as a source of legitimacy. The issues that divide the Nile valley elite and the Furs in Sudan are much more complex than religious ideology, and originate in deep ecological and socio-economic changes which, as Alex de Waal writes, effected profound shifts in the 'moral geography' of the country.[98] Once again, the realities that would be affected by war seem unimportant to some would-be humanitarian interventionists, who prefer to rely on ahistorical schemata drawn from the lexicon of 'anti-totalitarianism'.

The attempted annexation of South Lebanon

Speaking of Prime Minister Blair's stance over Israel's 2006 attack on Lebanon, Denis MacShane, Labour MP and member of the neoconservative Henry Jackson Society, explained: 'In geopolitical terms, calling for a ceasefire would not have stopped a single bomb from being dropped or a single rocket from being fired.' This was a downright falsehood, as MacShane surely knew. As the Israeli prime minister later admitted, they had planned the war in advance with Washington, and would not have proceeded without the support of Western states. At any rate, then Prime Minister Blair's refusal to endorse a UN Security Council resolution demanding a ceasefire, or even to call for one publicly, reflected his support for the venture.[99] Repeatedly challenged to call for a ceasefire, he explained that he could do so, but would not. This was one humanitarian intervention that the disgraced former prime minister could not see his way to, though it required the dropping of not a single bomb.

The war, allegedly a response to the capture of a soldier by Hezbollah, became an attempt at the ethnic cleansing and annexation of the south. Israel, which had a history both of ethnic purification and of occupying the south of Lebanon, was going for a new record. On 20 June 2006, the Israeli military ordered all Lebanese residents living south of the Litani river to evacuate within twenty-four hours. People did begin to flee, but they were bombed anyway, whether they were in cars or ambulances. Three days later, the IDF acknowledged that it was preparing to install a government of its own in the south of Lebanon. During the course of the war, the UN noted with horror that 'block after block' of civilian housing had been blasted to pieces. As civilians were slaughtered in plain view, the IDF's chief of Northern Command suggested 'not counting the dead'. The war targeted the civilian infrastructure and population centres, killing up to 1,300 civilians and displacing almost 1 million people. Israel's excuse was that Hezbollah was using civilians as human shields – a claim dismissed by Human Rights Watch monitors. By contrast, the Israeli human rights organization B'Tselem confirmed that Israel was using human shields in Gaza.[100] The evident aim was to conquer Lebanon as a preliminary strike in a proxy war against Syria and Iran, and the south of the country was to be annexed in the process.

This war introduced new depths of self-deception, nationalism and cruelty on the part of liberal warmongers. Michael Walzer, who had been mildly critical of the Iraq war but hoped for its success once it began, declared: 'War Fair'. Israel's wars never cease to be fair for Walzer, but in this case he relied on a simple reversal: if the capture of two soldiers was an act of war, then an act of war in return could not be considered illegitimate. The paucity of Just War theory is thus summarized: one could equally say that Israel, having kidnapped thousands of Palestinians and Lebanese in expansionist aggression, had no right to complain of similar actions in return. Norman Geras preferred to say that 'Israel does have just cause. This I don't argue for, I merely assert . . . no other country on the planet would be thought to be obliged to endure missile attacks on its population from a neighbouring country'. There is some consistency here: Geras has long argued against indiscriminate attacks on civilians even in just wars. It is unlikely that Geras, a long-time supporter of Israel, regarded Hezbollah's war as just, and he clearly held them responsible for illegitimate tactics in the context of that war. However, in this case he appeared to have forgotten that missile attacks on Israel's population centres began *after* the Israeli invasion. (It subsequently emerged that, while Israel had accused Hezbollah of hiding behind civilians, the reverse was actually true: Hezbollah had ordered its men and equipment away from civilian areas, while Israel had located prime military facilities used to attack Lebanon in civilian population areas.)[101]

By neglecting the fact that Israel was the aggressor, Geras could construe Israel's war as a legitimate defensive exercise. But he went further: having signalled a growing concern for his Jewish identity during the 1990s, he was now in the position of dispensing communalist reprimands to organizations like Jews for Justice for the Palestinians, which had marched against Israel's war. In an open letter co-written with other supporters of Israel, he accused the organization of 'Jewish sycophancy', reminding them of 'one of Hillel's central precepts, recorded in Perkei Avoth (Ethics of the Fathers): Do not separate yourself from the community.'[102] In its best light, this was an unpleasant attempt at disciplining even the mildest Jewish critics of Israel. It also appealed to precisely the religious particularism for which these authors upbraid political Islam.

Christopher Hitchens, as a long-standing advocate for the Palestinians, still describes himself as one of the few people of Jewish descent who thinks Zionism would have been a mistake even if there had been no Palestinians. He knows better than most journalists living in Washington what Israel has been up to in Lebanon and elsewhere. Yet he remained curiously silent about this war, raising no protest. In the end, he chose to fantasize that Israeli right-wingers admitted 'that Israeli colonization of Arabs is demographically impossible and morally wrong', and that Syria and Iran were using proxies to attack Israel. He did not like the war's 'promiscuity' and 'lack of proportion', but he nevertheless blamed Hamas and Hezbollah for it. This is hardly any less self-deceiving than the belief that US Marines could simply march into Baghdad and deliver liberation and laptop computers (never mind the electricity to run them on); but it is a predictable conclusion from someone who is obsessed these days with 'Islamic imperialism'.[103]

Nukes and terror (again)

Imperial projection continues to define Western discussions of war and peace, especially in the attempt to salvage the dignity of humanitarian imperialism from the ruins of Iraq. Christopher Hitchens repeated as late as 2007 that Saddam Hussein had been funding the Abu Sayyaf network in the Philippines, supposedly an al-Qaeda affiliate, and that he had given 'hospitality' to one of the bombers of the World Trade Center in 1993. The first claim had originated some months before the attack on Iraq, when an Iraqi defector named Hisham Hussein came forward with it, and it was repeated in testimony to Congress by Deputy Assistant Secretary of State for East Asian and Pacific Affairs Matthew Daley, as the war was going on. In fact, the only documentary evidence adduced by Hayes suggests that any relationship between the Baath regime and the Sayyaf outfit had been terminated, and it provides no indication that any networks of support had been created. A subsequent extensive study by US intelligence of Iraqi documents found no trace of any connection between Saddam Hussein's regime and any component of al-Qaeda.[104]

But, although the speculation as to possible connections between Saddam Hussein's government and various Islamist movements has yielded scanty evidence to date, little attention is paid by the self-professed opponents of terrorism – especially that carried out by Muslims – to the US government's extensive involvement with terrorist organizations. Iyad Allawi, before he was appointed head of the Iraqi Interim Government, had been a terrorist working for the Central Intelligence Agency. His Iraqi National Accord penetrated the cities of Iraq and planted 'car bombs and other explosive devices', one of which exploded in a cinema. Another bombing targeted a school bus.[105] In 2005 an alliance was formalized between the US government and the Jundullah militia. Jundullah is a Salafist group that operates from Waziristan, in the south-east of Pakistan. It has also been known to be active in Afghanistan. Its leader, Abd el Malik Regi, is a former Taliban fighter. It runs the Ummat studio, which produces video footage of gory beheadings, as well as anti-government propaganda. It is described in the Pakistani press as having links with the al-Qaeda network. Its main service to the United States, however, has been a series of bloody bomb attacks in Balochistan, in the south of Iran. It also takes credit for having kidnapped and executed hundreds of Iranian troops and officials. The US alliance with the group, which involved providing oversight and intelligence, as well as directing funds to the group from Iranian exiles, fits into its broader strategy of supporting separatist groups in Iran, many of them violent. The funding for these groups reportedly comes from the CIA's classified budget. Israel and America are also reported to be supporting a small Kurdish militia called the Party for Free Life in Kurdistan, which has conducted raids across the Iranian border. They were supplied with 'a list of targets inside Iran of interest to the US'.[106] It might be asked why Iran is not being urged to prosecute a 'war on terror'.

Albert Memmi wrote in *The Colonizer and the Colonized*: 'While it is pardonable for the colonizer to have his little arsenals, the discovery of even a rusty weapon among the colonized is cause for immediate punishment.' Progress being what it is, the Bush administration, possessor of 'mini-nukes' as well as quite a few ordinary-sized ones, made Iraq's rusty old weapons programmes its central *casus belli*. Mushroom clouds were, figuratively, in the air. It was asserted that the transfer of nuclear material to a waiting Islamist group by the Baath regime was only a matter of time. Again, the liberal interventionists were on hand to assist, especially when the case crumbled. 'Waiting for this sort of regime to obtain weapons of mass destruction would be plain recklessness', explained Adam Michnik in his defence of Bush in *Gazeta Wyborcza* in 2003. In the same year, Christopher Hitchens recited the finding of elements of a nuclear centrifuge hidden in an Iraqi scientist's back garden, warned that Saddam had indeed been attempting to 'reconstitute' his WMD programmes, and referred to the 'clear and present danger of Iraq giving lethal material to terrorist groups'.[107] Ignatieff also ventilated in Bush's defence:

> It is ideological claptrap to suppose that the Bush administration made up the risk. Saddam has been a security threat in the Gulf for 20 years. His desire to acquire these weapons was unquestionable; there isn't a serious analyst who doesn't think he'd wanted to have them.[108]

Ignatieff is intelligent enough to realize that the case for war would have been less persuasive had it been reduced to the claim that Saddam *wanted* weapons.

Although Saddam Hussein's putative threats with weapons of mass destruction were constantly raised and invented by the supporters of war, the threats were almost entirely the other way. In February 2003, the British defence secretary, Geoff Hoon, explained for the second time that the UK would be willing to use nuclear weapons against Iraq in 'extreme self-defence'. This raises the question, as it was surely designed to, of what Iraq could possibly do to mandate the annihilation of its population centres with nuclear weapons. Claims about an Iranian nuclear weapons programme are also widely bruited. Paul Berman has recently complained that 'the more Ahmadinejad threatened to obliterate Israel and build nuclear weapons the more people around the world wrote about . . . Bush! "Oh, no! What is Bush going to do?" As if the problem here was Bush!'[109] It is obviously of little relevance that the Iranian president did not threaten to obliterate Israel, and has energetically denied building nuclear weapons (a denial supported by the US National Intelligence Estimate in 2007, which concluded that any nuclear build-up had ceased in 2003, two years before Ahmadinejad was elected).[110] What Berman appears to mean is that the more Western propaganda held that Ahmadinejad was ready for nuclear genocide in the Middle East, the more people questioned that propaganda and wondered about its purpose – which is a source of ungovernable outrage. Iran is currently enemy number one for the United States government, and for the neoconservatives; so – in

Berman's 'anti-totalitarian' liberalism – the Left ought to behave itself and embrace the demonization campaign. The National Intelligence Estimate set back the cause of a military attack on Iran, but at the beginning of 2008 renewed sanctions were applied that targeted civilians.[111]

An ongoing saga, comparable to the vilification campaign against Iran, is the campaign to save Darfur. An extraordinary, spell-binding success, the coalition to save Darfur unites liberal celebrities such as George Clooney with reactionary American nationalists like John Bolton. The actress Mia Farrow runs a website devoted to the issue of Darfur, while Don Cheadle, the star of *Hotel Rwanda*, has been a vocal advocate on the topic. The celebrity spectacle is a slightly more politicized version of the 'Save Africa' spirit that moved Bono and Bob Geldof to produce such initiatives as Live 8 and Product Red. Reebok has even co-sponsored a video-game about it. More recently, it has induced Steven Spielberg to boycott the 2008 Olympics in China, because of the state's dealings with the Sudanese government. The political consensus is strikingly broad, ranging from liberals such as Ted Kennedy to right-wingers such as John McCain and Bob Dole. For Samantha Power, a key foreign policy advisor for Barack Obama, it is 'Another Problem From Hell'. Christian fundamentalists and Jewish organizations are also united on the issue, and are prominent forces in the Save Darfur coalition. Another supporter of intervention is the American Islamic Congress. The Congress comprises people like Kanan Makiya, Dr Hillel Fradkin of the American Enterprise Institute, and Zainab Al-Suwaij, one of the Iraqi exiles who worked with the neoconservative right to support war on Iraq.[112]

Alex de Waal, an expert on Sudan and co-author of *Darfur: A Short History of a Long War*,[113] argues that this says much more about American exceptionalism than it does about the situation in Darfur.

> There are two things to say here. One is that it is not coincidental that the villains in Darfur can be labelled as Arabs. It is hugely useful for American discourse, because no one in today's US political culture is going to stand up for Arabs. The second is that the Sudanese regime is indeed monstrous. It is in many ways guilty, and for worse things than Darfur today. Over the last three years, since the end of major hostilities at the end of 2004, between five and six thousand civilians have been killed in Darfur – that is a homicide rate comparable with Washington DC. So, it is not as if Darfur at the moment resembles the 'killing fields' of our

imaginations. But immediately prior, there were approximately seven to eight months in 2003 and 2004 when it came very close to that.

Given that the situation has so abated in intensity, the unabated intensity of calls for intervention demands an explanation other than unadulterated humanitarian outrage.

> About ten years ago, there was a domestic political consensus formed in the United States around Southern Sudan, which united the religious Right, the Israel Lobby, the Congressional Black Caucus, and liberals. It was unprecedented that they found such unity, and the issue over which they united was the plight of Christians in southern Sudan. But the focus moved to Darfur in part because after the arrival of peace in south Sudan, that issue couldn't fire people up, and the war in Darfur could. No one could deny that monstrosities were going on, but these were ready-made constituencies and the narrative happened to be extremely convenient for American political culture. It taps into the missionary zeal of American exceptionalism.
>
> The Bush administration is deeply divided on this. Bush would like to go in with all guns blazing, but some senior figures have argued effectively that the interventionist method is not going to work, and we need a negotiated peace deal with a covering international force. The main pressure for intervention is coming from outside the administration, partially from the Democrats, but also from right-wingers who think the administration is being held back by lily-livered bureaucrats.

And, with such a coalition behind it, the issue is likely to continue to be a central theme for US policymakers.

> The Save Darfur Coalition is in some disarray because it has had to choose a new leader, but as soon as the Democrats have chosen their candidate, these constituencies will be in action to ensure that it is an issue. Part of what is driving this is the desire to show that the Democrats can be tough; and part of it is to maintain claims for American supremacy in what may be the beginnings of decline.[114]

But the narrative of humanitarian action combined with a crusade against 'totalitarianism' does not always obtain when the US is 'saving Africa'. It does not apply to Somalia, for example, where US military interventions have served to replace a relatively stable Islamist government with an unpopular government of warlords. The situation has – uncontroversially, but also largely without comment – disintegrated into a catastrophe. In the worst areas of Somalia, the malnutrition rate exceeds that in Darfur. Instead of humanitarian intervention, therefore, the attack on Somalia is depicted as part of a war against al-Qaeda. But US engagement in Somalia did furnish some of the early impetus for liberal interventionism. It was during the United States' first intervention into Somalia, in which up to 10,000 people were killed by the US action, that Alex de Waal coined the term 'humanitarian international', and for reasons that are instructive.[115]

> I was working with Africa Watch, which was a component of Human Rights Watch, in 1992 when George Bush senior announced to great surprise that he was sending the troops into Somalia – it didn't seem like a vital US strategic interest. I wrote a column asking if the marines represented the vanguard of the humanitarian international or the storm-troopers of philanthropic imperialism. The opposition of myself and my colleague Rakiya to the US intervention caused us to lose our jobs – Rakiya was fired and I resigned. A few months later, when the confrontation with General Aideed's forces was heating up, I wrote about the violations of the Geneva Conventions by the UN troops there, and they tried to arrest me. Subsequently, a US military attorney who had been seconded to the UN explained that the UN troops would not be bound by the Geneva Conventions, as they had not written them.[116]
>
> It was clear that, given the US doctrine of overwhelming military force, and given its unwillingness to risk its own combat troops, all they could do was massacre large numbers of people. Yet, while most of the humanitarian international saw military action as a deviation from the necessary action to save lives, there were some who saw it as being the essential expression of humanitarianism, and who quietly saw it as being precisely what was needed.

Some of the arguments that then followed seemed to regurgitate the lexicon of colonialism.

> What you had in Somalia was a military intervention to protect the giver of aid. In Yugoslavia, UNPROFOR's role was to protect the UNHCR. It was out of a critique of that situation

that there developed the doctrine of the 'Responsibility to Protect'. The charge was that, as they were protecting aid workers, they ought to have protected civilians. That is in one way a slight advance. However, the discussion is always about what we can do for them, not what we might do to help them do it for themselves. And one right people might claim is a right to security, which might sometimes be served by intervention, but quite often will not be.[117]

The pristine culture of empire

There is a temptation to overstate the singularity of America's imperial ideology: the references to exceptionalism, Manifest Destiny, an evangelical crusade for a liberal world order, and so on, obscure as much as they reveal. It does matter that the United States government places emphasis on 'human rights' and cognate notions when it engages in overseas adventures, but there are structural reasons for this that are not specifically American. Ellen Meiksins Wood argues that this can be understood easily enough if we recall that capitalism does not need formal political inequalities – rather, domination and class rule are expressed as rights, specifically as property rights. The American empire is not a colonial one, instead seeking to sustain relations of domination through market transactions, guaranteed by an orderly global system of disciplined nation-states. It therefore seeks an ideology that legitimizes constant, open-ended interventions, requiring an *unprecedented* level of intervention and military build-up. The available ideological resources are narrowed by the formal disavowal of principles of inequality, so imperialists are obliged to draw on democratic and egalitarian ideologies.

The specifically American idea of democracy, as Wood has it, is extremely useful, since it is an impoverished notion, offering many strategies for insulating the public from the state. For example, formal elections were allowed to take place in Iraq (after considerable pressure), but the state is effectively controlled by networks of patrimonial tutelage, unelected 'reconstruction' bodies, and unaccountable bodies such as Ahmed Chalabi's Higher National Committee for the Eradication of the Baath Party. 'Advisors' from the Xanadu-like American embassy penetrate every ministry, while the basic political framework has been determined at every step by the coalition and its surrogates. Yet the belief that the US represents the sine qua non of democracy produces the assumption that the West, and America in particular, has the answers, and therefore a unique right to Americanize other states that the US deems threatening. Bush explained recently to Rush Limbaugh that, if America left Iraq, its oil resources would fall into the hands of those who would use them to blackmail America.[118] This carried two implicit assumptions: that a state not developed under American guidance would necessarily be irrational, undemocratic and bellicose; and that, because of this, America has a right to decide what happens to Iraq's resources and people. Genocidal levels of death are a price 'we' must pay for this right (even if 'we' don't pay it) – a consensus that also included Madeleine Albright. Liberal interventionists availing themselves of this ideology inhabit an almost impregnable moral fortress, from which they permit themselves to see only the empire's immense charity and benevolence.

It is long past time to drop the idea that empire is or can be a combination of social engineering, cultural therapy, feminist agitation, humanitarianism, internationalism, solidarity and enlightenment. It is none of these things – and nor, incidentally, is it of any benefit to ordinary Americans. At one time it was arguable that American primacy gave it the prosperity to improve the living conditions of most of its residents. However, the average American has experienced hardly any real wage growth for over thirty years, and has witnessed an especially dramatic contraction in income under Bush. The US has an iron curtain of military bases extending from Greenland, through Europe via the Balkans, into the Arab world and Africa, and right through Central Asia, many of them established through violent military interventions. The State Department's International Military Education and Training programme and similar programmes offer training to 70 per cent of the world's armies, and America's arms industries carefully direct weapons to surrogate armies, such as the warlords in Somalia and the death squads in Colombia.[119]

The American empire can be charged with its own triptych of crimes: connections to terrorism; colossal human rights abuses; and the development, proliferation, threat and use of weapons of mass destruction. It is the chief inheritor of the legacy of violent white supremacy. In addition to sustaining illiberal forms of domination and exploitation, it exacerbates global dangers, particularly the threat of nuclear elimination. We urgently need an international coalition of the willing, led by Americans, to take on the regime. As President Bush said in a different context, we do not want the smoking gun to become a mushroom cloud.

AFTERWORD TO THE
PAPERBACK EDITION

Shortly after the first edition of this book was published, I had the chance to gloat in the pages of the *Socialist Worker*: 'The pro-imperialist liberals, once vociferous and united in defence of US wars, are in a mess. The invasion of Iraq, on which so many of them waged their moral and intellectual credibility, has led to horrifying bloodletting. Numerous defections to the anti-war camp have left interventionists out in the cold. In their isolation they have degenerated into spiteful Islamophobic rhetoric. In truth, this pathetic faction has never looked less politically viable.'[1] Did I speak too soon? Is the recess of liberal bellicosity at an end?

Before considering this question, I want to state in brief, general terms what the hypotheses of this book have been. First, that today's pro-war liberal intellectuals stand in a tradition extending over roughly half a millennium. We have seen that their humanitarian support for imperialism is underpinned by the dehumanization of its opponents, and thus all too readily segues into bloody and vengeful rhetoric, and ultimately support for violent repression. Yet all the failings of today's liberal warriors have, as it were, a genetic origin. Liberalism was born one of a conjoined quintuplet, linking capitalism, European colonialism, slavery and 'race' ideology. Being in some respects an ideology of freedom and equality, it has nonetheless operated what Domenico Losurdo calls 'exclusion clauses', such that it was complicit in racial tyranny, imperialism and class domination.[2]

From Locke to Mill and Tocqueville, early to modern liberalism justified colonialism, usually on the grounds of its 'improving' character and beneficial effect for natives. Much of the early European Left and labour movement, particularly those elements of it closest to liberalism, were influenced by this pro-colonial chauvinism. Nor was it purely a European affair, as such supremacism was never more pungent than in its Wilsonian form. The Russian Revolution, subsequent anti-colonial revolutions and the US Civil Rights movement, weakened the hold of this ideology. Yet it has survived through adaptation and the modification of its terms. This is because the ideology of liberal imperialism has a structural role in explaining, justifying and consolidating a liberal world system that is necessarily an imperialist system.[3]

Second, that the pro-war liberals perform a role of advocacy, communicating ideas to strategically important audiences that are less likely to be reached by Pentagon spokespersons or Donald Rumsfeld. This point was perhaps underdeveloped in the first edition, so I will flesh it out a little here. In Gramscian terms, the liberal imperialists described in this book form part of a family of intellectuals and ideological producers who help consolidate the rule of the dominant classes. These are the 'organic intellectuals' of the bourgeoisie. This notion of Gramsci's was central to his arguments about hegemony. A ruling class, he argued, constantly works to construct hegemony by incorporating allied classes and class fractions into a wider bloc which dominates the excluded, subaltern classes. The unity of this bloc is secured partially by a hegemonic discourse produced by intellectuals who explain to the power bloc what its interests are, why its interests are universally valid and how they must be fought for and defended. Obviously, within such a bloc there is no clear, determinate interest that unites everyone, much less agreement on a particular strategy. This is why organic intellectuals are required, in various modes of specialization and reaching various kinds of audience, to provide moral and intellectual leadership.[4]

The subjects of this book vary greatly in terms of their locus of operation, their audience and their degree of specialization. Some, such as Michael Ignatieff and Samantha Power, successfully traverse the different fields of academia, opinion journalism and work within the state bureaucracy. Bernard Kouchner has migrated between the human rights industry, the French state and the UN with no great difficulty. Bernard-Henri Lévy, with the resources of a member of the French *haute bourgeoisie* at his disposal, is at will a philosopher, a documentary-maker, a diplomat, a publisher, a politician, a businessman, a journalist. Others such as Christopher Hitchens and Paul Berman are content in the role of polemical journalist in the pamphleteering tradition. And while Ignatieff, Kouchner and Power have tended to focus mainly on human rights in foreign policy, Hitchens, Berman and Lévy dilate comfortably on a variety of subjects. What they have in common is that the aspect of ruling-class power that they labour on is its international, imperialist power and that they operate not as isolated individuals, but as intellectual producers within larger systems (media conglomerates, academic institutions, state apparatuses) who disseminate their product to relatively privileged and powerful audiences. In this respect, they are not dissimilar to the neoconservatives with whom, I maintain, they share a vocabulary. The neoconservatives are also highly motivated but diverse intellectual producers, operating as much in the press as in the high mandarin departments of state and universities, and also work mainly on issues relating to imperial power. And of course, the neocons also suffered a tremendous blow as a result of the failure of Operation Iraqi Freedom.

That said, are the they and their liberal allies on the brink of resurgence? Do they now have a project capable of uniting them, and has their credibility recovered? Until very recently, the moralistic militarism that constituted the sharp edge of US global domination during Bush's tenure did seem to have lost much of its power. The US lacked the political capital, and its military was too overstretched, to countenance another war of liberation. Its inability to prevent a Russian victory over Georgia, when the latter's brutish ruler picked a fight over the ownership of South Ossetia, confirmed its newly limited power. Even Israel, Washington's prized asset in the Middle East, began to act erratically in an attempt to restore its lost deterrent capacity after the 2006 Lebanon war, its atrocities during Cast Lead and aboard the *Mavi Marmara*, costing it global support and causing division with its former ally Turkey. Lastly, far from being a proactive agent of change in the Middle East, the US was compelled to react, often in a delayed and incoherent fashion, as revolution struck at the heart of its regional hegemony.

While Tunisia was not central to US interests, the fall of its dictator, Zine El Abidine Ben Ali, accelerated the collapse of Hosni Mubarak's regime in Egypt. Egypt was the number-one recipient of US military aid in the world after Israel. Its strategic position as America's most-prized dictatorship was confirmed as the US refused to withdraw support and funding for the regime, even as the protests against it involved millions, and even as the dictator Hosni Mubarak launched his attempts to drown the revolt in blood.[5] A major worry for the US was that pro-Palestinian political forces would come to power, abrogate the Camp David Accords and cease to cooperate with Israel in its containment of the Palestinians. This cordial relationship, in crisis since Mubarak's overthrow, had seen Egypt collaborate with Israel's blockade of the Gaza Strip, and it was central to US strategy in the region. In its ideological expression, this geostrategic concern took the form of berating the Muslim Brotherhood and 'extremism', an articulation that naturally appealed to liberal advocates of war.

More broadly, the chain of pro-US regimes in the Middle East was being tested by the failure of the 'Washington Consensus' centred on neoliberal policies. The global recession, beginning with the credit crunch in 2007, had unleashed what David McNally refers to as a 'mutating crisis', in which the locus of the crisis was progressively displaced from subprime to the whole financial sector, before being transferred to states in the form of bailouts.[6] Finally, through 'austerity' measures, the crisis was shifted to the working class – in order to re-capitalize the banks, living standards for the majority had to come down. Several aspects of this crisis were concentrated in the regimes that fell, as high unemployment, low wages and soaring food prices added acute pressures to chronic problems in these societies. The social base of the regimes had become narrower as a result of their implementation of said neoliberal policies – privatization, deregulation and spending cuts – which tended to consolidate wealth and power among ever narrower elites. To implement these nostrums, the regimes had been forced to resort to intensified repression. Their internal security apparatuses, equipped and funded by the United States, worked to disorganize oppositional forces and thus erode any friction to the passage of such policies. Yet the long-term effect was to weaken the regimes' civil society base and to broaden the range of excluded subaltern layers. When the global crisis struck, those layers were fused into a mutinous multitude. Thus, if the proximate targets of their revolt were authoritarian patriarchs, in the background were the IMF, Wall Street and the regional systems sustaining US hegemony. This is why, far from the US leading a 'democratic' or 'Jeffersonian' revolution in the Middle East, it was at the vertex of an array of counterrevolutionary forces, as it struggled to buttress the crumbling battlements of these ancient regimes.

Given this constellation of circumstances, with the scope for US action so limited, there was little for the poetasters of empire to rally behind. Indeed, those neoconservatives and liberal bombers whom we might, following Martin Amis, brand the 'megadeath intellectuals' were surely consigned to irrelevance. If a popular-democratic revolution could overthrow an entrenched dictatorship, with nary a cruise missile in sight, these people who had bet all on the 101st Airborne surely had nothing useful to say. Yet, given the longevity of the tradition I've described and its structural relationship to the global system, the quietus of liberal imperialists cannot be taken for granted. There will always be opportunities for imperialist violence, and thus for its moralization. For when the revolt spread to Libya, the 'humanitarian interventionists' of the Obama administration found an avenue for the revival of US power allied with the anti-Gaddafi opposition. We will return to this later.

In the ensuing sections, we will examine a series of crises confronting US hegemony over the last three years, specifically in the Middle East; the resourceful response of the Obama administration; and the revival of liberal imperialism, and its limits.

The end of the Bush era

The Bush administration was staggering through its last days, the imperial triumphalism of its early years a despised and embarrassing memory. The conclusion to the first edition of this book, completed in 2008, itemized the backpedalling of some of the administration's liberal supporters. By and large, they retreated to the Democratic fold. The Democrats had won the 2006 congressional midterms, with the efforts of anti-war activists contributing significantly to their success. Barack Obama, a centrist Democrat who had opposed the Iraq war, was contesting the presidential election on a 'peace' mandate. To this extent, there was a precious irony in some of the most belligerent commentators finding themselves corralled into the camp of 'Obamamania'.

Yet, the most striking thing about Obama's foreign policy comportment was how conventional he was. He intended to continue the war in Afghanistan and Pakistan, and was surrounded by Clintonite retreads. The foreign policy group chosen by the incoming administration comprised a mixture of Realpolitikers and liberal interventionists. Among the Realists was Robert Gates, a survivor from the Bush administration chosen by Obama as defence secretary. General James Jones is another of that ilk, a seemingly low-key but significant appointment to the National Security Council – as it was Jones who led the Marines into the Iraq war. Unofficial advisors were said to include General Brent Scowcroft, a GOP Realist who opposed the Iraq war, and Zbigniew Brzezinski, a long-standing Democratic strategist and author of a severe indictment of the Bush administration from the perspective of an experienced mandarin deeply embedded in the foreign affairs establishment.[7]

Among the liberal interventionists were Susan Rice, Samantha Power and Anne-Marie Slaughter. Slaughter, dean at the Woodrow Wilson School of Public and International Affairs at Princeton University, was offered a position under Secretary of State Hillary Clinton. Susan Rice, a former Clintonite national security advisor, protégé of Madeleine Albright and strong advocate of intervention in Sudan, was appointed ambassador to the United Nations. Rice played an important role in supporting the partition of Sudan. Samantha Power, who is believed to have been a key advocate within the administration of intervention in Libya, was made a national security advisor. And there were many outside the administration pressing for a revived focus on humanitarian intervention. Former Clinton officials William Cohen and Madeleine Albright were heading the Genocide Prevention Task Force, who urged the incoming Obama administration to set up a 'genocide alert' system that would be used to trigger intervention into crisis situations. Both had been responsible for the implementation of the genocidal sanctions policy toward Iraq.[9]

Such an assembly of forces in the Obama administration suggested not a peace presidency, but rather a shift in strategy. US power would be resuscitated through a more cautious multilateral policy focused on winning consent among allies, with the doctrine of 'pre-emptive strikes' talked down.[10] America's immense military arsenal would be deployed more carefully – but it would be deployed. An important aspect of this story is the effect that the incoming administration had on those popular forces that had been ranged against Bush's foreign policy.

Historically, anti-war movements in the United States have tended to find themselves being conducted into the electoral strategies of one of the two dominant capitalist parties, usually the Democrats. So it was with the enormous anti-war coalitions of the Bush era. An important study of the US anti-war movement shows that, after 2006, the mainstream of the anti-war movement began to defect from the streets to the Democrats' election campaigns. This contributed to the loss of critical mass for the anti-war movement, particularly after 2008. There were other factors at work, including the stabilization of the occupation of Iraq after 2007, with a US 'tilt' toward Sunni leaders and a truce with the Mahdi Army drastically reducing the rate of insurgent attacks. In addition, the global recession, which began with the credit crunch in 2007, turned the attention of Americans toward 'bread and butter' issues. So it was that the Democratic Party took maximum advantage of dissatisfaction with the Bush administration among both elite and popular constituencies, and the mass movements of the Bush era melted away.[11] This has been an important precondition for the revival of liberal imperialism. Anti-war opinion remained strong for a number of reasons; but the ability of anti-war movements to reach critical mass, or even to move beyond small groups of hard-core activists, was fatally weakened.

From *Cast Lead* to the Mavi Marmara

Obama has had the misfortune to be president during a series of unprecedented crises for America's hegemony in the Middle East. Before the Arab Spring, the behaviour of its regional client Israel was the major bugbear. The assault on Gaza, known as Operation Cast Lead, beginning in December 2008, provoked the first crisis, causing a significant sector of liberal opinion to have doubts about Israel. Roger Cohen of the *New York Times* is typical of this trend. Normally pro-Israel, he called the Gaza war 'a travesty; I have never previously felt so shamed by Israel's actions. No wonder Hamas and Hezbollah are seen throughout the Arab world as legitimate resistance movements.'[12] Wider US public opinion was almost evenly divided, with 44 per cent of people saying they approved of the attacks, and 41 per cent opposed; a significant shift in a normally pro-Israel society.[13] In the UK, where opinion had already been shifting against Israel, a leading member of Labour Friends of Israel argued that the Ehud Olmert government had 'gone too far'. The attack was 'wrong in principle, erratic in practice and now damaging to longer-term peace prospects'.[14] It was, in many ways, a Budapest moment.

The sheer disbelief on the part of Israel's supporters can be accounted for by the unprovoked fury of the assault. Israel's rationale for attacking Gaza was that Hamas had broken a truce and was firing rockets into its southern population centres. In reality, the tentative truce, negotiated in June 2008, had already been broken. In exchange for a relaxation of an Israeli-imposed blockade on the Gaza Strip, Hamas had agreed to suppress rocket attacks on southern Israel. The blockade remained in place, with devastating consequences for the civilian population. The result was not merely that nine out of ten Palestinians in Gaza were forced below the poverty line, but, in the words of former UN Humanitarian Coordinator Mary Robinson, 'their whole civilization has been destroyed. I'm not exaggerating. It's almost unbelievable that the world doesn't care while this is happening.'[15]

Nonetheless, the unstable truce held until 4 November, when Israel unilaterally blocked all crossings into Gaza, preventing aid and trade, and began a series of bombing raids. Richard Falk, the UN human rights coordinator, characterized the action as a 'crime against humanity'. For his trouble, he was prevented by Israel from entering Gaza and detained. Finally, after a series of raids in December, Hamas returned rocket fire, as Israel intended. As a former IDF commander put it: 'You cannot just land blows, leave the Palestinians in Gaza in the economic distress they're in, and expect that Hamas will just sit around and do nothing.'[16] Only at this point was it widely acknowledged that the truce had been breached, and Hamas was duly blamed for it.[17] Even so, for all the bias of the Anglophone media and political classes, nothing could conceal the tremendous disproportion between Qassam rocket attacks, which rarely injured or killed anyone, and a premeditated aerial assault and invasion.

The military rationale for the attack was the need to counter a decline in Israel's 'deterrent capacity' following a series of setbacks, including its loss of southern Lebanon in 2000, and the catastrophic failure of the invasion in Lebanon in 2006 against a force largely composed of Lebanese volunteers rather than Hezbollah regulars. As importantly, though, Israel needed to counter Hamas's 'peace offensive'. The diplomatic strategy embarked on by Hamas to secure a relaxation of the blockade was in danger of proving viable. Hamas's success in curtailing rocket fire undermined the rationale for maintaining a system of collective punishment against Gaza, and threatened to legitimize a political movement that continued to resist Israeli aggression while Fatah, controlling the West Bank, merely acquiesced.[18]

The bombing focused on densely populated urban areas and was timed, moreover, in the most grotesque way. As the Israeli journalist Amira Hass wrote:

> This isn't the time to speak of ethics, but of precise intelligence. Whoever gave the instructions to send 100 of our planes, piloted by the best of our boys, to bomb and strafe enemy targets in Gaza is familiar with the many schools adjacent to those targets – especially police stations. He also knew that at exactly 11:30 A.M. on Saturday, during the surprise assault on the enemy, all the children of the Strip would be in the streets – half just having finished the morning shift at school, the others en route to the afternoon shift.[19]

The campaign began as it was intended to go on. UNRWA-run schools were routinely attacked. Rather than deny responsibility, Israel cheerfully admitted to attacking schools, on the pretext that Hamas had used these buildings to fire on the invading army – claims which the UN rejected.[20] In one of the most shocking incidents, the Red Cross reported that four children had been found starving next to their dead mother in a property in Zeitoun, where the IDF had sealed off the area before attacking it and preventing access for aid workers over several days.[21] The Israeli attack seemed to redefine the category of civilian, as adult males were automatically considered combatants by the military.[22] The doctrinal basis for this appeared to have been laid out by General Gadi Eisenkot in his elaboration of the 'Dahiya doctrine':

> What happened in the Dahiya quarter in Beirut in 2006 will happen in every village from which Israel is fired upon. We will apply disproportionate force upon it and cause great damage and destruction there . . . *From our standpoint, these are not civilian villages, they are military bases.* This is not a recommendation. This is a plan. And it has been approved.[23]

At the end of the bloodletting, the UN commissioned Richard Goldstone – himself a Jewish supporter of Israel – to investigate possible Israeli war crimes during the prosecution of Cast Lead. The report itemized dozens of war crimes, stating that the war was against 'the people of Gaza as a whole', and specifically 'aimed at punishing the Gaza population for its resilience and for its apparent support for Hamas'.[24]

Given this grisly reality, the reaction of much of the liberal establishment might have been expected to find some echo in Obama's response. Yet Obama said nothing. The president-elect was already putting his immense political capital at the service of the outgoing Bush administration and its bank bailouts. Yet, on Cast Lead, he insisted that he would have nothing to say. 'One president at a time', he had argued, implying that he would take no political stance on major issues until inaugurated come January.

The more plausible explanation for Obama's silence is that, in his election campaign, he had been even more pro-Israel than the Bush administration, telling the American Israel Public Affairs Committee (AIPAC) that Jerusalem would remain the 'undivided' 'capital of Israel'. This was an astonishing claim given that Jerusalem is not the capital of Israel and is the subject of ongoing negotiations. Under criticism, Obama was compelled to backtrack – but the signal had been sent to the correct constituency: Obama would be a 'true friend' to Israel.[25]

Yet if Obama's silence was merely tactful, there were those whose usual war lust failed them. Christopher Hitchens, for whom the bracing moral clarity of the 'war on terror' had revived his otherwise sagging political zeal, lost his afflatus. He wrote a single article on the subject, in which, unable to articulate a case for Israel's war and wholly lacking sympathy for the political forces dominant in the Gaza strip, he opted to belabour both sides.[26] In addition to constituting the sort of liberal prevarication for which he has habitually exhibited contempt, this also represented a further retreat on Hitchens's part from his previous uncompromising support for the Palestinians.[27]

However, Hitchens did not damn both sides equally. As in Israel's 2006 invasion of Lebanon, he held the usual local culprits – Iran, Hezbollah, Hamas – largely responsible for the situation. The forces of 'fundamentalism' were if anything more suspect than those of Zionist expansionism. Citing a self-pitying article by the Israeli historian Benny Morris (whose racism toward Arabs and support for ethnic cleansing is likely to be well known to Hitchens), he asserted in all seriousness that Israel was under existential threat from its neighbours.[28] War under such circumstances was inevitable. His main regret was the cynicism of its timing on Israel's part, as well as the dangerous messianism of the Israeli right. Hitchens's 'theophobia' has played the same role in his political trajectory as 'Stalinophobia' once played in the apostasy of the Cold War ex-communists.

Paul Berman, whom last we witnessed blending Arab nationalism and political Islam into a gruel-thin puree called 'Muslim totalitarianism', was more comfortable with the assault on Gaza. He had most recently written on the subject of Islamism's supposed insidious colonization of the European Left through the vector of the progressive Islamist Tariq Ramadan.[29] His concern with the 'Muslim branch of totalitarianism' was relevant in Gaza. Berman suggested that the suitability of Cast Lead depended on whether or not one judged Hamas to be a serious long-term threat, potentially capable of reinforcing the anti-Semitism of its charter through an alliance with a nuclear Iran and a resurgent Hezbollah. This hinged on an assessment of the future in which 'we stand in the dark, and we make guesses'. Thus: 'Those of us who look on the Gaza war from thousands of miles away enjoy the luxury of speculating this way or that way . . . Israel is in a bind. No matter what the Israelis choose to do, they have to recognize that they might be tragically wrong – either in their failure to defend themselves, or in the suffering they inflict on other people.'[30] Berman stopped short of simply endorsing Israel's strategic calculation, but he clearly felt it was theirs to make, and that the pummelling of UNRWA schools, the premeditated murder of families, and the blasting of ambulances and apartment buildings may yet be redeemed in the evaluation of informed historians.

If both Hitchens and Berman have their arguments with Israel's conduct, this could not be said of Bernard-Henri Lévy. As we have seen, he is apt to charge Israel's critics with anti-Semitism. During Cast Lead, he marched into Gaza with the Israeli army and reported on the war from their perspective. The last sighting of BHL in a war zone had been when, continuing his erratic journalistic career, he distinguished himself during the brief, armed contretemps between Russia and Georgia, by reporting on events in the shattered Georgian city of Gori, direct from the Marriott Hotel some eighty-five kilometres away in Tbilisi.[31] Assuming, then, that his reporting from Gaza was not conducted from a suite in Tel Aviv, it was nonetheless just as preposterous.

Israel, he vouched, was working overtime to protect civilians – the mere appearance of a grandmother hobbling out of a Hamas stronghold was enough to have any bombing raid cancelled, the pilot returned to base. He reminded us, moreover, that 'no other State in the world' would tolerate having rockets rained on its citizens. This, a common theme in Israeli *hasbara*, neglected to say what other people in the world would tolerate permanent occupation and blockade.[32] Israel's treatment of Arab minorities during the conflict was particularly worthy of 'admiration' according to BHL. Israel has been in a constant state of war since inception, yet 'it never gave up on the democratic values at its core'.[33]

The hosannas for Israel's democracy call to mind George Orwell's rebuke to pseudo-democratic cant during World War II: 'The unspoken clause is always "not counting niggers".'[34] Still, it would be churlish to deny BHL's credentials as a philosopher of war. He was then the recent author of *On War in Philosophy*, in which he described Immanuel Kant, the pioneer of 'democratic peace' theory, as an unhinged 'fake'. In support of this judgment, he copiously cited the work of the renowned philosopher Jean-Baptiste Botul. Botul was not merely a biographer and critic of Kant, but the founder of an intellectual tradition known as 'Botulism'. Lamentably, Botul, whose works included *The Sex Life of Immanuel Kant*, was also a fictional character, created by the satirist Frédéric Pagès. When his latest pratfall was disclosed, Lévy insisted that Pagès had invented a truer than real life Kant.

Michael Ignatieff, the doyen of 'humanitarian empire' and apologist for torture, had been made interim leader of the opposition Liberal Party in Canada when the war began.[36] Having made what he felt was 'an error' in criticizing Israeli war crimes in Lebanon, he was anxious not to be outflanked by the ruling Conservative Party on its support for Israel.[37] As such, he supported Israel's position, asserted that Gaza had been attacking Israel for ten years, and claimed that 'there is no occupation' in Gaza – a position not shared by the UN. And he blamed Hamas for civilian casualties during Cast Lead, accusing them of 'sheltering among civilian populations', a time-honoured technique for defending war crimes. Rejecting calls for negotiations, he said he 'wouldn't touch Hamas with a ten-foot pole.'[38] Thus, by and large the pro-war liberals articulated the Israeli propaganda position, which held that Hamas had caused the war and was not a 'partner for peace'.

As noted, though, Israel's supporters and apologists were marginalized, with little to fall back on but dire warnings of a Hamas-inspired Shoah that fewer and fewer people credited, particularly with Israeli ministers threatening Gaza with a 'holocaust'.[39] A result of this was an upsurge in sympathy for and activism on behalf of Gaza. The Israeli-imposed blockade was the natural target of such activism. A report by sixteen charities and humanitarian organizations a year after Cast Lead noted that the reconstruction of Gaza had been obstructed by the ongoing blockade. It stated:

> In the first three months after the offensive, joblessness in Gaza had crossed 40% of the workforce . . . With jobs and income plummeting and prices for many basic items rising, also because of the blockade, it is not hard to see why so many people in Gaza have been squeezed into a poverty trap. Even in May 2008, a survey showed that 70% of families were living on a dollar a day.[40]

In response to the grinding brutality of the blockade, a coalition of international activists organized around the Free Gaza Movement embarked on a series of missions, with flotillas sailing to Gaza to supply humanitarian aid. Beginning in 2008, they repeatedly attempted to reach Gaza's shores, including twice during Cast Lead, and were each time intercepted by Israeli forces. But in May 2010, a ship named the MV *Mavi Marmara* was acquired by the Turkish NGO IHH Humanitarian Relief Foundation, as part of a flotilla commandeered by the Free Gaza Movement to take supplies to Gaza. Israeli officials rushed to characterise the IHH as a terrorist-supporting organisation linked to al-Qaeda. Though evidence for this was negligible, it supplied the desired image of terrorists descending on Gaza with crates of weapons.[41]

At 4.30 a.m. on 30 May 2010, Israeli forces initiated an assault on the *Mavi Marmara* while it was in international waters. The ship was attempting to flee when it was attacked. By the end of the siege, nine volunteers had been shot dead by Israeli special forces, and dozens wounded. Five of the dead were shot in the head, and totalled thirty bullet wounds between them. The IDF alleged that the soldiers had been attacked first, and only responded with fire afterwards. In fact, an Al Jazeera journalist who was present reported that there had been fire from the air as Israeli forces descended on the ship. Several eyewitness accounts stated that the IDF opened fire indiscriminately and without provocation.[42] Nor did the killings look like the unpremeditated acts of men acting in self-defence. A UN fact-finding mission published in September 2010 confirmed numerous execution-style killings. For example, the nineteen-year-old Turkish-American citizen Furkan Doğan was shot five times. All but one shot hit him in the back. The other, which entered his face, was fired at point-blank range. But the very fact that the passengers resisted their assault, once it was underway, was used to damn them. A press release on the IDF website later claimed: 'Attackers of the IDF Soldiers Found to be Al Qaida Mercenaries'. This claim was later dropped after IDF spokespeople admitted, 'We don't have any evidence.'[44] The IDF also doctored an audio track of the siege to give the impression that flotilla passengers had told the soldiers to 'go back to Auschwitz'.[45] They also ineptly used a picture taken in 2006 to establish a connection between the flotilla and the global Jihad.[46] This was possibly the most ham-fisted PR effort Israel had ever embarked upon.

This siege, undoubtedly intended – like Cast Lead – to reinforce Israel's 'deterrent capacity', seems to have had the opposite effect of consolidating the range of forces opposed to it. The Palestinian writer and human rights activist Omar Barghouti wrote that the massacre was 'not only categorically immoral and patently illegal but undeniably irrational, too. It is swelling the ranks of those who support boycott, divestment and sanctions against Israel until it supports international law and basic human right.'[47]

Still, there were those who kept the faith. The overlap between Israel's propaganda and the attitudes of liberal intellectuals criticizing the Free Gaza activists was remarkable. For example, it was an article of faith among Israel's supporters that the activists were, had to be, *asking for it*. The prevailing view was that they were fanatics looking for violence – and they got it. Thus, the liberal Israeli commentator and novelist David Grossman marvelled that 'a small Turkish organization, fanatical in its religious views and radically hostile to Israel', had 'managed to lure Israel into a trap, precisely because it knew how Israel would react, knew how Israel is destined and compelled, like a puppet on a string, to react the way it did.'[48]

Seth Freedman, writing in the *Guardian*, asserted that Israel had 'no choice' but to murder the aid workers because they had 'issued threat after threat against the IDF in the days building up to this morning's clash' and on the day were using 'iron bars and other weapons to assault the troops and giving the IDF carte blanche to respond with

force against them.'[49] The figure of a helpless Israel compelled by
vicious opponents into killing them has a venerable history, going back
to Golda Meir's infamous suggestion that she would never forgive the
Arabs for making Israel kill their children.[50]

For Hitchens, Israel's action was not malicious – the soldiers only
shot 'when panicked'. At most, it was 'stupidity', running straight into
'a preplanned riot'. He reserved his bombast for Israel's opponents and
his insinuating contumely for its victims. More than the murder of
unarmed civilians aboard a civilian vessel in international waters, he
was vexed by the prospect of construction equipment being delivered
to Hamas: 'is it really humanitarian to make contributions to a ruling
party that has a totalitarian and racist ideology and is in regular receipt
of nonhumanitarian aid from Syria and Iran, two of the most retrograde and aggressive dictatorships in the world?'[51]

BHL, too, insisted that the action was 'stupid', chiefly because it had
handed a propaganda coup to its opponents. The world urgently
needed to be told that Israel was not imposing a vicious blockade on
the Palestinians, that 'the blockade concerns only arms and the material needed to manufacture them' and that 'it is a lie to state that people
are "dying of hunger" in the streets of Gaza City' – no matter that
numberless humanitarian agencies assert the contrary. With a sense of
proprietary outrage, he also intimated that he had helped organize
such symbolic humanitarian actions in the past and found this version
a tawdry imitation.[52]

The precedent set by the assault on the Mavi Marmara is not always
seen as a bad one. For instance, British author Howard Jacobson took
issue with the African American author Alice Walker in June 2011 about
her plans to join a Gaza freedom flotilla. He charged, in typically pneu-
matic prose, that the flotilla bore 'a cargo of intention . . . freighted with
political sympathy and attitude'. It was 'a provocation', 'half inviting a
violence which can then be presented as a slaughter of the innocents.'
Had there been a repeat of the Gaza flotilla raid, with the accompanying
carnage, it would have been the fault of the activists for 'luring the Israeli
military into action which can be represented as brutal'.[53] Once again,
Israel's victims are asking for it. This is the rationale that Alexei Sayle
characterized as 'the psychology of the murderer . . . the psychology of
the rapist . . . the psychology of the bully'.[54]

Nonetheless, the tendency following the event was very much as
depicted by Omar Barghouti. The strategic cleavage with Turkey resulting from the massacre hinted that Israel's regional power was weakening.
Yet this was as nothing compared to the rude awakening that both
Israel and its US sponsor were about to receive.

The 'Arab Spring', and Libya's revolution hijacked

While it is fair to say that the pro-war liberals have evinced little but contempt for Palestinian human rights and democracy (particularly if they vote for Hamas), the series of revolts dubbed the 'Arab Spring' in late 2010 and early 2011 produced, at least in some quarters, a renewed fervour for Arab democracy. Within the Obama administration, the humanitarian interventionists began to see ways in which the US could realize its longer-term interests by shifting its support away from the dictators. By February, they had found a cause on account of which the US could lead the world into war with a moral mandate.

Liberal imperialists were in a potentially difficult situation, as the first two regimes to fall, Tunisia and Egypt, were US allies whose opponents included the hated Islamists. Other threatened regimes in Yemen and Bahrain also comprised important links in the chain of repressive states supported by the US. Since these pundits had bet on the US armed forces as an agent of liberation, the prospect of the US being an openly counterrevolutionary force was an unsettling one. Moreover, the contrast between the chaos of Afghanistan and Iraq with the genuine emancipatory thrill of Tahrir Square was striking. Consider that, according to a recent study by the humanitarian organization Relief International, the war on Iraq produced one million widows. This establishes a minimum of a million adult males killed by the occupation.[55] Consider also that many of those who died would have been children, women or unmarried adult males, and the death toll looks considerably higher. It becomes evident that what was billed as 'liberation' was an atrocity comparable with some of the worst in the twentieth century. Some of the soi-disant democrats and humanitarians such as Ignatieff and BHL could certainly greet the Middle East revolutions with jubilation.[56] But they could not do so without a certain amount of hypocrisy and bad faith.

A particularly striking example of this was Paul Berman's argument that the Arab Spring confirmed that 'the pathologies of totalitarian movements' should be opposed 'by argument, above all'. Arabs and Iranians had been increasingly won over by anti-dictatorial arguments, and this was 'the only way that a true solution of these various problems was ever going to be found'.[57] This does not mean that Berman relents on the 'necessary wars' in Iraq and Afghanistan. He has backpedalled, gracelessly, but never recanted on supporting these wars.[58] Rather, he simply chooses not to acknowledge that there is a contradiction between supporting popular, democratic movements as a solution to dictatorship and supporting brutally repressive wars as a solution to dictatorship.

And the jubilation was not unmixed. Indeed, as the bloodletting began, Egyptians had to hear two of the world's most bellicose (and, at different stages, powerful) liberals lavish praise on Mubarak. Vice President Joseph Biden declared that Mubarak was not a dictator, and should not step down. He was an 'ally of ours' who was valuable because of his relationship with Israel.[59] Tony Blair (a man with a 'moral pulse' – *dixit* Christopher Hitchens) remarked that Mubarak was 'immensely courageous and a force for good' due to his support for Israel. Blair also warned against rapid change or elections because 'if you open up a vacuum, anything can happen'. The 'extremists', by whom he meant the Muslim Brotherhood, might win an election.[60] On the face of it, it is surprising that Tony Blair should be so concerned about Islamists governing Egypt. He has shown remarkable understanding toward a well-known authoritarian Islamist government, the Saudi regime. Challenged about its habit of beheading disorderly subjects, Blair retorted, 'They have their culture, their way of life.'[61]

The unsettling effect of the revolutions can also be seen in the writing of Christopher Hitchens. While broadly sympathetic to the uprisings, his support for imperialism and his obsession with the Islamist folk-devil clearly affected his stance. His writing on Tunisia prior to its 'Jasmine Revolution' had been lyrical and evocative concerning this 'frontline territory between Europe and Africa'. Acknowledging that the country had a dictatorship, he nonetheless vouched that 'people do not lower their voices or look over their shoulders . . . before discussing these questions.' Celebrating its accomplishments, he lauded its banning of the Islamist opposition and complained that Rachid Ghannouchi, the leader of the Islamist party al-Nahda, was unwelcome in Tunisia but 'allowed to broadcast his hysterical incitements into Tunisia from a London station.'[62] After all:

> Why pick on mild Tunisia, where the coup in 1987 had been bloodless, where religious parties are forbidden, where the population grows evenly because of the availability of contraception, where you can see male and female students holding hands and wearing blue jeans, and where thousands of Americans and more than four million Europeans take their vacations every year?[63]

And so, unsurprisingly, Hitchens greeted the 2010–11 uprising by remarking that Tunisia was the 'most civilized dictatorship' in the Middle East, whose subjects rebelled because 'they knew they could. There was scant likelihood of the sort of all-out repression and bloodshed that was met by, say, the protesters against the Iranian mullahs.'[64]

(This was untrue: the death toll from the Tunisian revolution stood at 224 by its end. The death toll from the suppression of the Iranian Green movement was 72 according to the opposition.)[65] And for all that he welcomed the revolt, he expressed unease at the emergence of al-Nahda leaders from exile to participate in the new democracy. Hitchens's evasions and revisions on Tunisia segued neatly into his pouring cold water on the Egyptian revolution, which he suggested (writing in early February) would likely fail, as 'the Arab world is almost completely unlettered and unversed' in 'the language of civil society'.[66]

In general, the pro-war liberals did not choose to disparage the revolution, laud Mubarak or openly fret about a vacuum, as Blair and Biden did. Yet, it was to be the failure of a revolt against Colonel Gaddafi, only a recent ally of the United States, which really energized them.

The first opportunity for the US to intervene in the Middle East revolutionary process arose when the revolt in Libya began to falter. Its difficulties, and hence its vulnerability to an offshore takeover, are worth examining in some detail. The revolution that began on 17 February 2011, in its initial phase, resembled its immediate predecessors in some aspects of its composition. The leading figures were middle-class human rights activists, lawyers and professionals ranged against a dictatorship that allowed almost no political liberty whatever. The mass base was the working classes, concentrated mainly in the eastern cities and towns, though they lacked any independent organization, such as parties or unions. This points to a significant contrast with Egypt and Tunisia. In the Jamahiriya, political parties and trade unions were banned as, in theory, the direct democracy of 'people's committees' needed no mediation by such hierarchies. Of course, the committees were stuffed with Gaddafi's supporters. This meant that the revolution, when it began, had no organized labour movement, and no left wing. The emergent 'popular committees' were the main form of popular organization, but these were disarticulated, disunited and no match for a centralized state that Gaddafi could mobilize.

Meanwhile, the dictatorship was a fairly typical oil rentier state, and had been so since oil was first discovered in the country in the late 1950s. Its monopoly of energy and related services gave the state a particular prominence in the economy, and meant that the larger sections of the Libyan ruling class were integrated into the state. This did not change with the coming to power of Gadaffi and the Free Officers in a bloodless coup in 1969. Promising to meet popular demands, and tapping into popular suspicion of the metropolitan, central state rooted in the colonial era, Gaddafi nonetheless built a national security state like its neighbours', ruthlessly persecuting dissidents and spending over a tenth of the country's GDP on the military.[67]

Though the regime had won recognition from the Nixon White House for its anti-communism, its policy of supporting Third World liberation movements, opposing the Camp David Accords and purchasing weapons from the USSR was enough to earn it the hostility of the Reagan White House. The US attempted to subvert the regime in various ways, supporting rebel armies, bombing the country in 1986 over spurious charges of a terrorist bombing in a Berlin nightclub, and getting UN sanctions applied after the Lockerbie bombing, which was dubiously blamed on Libyan suspects.[68] More than any other policy, it was sanctions, costing the Libyan government between $18 billion and $33 billion, that forced Gaddafi to seek rapprochement with the EU and US. In the context of the 'war on terror', he referred to his own battles with an Islamist insurgency beginning in the 1990s, and pledged to join the fight against 'al-Qaeda'. This allowed Libya to join the caste of favoured nations without engaging in any dangerous political liberalization.[69]

The ensuing nuptials with Blair and Bush resulted in platoons of lobbyists, oil industry flaks, economists, statesmen and neoliberal technocrats working to accelerate the development of a private sector capitalist elite. Among those flocking to Gaddafi's side were neoconservatives Richard Perle, Francis Fukuyama and Bernard Lewis; former US Vice President Dick Cheney; Democratic strategist Joseph Nye; and 'Third Way' thinker Anthony Giddens, who remarked that 'As one-party states go, Libya is not especially repressive. Gaddafi seems genuinely popular ... Will real progress be possible only when Gaddafi leaves the scene? I tend to think the opposite.'[70]

The neocons and liberals who flocked to Gaddafi believed that the regime was stable, but its social basis was actually undergoing a slow disintegration. Its refusal to permit legal opposition meant that its most serious challenges came in the form of armed rebellion, in which terrain it had a clear advantage. Further, these challenges tended to be regionally concentrated in the east, and did not spread more widely. However, the punitive policies and persistent underdevelopment of the east created a bedrock of opposition from which revolt could spread. And the neoliberal reform project embarked upon under the stewardship of Saif al-Gaddafi resulted in a strategic cleavage in Libya's ruling class between a relatively conservative state capitalist elite and a neoliberal elite rooted more in the private sector and with fresh-minted connections to Euro-American power. The regional uprisings accelerated this fissure, while giving heart to Libya's dissidents.

Thus, when Gaddafi's forces responded to the Day of Rage by Libyan protesters with machine-gun fire, it had the effect of widening the cracks in the regime. The rebellion, far from remaining localized, spread. The ruling class split became a chasm, as regime elements began to break away and side with the rebels. These included the former Interior Minister General Abdel Fatah Younes and sections of the armed forces. It was partly because of this that the Libyan rebels were able to quickly achieve an advantage that the Egyptian revolutionaries lacked – dual power, founded on the control of major urban centres. The absence of popular organization meant that it was the former-regime elements, such as businessmen, military figures and professionals – in a word, those who were already powerful – who stepped in to form the nucleus of a rival government, the National Transitional Council (NTC). And though this outfit struggled to stamp its authority on the rebellion, it remains the sole national representative body that has developed.[71]

A combination of military weakness and the dominance of conservative elites resulted in a series of setbacks for the rebels and the appearance of behaviour among them wholly incompatible with the emancipatory thrust of the revolution. Gaddafi had attempted, by forcing the issue into a terrain in which his military superiority gave him the advantage, to finish the rebellion quickly and painfully. Though initially this only exacerbated his woes, he did gain the upper hand, thwarting any insurgency in Tripoli and retaking lost cities. And as this happened, the space for political paranoia opened among the rebels. The leadership began to spread rumours that 'African mercenaries' were being used as an alien element against the rebellion. In this context, 'African' meant 'black'. The rumours were largely unfounded, but a series of lynchings, beatings and mass arrests of black workers and migrants began in rebel-controlled areas. After Gaddafi's downfall, the process seemed to accelerate, with gruesome killings, thousands of black workers and immigrants being rounded up, and even ethnic cleansing in some areas taking place.[72]

Unfortunately, this related to a wider tendency to racialize the conflict, as anti-Gaddafi graffiti often depicted him as a demonic Jew. The racism in Libyan society could have potentially been overcome by political forces of the Left, or by labour organisation, arguing for unity among the oppressed. Unfortunately, the initiative was in the hands of ruling-class factions who had profited from Libya's class-divided society and the exploitation of migrant workers. Indeed, among the rebel leaders were former Foreign Secretary Moussa Koussa, who had implemented Libya's harsh policies toward migrants. The rebel leadership would later promise EU powers to keep these policies in place.[73]

With the regime making a comeback, a number of leading figures began to call for external intervention to protect the revolution. This had been the position of some from quite early on. Libyan diplomat Ibrahim Dabbashi called for a no-fly zone after the first week of fighting, though he was isolated at that stage. By 1 March, with the rebellion in retreat, General Abdel Fatah Younes was calling for air strikes. Still, there was widespread opposition in Libya to foreign intervention. Hafiz Ghoga expressed the sentiment clearly: 'We are completely against foreign intervention. The rest of Libya will be liberated by the people and Gaddafi's security forces will be eliminated by the people of Libya.' Signs appeared in Benghazi, the liberated capital of the rebellion, warning against intervention.[74]

It required constant setbacks for the rebels before the majority acquiesced in what seems to have been a deal between the NTC leadership and NATO powers. Not that the imperialist powers waited for a say-so, or a UN vote, to begin coordinating their involvement. The political pressure for a no-fly zone, coming from the former colonial powers Britain and France, began quite soon after the rebellion took off. NATO planning for such a possibility began in late February. All indications are that warships were already being dispatched, and intelligence and special forces were on the ground, from the beginning of March.[75]

'In my opinion,' Defence Secretary Robert Gates warned, 'any future defense secretary who advises the president to again send a big American land army into Asia or into the Middle East or Africa should "have his head examined", as General MacArthur so delicately put it.' This quip, uttered amid revolutions that the US seemed powerless to put down or control, seemed to signal a serious ideological 'drawdown', as the Realpolitikers in the Obama administration brought Bush-era adventurism to a close. Foreign policy Realists such as Stephen Walt, co-author with John Mearsheimer of *The Israel Lobby*, had long been encouraged by 'hints of realism emerging from the Obama administration', quite in contrast to the 'fits of hubris' that had marked US foreign policy under Bush.[76]

This stance made the liberal interventionists very unhappy. Anne-Marie Slaughter complained that the US was 'defining "vital strategic interest" in terms of oil and geography, not universal values.' This would 'come back to haunt us'.[77] Yet, by the end of March, Slaughter

could exult in Obama's decision to intervene in Libya. This she celebrated in classically Wilsonian cadences. The president, she suggested,
had shown it was possible to defend American interests in a way that
also reflected American values. Both for reasons of prudence and principle, the US should be seen to side with the aspirations of the young
people who represent 60 per cent of the Middle East population, and
not the dictators. Supporting a liberal world order would engender
greater security and bolster US hegemony. Now, far from worrying that
Obama was selling out the cause to Realpolitik, Slaughter paid tribute
to Obama as a man of principle who 'came to power vowing to reject
torture and close Guantánamo (though that has proven difficult to
accomplish in practice)'.[78] This careful airbrushing, as well as the
narcissism of a perspective in which every global problem is ultimately
defined as an American dilemma, is reflexive. And it would seem
pedantic to note that Obama has vigorously conserved the use of
torture and expanded the executive powers that facilitate it.[79]

What made the difference between February and March? A number
of things, it seems. To begin with, the governments of Britain and
France forcefully lobbied for intervention, thus making a multilateral
force possible. Indeed, France preempted its allies in recognizing the
Benghazi-based opposition as the legitimate government of Libya,
following a high-profile meeting with opposition leaders in the Elysée
Palace facilitated by Bernard-Henri Lévy (of which more later).[80]

Further, the opposition leadership was increasingly composed of
former regime elements known to be pro-US. These included such
figures as Mahmoud Jibril, the chair of the National Transitional
Council who had previously headed Libya's Economic Development
Board, a pro-privatization initiative jointly launched by Saif al-Gaddafi
and Michael Porter of the Harvard Business School. Jibril had been
one of the neoliberal reformers of the regime, advocating a new relationship with the US based on 'more than oil'.[81] These were the people
requesting intervention by mid-March, and whatever was said in negotiations, they evidently dispelled any lingering distrust that Washington
may have had of them.

And the intervention would be mandated by the United Nations and
would not involve a land invasion, but air strikes with intelligence and
special forces coordinating on the ground to assist an indigenous army.
Finally, presumably in light of the foregoing, the State Department
under Hillary Clinton shifted decisively behind intervention. Clinton
seems to have sided with the supporters of 'humanitarian intervention'
in the cabinet very late in the day, and taken no more than a few hours
to lobby Obama into changing his position on the Monday. In doing so,

she sided against the Realists in the administration like Robert Gates and National Security Advisor Timothy Donilon, who argued that Libya was not vital to US national interests and that Qaddafi's replacements could be linked to 'al-Qaeda'.[82]

This was not therefore a premeditated master plan to grab Libya's oil or dispose of an unreliable flake. It was one of a series of improvised, uncertain and highly contested responses by US power to the unfolding revolt in an attempt to manage the process. Importantly, these responses were not separate from one another, but co-dependent. For example, in order to win Arab League backing for intervention, it is reported that Hillary Clinton lobbied Saudi Arabia, offering them a deal in which the US would support the Saudi invasion of Bahrain to murder the peaceful uprising that had begun on the archipelago.[83] Nor should the proximity of avowed humanitarian, even revolutionary, motives to extreme repression and bloodshed be at all surprising. We have seen US imperialism in its 'revolutionary' guise before.

The relief of pro-war commentators was palpable. What is striking, though, is that their major concern was usually not Libya itself. Their analysis of the situation in Libya was usually thin and often cursory. They were much more interested in restoring the (moral, political and military) capacity of the states they supported. The bombing was thus hailed by the Henry Jackson Society, a lobby uniting liberals and neoconservatives in support of 'Western values', as 'The Welcome Return of Interventionism': 'The so-called "lessons of Iraq" and the faltering of the mission in Afghanistan suggested that interventionism was out of fashion. However, events in the Middle East rendered this stance redundant.'[84]

Bernard Kouchner was just as delighted. In the last few years, the founder of 'humanitarian intervention' had been dogged by revelations regarding his business dealings with the corrupt dictatorships in Gabon and the Democratic Republic of Congo, and with his work for the Total oil company in Burma, among other things. (Kouchner responded in fine fashion by accusing the author of said revelations of being anti-Semitic.)[85] Still, with war underway under a humanitarian rubric, Kouchner was in his element. For him, the key issue was not really whether Libyans could be left to die 'in full view of our TV cameras'. It was what would become of Europe. Libya 'highlights the need for the EU to grow stronger and gain greater coherence, in keeping with the promise of the Lisbon treaty.' 'We all know', he suggested, 'there could be nothing worse than a warmongering Europe . . . except perhaps a powerless Europe.' Thus, a 'middle course' must allow Europe to assert itself in world affairs. Libya was merely the fortunate testing ground for this middle course.[86]

Yet, as we might put it to Christopher Hitchens, why pick on Libya? In theory, there was much for Hitchens to like about Gaddafi's regime. Here was a society where religious parties were banned (because all opposition parties were banned), where the regime came to power as a result of a bloodless coup, where women had more freedom than in many neighbouring states, and where Islamists were killed. Yet, when it came to Gaddafi's meltdown, there was suddenly a fresh energy in Hitchens's prose and his indictments of the White House. Obama 'dithered' over Tunisia and Egypt, and now did nothing while Gaddafi, 'an all-round stinking nuisance and moreover a long-term *enemy*', hunted the opposition. Railing against the cautious Realists, he insisted: 'In the Mediterranean, the United States maintains its Sixth Fleet, which could ground Qaddafi's air force without breaking a sweat . . . The United States, with or without allies, has unchallengeable power in the air and on the adjacent waters. It can produce great air lifts and sea lifts of humanitarian and medical aid, which will soon be needed anyway along the Egyptian and Tunisian borders, and which would purchase undreamed-of goodwill. It has the chance to make up for its pointless, discredited tardiness with respect to events in Cairo and Tunis.'

Thus, for Hitchens – who does not wear his new-found nationalism lightly – this was as much an opportunity to revive America's global reputation as anything else. In fact, he took the opportunity to recuperate the Iraq war from widespread ignominy, suggesting that the overthrow of Saddam had been 'an unnoticed and unacknowledged benefit' to the revolution 'whose extent is impossible to compute'.[87] (Hitchens, a stylist in the tradition of Orwell, seems to have forgotten the guru's injunction not to 'say anything outright barbarous'.) Nor were the wishes of Libyans decisive in his view. Acknowledging, in early March, that the revolutionaries still appeared 'to want this achievement [the overthrow of Gaddafi] to represent their own unaided effort', he insisted that 'it doesn't excuse us from responsibility'. This was because Gaddafi's 'revolutionary' foreign policy was a security menace. 'Even if Gaddafi basked in the unanimous adoration of his people, he would not be entitled to the export of violence,' he observed. Accepting that Hitchens is indeed scandalized by the 'export of violence', it is odd that he chose to cite policies long since abandoned, dropped when the Gaddafi regime began making eyes at the US. As ever, there was also an element of egocentrism in Hitchens's position: 'I am sure I am not alone in feeling rather queasy about being forced to watch the fires in

Tripoli and Benghazi as if I were an impotent spectator.'[88] America should bomb someone so Hitchens doesn't feel impotent. Alas, he is not an international diplomat like the *gaffeur* Bernard-Henri Lévy.

BHL, an old friend of Nicolas Sarkozy, evidently had no doubt that if he called the Elysée Palace switchboard on 27 February, he'd be put through to the president. He was. He told le petit Nicolas that he was on his way to Benghazi. Sarkozy wanted BHL to do him a favour – look out for rebel leaders that the French state could deal with. And so he did, arriving in Benghazi with the usual photographers on hand to record his doings, before addressing a rebel meeting and offering to take the leaders to meet the French president. He then introduced Sarkozy to the "Libyan Massouds", referring to his alliance with the Northern Alliance leader Ahmed Shah Massoud. Thus, he precipitated France's rush to intervene in Libya.

Taking this story with an advisable pinch of salt, for it is one spun by BHL himself, it is not unlike the man to engage in dramatic diplomacy. As with Bosnia, self-promotion is involved. It was on account of his habit of sweeping in and out of war zones flanked by cameras and entourage that Susan Sontag used to call BHL 'DHS', meaning 'Deux Heures à Sarajevo'. There was also the stink of hypocrisy, as *Le Monde Diplomatique* pointed out, since BHL had never shown the slightest interest in Arab democracy when it was contrary to Israel's interests. Of course, for BHL, his sweat purchased a stay of execution for a population facing a 'bloodbath'. However, the long-term benefit that he sees as coming out of the intervention is the international validation of the principle of '*droit d'ingérence*' (right of interference), devised by Bernard Kouchner and Mario Betatti: "For the first time this concept was endorsed by the Arab League, by the African Union and by the UN security council. This is huge."[89] After all these years, and all these wars, BHL is still worried that powerful states may not be sufficiently empowered to intervene in the affairs of others.

It was predictable that the cruise missile liberals would seize on any chance to reorganise and revitalise 'Western' power. Whether working inside the Obama administration, networking with Sarkozy or writing for privileged audiences, nothing enlivens such people like a 'just war'. Yet, have we really witnessed the 'return of interventionism'? It is true that the bombing of Libya was supported by the leadership of a popular rebellion. It is also true that the bombing was relatively light and probably incurred relatively few casualties as wars go (none on the NATO side). Further, by preventing troop concentrations on Gaddafi's side, clearing the way for rebel advances and keeping pressure on the regime to ensure its eventual disintegration, the NATO intervention ensured the opposition's success, which would otherwise have been impossible. Lastly, this regime change was effected at remarkably little cost in Pentagon terms – a mere $1 billion. This would suggest that Obama is a far better imperialist than Bush was. It also seems to open the path for further wars elsewhere, perhaps in Syria.

Furthermore, the fragmentation of opinion among the antiwar Left over this issue has been remarkable. On the one hand, some anti-war forces controversially saw Gaddafi's regime as relatively 'progressive'.[90] Some defended the revolution against the pro-Gaddafi voices, but argued that the intervention was liable to usurp the initiative and power of the masses and transfer it to a handpicked elite. If the opposition was to defeat Gaddafi, they needed weapons, not NATO.[91] And others, for some excellent reasons and a few poor ones, regarded military intervention in Libya as a necessary evil. Analysts as different as Gilbert Achcar and Juan Cole, while acknowledging the dangers of empowering imperialist states in this situation, nonetheless insisted that the rebel leadership had a right to solicit outside help, that it was necessary to prevent the massacre of revolutionaries in Benghazi, and that it would enable the momentum to continue and spread beyond Libya.[92] Such divisions are perhaps not so consequential, since the Left is almost materially powerless to do anything but have an opinion in this situation. Yet, if even a few on the Left are defending intervention in a way that hasn't been the case since the Kosovo war, there is a case for saying that the liberal imperialists are back in their element.

Before declaring the carcass of pro-war liberalism reanimated, however, there are a few considerations that we have not yet looked at. The conditions that made the Libyan intervention so successful on its own terms are unlikely to be reproduced elsewhere. The presence of dissident ruling-class factions with ties to the US and EU was an unusual feature brought about by the period of 'engagement' with Gaddafi prior to the revolution. There was also a considerable stroke of luck for NATO in Gaddafi falling just when he did, as it cut through the strained negotiations between the NTC and regime officials. NATO was running out of bombing targets, the rebels had lost momentum, and the most likely outcome was either some sort of diplomatic carve-up or the de facto partition of Libya.[93] By most analyses it was quite possible for the Gaddafi regime to have held on, and prior to its implosion it was in fact making territorial gains.[94] Had it done so, the view of military commanders such as General Carter Ham was that it was unlikely that Gaddafi could be shifted without a ground invasion, which the opposition leadership didn't want.[95] The fact that both the US and its allies worked to avoid a land invasion suggests that the 'Iraq syndrome' is not going to disappear any time soon. In this respect, Hitchens is absolutely right to say that the invasion of Iraq benefited Libya.

It is also striking that this war did not carry public support. By and large, European publics favoured 'humanitarian intervention' in Yugoslavia. But in neither the US nor the UK did majorities support the bombing campaign in Libya.[96] This is the other side of the 'Iraq syndrome'. Further, for a war that was ostensibly aimed at narrow humanitarian objectives, the intervention failed one of the most elementary humanitarian tests – the exhaustion of all peaceable alternatives. Almost as soon as the bombs started flying, there was suddenly talk of a possible negotiated settlement, as if it had only just been thought of.[97]

Further, the humanitarian rationale suffered not only when it emerged that the rebels were engaging in atrocities, but also when many of the claims about Gaddafi's atrocities turned out to be falsified.[98] One of the remarkable benefits of the revolution had been the ability to turn free cities into independent media centres. But as soon as winning the support of overseas power became an imperative, these became sources of propaganda. For example, it was claimed early on by rebel leaders that Gaddafi was carrying out a 'genocide', and that should he take Benghazi he would kill up to half a million people.[99] There was no precedent for such a scale of barbarism in Gaddafi's previous crackdowns, nor had anything like this level of atrocity been evident in the rest of Libya during the uprising. And while the rebel leadership claimed a total of 50,000 deaths resulting from the war as Gaddafi fell, the *New York Times* reporters investigating the country's mortuaries were able to find no evidence of this. Even the specific justification for a no-fly zone looked threadbare when it emerged that, as Patrick Cockburn reported, 'There is no evidence that aircraft or heavy anti-aircraft machine guns were used against crowds.'[100]

This is emphatically not to minimize the actual crimes of the regime as it embarked on a pitiless counterinsurgency. It is to say that the true nature of this was exaggerated and distorted to justify intervention. Moreover, while one would expect the crimes to come to an end once the regime had fallen, it is reported that graves are filling up with people deemed to have been pro-Gaddafi, with no explanation offered as to the cause of death.[101] Among these will be the many black men being rounded up and slaughtered by the newly empowered opposition forces. As Alex Thomson reported for Channel 4 News, 'This is a bad time to be a black man in Libya'.[102]

Once the humanitarian rationale is stripped away, what is left is the politics of intervention. And this must be assessed in the wider context of the Arab Spring. Washington, unable to prevent the toppling of client regimes, has attempted to provide its alternative to the thronging, vibrant democracy of Tahrir Square, the city within a city that withstood waves of assault from the dictatorship. The group of 'humanitarian interventionists' are correct to diagnose that this is what the US must do if it is to have any power in the new Middle East. But the alternative is roughly that signposted by Tony Blair: gradual reform, managed by trusted elites. The population is untrustworthy, susceptible to extremism, apt to have 'the wrong idea and a closed idea'.[103] NATO has brought to power not the population of Libya, but an alliance of regime elements, businessmen and professionals with whom Euro-American powers share some interests. The old regime is being reconstituted and fast-forwarded through the kind of reform process that Saif al-Gaddafi was once entrusted with. At the same time, the repression continues in Yemen and Bahrain with US support.

Yet, the US remains a declining power, its limitations evident in the cautiousness of its role in Libya. The administration has been unable to reach a convincing victory, or even conclusion, in Afghanistan, and has not reclaimed America's lost power in Latin America. And as such, while Libya may have temporarily cheered up the liberal imperialists, it seems unlikely that there will be a basis for their ideological revival in the immediate future. In their narrow, frequently nationalist purview, their often barbarous cadences, their hypocrisy and their inability to absorb salient political realities, they remain as wrong, and as unsightly, as ever.

NOTES

Prologue: September 11 and Kriegsideologie

1   J. Glazov, 'Frontpage Interview: Christopher Hitchens', *FrontPage magazine.com*, 10 December 2003.

2   See, for example, N. Cohen, 'Ken has a lot to be sorry for', *Observer*, 20 February 2005.

3   J. Bricmont, *Humanitarian Imperialism: Using Human Rights to Sell War* (Monthly Review Press, 2006).

4   F. Fukuyama, *The End of History and the Last Man* (Penguin, 1993); G. Elliott, *Ends in Sight: Marx/Fukuyama/Hobsbawm/Anderson* (Pluto Press, 2008), p. 38; 'To Paris, U.S. Looks Like a "Hyperpower"', *International Herald Tribune*, 5 February 1999.

5   One of the most ill-informed examples of this literature was also one of the most popular. Francis Wheen's *How Mumbo-jumbo Conquered the World: A Short History of Modern Delusions* (Fourth Estate, 2004) purports to provide a critique of Derrida on the basis of some second-hand misconstructions; attacks Max Horkheimer and Theodor Adorno for rejecting Enlightenment, apparently missing the first page of their *Dialectic of Enlightenment* (Verso, 2002), in which the authors state that 'social freedom is inseparable from enlightened thought'; and lambasts Noam Chomsky on long-discredited claims that he supported the Khmer Rouge (for a comprehensive rebuttal of these claims, see none other than Christopher Hitchens, 'The Chorus and Cassandra', *Grand Street* <www.zmag.org/Chomsky/other/85–hitchens.html>). For a scathing critique of this extolment of a 'historically disembodied' and 'bowdlerized' Enlightenment in the service of power, see Dan Hind, *The Threat to Reason: How the Enlightenment Was Hijacked and How We Can Reclaim It* (Verso, 2007).

6   P. Berman, quoted in R. Neumann, 'The Empire Strikes Back', *Village
        Voice*, 9 October 2001.

7   Quoted in C. Robin, 'Liberalism at bay, conservatism at play: fear in the
        contemporary imagination', *Social Research*, Winter 2004; quoted in C.
        Robin, 'Remembrance of Empires Past' in Ellen Schrecker, ed., *Cold
        War Triumphalism: The Misuse of History after the Fall of
        Communism* (New Press, 2004).

8   The PNAC had called for the US government to take the 'unprecedented
        strategic opportunity' in the absence of an 'immediate great-power
        challenge' to build up military forces, and especially to expand the
        already extensive range of US military bases since 'landpower is the
        essential link in the chain that translates U.S. military supremacy into
        American geopolitical pre-eminence'. 'Rebuilding America's Defenses:
        Strategy, Forces and Resources for a New Century', A Report of the
        Project for a New American Century, September 2000 <http://www.
        newamericancentury.org/RebuildingAmericasDefenses.pdf>; W. Kristol
        and R. Kagan, 'National Interest and Global Responsibility', in I.
        Stelzer, ed., *Neoconservatism* (Atlantic Books, 2004); Robin,
        'Remembrance of Empires Past'.

9   J. Atlas, 'The World: Among the Lost; Illusions of Immortality', *New
        York Times*, 7 October 2001; C. Hitchens, 'Facing the Islamist Menace',
        City Journal, Winter 2007; S. Harris, 'Head-in-the-Sand Liberals:
        Western civilization really is at risk from Muslim extremists', *Los
        Angeles Times*, 18 September 2006.

10   See S.P. Huntington, *Political Order in Changing Societies* (Yale
        University Press, 1996) pp. 1–11, 136–7, 192–6; 'The Clash of
        Civilizations?', *Foreign Affairs*, Summer 1993, reproduced in *America
        and the World: Debating the New Shape of International Politics* (W.W.
        Norton & Co., 2002). Huntington's essay is not particularly enlighten-
        ing. Aside from the fact that most people on the planet, from whichever
        'civilization', appear to want no part of this clash (see 'Global Poll
        Finds that Religion and Culture are Not to Blame for Tensions between
        Islam and the West', *WorldPublicOpinion.org*, 16 February 2007), there
        is no attempt anywhere to justify Huntington's conception of a
        'civilization'. Its existence and coherence as a unit is simply assumed,
        without qualification. Arguably, there are loose 'cultural entities' – but
        as Mary Midgley points out, these are more likely to resemble weather
        fronts than geographical boundaries. Huntington does not cite Oswald
        Spengler, but the cultural determinism is redolent of the latter's claim
        that 'every Culture has *its own* Civilization', which is its 'inevitable
        destiny'. The ideas that Huntington accrues, somewhat triumphantly,
        to 'the West', have historically been challenged and violated as much in

'the West' as elsewhere. Economic regionalism has done as much to divide 'the West' internally (the EU versus NAFTA, for example) as it does to unite putative 'civilizations'. As for the 'Islamic–Confucian' connection, it is certainly true that China helped supply Iran with arms, but then so has Russia, and China has also sold weapons to Israel. Big business does not seem to gravitate according to these civilizational poles or alliances either, since China is one of 'the West's' primary markets, while it increasingly depends on oil purchases from parts of the Latin American 'civilization'. Despite the appearance of Chinese-made armaments in the Middle East, the US remains the largest supplier of weapons.

It is also significant that Huntington sees this as a potential domestic problem for the United States, whose 'unity' has 'historically rested on the twin bedrock of European culture and political democracy'. (Quoted in A. Kalam, 'Huntington and the World Order: Systemic Concern or Hegemonic Vision?', in S. Rashid, ed., *The Clash of Civilizations'? Asian Responses* (The University Press Limited, 1997) pp. 41–2.)

11 R. Kaplan, 'The Coming Anarchy', *Atlantic Monthly*, February 1994, reproduced in Foreign Affairs, *America and the World: Debating the New Shape of International* Politics (W.W. Norton & Co., 2002); C. Cramer, *Civil War Is Not A Stupid Thing: Accounting for Violence in Developing Countries* (Hurst & Co., 2006), p. 30; see N. Larsen's review, 'Poverties of Nation: The Ends of the Earth, "Monetary Subjects without Money," and Postcolonial Theory', *Cultural Logic*, Vol. 1, No. 1, Fall 1997 <http://clogic.eserver.org/1–1/larsen.html>.

12 Kaplan's analysis, if it abstracts problems of 'scarcity' and 'over-population' from their socioeconomic context (or, rather, collapses the social and economic context into 'scarcity' and 'overpopulation'), is not completely lacking an historical sense, as is made clear in his latest book, *Imperial Grunts: The American Military on the Ground* (Random House, 2005). The situation calls for old-fashioned imperial expansion.

13 See G. Gerstle, 'In the Shadow of Vietnam: Liberal Nationalism and the Problem of War', in M. Kazin and J. McCartin, eds, *Americanism: New Perspectives on the History of an Ideal* (University of North Carolina Press, 2006), pp. 130, 136–7; J. Shulevitz, 'The Way We Live Now: 9–23–01: Close Reading: Elements of Tragedy; The Thrill', *New York Times*, 23 September 2001; H. Allen, 'The Message in the Smoke', *Washington Post*, 12 September 2001.

14 R. Gerecht, 'Bin Laden, Beware', *Weekly Standard*, 24 September 2001; R. Rosenblatt, 'The Age of Irony Comes to an End: No longer will we

fail to take things seriously', *Time*, 24 September 2001; David Beers, 'Irony is dead! Long live irony!', *Salon.com*, 25 September 2001.

15   K. Mattson, 'American Culture Since 9/11', *Dissent*, Winter 2003; Hendrik Hertzberg, 'Lost Love', *New Yorker*, 11 September 2006.

16   M. Chishti, D. Meissner, D. Papademetriou, J. Peterzell and M. Wishnie, 'AMERICA'S CHALLENGE: Domestic Security, Civil Liberties, and National Unity after September 11', *Migration Policy Institute*, 2003. Regrettably, precise figures for the numbers detained do not exist, since the US government has kept the information secret; Aaron Glantz, 'U.S. Military Spied on Hundreds of Antiwar Demos', *Common Dreams*, 25 January 2007.

17   S. Hersh, 'Lunch With the Chairman: Why was Richard Perle meeting with Adnan Kashoggi?', *New Yorker*, 17 March 2003; C. Hitchens, 'The fascist sympathies of the soft left', *Spectator*, 29 September 2001; T. Gitlin, 'Blaming America First', *Mother Jones*, January/February 2002; M. Walzer, 'Can There Be A Decent Left?', *Dissent*, vol. 49, no. 2 (Spring 2002); M. Cooper, *Los Angeles Times*, 14 October 2001; 'Marxism, the Holocaust and September 11: An Interview with Norman Geras', *Imprints*, vol 6, no. 3 (2002).

18   Julian Go explains,

> The phrase 'American empire' appeared in 1,000 news stories over a single six-month period in 2003 . . . In 2000, Richard Haas of the State Department urged Americans to 're-conceive their global role from one of a traditional nation-state to an imperial power.' Two years later, a senior-level advisor to the U.S. President stated: 'We're an empire now, and when we act, we create our own reality.'

J. Go, 'The Provinciality of American Empire: "Liberal Exceptionalism" and U.S. Colonial Rule, 1898–1912', *Comparative Studies in Society and History*, 2007, 49(1), pp. 74–108.

19   See M. Boot, 'American Imperialism? No Need to Run Away from Label', *USA Today*, 6 May 2003, and 'Neither New nor Nefarious: The Liberal Empire Strikes Back,' *Current History*, vol. 102, no. 667, November 2003; R. Kagan, *Paradise and Power: America and Europe in the New World Order* (Vintage, 2004); Grover Norquist and Will Hutton, 'The Right to be Different', *OpenDemocracy*, 30 July 2004.

20   C. Hitchens, 'Imperialism: Superpower dominance, malignant and benign', *Slate.com*, 10 December 2002.

21   M. Ignatieff, *Empire Lite: Nation-Building in Bosnia, Kosovo and Afghanistan* (Vintage, 2003); J. Geddes, 'Smart Guy, Eh?', *Macleans*, 23

June, 2003; M. Ignatieff, 'US Becoming an Empire – in Word and Deeds', *Seattle Post-Intelligencer*, 2 February 2003. Ignatieff suggests that '[s]ince 1945, America has displayed exceptional leadership in promoting international human rights.' He acknowledges that the US 'has also supported rights-abusing regimes from Pinochet's Chile to Suharto's Indonesia', adding that it exempts itself from the provisions of international human rights legislation that it holds others to, 'judging itself and its friends by more permissive criteria than it does its enemies'. However, he maintains that the United States is exceptional not on account of its support for brutality or 'double standards', but its 'strongly messianic vision of the American role in promoting rights abroad'. Ignatieff cites the Wilsonian vision of US power making the world safe for democracy, and Franklin Roosevelt's 'four freedoms'. International law operates 'not as a system of constraints on US power, but as a forum in which US leadership can be exercised and American intuitions about freedom and government can be spread across the world'. In fact, the apparent hypocrisy of the US, its conserving of its own sovereignty while abridging that of others, results from America's 'distinctive rights culture', 'anchored in the historical project of the American Revolution'. M. Ignatieff, ed., *American Exceptionalism and Human Rights* (Princeton University Press, 2005), pp. 1–14.

22 Quoted in J. Lloyd, 'Peaceniks No More', *New Statesman*, 29 October 2001; D. Hare, 'An Act of Faith', *Guardian*, 13 July 2002.

23 BHL's praise for the occupation of Afghanistan was reported in N. Boissenot, '"2nd Sartre" appeals for world's forgotten', *Japan Economic Newswire*, 1 February 2002. Lévy's encomiastic depiction of the United States usually has the effect of evincing his incuriosity. For example, he argues that '[i]t was French fascists who invented anti-Americanism in the 1920s and 1930s. They were partisans of a racially pure country against the cosmopolitan melting-pot America of blacks and Jews'. (M. Campbell, 'America, je t'aime toujours', *Sunday Times*, 2 November 2003.) However 'anti-Americanism' is construed, 'melting-pot' America not only had its own brand of far right on the rise before the French had ever seen a goose-step or a *ligue*, but it also had its admirers among the European far right for its handling of the 'race problem' in the South. Still, thanks to his 'anti-anti-Americanism' (or 'pro-Americanism' as it might less cumbersomely be called), he almost always accrues praise and puns in some measure when he is mentioned in American or British publications: 'Croque Monsieur' and 'French Toasts' were typical, while his 2002 visit to Afghanistan as Chirac's envoy produced 'I think therefore I am off to Afghanistan', and 'France's own smart bomb to help Afghans'. The coverage rarely fails to

mention BHL's appearance ('heart-throb', 'Byronic looks'), his trade-mark wide-open-necked white shirt, his trendy apartment on the Left Bank (or one of his other homes), his celebrity status ('superstar' is the usual breathless tribute), his model-cum-actress wife, and his fabulous personal wealth.

24   J. Graff, 'The Engaged Intellect', *Time*, 4 May 2003; BHL campaigned throughout the 1990s for the French government to support Ahmed Shah Massoud, one of the warlords who took part in the Afghan civil war in the 1990s and led the Northern Alliance against the Taliban. See P. Cohen, *BHL: une biographie* (Fayard, 2005), pp. 118–22, 408–14; see also William Dalrymple, 'Murder in Karachi', *New York Review of Books*, vol. 50, no. 19, 4 December 2003.

25   In a notable instance, Pierre Vidal-Nacquet excoriated Lévy's third book, *The Testament of God*, in *Le Monde Diplomatique*, accusing him of multiple falsehoods, not least of which was the citation of Himmler's 'deposition' to the Nuremberg tribunal, which actually began six months after the leading Nazi's suicide ('Une lettre du Pierre Vidal-Nacquet', *Le Monde Diplomatique*, 18 June 1979). This same laxity with the truth is evident in his recent journalistic work. Sometimes, caught in a misstatement, Levy will claim that if his work has drawn attention to suffering, it does not matter. Cohen writes: 'BHL takes freedoms with the facts that one undoubtedly does not tolerate in others. But what does it matter if it manages to force the world's powers to act on suffering that they would see!' It is the 'force of media attrac-tion' that legitimizes BHL's claim to be a journalist, rather than the ordinary rules of the profession. See Cohen, *BHL*, p. 405.

26   Bernard-Henri Lévy, *American Vertigo: Traveling America in the Footsteps of Tocqueville* (Random House, 2006), pp. 29, 212–17, 361. See Sam Stark, 'Mediocracy in America', *n+1*, 6 February 2006, for a mordant critique of Lévy's kitschy impressionism. It is important that Lévy disavows the existence of an American empire, since that implies a racial order which Lévy strenuously insists characterizes neither America's domestic make-up in any essential way nor its external relations. On the contrary, he admires the neoconservatives for their putative anti-racism: 'At least they're asserting that democracy isn't set aside for white people, Christians and Westerners'.

27   S. Rushdie, 'A Liberal Argument For Regime Change', *Washington Post*, 1 November, 2002; N. Cohen, *Observer*, 14 April 2002, 10 March 2002, 16 February 2003, and 13 July 2003. The March/April 2003 issue of *Amnesty* had raised the prospect of '50,000 civilian deaths', which in retrospect looks tremendously optimistic, and its campaigning had involved vigils on the theme of 'Iraq: The Human Cost of War'.

28 A. Gopnik, 'The Anti-Anti-Americans', *New Yorker*, 1 September 2003. Incidentally, the phrase 'anti-anti-American' was hardly used at all until the beginning of 2003. A LexisNexis search for the term yields 130 mentions going back to 1994, 119 of which occurred after the beginning of 2003.

29 N. Weill, 'The French Pro-War Intellectuals', *Le Monde*, 19 March 2003; P. Bruckner, A. Glucksmann and R. Goupil, 'Saddam must go, by choice or by force!', *Le Monde*, 3 March 2003; J. Ramos-Horta, 'War for Peace? It worked in My Country', *Sydney Morning Herald*, 25 February 2003, and 'Sometimes, a War Saves People: We must be willing to bring the fight to those who would do evil', *Wall Street Journal*, Opinion Journal, 13 May 2004; T. Cushman, 'Antitotalitarianism As A Vocation: An Interview With Adam Michnik', *Dissent*, Spring 2003; A. Michnik, *Gazeta Wyborcza*, 28 March 2003; G. Packer, *The Assassin's Gate: America in Iraq* (Faber & Faber, 2006); 'Kanan Makiya's War Diary', *New Republic Online*, 24 March 2003; 'Kanan Makiya, "All Levels of the Iraqi Government Were Complicit"', *Middle East Quarterly*, Spring 2005.

30 Quoted in 'Cakewalk', *Salon.com*, 28 March 2003; C. Hitchens, 'I Wanted It To Rain On Their Parade', *Mirror*, 18 February 2003; C. Hitchens, *The Long Short War: The Postponed Liberation of Iraq* (Plume, 2003), p. 5; C. Hitchens, 'Why We Must Keep Our Nerve', *Mirror*, 25 March 2003.

31 M. Ignatieff, 'America's Empire is an Empire Lite', *New York Times*, 10 January 2003; P. Berman interview, 'A War Against Totalitarianism? A War of Ideology?', *PBS Frontline* <http://www.pbs.org/wgbh/pages/frontline/shows/blair/liberal/2.html>; W. Stephenson, 'On Liberal Grounds', an Interview with Paul Berman, *PBS Frontline*, 24–31 March 2003.

32 J. Hari, 'WMD are irrelevant; Iraqis wanted the war', *Independent*, 11 July 2003. The ICG's account of its research did not in fact contain any information about the numbers of Iraqis who were willing to support an invasion. See 'Voices From The Iraqi Street', *Middle East Briefing No. 3*, Iraq Crisis Group, 4 December 2002. The report can be read at <http://www.crisisgroup.org/home/index.cfm?id=1825&l=1>. Hari recanted after an epidemiological survey suggested that at least 100,000 Iraqis had died as a result of the war. See J. Hari, 'After three years, after 150,000 dead, why I was wrong about Iraq', *Independent*, 18 March 2006.

33 One instance is the sudden emergence of the name 'Abu Musab al-Zarqawi' in Christopher Hitchens's writings, immediately after Colin Powell made his infamous presentation to the United Nations. For the

origins of the Zarqawi myth see N. Davies, *Flat Earth News* (Chatto & Windus, 2008), pp. 205–56.

34   P. Robertson, *The 700 Club*, Christian Broadcasting Network, 12 June 2007; 'Attacks on Muslims/Islam', *Media Matters for America*, retrieved on 20 June 2007 at <http://mediamatters.org/issues_topics/attacks_on_muslims_islam>.

35   'Writers issue cartoon row warning', *BBC News*, 1 March 2006; interview, *Jewish Chronicle*, 14 October 2006; A. Michnik, 'Forum 2000 Conference', Prague Castle, 17 October 2001, transcription at <http://www.forum2000.cz/conferences/2001/transcripts.php?id=177>. This astonishing claim came more than a month after the condemnations from Muslim scholars and even antagonistic Islamist groups had poured in. The day after the attacks, the State Department spoke of how 'Muslim American Groups Denounce Terrorist Attacks'. Two days later, a statement signed by such diverse groups as Hamas, the Egyptian Muslim Brotherhood, the Pakistani Jamaat-e-Islami, and dozens of Muslim scholars denounced the attacks as 'against all human and Islamic norms'. Shortly after that, a *fatwa* was signed by Sheikh Yusuf al-Qaradawi and others, denouncing the attacks as a crime in the eyes of Islamic law. P. Kurata, 'Muslim American Groups Denounce Terrorist Attacks', State Department, 12 September, 2001, at <http://usinfo.state.gov/is/international_security/terrorism/sept_11/sep t_11_archive/Muslim_American_Groups_Denounce_Terrorist_Attack s.html>. Al-Quds al-Arabi, 14 September 2001, republished by the Council of American–Islamic Relations website at <http://www.cair-net.org/html/911statements.html>. Council of American Islamic Relations, 'CAIR Statements on the Events of September 11', at <http://www.cair-net.org/html/911statements.html>.

36   Quoted in M. Amis, 'The age of horrorism', *Observer*, 10 September 2006.

37   C. Hitchens, 'Of Sin, the Left and Islamic Fascism', *Nation*, 24 September 2001.

38   C. Hitchens, debate with C. Hedges on 'Is God Great?', King Middle School, Berkeley, 24 May 2007; R. Pape, *Dying To Win: The Strategic Logic of Suicide Terrorism* (Random House, 2005); L. Ricolfi, 'Palestinians, 1981–2003', in D. Gambetta, ed., *Making Sense of Suicide Missions* (Oxford University Press, 2005), pp. 77–116. Farhad Khosrokavar, in his analysis of Muslim suicide attackers, emphasizes as a crucial factor the 'humiliation experienced by Palestinians' which 'goes far beyond the symbolic order . . . Objective factors give the subjective feeling of humiliation an objective substratum'. F. Khosrokavar, *Suicide Bombers: Allah's New Martyrs* (Pluto Press, 2005), p. 118.

39 C. Hitchens, *God Is Not Great: The Case Against Religion* (Atlantic Books, 2007). For his early anti-theism, see Hitchens's *Prepared for the Worst: Selected Essays and Minority Reports* (Chatto & Windus, 1989), pp. 143–7.

40 S. Harris, *The End of Faith: Religion, Terror and the Future of Reason* (Norton, 2004); 'Sam Harris on The Reality of Islam', *Truthdig*, 7 February 2006; S. Harris, 'Head-in-the-Sand Liberals'.

41 C. Hitchens, 'Facing the Islamist Menace', *City Journal*, Winter 2007.

42 W. Hutton, 'Why the Euston group offers a new direction for the left', *Observer*, 23 April 2006. The Euston Manifesto is a now dormant position statement on the 'war on terror' supported by a network of former left-wingers and liberals which reproves the Left for anti-Americanism and endorses the occupation of Iraq as a 'liberation'. W. Hutton, 'Why the West must stay true to itself', *Observer*, 17 June 2007.

43 In the UK, for instance, domestic violence claims the lives of two women each week, and accounts for 16 per cent of all violent crime in England and Wales. Home Office Statistical Bulletin, 'Crime in England and Wales 2004/2005', July 2005; 'Domestic Violence', Home Office website, retrieved 19 January 2007 at <http://www.homeoffice. gov.uk/crime-victims/reducing-crime/domestic-violence/>. In the United States, the Department of Justice estimates that three women are killed in domestic violence each day. Bureau of Justice Statistics Crime Data Brief, *Intimate Partner Violence, 1993–2001*, February 2003.

44 M. Amis, *Experience: A Memoir* (Vintage, 2000), pp. 256–65; 'The Age of Horrorism', *Observer*, 10 September 2006; quoted in D. Soar, 'Bile, Blood, Bilge, Mulch', *London Review of Books*, vol. 29, no. 1, 4 January 2007.

45 J. Brown, 'Amis launches scathing response to accusations of Islamophobia', *Independent*, 12 October 2007; 'I did not advocate harassing Muslims', *Guardian*, 12 October 2007.

46 A. Lieven, *America Right or Wrong: An Anatomy of American Nationalism* (HarperCollins, 2004), p. 53; quoted in Lieven, *American Right or Wrong*, p. 52.

47 This observation is adapted from Peter Blickle's discussion of the German idea of *Heimat* ('Homeland'). Peter Blickle, *Heimat: A Critical Theory of the German Idea of Homeland* (Camden House, 2002), pp. 130–49.

48 C. Hitchens, 'Londonistan Calling', *Vanity Fair*, June 2007; N. Cohen, 'We have to deport terror suspects – whatever their fate', *Observer*, 5 November 2006; G. Younge, 'Newspapers warn of threat to America from "Londonistan"', *Guardian*, 12 July 2005; C. Hitchens, 'Londonistan Calling'.

49 As of 2003, there were still 1,200 in captivity. M. Harrington, 'Arab and Muslim Immigrants Under Fire: Interview with Hatem Abudayyeh of

the Arab American Action Network', *Dollars and Sense*, 3 July 2003. Several lists have been made of individuals targeted for deportation, one of which, in February 2002, brought together 6,000 individuals from countries that the US believes al-Qaeda to operate in, whose visa had expired, or who had ignored a removal order, or who had never received the final removal order. Thus, many people were separated from jobs, families, and American-born children. N. Murray, 'Profiled: Arabs, Muslims and the Post-9/11 Hunt for the Enemy Within', in E. Hagopian, ed., *Civil Rights in Peril: The Targeting of Arabs and Muslims* (Haymarket Books & Pluto Press, 2004), pp. 36–7.

50   A. Taheri, 'A Colour Code for Iran's Infidels', *National Post*, 18 May 2006; C. Wattie, 'Iran Eyes Badges for Jews', *National Post*, 18 May 2006, and 'Experts say report of badges for Jews in Iran is untrue', *National Post*, 19 May 2006; *Editor and Publisher*, 10 August 2006; S. Goldenberg, 'Islamophobia Worse in America Now Than after 9/11, Survey Finds', *Guardian*, 10 March 2006.

51   S. Harris, 'In Defense of Torture', *Huffington Post*, 17 October 2005; N. Cohen, 'We have to deport terrorist suspects – whatever their fate', and 'A child is in mortal danger. This man can tell you where he is, but won't talk. What would you do?', *New Statesman*, 29 November 2004; M. Ludders, 'Columnist Hitchens Lectures on Political Dissent', *Kenyon Collegian*, 18 November 2004; 'An Interview with Christopher Hitchens ("Moral and Political Collapse" of the Left in the US)', *Washington Prism.org*, 16 June 2005.

52   J. Laksin, 'Christening the David Horowitz Freedom Center', *Frontpagemag.com*, 14 September 2006; C. Hitchens, 'Facing the Islamist Menace', op cit.

53   In fact, it is worth mentioning in this context that, although Hitchens presents his apologia as a reaction to someone else's aggression, he was already lionizing Senator Bob Kerrey back in May 2001, when there was widespread discussion of Kerrey's participation in the Thanh Phong massacre, in which a Vietnamese peasant family consisting of an elderly man, a woman and children under the age of twelve were stabbed to death with knives. Hitchens murmured to Fox viewers that 'he's my president', adding that

> none of the people he killed were raped. None of them were dismembered. None of them were tortured. None of them were mutilated, had their ears cut off. He never referred to them as gooks or slopes [afterwards]. So . . . for one day's work in a free-fire zone in the Mekong Delta, it was nothing like as bad as most days.

It would be hard to imagine Hitchens making a similar case for a Serbian soldier-cum-politician who had committed a similar act. Quoted in A. Cockburn, 'Kerrey, Scheer and Hitchens: Liberals Rush to Defend War Criminal', Counterpunch, 8 May 2001. For details of the massacre, see G. Vistica, 'One Awful Night in Thanh Phong', New York Times Magazine, 25 April 2001.

54   R. Kaplan, Imperial Grunts, p. 4; D. Rieff, 'The False Friends of the American Military: The Cowboy Culture', New Republic, 10 October 2005; R. Kaplan, Imperial Grunts, pp 1, 7–10.

55   Lieven, American Right or Wrong, pp. 22–3; D. Losurdo, Heidegger and the Ideology of War: Community, Death and the West (Humanity Books, 2001), pp. 11–12, 13.

56   D. Losurdo, Heidegger, p. 26; C. Thornhill, Karl Jaspers: Politics and Metaphysics (Routledge, 2002), p. 59; D. Losurdo, Heidegger, pp. 57, 48.

1: Forging Old Europe

1   Quoted in P. Levine, The British Empire: Sunrise to Sunset (Pearson Longman, 2007), p. ix.

2   The polyvalence of liberalism forbids allowing a blanket statement like this to go without at least clarifying that this is merely a statement about perception. Some traditions of liberalism do stress human equality, but, as will become clear throughout the text, many are highly inegalitarian.

3   Levine, British Empire, pp. 1–12, 16; D. Brion Davis, Inhuman Bondage: The Rise and Fall of Slavery in the New World (Oxford University Press, 2006), pp. 124–40; E. Meiksins Wood, The Origin of Capitalism: A Longer View (Verso, 2002), pp. 152–6; R. Tuck, The Rights of War and Peace: Political Thought and the International Order From Grotius to Kant (Oxford University Press, 1999), pp. 78–109.

4   Tuck, Rights of War and Peace, pp. 166–81.

5   B. Arneil, 'Trade, Plantations, and Property: John Locke and the Economic Defense of Colonialism', Journal of the History of Ideas, 1994, pp. 591–609; see also, Origin of Capitalism, pp. 96–100; quoted in R. Blackburn, The Making of New World Slavery: From the Baroque to the Modern 1492–1800 (Verso, 1997), p. 264; R. Bernasconi and A. Maaza Mann, 'The Contradictions of Racism: Locke, Slavery and the Two Treatises', in A. Valls, ed., Race and Racism in Modern Philosophy (Cornell University Press, 2005), p. 91.

6   D. Brion Davis, Inhuman Bondage, p. 233.

7   Ibid., pp. 241–2, 236, 245–7.

8   S. Muthu, Enlightenment Against Empire (Princeton University Press, 2003), pp. 172–258.

9   J. Pitts, *A Turn To Empire: The Rise of Imperial Liberalism in Britain and France* (Princeton University Press, 2005), pp. 59–100; N. B. Dirks, *The Scandal of Empire: India and the Creation of Imperial Britain* (The Belknap Press of Harvard University Press, 2006); Pitts, *Turn to Empire*, pp. 103–22.

10   Pitts, *Turn to Empire*, p. 2; J.S. Mill, 'On Liberty', in *On Liberty and Other Essays* (Oxford University Press, 1991), pp. 14–15; A. Ryan, 'Introduction', in M.I. Moir, D. M. Peers and L. Zastoupil, *J.S. Mill's Encounter With India* (University of Toronto Press, 1999), pp. 15–16; Pitts, *Turn to Empire*, pp. 133–62, 139–40.

11   R. Boesche, *Tocqueville's Road Map: Methodology, Liberalism, Revolution, and Despotism* (Lexington Books, 2006), p. 110; O. Le Cour Grandmaison, 'Liberty, equality and colony', *Le Monde Diplomatique*, June 2001; A. de Tocqueville, *Writings on Empire and Slavery*, transl. and intr. by J. Pitts (Johns Hopkins University Press, 2001), p. xiii–xv; 'First Letter on Algeria', Tocqueville, *Writings on Empire and Slavery*, pp. xvi–xvii, 5–13; Boesche, *Tocqueville's Road Map*, pp. 114–6.

12   Pitts, *Turn to Empire*, pp. 204–39; A. H. Nimtz, Jr, *Marx, Tocqueville, and Race in America: The 'Absolute Democracy' or 'Defiled Republic'* (Lexington Books, 2003), p. 45; 'Intervention in the Debate Over the Appropriation of Special Funding', 1846, in Tocqueville, *Writings on Empire and Slavery*, pp. 117–29; Grandmaison, 'Liberty, equality and colony'. Interestingly, however, Mill appears to have become increasingly hostile to the settlement of Australia, believing that the barbarity of the colonialists violated the principle of utility. See Katherine Smits, 'John Stuart Mill on the Antipodes: Settler Violence against Indigenous Peoples and the Legitimacy of Colonial Rule', *Australian Journal of Politics and History*, vol. 54, no. 1 (March 2008).

13   Nimtz, *Marx, Tocqueville, and Race in America*, p. 47; Boesche, *Tocqueville's Road Map*, p. 114; Pitts, *Turn to Empire*, p. 240.

14   L. James, *Raj: The Making and Unmaking of British India* (Little, Brown & Co., 1997), pp. 254–77; J. Newsinger, *The Blood Never Dried: A People's History of the British Empire* (Bookmarks, 2006), pp. 65–83; R. Ramesh, 'India's secret history: A holocaust, one where millions disappeared. . .', *Guardian*, 24 August 2007; M. Davis, *Late Victorian Holocausts: El Niño Famines and the Making of the Third World* (Verso, 2002), pp. 311–2; V. Chibber, 'The Good Empire: Should we pick up where the British left off?', *Boston Review*, February/March 2005.

15   D. Judd, *Empire: The British Imperial Experience from 1765 to the Present* (Phoenix Press, 1996), pp. 66–81; Levine, *British Empire*, p. 77.

16 G. Moore, *Dickens and Empire: Discourses of Class, Race and Colonialism in the Works of Charles Dickens* (Ashgate, 2004), pp. 94, 113, 167.

17 T. Ballantyne, *Orientalism and Race: Aryanism in the British Empire* (Palgrave Macmillan, 2002), pp. 1–59.

18 Ballantyne, *Orientalism and Race*, pp. 43–5, 133–4, 184; see also P. Chatterjee, *Nationalist Thought and the Colonial World: A Derivative Discourse* (Zed Books, 1993), pp. 75–7.

19 L. Gibbons, 'Race against time: racial discourse and Irish history', in C. Hall, ed., *Cultures of Empire: A reader: Colonizers in Britain and the empire in the nineteenth and twentieth centuries* (Manchester University Press, 2000), pp. 207–10. For an account of the torsions of ideology and classification that took place as the 'Aryan Model' was elaborated, see M. Bernal, *Black Athena: The Afro-Asiatic Roots of Classical Civilisation, Volume I: The Fabrication of Ancient Greece, 1785–1985*, Vintage, 1991. Nazi race classifications were also prone to confusion – the Gypsies, whom they wished to exterminate, were considered a part of the Indo-European lineage that the Nazi regime exalted, and its race scientists were obliged to contrive all sorts of embellishments to justify their slaughter. See Y. Arad, *Belzec, Sobibor, Treblinka: The Operation Reinhard Death Camps* (Indiana University Press, 1987), pp. 150–3.

20 See E. Said, *Orientalism* (Penguin, 2003); Disraeli quoted by E. Said in G. Viswanathan, ed., *Power, Politics and Culture: Interviews with Edward Said* (Bloomsbury, 2004), p. 48; Said, *Orientalism*, p. 234; V. Kiernan, *The Lords of Human Kind: European Attitudes to Other Cultures in the Imperial Age* (Serif, 1995), pp. 136–45; Said, *Orientalism*, pp. 227–8.

21 J. Robinson, M. Moir and Z. Moir, eds, *Writings on India by John Stuart Mill* (Routledge, 1990), p. 122–5; P. Anagol, *The Emergence of Feminism in India 1850–1920* (Ashgate, 2006), p. 19; V. Amos and P. Parmar, 'Challenging Imperial Feminism' and 'Many Voices, One Chant: Black Feminist Perspectives', *Feminist Review*, no. 17, Autumn 1984; Levine, *British Empire*, p. 145; C. Hall, 'Of Gender and Empire: Reflections on the Nineteenth Century', in P. Levine, ed., *Gender and Empire* (Oxford University Press, 2004), p. 50–5.

22 C. Midgely, 'Anti-slavery and the roots of "imperial feminism"', in C. Midgley, ed., *Gender and Imperialism* (Manchester University Press, 1998), pp. 161–77; A. Schaser, 'Women in a Nation of Men: the politics of the League of German Women's Associations (BDF) in Imperial Germany, 1894–1914', in I. Blom, K. Hagemann and C. Hall, eds, *Gendered Nations: Nationalisms and gender order in the long*

nineteenth century (Berg, 2006); J. Haggis, 'White women and colonialism: towards a non-recuperative history', in Midgley, 'Anti-Slavery', pp. 45–71; A. Burton, 'The White Woman's Burden: British Feminists and "The Indian Woman", 1865–1915', in N. Chandhuri and M. Strobel, *Western Women and Imperialism: Complicity and Resistance* (Indiana University Press, 1992), pp. 137–9.

23   Levine, *British Empire*, pp. 89–91; J. Newsinger, 'Liberal imperialism and the occupation of Egypt in 1882', *Race and Class*, vol. 49, no. 54 (2008). For a brief discussion of al-Afghani's influence, see Nazih Ayubi, *Political Islam: Religion and Politics in the Arab World* (Routledge, 1991), pp. 57–8.

24   Newsinger, 'Liberal imperialism'; H. Wesseling, *The European Colonial Empires, 1815–1919* (Longman Pearson, 2004), pp. 87–8; Newsinger, 'Liberal imperialism'. Mahdism was itself one of the modernizing currents in late-nineteenth-century Islam. See Said, *Orientalism*, p. 281 and Ayubi, *Political Islam*, pp. 101–2.

25   W. Churchill, *Marxism and Native Americans* (South End Press, 1984), p. 160; Said, *Orientalism*, pp. 153–5. This view of Marx is also accepted, and celebrated, by Bill Warren, who argues that colonialism was indeed a progressive moment that disseminated capitalism and raised the living standards of the colonized: Bill Warren, *Imperialism: Pioneer of Capitalism* (Verso, 1980). It is also praised by Christopher Hitchens: 'The Grub Street years', *Guardian*, 20 June 2007.

26   F. Engels, 'Extraordinary Revelations – Abd-El-Kader – Guizot's Foreign Policy', *Northern Star*, 22 January 1848, reproduced at the Marxists Internet Archive: <http://www.marxists.org/archive/marx/works/1848/01/22.htm>.

27   F. Engels, 'The Movements of 1847', *Deutsche-Brüsseler-Zeitung*, 23 January 1848, reproduced in A. Ahmad, ed., *Karl Marx and Frederick Engels on the National and Colonial Questions: Selected Writings* (Left Word, 2001), p. 50; quoted in R. Munck, 'Marx and Latin America', Review of *Marx y América Latina* by A. José, *Bulletin of Latin American Research*, vol. 3, no. 1 (January 1984), pp. 141–2; K. Marx, 'The Future Results of the British Rule in India', *New York Daily Tribune*, 8 August 1853, reproduced in Ahmad, *Karl Marx and Frederick Engels*, p. 70; Marx, 'Future Results of British Rule', pp. 65–6.

28   Marx, 'Future Results of British Rule', p. 6; P. Anderson, *Lineages of the Absolutist State* (Verso, 1979), pp. 468–77. Hegel, for whom 'it is the necessary fate of Asiatic Empires to be subjected to Europeans', maintained that Indian society was static, a system of dormant village communes that sustained a specifically Asiatic kind of despotism. The full array of racist conceptions about Indians is deployed: they are

amoral, given to infanticide, irrational, tend towards deceit and cunning, and so on. G. Hegel, *The Philosophy of History* (Prometheus Books, 1991), pp. 139–67; I. Habib, *Essays in Indian History: Towards a Marxist Perception* (Anthem Press, 2002), pp. 297–9; Marx, 'Future Results of British Rule', p. 71; quoted in M. Harrington, *Socialism Past and Future* (Pluto Press, 1989), p. 88.

29 For an extensive discussion of Said's treatment of Marx, see A. Ahmad, 'Marx on India: A Clarification' in *In Theory: Nations, Classes, Literatures* (Verso, 2008), pp. 221–42. For an acerbic critique of Said's oeuvre, see pp. 159–219; Marx, 'Future Results of British Rule', pp. 74, 75; K. Marx, 'The Indian Revolt', *New York Daily Tribune*, 16 September 1857, reproduced in Ahmad, *In Theory*, p. 82; K. Marx, 'Investigation of Tortures in India', *New York Daily Tribune*, 28 August 1857, reproduced in Ahmad, *In Theory*, p. 90.

30 Marx, 'Future Results of British Rule', p. 73; quoted in 'Introduction', Ahmad, *In Theory*, p. 19.

31 A. Nimtz, Jr, *Marx, Tocqueville, and Race in America: The 'Absolute Democracy' or 'Defiled Republic'* (Lexington Books, 2003), pp. 44–6, 99–101, 154–5; 'Marx to Sigfrid Meyer and August Vogt in New York', K. Marx and F. Engels, *Selected Correspondence* (Progress Publishers, 1975), pp. 220–4, reproduced at <http://www.marxists.org/archive/marx/works/1870/letters/70_04_09.htm>; V. Lenin, 'The Right of Nations to Self-Determination', *Lenin, Collected Works* (Progress Publishers, 1972) vol. 20, pp. 393–454, reproduced at <http://www.marxists.org/archive/lenin/works/1914/self-det/>.

32 P. Kelemen, 'Planning for Africa: The British Labour Party's Colonial Development Policy, 1920–1964', *Journal of Agrarian Change*, vol. 7, no. 1 (January 2007), pp. 76–98; F. Schneider, 'Fabians and the Utilitarian Idea of Empire', *Review of Politics*, vol. 35, no. 4 (1973), pp. 501–22; D. Judd and K. Surridge, *The Boer War* (John Murray, 2002), pp. 17–32.

33 Judd and Surridge, *Boer War*, pp. 32–50; B. Nasson, *The South African War, 1899–1902* (Arnold, 1999), pp. 220–1; Judd and Surridge, *Boer War*, pp. 194–6. See, for example, A. Ashforth, *The Politics of Official Discourse in Twentieth-Century South Africa* (Clarendown Press, 1990); M. Lacey, *Working for Boroko: The origins of a coercive labour system in South Africa* (Ravan Press, 1981); and C. Feinstein, *An Economic History of South Africa: Conquest, Discrimination, and Development*, (Cambridge University Press, 2005).

34 Judd and Surridge, *Boer War*, pp. 238–41; E. Pease, *The History of the Fabian Society* (A. C. Field, 1916), pp. 131–2; G. Bernard Shaw, ed., *Fabianism and the Empire: A Manifesto By the Fabian Society* (Grant Richards, 1900), p. 6; Pease, *History of the Fabian Society*, p. 135.

35 Shaw, *Fabianism and the Empire*, pp. 15–21.

36 Shaw, *Fabianism and the Empire*, p. 22; Pease, *History of the Fabian Society*, p. 128; Shaw, *Fabianism and the Empire*, pp. 31–8, 44–9.

37 F. Lee, *Fabianism and Colonialism: The Life and Political Thought of Lord Sydney Olivier* (Defiant Books, 1988), p. 165; M. Nuri El-Amin, 'Sydney Olivier on Socialism and the Colonies', *Review of Politics*, vol. 39, no. 4 (October 1977), p. 522; Lee, *Fabianism and Colonialism*, pp. 111, 171–5; M. Olivier, ed., *Sydney Olivier: Letters and Selected Writings* (George Allen & Unwin, 1948), pp. 189–95.

38 Quoted in R. Hinden, 'Socialism and the Colonial World', in A. Creech Jones, ed., *New Fabian Colonial Essays* (Hogarth Press, 1959), pp. 9, 12–13.

39 R. Vickers, *The Labour Party and the World, Volume 1: The evolution of Labour's foreign policy, 1900–51* (Manchester University Press, 2003), pp. 40, 35, 43; J. Ramsay MacDonald, 'Labour and the Empire', in J. Keir Hardie and J. Ramsay MacDonald, *From Serfdom to Socialism* (Farleigh Dickinson University Press, 1974), pp. 18, 27, 39; quoted in José Harris, *Civil Society in British History: Ideas, Identities, Institutions* (Oxford University Press, 2003), p. 163. The entire text of the Manifesto is reproduced at <http://www.labour-party.org.uk/manifestos/1918/1918–labour-manifesto.shtml>.

40 W. Cohen, *The French Encounter with Africa: White Responses to Blacks, 1830–1880* (Indiana University Press, 2003), pp. 270–5.

41 D. Thompson, *France, Empire and Republic, 1850–1940: Historical Documents* (Macmillan, 1968), pp. 305–7; M. Agulhon, *The French Republic, 1879–1992* (Blackwell, 1993), p. 45.

42 R. Tombs, *France: 1814–1914* (Longman, 1996); Wesseling, *European Colonial Empires*, pp. 132–3, 149–50, 193–4; quoted in M. Silverman, *Deconstructing the Nation: Immigration, Racism and Citizenship in Modern France* (Routledge, 1992), p. 31.

43 Tombs, *France*, p. 446; Thompson, *France*, pp. 308–9. There is an early echo here of Lenin's theory of imperialism as a stage of capitalist development requiring the export of capital.

44 C. Andrew, 'The French Colonialist Movement during the Third Republic: The Unofficial Mind of Imperialism', *Transactions of the Royal Historical Society*, 5th Series, vol. 26 (1976), pp. 143–66; H. Goldberg, *The Life of Jean Jaurès* (Wisconsin University Press, 1962), p. 212; M. Ferro, *Colonization: A Global History* (Routledge, 1997), p. 175; W. Cohen, 'The Colonial Policy of the Popular Front', *French Historical Studies*, vol. 7, no. 3 (1972), p. 369.

45 J. Hecht, 'Vacher de Lapouge and the Rise of Nazi Science', *Journal of the History of Ideas*, vol. 61, no. 2 (April 2000), pp. 285–304.

46 R. Stuart, *Marxism and National Identity: Socialism, Nationalism and National Socialism during the French Fin de Siècle* (SUNY Press, 2006), pp. 14, 26, 30, 128–30, 124. Guesde's antics in 1914 prompted Lenin to remind European socialists of what he had said of imperialist war in 1911:

> It is chiefly a war between the capitalists of all countries for profits and possession of the world market, and it is fought at the price of our blood. Now, just imagine that in each of the capitalist countries of Europe, this mutual slaughter for the sake of plunder is directed by a socialist! Just imagine an English Millerand, an Italian Millerand, a German Millerand, in addition to a French Millerand, working to embroil the proletarians in this capitalist brigandage and make them fight each other! What would remain I ask you, comrades, of international solidarity?

Quoted in V. I. Lenin, 'An Open Letter to Boris Souvarine', *Lenin, Collected Works* (Progress Publishers, 1964), vol. 23, pp. 195–204, republished by the Marxist Internet Archive at <http://marxists.org/archive/lenin/works/1916/dec/15b.htm>.

47 N. Stargardt, *The German Idea of Militarism: Radical and Socialist Critics, 1866–1914* (Cambridge University Press, 1994), pp. 49–55, 66.

48 Stargardt, *German Idea of Militarism*, pp. 57–8; quoted in H. Koch, review of Roger Fletcher, *Revisionism and Empire: Socialist Imperialism in Germany, 1897–1914* (George Allen & Unwin, 1984), in *English Historical Review*, vol. 102, no. 403 (April 1987), pp. 526–7; Stargardt, *German Idea of Militarism*, p. 59; W. Pelz, review of M. Steger, 'The Quest for Evolutionary Socialism: Eduard Bernstein and Social Democracy', *American Historical Review*, vol. 103, no. 5 (December 1998), pp. 1,624–5; quoted in L. Proyect, 'Looking Back at The Battle of Algiers', *MRZine*, 12 August 2005.

49 R. Fletcher, *Revisionism and Empire: Socialist Imperialism in Germany, 1897–1914* (George Allen & Unwin, 1984), pp. 127–59; quoted in ibid., p. 160.

50 Ibid., pp. 160–5.

51 J. Riddell, ed., *Lenin's Struggle for a Revolutionary International, Documents: 1907–1916, The Preparatory Years* (Monad Press, 1984), p. 10; M. Wadsworth, 'Black politics: a historical perspective', *Race and Class*, no. 34 (1992), p. 63–74.

52 Riddell, *Lenin's Struggle*, pp. 5–6, 12.

53 Riddell, *Lenin's Struggle*, pp. 5, 14; E. Hansen, 'Marxists and

Imperialism: The Indonesian Policy of the Dutch Social Democratic Workers Party, 1894–1914', *Indonesia*, vol. 16 (October 1973), pp. 81–104; E. Hansen, 'The Dutch East Indies and the Reorientation of Dutch Social Democracy, 1929–40', *Indonesia*, vol. 23 (April 1977), pp. 59–85.

54   Riddell, *Lenin's Struggle*, pp. 14–15.

55   Vickers, *Labour Party*, pp. 56–7; P. Stansky, *The Left and War: the British Labour Party and World War I* (Oxford University Press, 1969), p. 58.

56   Vickers, *Labour Party*, pp. 57–67; H. Pelling, *A Short History of the Labour Party*, 9th edn (Macmillan, 1991), p. 37; G. Braybon, *Evidence, History and the Great War: Historians and the Impact of 1914–18* (Berghahn Books, 2005), p. 79.

57   Vickers, *Labour Party*, pp. 58, 63, 66. On 'doormat incident', see Stanksy, *Left and the War*, p. 201; Vickers, *Labour Party*, pp. 66–7.

58   D. Silbey, *The British Working Class and Enthusiasm for War, 1914–1916* (Routledge, 2005), pp. 7–15, 38–9, 69–104; 15–18.

59   M. Seligman and R. MacLean, *Germany from Reich to Republic, 1871–1918* (Macmillan Press, 2000), p. 158; M. Fulbrook, *A Concise History of Germany* (Cambridge University Press, 1991), p. 151; J. Winter, *The Experience of World War* (Oxford University Press, 1988), pp. 164–6; J. Joll, *The Origins of the First World War* (Longman, 1984), p. 184; J. Verhey, *The Spirit of 1914: Militarism, Myth, and Mobilization in Germany* (Cambridge University Press, 2000).

60   Joll, *Origins*, pp. 180–1; A. Hall, 'By Other Means: The Legal Struggle Against the SPD in Wilhelmine Germany 1890–1900', *The Historical Journal*, 1974, pp. 365–86; H. Wehler, *The German Empire, 1871–1918* (Berg Publishers, 1985), pp. 157–8; Joll, *Origins*, p. 117.

61   Koch, review, *EHR*, p. 526; C. Schorske, *German Social Democracy 1905–1915: The Development of the Great Schism* (Harvard University Press, 1983), pp. 59–108; G. Eley, *Reshaping the German Right: Radical Nationalism and Political Change after Bismarck* (University of Michigan Press, 1991), p. 254; V. Berghahn, *Imperial Germany: Economy, Society, Culture and Politics, 1871–1914* (Berghahn Books, 1994), p. 292; Joll, *Origins*, p. 117; Schorske, *German Social Democracy*, p. 63.

62   W. Walling, *The Socialists and the War: A Documentary Statement of the Position of the Socialists of All Countries with Special Reference to their Peace Policy* (Adamant Media Corporation, 2001), p. 143.

63   M. Fainsod, *International Socialism and the World War* (Octagon Books, 1973), pp. 21–2, 32, 52–3, 61–2, 102–3, 110–1, 133–5; G. Haupt, *Socialism and the Great War: The Collapse of the Second International* (Clarendon Press, 1972), p. 119.

64   H. Strachan, *The First World War, Volume I: To Arms* (Oxford University Press, 2003), pp. 126–63; L. Haimson and G. Sapelli, *Strikes, Social Conflict and the First World War: An International Perspective* (Feltrinelli Editore, 1992).

65   M. Clark, *Mussolini* (Pearson Longman, 2005), pp. 15–17; A. De Grand, *The Italian Left in the Twentieth Century: A History of the Socialist and Communist Parties*, (Indiana University Press, 1989), pp. 23–4; S. Lindquist, *A History of Bombing* (Granta Books, 2001), pp. 76–8; P. O'Brien, *Mussolini In The First World War: The Journalist, The Soldier, The Fascist* (Berg Publishers, 2005), p. 31.

66   O'Brien, *Mussolini*, pp. 31–59; De Grand, *Italian Left*, pp. 28–9; O'Brien, *Mussolini*, p. 186; 11–12.

67   R. Paxton, *The Anatomy of Fascism* (Penguin Books, 2004), p. 28.

68   V. Lenin, 'The European War and International Socialism', *Lenin, Collected Works* (Progress Publishers, 1974), vol. 21, pp. 20–4, reproduced by the Marxist Internet Archive at <http://marxists.org/archive/lenin/works/1914/aug/x02.htm>. See, for example, R. Craig Nation, *War On War: Lenin, The Zimmerwald Left, and the Origins of Communist Internationalism* (Duke University Press, 1989), pp. 205–36.

69   Cohen, 'Colonial Policy', p. 368; 'Introduction', T. Schafer and A. Sackur, eds, *French Colonial Empire and the Popular Front: Hope and Disillusion* (St Martin's Press Inc, 1999), pp. 1–16; G. Wilder, 'The Politics of Failure: Historicising Popular Front Colonial Policy in French West Africa', Schafer and Sackur, *French Colonial Empire*, p. 33.

70   P. Norindr, 'The Popular Front's Colonial Policies in Indochina: Reassessing the Popular Front's "Colonisation Altruiste"', in Schafer and Sackur, *French Colonial Empire*, pp. 232–4; A. Colás, 'The Popular Front and Internationalism: the Tunisian Case in Comparative Perspective', in Schafer and Sackur, *French Colonial Empire*, pp. 96–103.

71   Colás, 'Popular Front and Internationalism', pp. 90–1; D. Slavin, 'The French Left and the Rif War, 1924–25: Racism and the Limits of Internationalism', *Journal of Contemporary History*, vol. 26, no. 1 (1991), pp. 5–32; J. Hargreaves, 'The Comintern and Anti-Colonialism: New Research Opportunities', *African Affairs*, vol. 92, no. 367 (April 1993), p. 259; T. Shepard, *The Invention of Decolonization: The Algerian War and the Remaking of France* (Cornell University Press, 2006), p. 39; M. Adereth, *The French Communist Party: A Critical History (1920–84), from Comintern to 'the Colours of France'* (Manchester University Press, 1984), p. 50–3.

72   D. Caute, *Communism and the French Intellectuals 1914–1960* (Andre Deutsch, 1964), pp. 206–7.

73   Hargreaves, 'The Comintern', pp. 260–1; J. Hargreaves, 'The Africanist International and the Popular Front', in Schafer and Sackur, *French Colonial Empire*, pp. 74–5.

74   Colás, 'Popular Front and Internationalism', p. 101.

75   H. Batatu, *The Old Social Classes and the Revolutionary Movements of Iraq: A Study of Iraq's Old Landed and Commercial Classes and of its Communists, Ba'athists and Free Officers* (Saqi, 1978), pp. 725–7.

76   For the fullest account yet of this tragic episode, see S. Balfour, *Deadly Embrace: Morocco and the Road to the Spanish Civil War* (Oxford University Press, 2002).

77   P. Preston, *The Coming of the Spanish Civil War: Reform, Reaction and Revolution in the Second Republic*, 2nd edn (Routledge, 1994), pp. 16–32.

78   J. Keene, *Fighting For Franco: International Volunteers in Nationalist Spain During the Spanish Civil War* (Leicester University Press, 2001), pp. 18–21; S. Mangini, *Memories of Resistance: Women's Voices from the Spanish Civil War* (Yale University Press, 1995), pp. 3–24; A. Beevor, *The Spanish Civil War* (Orbis Publishing, 1982), p. 27.

79   Keene, *Fighting For Franco*, pp. 22–31; Beevor, *Spanish Civil War*, pp. 51–2.

80   C. Pennell, 'Ideology and Practical Politics: A Case Study of the Rif War in Morocco, 1921–1926', *International Journal of Middle East Studies*, vol. 14, no. 1 (February 1982), pp. 19–33; Beevor, *Spanish Civil War*, pp. 52–63.

81   On the origins of World War II, and particularly the British strategy of 'appeasement', which was in reality a policy of collaboration with the fascist powers intended to divert Hitler into a conflict with the USSR, see P. Hehn, *A Low, Dishonest Decade: The Great Powers, Eastern Europe, and the Economic Origins of World War II, 1930–1941* (Continuum, 2002), pp. 394–402; on Britain's acceptance of Franco's propaganda and willingness to join Italy and Germany if either Spain or France were 'menaced by Bolshevism', see A. Durgan, *The Spanish Civil War* (Palgrave Macmillan, 2007), pp. 56–60.

82   Beevor, *Spanish Civil War*, pp. 90–1, 120–1; E. Carr, *The Comintern and the Spanish Civil War* (Macmillan, 1984), pp. 10–28; Mangini, *Memories of Resistance*, p. 18; G. Orwell, *Homage to Catalonia* (Penguin Books, 2003), p. 167.

83   For example, of the SPD's role in the collapse of the Weimar Republic, Peter Stachura writes that its timidity resulted from its strategy of constitutionalism, its non-violence, and its distance from extra-parliamentary activity, which the Social Democrats saw as beneath them. See P. Stachura, 'The SPD and the Collapse of the Weimar Republic', in R.

Fletcher, ed., *Bernstein to Brandt: A Short History of German Social Democracy* (Edward Arnold, 1987), pp. 164–5.

84   E. Traverso, *The Origins of Nazi Violence* (The New Press, 2003), pp. 51–2, 54–63; E. Barkan, 'Genocides of Indigenous Peoples: Rhetoric of Human Rights', in R. Gellately and B. Kiernan, eds, *The Specter of Genocide: Mass Murder in Historical Perspective* (Cambridge University Press, 2003), pp. 117–139; quoted in C. Koonz, *The Nazi Conscience* (The Belknap Press of Harvard University Press, 2003), p. 7.

85   Koonz, *Nazi Conscience*, p. 8; H. Trevor Roper, ed., *Hitler's Table Talk, 1941–1944, His Private Conversations* (Phoenix Press, 2000), p. 354, 15.

86   Trevor Roper, *Hitler's Table Talk*, p. 24; A. Hitler, *Mein Kampf* (Hurst & Blackett, 1935), p. 121.

87   P. Grosse, 'What Does German Colonialism Have to Do with National Socialism?', in E. Ames, M. Klotz and L. Wildenthal, eds, *Germany's Colonial Pasts* (University of Nebraska Press, 2004), pp. 127–8; S. Lindquist, *'Exterminate All The Brutes'* (Granta Books, 1996), p. 149; H. Arendt, *The Origins of Totalitarianism* (George Allen & Unwin, 1966). See Domenico Losurdo's scintillating essay, 'Towards a Critique of the Category of Totalitarianism', *Historical Materialism*, vol. 12, no. 2 (2004).

88   L. Butler, *Britain and Empire: Adjusting to a Post-Imperial World* (I.B. Tauris, 2002), pp. 48, 28.

89   See I. Pappé, *The Ethnic Cleansing of Palestine* (One World, 2006), pp. 15–17; D. Hirst, *The Gun and the Olive Branch: The Roots of Violence in the Middle East* (Faber & Faber, 2003), pp. 227–9; J. Rose, *The Myths of Zionism* (Pluto Press, 2004), pp. 129–31; Newsinger, *The Blood Never Dried*, p. 139; Pappé, *Ethnic Cleansing*, p. 87.

90   See, for example, A. Shlaim, *The Iron Wall: Israel and the Arab World* (Penguin Books, 2000); Pappé, *Ethnic Cleansing*; I. Pappé, *The Making of the Arab–Israel Conflict: 1947–1951* (I.B. Tauris, 2001); B. Kimmerling and J. Migdal, *The Palestinian People: A History* (Harvard University Press, 2003); I. Pappé, *A Modern History of Palestine: One Land, Two Peoples* (Cambridge University Press, 2004).

91   Pappé, *Ethnic Cleansing*, pp. 191–3.

92   See C. Hitchens, 'Broadcasts', in E. Said and C. Hitchens, eds, *Blaming the Victims: Spurious Scholarship and the Palestine Question* (Verso, 1986), pp. 73–83.

93   Newsinger, *The Blood Never Dried*, p. 135; J. Gorny, *The British Labour Movement and Zionism, 1917–1948* (Routledge, 1983), pp. 8–11; B. Morris, 'Revisiting the Palestinian Exodus of 1948', in E. Rogan and A. Shlaim, eds, *The War on Palestine: Rewriting the History of 1948* (Cambridge University Press, 2001), pp. 46–7; Hirst, *The Gun and the*

Olive Branch, p. 255; Newsinger, *The Blood Never Dried*, p. 135; Pappé, *Ethnic Cleansing*, pp. 124–5. J. Edmunds, 'The Evolution of British Labour Party Policy on Israel from 1967 to the Intifada', *Twentieth Century British History*, vol. 11, no. 1 (2000), pp. 23–41.

94 Ze'ev Sternhell, *The Founding Myths of Israel* (Princeton University Press, 1998).

95 Pappé, *Making of the Arab–Israel Conflict*, pp. 36–7; P. Kelemen, 'British Communists and the Palestine Conflict, 1929–1948', *Holy Land Studies*, 5.2 (2006), pp. 131–53; W. Thompson, *The Good Old Cause: British Communism 1920–1991* (Pluto Press, 1992), pp. 75–6, 97; K. Laybourn and D. Murphy, *Under The Red Flag: A History of Communism in Britain, c. 1849–1991* (Sutton Publishing, 1999), p. 142.

96 D. Sassoon, *One Hundred Years of Socialism: The West European Left in the Twentieth Century* (I.B. Tauris, 1996), pp. 167–9; A. Dobson, 'Labour or Conservative: Does It Matter in Anglo-American Relations?', *Journal of Contemporary History*, vol. 25, no. 4 (1990), p. 391; Newsinger, *The Blood Never Dried*, pp. 216–7; Sassoon, *One Hundred Years of Socialism*, p. 171; L. Black, '"The Bitterest Enemies of Communism": Labour Revisionists, Atlanticism and the Cold War', *Contemporary British History*, vol. 15, no. 3 (Autumn 2001), pp. 26–62.

97 H. Wilford, *The CIA, the British Left, and the Cold War: Calling the Tune?* (Frank Cass Publishers, 2003); Black, '"The Bitterest Enemies"'; Butler, *Britain and Empire*, p. 176; Newsinger, *The Blood Never Dried*, p. 223; Butler, *Britain and Empire*, pp. 176–7; M. Curtis, *Web of Deceit: Britain's Real Role in the World* (Vintage, 2003), pp. 414–31.

98 A. Shennan, *Rethinking France: Plans for Renewal, 1940–1946* (Oxford University Press, 1989), p. 93. Caute, *Communism and the French Intellectuals*, p. 208; M. Harbi, 'Massacre in Algeria', *Le Monde Diplomatique*, May 2005; Caute, *Communism and the French Intellectuals*, p. 209; P. Leymarie, 'Painful Memories of the Revolt of 1947: Deafening silence on a horrifying repression', *Le Monde Diplomatique*, March 1997.

99 Shepard, *Invention of Decolonization*, pp. 64–5; D. Joly, *The French Communist Party and the Algerian War* (Macmillan, 1991), p. 9; M. Scott Christofferson, *French Intellectuals Against the Left: The Antitotalitarian Movement of the 1970s* (Berghahn Books, 2004), pp. 30–1; quoted in D. Bell and B. Criddle, *The French Communist Party in the Fifth Republic* (Clarendon Press, 1994), p. 82; I. Birchall, *Sartre Against Stalinism* (Berghahn Books, 2004), p. 188. Trade surpluses with Algeria, Morocco and Tunisia, respectively, were 56.62 billion, 26.33 billion, and 13.27 billion francs. See C. Harrison, 'French Attitudes to Empire and the Algerian War', *African Affairs*, vol. 82, no.

326 (1983), p. 76; Shepard, *Invention of Decolonization*, p. 79; Joly, *French Communist Party*, p. 70.

100 R. Aronson, *Camus and Sartre: The Story of a Friendship and the Quarrel that Ended It* (University of Chicago Press, 2004), p. 186; B. Stora, *Algeria, 1830–2000: A Short History* (Cornell University Press, 2001), p. 20; M. Evans, *The Memory of Resistance: French Opposition to the Algerian War (1954–1962)* (Berg Publishers, 1997), p. 137.

101 Aronson, *Camus and Sartre*, p. 25; quoted in D. Carroll, 'Camus's Algeria: Birthrights, Colonial Injustice, and the Fiction of a French–Algerian People', *MLN*, vol. 112, no. 4 (1997), p. 525; J. Le Sueur, *Uncivil War: Intellectuals and Identity Politics During the Decolonization of Algeria* (University of Pennsylvania Press, 2001), p. 111.

102 Le Sueur, *Uncivil War*, p. 120.

103 Birchall, *Sartre Against Stalinism*, pp. 159, 173–4; Bell and Criddle, *French Communist Party*, pp. 83–4.

104 J.-P. Sartre, 'Colonialism is a System', *Les Temps Modernes*, no. 123 (March–April 1956), reproduced in Sartre, *Colonialism and Neocolonialism* (Routledge, 2001).

105 J.-P. Sartre, 'Preface', in F. Fanon, *The Wretched of the Earth* (Penguin Books, 1963), pp. 7–26; J.-P. Sartre, 'Lumumba et le neo-colonialisme', preface to *Discours de Lumumba* (Presence africaine, 1938), reproduced in Sartre, *Colonialism and Neocolonialism*, pp. 156–200.

106 Le Sueur, *Uncivil War*, p. 132; D. Bell and B. Criddle, *The French Socialist Party: The Emergence of a Party of Government* (Clarendon Press, 1988), p. 21; 'Minutes of a Meeting between the FLN and the PCF', in H. Hamon and P. Rotman, *Les Porteurs de Valises* (Albin Michel, 1979), reproduced at <http://www.marxists.org/history/algeria/1958/minutes-fln-pcf.htm>; H. Spruyt, *Ending Empire: Contested Sovereignty and Territorial Partition* (Cornell University Press, 2005), p. 114; Shepard, *Invention of Decolonization*, pp. 78, 80; Spruyt, *Ending Empire*, p. 99; Shepard, *Invention of Decolonization*, p. 80; Spruyt, *Ending Empire*, p. 99; I. Wall, 'The French Communists and the Algerian War', *Journal of Contemporary History*, vol. 12, no. 3 (1977), pp. 523–4; Shepard, *Invention of Decolonization*, p. 45.

107 Spruyt, *Ending Empire*, p. 2; Curtis, *Web of Deceit*, pp. 334–45; M. Curtis, *Unpeople: Britain's Secret Human Rights Abuses* (Vintage, 2004), p. 313.

108 H. Brailsford, 'Socialists and Empire', in R. Hinden, ed., *Fabian Colonial Essays* (George Allen & Unwin, 1945), pp. 19–21; A. Creech Jones, in Hinden, 'Socialism and the Colonial World', p. 10; Kelemen, 'Planning for Africa', p. 76.

109   Hinden, *New Fabian Colonial Essays*, pp. 9, 12–13; Hinden, 'Socialism and the Colonial World',, p. 13.

110   R. Parry, 'So Iraq Was About the Oil', *Consortium News*, 8 November 2005.

111   Hinden, *New Fabian Colonial Essays*, p. 14–16; C. Elkins, *Britain's Gulag: The Brutal End of Empire in Kenya* (Pimlico, 2005).

112   Hinden, *New Fabian Colonial Essays*, pp. 17–18.

113   Quoted in R. Emerson, 'The Fate of Human Rights in the Third World', *World Politics*, vol. 27, no. 2 (January 1975), pp. 201–226.

114   A. Dawisha, *Arab Nationalism in the Twentieth Century: From Triumph To Despair* (Princeton University Press, 2003), pp. 175–80; O. Arne Westad, *The Global Cold War* (Cambridge University Press, 2007), pp. 104–5; S. Aburish, *Nasser: The Last Arab* (Duckworth, 2004), pp. 104–11. Regarding the decision to isolate Nasser, see in particular the 'OMEGA' memorandum, United States Department of State, *Foreign relations of the United States, 1955–1957. Arab-Israeli dispute, January 1–July 26, 1956*, volume XV, 1955–1957.

115   Levine, *British Empire*, pp. 199–200; Newsinger, *The Blood Never Dried*, pp. 84–99, 164–81; N. Ayubi, *Over-stating the Arab State: Politics and Society in the Middle East* (I.B. Tauris, 1995), p. 96; Aburish, *Nasser*, p. 111.

2: Creating an Imperial Constituency

1   R. Bourne, 'The War and the Intellectuals', in C. Resek, ed., *War and the Intellectuals: essays by Randolph Bourne, 1915–1919* (Harper & Row, 1964), p. 5.

2   C. Hitchens, 'Minority Report', *Nation*, 19 October 1992.

3   A. Hoogenboom, 'American Exceptionalism: Republicanism as Ideology', in E. Glaser and H. Wellenreuther, eds, *Bridging The Atlantic: American Exceptionalism in Perspective* (German Historical Institute, Washington DC, and Cambridge University Press, 2002).

4   C. Hitchens, 'Anti-Americanism: Varieties Right and Left, Foreign and Domestic', *Slate.com*, 27 November 2002.

5   Quoted in G. Packer, *The Assassin's Gate: America In Iraq* (Faber & Faber, 2006), p. 58.

6   M. Ignatieff, ed., *American Exceptionalism and Human Rights* (Princeton University Press, 2005), pp. 1–14.

7   See, for example, P. Linebaugh and M. Rediker, *The Many-Headed Hydra: Sailors, Slaves, Commoners, and the Hidden History of the Revolutionary Atlantic* (Beacon Press, 2000), pp. 211–47.

8   D. Brion Davis, *The Problem of Slavery in Western Culture* (Oxford University Press, 1966), pp. 3–4; M. Krenn, *The Color of Empire: Race*

and American Foreign Relations (Potomac Books Inc., 2006), pp. 13–23; quoted in R. Van Alstyne, 'The American Empire: Its Historical Pattern and Evolution', *Historical Association*, no. 43 (Cox & Wyman, 1960), p. 5; G. Marsh Frederickson, *The Black Image in the White Mind: The Debate on Afro-American Character and Destiny, 1817–1914* (Wesleyan University Press, 1987), pp. 1–2; Krenn, *Color of Empire*, p. 6.

9   For example, A. Lieven, *America Right or Wrong: An Anatomy of American Nationalism* (HarperCollins Publishers, 2004), p. 41; D. Losurdo, 'Lenin and *Herrenvolk* Democracy', in S. Budgen, S. Kouvelakis and S. Zizek, eds, *Lenin Reloaded: Towards a Politics of Truth* (Duke University Press, 2007), pp. 239–52.

10   G. Horne, *The Deepest South: The United States, Brazil, and the African Slave Trade* (New York University Press, 2007), p. 2.

11   D. Brion Davis, *Inhuman Bondage: The Rise and Fall of Slavery in the New World* (Oxford University Press, 2006), pp. 268–9.

12   D. Brion Davis, *Inhuman Bondage*, pp. 269–70; Krenn, *Color of Empire*, pp. 25–34; R. Horsman, *Race and Manifest Destiny: The Origins of American Racial Anglo-Saxonism* (Harvard University Press, 1981), p. 233.

13   Horne, *Deepest South*, pp. 1–4.

14   Ibid., pp. 5–6.

15   Ibid., pp. 173–97.

16   M. Estes, *A Defense of Negro Slavery As It Exists in the United States* (Press of the Alabama Journal, 1846); J. D. Smith, ed., *Anti-Black Thought, 1863–1925, 'The Negro Problem', An Eleven Volume Anthology of Racist Writings, Volume Four: The 'Benefits' of Slavery, The New Proslavery Argument, Part II* (Garland Publishing Inc, 1993), p. 6.

17   Smith, ed., *Anti-Black Thought*, pp. 244–54.

18   G. Fitzhugh, *Cannibals, All! Or, Slaves Without Masters*, Harvard University Press, 1960

19   Horne, *Deepest South*, pp. 198–221; J. Eperjesi, *Visions of Asia and the Pacific in American Culture* (Dartmouth College Press, 2005); W. LaFeber, *The Clash: US–Japanese Relations Throughout History* (WW Norton & Company, 1997), pp. 27–41.

20   G. Horne, *The White Pacific: US Imperialism and Black Slavery in the South Seas After the Civil War* (University of Hawaii Press, 2007) pp. 160–78.

21   R. Horsman, *Expansion and American Indian Policy 1783–1812* (University of Oklahoma Press, 1967); A. Vaughan, *Roots of American Racism: Essays on the Colonial Experience* (Oxford University Press, 1995), pp. 7–22; Horsman, *Expansion and American Indian Policy*.

22   Krenn, *Color of Empire*, pp. 23–4.

23   W. Williams, 'United States Indian Policy and the Debate over Philippine Annexation: Implications for the Origins of American Imperialism', *Journal of American History*, vol. 66, no. 44 (1980), pp. 810–31; Krenn, *Color of Empire*, pp. 47–8.

24   R. Slotkin, *The Fatal Environment: The Myth of the Frontier in the Age of Industrialisation: 1800–1890* (Atheneum, 1985), p. 15; Krenn, *Color of Empire*, p. 42; S. Phillips, 'Antebellum Agricultural Reform, Republican Ideology, and Sectional Tension', *Agricultural History*, vol. 74, no. 4 (2000), pp. 799–822; Library of Congress: <http://www.loc.gov/rr/program/bib/ourdocs/Homestead.html>; R. Weigley, *The American Way of War: A History of United States Military Strategy and Policy* (Indiana University Press, 1973).

25   M. Dubovksy and F. Dulles, *Labor in America: A History* (Harlan Davidson Inc., 1984), pp. 104–9; M. Beaud, *A History of Capitalism 1500–2000* (Monthly Review Press, 2000); Krenn, *Color of Empire*, p. 36; D. Jenkins, *The Final Frontier: America, Science and Terror* (Verso, 2002), pp. 97–128.

26   M. Frye Jacobson, *Barbarian Virtues: The United States Encounters Foreign Peoples at Home and Abroad 1876–1917* (Hill & Wang, 2000), pp. 183–90; D. Roediger, *Working Toward Whiteness: How America's Immigrants Become White. The Strange Journey from Ellis Island to the Suburbs* (Basic Books, 2005), pp. 3–33; J. Pfaelzer, *Driven Out: The Forgotten War Against Chinese Americans* (Random House, 2007); Krenn, *Color of Empire*, p. 54; Jacobson, *Barbarian Virtues*, pp. 193–4, 195; M. Ngai, *Impossible Subects: Illegal Aliens and the Making of Modern America* (Princeton University Press, 2004), pp. 1–49; W. Wu, *The Yellow Peril: Chinese Americans in American Fiction 1850–1940* (Archon Books, 1982); Krenn, *Color of Empire*, p. 51.

27   Krenn, *Color of Empire*, pp. 57–8; J. Tyner, *Oriental Bodies: Discourse and Discipline in US Immigration Policy, 1875–1942* (Lexington Books, 2006), pp. 1–19; I. Dowbiggin, *Keeping America Sane: Psychiatry and Eugenics in the United States and Canada, 1880–1940* (Cornell University Press, 1997); W. Kline, *Building a Better Race: Gender, Sexuality, and Eugenics from the Turn of the Century to the Baby Boom* (University of California Press, 2001); C. Cogdell, *Eugenic Design: Streamlining America in the 1930s* (University of Pennsylvania Press, 2004); E. Black, *War Against the Weak* (Four Walls Eight Windows, 2003), pp. 247–58, ch. 15.

28   Amy Greenberg, *Manifest Manhood and the Antebellum American Empire*, (Cambridge University Press, 2005).

29   Jenkins, *Final Frontier*, pp. 97–101.

30   Quoted in Jacobson, *Barbarian Virtues*, p. 3; T. Roosevelt, 'The Strenuous Life', speech to the Hamilton Club, Chicago, 10 April 1899: <http://teachingamericanhistory.org/ >.

31   M. Lake and H. Reynolds, *Drawing the Global Colour Line: White Men's Countries and the International Challenge of Racial Equality* (Cambridge University Press, 2008), pp. 96–7, 100–3.

32   T. Roosevelt, 'The New Nationalism', speech before the Grand Army, 1910: <http://teachingamericanhistory.org/ >; T. Roosevelt, *The Rough Riders* (Charles Scribner's Sons, 1903), pp. 4, 9–11, 15, 168–9; 232–3.

33   Quoted in M. Jacobson, *Barbarian Virtues: The United States Encounters Foreign Peoples at Home and Abroad 1876–1917* (Hill & Wang, 2000), p. 3; quoted in N. Yuval-Davis, *Gender and Nation* (Sage Publications, 1997), p. 30; A. McClintock, 'No Longer in a Future Heaven': Nationalism, Gender and Race', in G. Eley and R. Suny, eds, *Becoming National: A Reader* (Oxford University Press, 1996), p. 262; T. Roosevelt, 'On American Motherhood', 13 March 1905, transcript reproduced by the National Centre for Public Policy Research: <http://www.nationalcenter.org/TRooseveltMotherhood.html>; quoted in S. Lyons Watts, *Rough Rider in the White House: Theodore Roosevelt and the Politics of Desire* (University of Chicago Press, 2003), p. 22.

34   L. Pérez, Jr, *The War of 1898: The United States and Cuba in History and Historiography* (University of Carolina Press, 1998), pp. 2–7; K. Hoganson, *Fighting American Manhood: How Gender Politics Provoked the Spanish–American and Philippine–American Wars* (Yale University Press, 1998), p. 2; Pérez *War of 1898*, pp. 8–11.

35   Pérez *War of 1898*, pp. 13–14; Krenn, *Color of Empire*, pp. 46, 17–21.

36   Jacobson, *Barbarian Virtues*, pp. 243–4, 223; Hoganson, *Fighting American Manhood*, pp. 134–7; Jacobson, *Barbarian Virtues*, p. 222; Hoganson, *Fighting American Manhood*, p. 134; P. Kramer, 'Empires, Exceptions and Anglo-Saxons: Race and Rule Between the British and US Empires, 1880–1910', in J. Go and A. Foster, eds, *The American Colonial State in the Philippines: Global Perspectives* (Duke University Press, 2003), p. 61; P. Kramer, *The Blood of Government: Race, Empire, the United States and the Philippines* (University of North Carolina Press, 2006), p. 10–11.

37   P. Foner and R. Winchester, eds, *The Anti-Imperialist Reader: A Documentary History of the United States, Volume I, From the Mexican War to the Election of 1900* (Holmes & Meier Publishers Inc., 1984), pp. 3, 69, 103, 425; J. De Veyra, 'Address Before the Nineteenth Annual Meeting of the Anti-Imperialist League', Report of the Nineteenth Annual Meeting of the Anti-Imperialist League (Boston:

Anti-Imperialist League, 1917): <http://www.boondocksnet.com/ai/ >; J. Zwick, ed., *Anti-Imperialism in the United States, 1898−1935*: <http://www.boondocksnet.com/ai/>, p. 107.

38   J. Zwick, ed., *Mark Twain's Weapons of Satire: Anti-Imperialist Writings on the Philippine–American War* (Syracuse University Press, 1992).

39   Foner and Winchester, *The Anti-Imperialist Reader*, pp. 425−43; Kramer, 'Empires, Exceptions and Anglo-Saxons', p. 65.

40   Jacobson, *Barbarian Virtues*, p. 221; R. Grossman, '"The Blood of the People'": The Guardia Nacional's Fifty-Year War against the People of Nicaragua, 1927−1979', in C. Menjívar and N. Rodriguez, eds, *When States Kill: Latin America, the US, and Technologies of Terror* (University of Texas Press, 2005), pp. 60−1; Anti-Imperialist League, 'Against Intervention in Nicaragua,' Report of the Fourteenth Annual Meeting of the Anti-Imperialist League (Anti-Imperialist League, 1913), at <http://www.historyillustrated.com/ai/ >; in J. Zwick, ed., *Anti-Imperialism in the United States*; M. Renda, *Taking Haiti: Military Occupation and the Culture of US Imperialism, 1915−1940* (University of California Press, 2001), pp. 10−11; H. Schmidt, *The United States Occupation of Haiti, 1915−1934* (Rutgers University Press, 1995), pp. 7, 15−16, 64−5, 70, 84; Renda, *Taking Haiti*, p. 10; H. Seligmann, 'The Conquest of Haiti', *Nation*, 111 (10 July 1920); http://www.boondocksnet.com/ai/; J. Zwick, ed., *Anti-Imperialism*; R. Pettigrew, 'The U.S. and the Course of Empire', *Imperial Washington* (Charles H. Kerr & Co., 1922); <http://www.boondocksnet.com/ai/ >, cited in J. Zwick, ed., *Anti-Imperialism in the United States, 1898−1935*.

41   Jacobson, *Barbarian Virtues*, p. 221; R. Grossman, '"The Blood of the People": The Guardia Nacional's Fifty-Year War against the People of Nicaragua, 1927−1979', in C. Menjívar and N. Rodriguez, eds, *When States Kill: Latin America, the US, and Technologies of Terror* (University of Texas Press, 2005), pp. 60−1; Anti-Imperialist League, 'Against Intervention in Nicaragua,' Report of the Fourteenth Annual Meeting of the Anti-Imperialist League (Boston: Anti-Imperialist League, 1913), at <http://www.historyillustrated.com/ai/ >; in Zwick, ed., *Anti-Imperialism*; M. Renda, *Taking Haiti: Military Occupation and the Culture of US Imperialism, 1915−1940* (University of California Press, 2001), pp. 10−11; H. Schmidt, *The United States Occupation of Haiti, 1915−1934* (Rutgers University Press, 1995), pp. 7, 15−16, 64−5, 70, 84; Renda, *Taking Haiti*, p. 10; H. Seligmann, 'The Conquest of Haiti', *Nation*, 111 (10 July 1920); <http://www.boon docksnet.com/ai/>; Zwick, ed., *Anti-Imperialism*; R. Pettigrew, 'The U.S. and the Course of Empire', *Imperial Washington* (Charles H. Kerr

& Co., 1922); <http://www.boondocksnet.com/ai/ >, cited in J. Zwick, ed., *Anti-Imperialism*; Renda, *Taking Haiti*, pp. 13–19; Haiti-Santo Domingo Independence Society, 'Why Should You Worry About Haiti?', *Nation* 113 (9 November 1921); <http://www.historyillustrated.com/ai/>, in Zwick, ed., *Anti-Imperialism*.

42   P. Berman, *Terror and Liberalism* (WW Norton, 2004), p. 198; quoted in D. Keen, *Endless War? Hidden Functions of the 'War on Terror'* (Pluto Press, 2006), pp. 190–1; D. Rieff, *At The Point of a Gun: Democratic Dreams and Armed Intervention* (Simon & Schuster, 2005), p. 54. M. Ignatieff, *Virtual War: Kosovo and Beyond* (Vintage, 2000), p. 209; M. Ignatieff, *The Warrior's Honor: Ethnic War and the Modern Conscience* (Chatto & Windus, 1998), p. 91; Ignatieff, *American Exceptionalism*, p. 13.

43   K. O'Reilly, 'The Jim Crow Policies of Woodrow Wilson', *Journal of Blacks in Higher Education*, no. 17 (1997), pp. 117–21; A. Gaughan, 'Woodrow Wilson and the Rise of Militant Interventionism in the South', *Journal of Southern History*, vol. 65, no. 4 (1999), pp. 771–808; quoted in D. Heater, *National Self-Determination: Woodrow Wilson and his Legacy* (St Martin's Press, 1994), p. 15; S. Freud and W. Bullitt, *Thomas Woodrow Wilson, Twenty-eighth President of the United States: A Psychological Study* (Weidenfeld & Nicolson, 1967), pp. 45, 47, 51–4, 147.

44   Quoted in N. Aage Thorsen, *The Political Thought of Woodrow Wilson 1875–1910* (Princeton University Press, 1988), p. 179.

45   A. Thorsen, *Political Thought of Woodrow Wilson*, p. 177; Heater, *National Self-Determination*, pp. 19–20; N. Levin, Jr, *Woodrow Wilson and World Politics: America's Response to War and Revolution* (Oxford University Press, 1968); C. Miéville, *Between Equal Rights: A Marxist Theory of International Law* (Brill, 2005), pp. 20–1; F. Ninkovich, *The Wilsonian Century: U.S. Foreign Policy Since 1900* (University of Chicago Press, 1999), p. 51.

46   R. Pestritto, ed., *Woodrow Wilson: the Essential Political Writings* (Lexington Books, 2005), 32–5; quoted in D. Flamming, *Bound for Freedom: Black Los Angeles in Jim Crow America* (University of California Press, 2005), p. 88.

47   Thorsen, *Political Thought of Woodrow Wilson*, pp. 99–164, 166, 168, 171, 165–6, 174–7.

48   Thorsen, *Political Thought of Woodrow Wilson*, pp. 164–5; Heater, *National Self-Determination*, pp. 24–5.

49   Thorsen, *Political Thought of Woodrow Wilson*, pp. 174–5.

50   R. Watson Curry, 'Woodrow Wilson and Philippine Policy', *Mississippi Valley Historical Review*, vol. 41, no. 3 (1954), pp. 435–52; A. Link,

Woodrow Wilson and the Progressive Era, 1910–1917 (Harper & Brothers, 1954), pp. 227–8; E. Manela, *The Wilsonian Moment: Self-Determination and the International Origins of Anticolonial Nationalism* (Oxford University Press, 2007), pp. 24, 30.

51 N. Smith, *American Empire: Roosevelt's Geographer and the Prelude to Globalization* (University of California Press, 2003), p. 115.

52 M. Beaud, *A History of Capitalism: 1500–2000* (Monthly Review Press, 2002), chapter 4; E. Hobsbawm, *Industry and Empire* (History Book Club, 1968), chapter 12.

53 Smith, *American Empire*, pp. 115–55; Manela, *Wilsonian Moment*, p. 42.

54 Manela, *Wilsonian Moment*, pp. 38–9, 48–52, 181–2, 220.

55 For example, the British were successfully able to characterize the anti-colonial disturbances as 'Bolshevism', or 'rapidly developing into Bolshevism' as the US consul general in Cairo put it. Manela, *Wilsonian Moment*, pp. 154–6.

56 G. Horne, *Race War: White Supremacy and the Japanese Attack on the British Empire* (New York University Press, 2004), pp. 187–219.

57 J. Thompson, *Reformers and War: Progressive Publicists and the First World War* (Cambridge University Press, 1987), pp. 117–77; C. Resch, ed., *War and the Intellectuals: Essays by Randolph Bourne, 1915–1919* (Harper & Row, 1964), pp. 3–9.

58 M. Ruotsila, *John Spargo and American Socialism* (Palgrave MacMillan, 2006), pp. 10–15, 49–72.

59 Ruotsila, *John Spargo*, pp. 73–9.

60 Ruotsila, *John Spargo*, pp. 79–93; J. Spargo, *Russia As An American Problem* (Harper, 1920).

61 Ruotsila, *John Spargo*, pp. 91–211. On Wilson's non-recognition, see K. Amelia and S. Sibley, *Loans and Legitimacy: The Evolution of Soviet–American Relations, 1919–1933* (University of Kentucky Press, 1996), p. 47. For a lengthy review, see R. Radosh, 'John Spargo and Wilson's Russian Policy, 1920', *Journal of American History*, vol. 52, no. 3 (December 1965), pp. 548–65. Radosh, once a socialist, has since followed in Spargo's footsteps.

62 M. Ellis, *Race, War, and Surveillance: African Americans and the United States Government during World War I* (Indiana University Press, 2001), pp. xiii–46, 228–30.

63 Thompson, *Reformers and War*, p. 179; S. Ewens, *PR! A Social History of Spin* (Basic Books, 1998), chapter 1.

64 G. Creel, *How we advertised America; the first telling of the amazing story of the Committee on public information that carried the gospel of Americanism to every corner of the globe* (Harper & Brothers, 1920).

65 Creel, *How we advertised America*, pp. 5, 87, 109, 172–3; R. Mock, *Words That Won the War: The Story of the Committee on Public Information, 1917–1919* (Princeton University Press, 1939), pp. 112–13.

66 *Washington Post* editorial, 1 January 1917, reproduced in I. Bennett, *Editorials from the Washington Post, 1917–1920* (Washington Post Company, 1921), pp. 1–2; *Washington Post* editorials, 2 February 1917, 5 February 1917, Bennett, *Editorials*, pp. 3–7; *Washington Post* editorial, 16 April 1918, Bennett, *Editorials*, p. 205; *Washington Post* editorial, 5 February 1917, Bennett, *Editorials*, p, 7.

67 Quoted in Gaughan, 'Woodrow Wilson', p. 789.

68 R. Schmidt, *Red Scare: The FBI and the Origins of Anticommunism in the United States, 1919–1943* (Museum Tusculanum Press, 2000), pp. 24–5, 213; S. Newsome, 'Seattle Minute Men: Amateur Spies, Gossip and Lies', *Seattle General Strike Project* (Washington University, 1999); Schmidt, *Red Scare*, pp. 26–35, 128–9; J. Woods, *Black Struggle, Red Scare: Segregation and Anti-Communism in the South, 1948–1968* (Louisiana State University Press, 2004).

69 R. Vallely, *The Two Reconstructions: The Struggle for Black Enfranchisement* (University of Chicago Press, 2004), pp. 1–11.

70 J. Higham, *Strangers in the Land: Patterns of American Nativism, 1860–1925* (Rutgers University Press, 2002), pp. 13, 265; M. Chalmers, *Hooded Americanism: The History of the Ku Klux Klan* (Duke University Press, 1987), p. 281; K. Kusner, 'Toward a Comparative History of Racism and Xenophobia in the United States and Germany, 1865–1933', in Glaser and Wellenreuther, *Bridging the Atlantic*, pp. 148–71.

71 'Americanizing the Moros', *New Republic* 65 (21 January1931), at <http://www.boondocksnet.com/ai/ >; J. Zwick, ed., *Anti-Imperialism*; J. Ehrman, *The Rise of Neoconservatism: Intellectuals and Foreign Affairs, 1945–1994* (Yale University Press, 1995), pp. 1–5; M. Nash and M. Small, *The Good Fight Continues: World War II Letters From the Abraham Lincoln Brigade* (New York University Press, 2006), pp. 1, 116–17; A. Wald, *Trinity of Passion: The Literary Left and the Anti-Fascist Crusade* (University of North Carolina Press, 2007), pp. 108–10.

72 D. Cesarani, *Arthur Koestler: The Homeless Mind* (Vintage, 1999), p. 172; A. Gleason, *Totalitarianism: The Inner History of the Cold War* (Oxford University Press, 1995), pp. 55–73.

73 R. Drinnon, *Keeper of Concentration Camps: Dillon S. Meyer and American Racism* (University of California Press, 1987), p. xxi; Krenn, *Color of Empire*, pp. 59–60, 61, 63–5; LaFeber, *The Clash*, pp. 124–5.

74 R. Bosworth, *Explaining Auschwitz and Hiroshima: History Writing and the Second World War, 1945–1990* (Routledge, 1993), pp. 169–79; G. Horne, *Race War*, pp. 1–5.

75   R. Drayton, 'An Ethical Blank Check: British and US Mythology About the Second World War Ignores Our Own Crimes and Legitimizes Anglo-American Warmaking', *Guardian*, 10 May 2005; Ngai, *Impossible Subjects*, p. 175; Drinnon, , pp. 4–6, 32, 30–1, 33; Horne, *Race War*, p. 128.

76   Ngai, *Impossible Subjects*, p. 175; Drinnon, *Keeper of Concentration Camps*, p. 34; Grossman, '"The Blood of the People"', pp. 60–1. Drinnon, *Keeper of Concentration Camps*, p. 34, 33; M. Schaller, *The American Occupation of Japan: The Origins of the Cold War in Asia* (Oxford University Press, 1985), p. 45; Drinnon, *Keeper of Concentration Camps*, pp. xxiv, 4, 9, 10, 8–9, 56–7; Ngai, *Impossible Subjects*, p. 179; Drinnon, *Keeper of Concentration Camps*, p. 9.

77   J. Dower, *War Without Mercy: Race and Power in the Pacific War* (Pantheon Books, 1986), pp. 17, 53; Horne, *Race War*, pp. 5–6; Dower, *War Without Mercy*, pp. 15–37; Krenn, *Color of Empire*, pp 66–7; Dower, *War Without Mercy*, pp. 38, 40–1.

78   G. Alperovitz, *Atomic Diplomacy: Hiroshima and Potsdam: The Use of the Atomic Bomb and the American Confrontation with Soviet Power* (Pluto Press, 1995); G. Alperovitz, 'Hiroshima: Historians Reassess', *Foreign Policy*, no. 99, (Summer 1994), pp. 18–19; Schaller, *American Occupation of Japan*, p. 8.

79   H. Stimson, 'The decision to use the atomic bomb', *Harper's Magazine*, February 1947, pp. 97–107; M. Isserman, *Which Side Were You On? The American Communist Party During the Second World War* (Wesleyan University Press, 1982), pp. 123–4; Alperovitz, *Atomic Diplomacy*, pp. 427–8; Schaller, *American Occupation of Japan*, p. 3.

80   D. Josefson, 'US compensates subjects of radiation experiments', *British Medical Journal*, 7 December 1996; R. Faden, 'The Advisory Committee on Human Radiation Experiments: Reflections on a Presidential Commission', *Hastings Center Report*, vol. 26, no. 5 (1996), pp. 5–10; W. Moss and R. Eckhardt, 'The Human Plutonium Injection Experiments', *Los Alamos Science*, no. 23 (1995).

3: Neocons and Apostates

1   F. Stonor Saunders, *Who Paid the Piper?: The CIA and the Cultural Cold War* (Granta Books, 1999); C. McGrath, 'A Liberal Beacon Burns Out', *New York Times*, 23 January 2006; letter addressed by Socialist Party presidential candidate Norman Thomas to President Harry S. Truman, dated 11 September 1948, *The Truman Library*: <http://www.trumanlibrary.org/>.

2   Stonor Saunders, *Who Paid the Piper?*; M. Heale, *McCarthy's*

Americans: Red Scare Politics in State and Nation, 1935–1965
(Macmillan Press, 1998), p. 55.

3   G. Dorrien, The Neoconservative Mind: Politics, Culture, and the War
     of Ideology (Temple University Press, 1993), pp. 79–84.

4   M. Sperling McAuliffe, Crisis on the Left: Cold War Politics and
     American Liberals, 1947–1954, (University of Massachussetts Press,
     1970), pp. 6–7; M. Friedman, The Neoconservative Revolution: Jewish
     Intellectuals and the Shaping of Public Policy (Cambridge University
     Press, 2005), p. 66; 'X' (G. Kennan), 'The Sources of Soviet Conduct',
     Foreign Affairs, July 1947: <http://www.foreignaffairs.org/>.

5   A. Schlesinger, Jr, The Vital Center: The Politics of Freedom (Andre
     Deutsch, 1970), pp. 1, 51–67.He was prescient, too, when he noted that
     a version of Marx could be appropriated by 'the democratic tradition'
     (ibid., pp. 63–4).

6   Ibid., pp. 68–71, 72. Trotsky did indeed mock the 'priestly–Kantian veg-
     etarian–Quaker prattle about the sacredness of human life', on more
     than one occasion. The most notable instance is in his riposte to the
     German social democrat Karl Kautsky, who had counterposed the
     Kantian tradition of liberalism and its respect for the 'sanctity of
     human life' to Bolshevism and its use of terror to win the civil war. See
     K. Kautsky, 'Terrorism and Communism: A Contribution to the
     Natural History of Revolution', 1919, chapter 7, reproduced by the
     Marxist Internet Archive at <http://www.marxists.org/ >. Trotsky's
     response can be found in Terrorism and Communism: A Reply to Karl
     Kautsky (Verso, 2007), pp. 61–2. Trotsky's critique is actually quite
     simply to assert the right of self-defence. He points out that Kautsky
     not only supported his government in World War I, but condemned the
     Bolsheviks for the Brest–Litovsk treaty: '[I]n his opinion we ought to
     have continued war. But what then becomes of the sacredness of human
     life? Does life cease to be sacred when it is a question of people talking
     another language, or does Kautsky consider that mass murders organ-
     ized on principles of strategy and tactics are not murders at all?'

7   Thus, in one line of argument (Vital Center, pp. 68–72), Schlesinger
     implies that Marx and Engels opposed the formation of a separate
     Communist party opposed to other working class parties, whereas his
     source indicates that Marx and Engels felt there ought to be a commu-
     nist party differing on some principles; imputes a statement to Lenin on
     the basis of a statement made by Stalin, who was then busily trying to
     appropriate Lenin's legacy in defence of his own policies; and again,
     relying on a secondary source, misquotes Lenin thus: 'Whoever
     attempts to achieve socialism by any other route than that of political

democracy will inevitably arrive at the most absurd and reactionary results, both political and economic.' This is to suggest that Lenin had a premonition of what might happen to socialism if political democracy was suspended. Lenin had in fact stated 'Anyone who attempts to achieve socialism by any other route without passing through the stage of political democracy, will inevitably arrive at the most absurd and reactionary conclusions, both economic and political.' In this he was upbraiding Trotsky for his call for an immediate workers' government in 1905, and insisting on the need for a bourgeois revolution before a socialist revolution could be achieved.

8   'The sin of racial pride still represents the most basic challenge to the American conscience. . .', Schlesinger, *Vital Center*, pp. 190, 189–218, 256.

9   Schlesinger, *Vital Center*, p. 159; J. Ehrman, *The Rise of Neoconservatism: Intellectuals and Foreign Affairs, 1945–1994* (Yale University Press, 1996), pp. 11–15; Schlesinger, *Vital Center*, pp. 12, 14, 161, 222, 224, 232.

10   Ehrman, *Rise of Neoconservatism*, p. 1–5; Schlesinger, *Vital Center*, pp. 137–8; McAuliffe, *Crisis on the Left*, p. 27; Stonor Saunders, *Who Paid the Piper?*; A. Wald, *The New York Intellectuals* (University of North Carolina Press, 1987), p. 257.

11   J. Neale, *A People's History of the Vietnam War* (The New Press, 2004), p. 55; Heale, *McCarthy's Americans*, pp. 21, 28–9, 56–60, 181–6, 193–205.

12   Typically, the CPUSA had done some of the dirty work itself here, by supporting the government's suppression of the Socialist Workers Party on the grounds that they were Trotskyists, and therefore objectively pro-fascist. They did not foresee – because they had expected the postwar continuation of the Grand Alliance – that they would in their turn become the victims of such legislation. See M. Belknap, *Cold War Political Justice: The Smith Act, the Communist Party, and American Civil Liberties* (Greenwood Press, 1977), p. 41.

13   M. Isserman, *Which Side Were You On? The American Communist Party During the Second World War* (University of Illinois Press, 1993), pp. 127–87; J. Duclos, 'On the Dissolution of the Communist Party of the United States', *Cahiers du Communisme*, April 1945, reproduced by the Marxist Internet Archive at <http://www.marxists.org/>; M. Isserman, *If I Had a Hammer: The Death of the Old Left and the Birth of the New Left* (University of Illinois Press, 1995), pp. 3–31.

14   Wald, *New York Intellectuals*, p. 316.

15   'Intellectuals in Retreat', *New International*, vol. 5, no. 1 (January 1939), pp. 3–22, republished by the Marxist Internet Archive at

<http://www.marxists.org/>; Christopher Hitchens, *Blood, Class and Nostalgia: Anglo-American Ironies* (Farrar, Straus and Giroux, 1990); I. Deutscher, 'The Conscience of the Ex-Communist', review of *The God That Failed* in *The Reporter*, April 1950.

16 W. Mayer, *The Changing American Mind: How and Why American Public Opinion Changed Between 1960 and 1988* (University of Michigan Press, 1993), pp. 47–55.

17 On the Greek Civil War, see G. Kolko, *The Politics of War: The World and United States Foreign Policy, 1943–1945* (Vintage Books, 1968), pp. 172–93; on the support for Franco, see Schmitz, *Thank God They're On Our Side: The United States and Right-Wing Dictatorships, 1921–1965* (University of North Carolina Press, 1999), pp. 153–68; on the division of Europe and the Berlin Blockade, see C. Eisenberg, 'The Myth of the Berlin Blockade and the Early Cold War', in E. Schrecker, ed., *Cold War Triumphalism: The Misuse of History After the Fall of Communism* (The New Press, 2004), pp. 174–200; on the confrontation with Khrushchev over Berlin and the rejection of proposals to normalize the situation of Germany, reunifying it under an elected government outside the competing military alliances, see H. Harrison, *Driving the Soviets Up the Wall: Soviet–East German Relations, 1953–1961* (Princeton University Press, 2003).

18 The US initially maintained a right of military intervention in Cuba to keep the government friendly to American interests through the Platt Amendment, which was dropped in 1934 by Franklin Delano Roosevelt, as part of the 'Good Neighbor Policy' launched *avant la lettre* under Hoover in the 1920s. It also involved withdrawal of troops from Haiti in 1934; the withdrawal from the Dominican Republic in 1924, and the maintenance of good terms with the Trujillo regime that came to power in 1930, and neutrality during its genocide against Haitian workers; and withdrawal from Nicaragua, after repeated interventions, in 1937. In every case, the withdrawal of direct military intervention had been preceded by the erection of a local national security apparatus which empowered pro-US dictatorships. See T. Wright, *Latin America in the Era of the Cuban Revolution* (Greenwood Publishers, 2000), p. 4; G. White, Jr, *Holding the Line: Race, Racism, and American Foreign Policy toward Africa, 1953–1961* (Rowman & Littlefield, 2005), p. 9; E. Roorda, *The Dictator Next Door: The Good Neighbor Policy and the Trujillo Regime in the Dominican Republic, 1930–1945* (Duke University Press, 1998).

19 D. Schmitz, *Thank God They're On Our Side: The United States and Right-Wing Dictatorships, 1921–1965* (University of North Carolina Press, 1999).

20   M. Krenn, *The Color of Empire: Race and American Foreign Relations* (Potomac Books, 2006), pp. 79–80.

21   G. Horne, *Cold War in a Hot Zone: The United States Confronts Labor and Independence Struggles in the British West Indies* (Temple University Press, 2007), pp. 1–14.

22   O. Arne Westad, *The Global Cold War: Third World Interventions and the Making of Our Times* (Cambridge University Press, 2007), pp. 170–6; S. Stern, *The Week The World Stood Still: Inside the Secret Cuban Missile Crisis* (Stanford University Press, 2005); 'Table of Global Nuclear Weapons Stockpiles, 1945–2002', Natural Resources Defense Council, 2002, at <http://www.nrdc.org/>.

23   P. Beinart, 'The Rehabilitation of a Cold War Liberal', *New York Times*, 30 April 2006; G. Grandin, *The Last Colonial Massacre: Latin America in the Cold War* (University of Chicago Press, 2004), pp. 38–86.

24   G. Grandin, *Empire's Workshop: Latin America, the United States and the Rise of the New Imperialism* (Metropolitan Books, 2006), pp. 48, 94–5, 96; quoted in N. Chomsky, 'Objectivity and Liberal Scholarship', reproduced in *American Power and the New Mandarins* (The New Press, 2002), p. 129; Grandin, *Empire's Workshop*, p. 49.

25   D. Little, *American Orientalism: The United States and the Middle East Since 1945* (I.B. Tauris, 2002), pp. 26–8; *New York Times* editorial, 6 August 1954, quoted in N. Chomsky, *Human Rights and American Foreign Policy* (Spokesman Books, 1978), p. 18.

26   C. Klein, *Cold War Orientalism: Asia in the Middlebrow Imagination, 1945–1961* (University of California Press, 2003), pp. 1–7, 13, 30, 36–7, 40–3, 51, 152–62; A. Schlesinger, Jr, *Bitter Heritage: Vietnam and American Democracy, 1941–1966* (Sphere Books, 1966), p. 20.

27   M. Schaller, *The American Occupation of Japan: The Origins of the Cold War in Asia* (Oxford University Press, 1985), p. 4.

28   Schaller, *American Occupation of Japan*, p. 27.

29   Schaller, *American Occupation of Japan*, pp. 5, 21–51, 122–8.

30   Quoted Westad, *Global Cold War*; S. Lee, *The Korean War* (Longman Pearson, 2001), p. 21; C. Armstrong, *The North Korean Revolution, 1945–1950* (Cornell University Press, 2003), pp. 12–14, 17; B. Cummings, *The Origins of the Korean War, vol. I: Liberation and the Emergence of Separate Regimes, 1945–1947* (Princeton University Press, 1981), pp. xx–xxi.

31   H. Deane, *The Korean War, 1945–1953* (China Books, 1999), pp. 12–14; Armstrong, *North Korean Revolution*, pp. 2, 142–5, 244; Cummings, *Origins of the Korean War, vol. I*, pp. 199, 209–13; Lee, *Korean War*, pp. 22–3; Cummings, *Origins of the Korean War, vol. I*, p. xxvi; J.

Merrill, 'Internal Warfare in Korea, 1948–1950: The Local Setting of the Korean War', in B. Cummings, ed., *Child of Conflict: the Korean–American Relationship: 1943–1953* (University of Washington Press, 1983), p. 136.

32 Deane, *Korean War*, p. 64; Merrill, 'Internal Warfare', pp. 140, 137–9, 144–5, 141, 137; B. Cummings, *The Origins of the Korean War, vol. II: The Roaring of the Cataract, 1947–1950* (Princeton University Press, 1990); B. Cummings, *Korea's Place in the Sun: A Modern History* (W.W. Norton & Co., 1997), p. 255.

33 Cummings, *Korea's Place in the Sun*, p. 248; Lee, *Korean War*, pp. 41–3; Deane, *Korean War*, p. 82. Even right-wing international relations scholar John Lewis Gaddis acknowledges that the intervention was at the behest of the North Korean leadership rather than Soviet aggression – but he does not acknowledge the raging civil war, the contested legitimacy of the southern state, or the repeated border assaults by the south. See J. Gaddis, *We Now Know: Rethinking Cold War History* (Oxford University Press, 1997), pp. 70–5.

34 Ehrman, *Rise of Neoconservatism*, pp. 16–17; Lee, *Korean War*, pp. 43–4; I. Stone, *The Hidden History of the Korean War* (Monthly Review Press, 1952), pp. 1–2.

35 Cummings, *Korea's Place in the Sun*, pp. 264–5; A. Offner, *Another Such Victory: President Truman and the Cold War, 1945–1953* (Stanford University Press, 2002), p. 371; P. Pierpaoli, Jr, *Truman and Korea: The Political Culture and the Early Cold War* (University of Missouri Press, 1999), pp. 2, 9–21, 84–92, 225–32.

36 Cummings, *Korea's Place in the Sun*, p. 263; A. Schlesinger, *A Thousand Days: John F. Kennedy in the White House* (Houghton Mifflin, 2002), pp. 299, 308; L. Wittner, *Rebels Against War: The American Peace Movement, 1941–1960* (Columbia University Press, 1969), pp. 127–8, 201–2; H. Zinn, *A People's History of the United States: 1492–Present* (Harper Perennial, 2003), p. 128.

37 P. Drucker, *Max Shachtman and His Left: A Socialist's Odyssey Through the 'American Century'* (Humanity Books, 1994), pp. 223, 244–9.

38 D. McCann and B. Strauss, eds, *War and Democracy: A Comparative History of the Korean War and the Peloponnesian War*, (M.E. Sharpe, 2001), p. 206.

39 Cummings, *Korea's Place in the Sun*, pp. 277, 278–82.

40 Offner, *Another Such Victory*, p. 381; Cummings, *Korea's Place in the Sun*, pp. 284–9; Offner, *Another Such Victory*, pp. 381–2; Cummings, *Korea's Place in the Sun*, pp. 289–92.

41 Cummings, *Korea's Place in the Sun*, pp. 293–5, 298.

42   Cited in N. Ferguson, *Colossus: The Rise and Fall of the American Empire* (Penguin, 2004), p. 94.

43   G. Kolko, *Anatomy of a War: Vietnam, the United States, and the Modern Historical Experience* (Pantheon Books, 1985), pp. 26, 27–39.

44   For a detailed account of the rebellion's dynamic and appeal, see B. Tria Kerkvliet, *The Huk Rebellion: A Study of Peasant Revolt in the Philippines* (Rowman & Littlefield, 2002).

45   Kolko, *Anatomy of War*, pp. 80–2.

46   Kolko, *Anatomy of War*, pp. 83–93, 111–3; D. Elliott, *The Vietnamese War: Revolution and Social Change in the Mekong Delta, 1930–1975* (M.E. Sharpe, 2003), p. 387; S. Jacobs, *Cold War Mandarin: Ngo Dinh Diem and the Origins of America's War in Vietnam, 1950–1963* (Rowman & Littlefield, 2006), pp. 135–6.

47   E. Hobsbawm, *Age of Extremes: The Short Twentieth Century, 1914–1991* (Michael Joseph, 1994), p. 244; Jacobs, *Cold War Mandarin*, p. 135; C. Neu, *America's Lost War: Vietnam, 1945–1975* (Harlan Davidson Inc., 2005), pp. 99–101; Neale, *A People's History*, pp. 62–3.

48   Kolko, *Anatomy of War*, pp. 122–5; Neale, *A People's History*, pp. 66–9.

49   Neale, *A People's History*, pp. 70–1; G. Kolko, *Vietnam: Anatomy of a Peace* (Routledge, 1997), p. 2; S. Lindquist, *A History of Bombing* (Granta Books, 2001), p. 346; Neale, *A People's History*, pp. 75–6, 80; Kolko, *Vietnam: Anatomy of a Peace*, p. 2.

50   Krenn, *Color of Empire*, p. 89; Kolko, *Anatomy of a War*; D. Roediger, *Toward the Abolition of Whiteness: Essays on Race, Politics and Working Class History* (Verso, 1994), pp. 117–20.

51   Krenn, *Color of Empire*, pp. 90–2; Kolko, *Anatomy of a War*, p. 117; M. Harrington, *Socialism Past and Future* (Pluto Press, 1989), pp. 86–7.

52   J. Young, *Socialism Since 1889: A Biographical History* (Rowman & Littlefield, 1998), p. 206; P. Berman, *Power and the Idealists* (Soft Skull Press, 2005); G. Gerstle, 'In the Shadow of Vietnam: Liberal Nationalism and the Problem of War', in M. Kazin and J. McCartin, eds, *Americanism: New Perspectives on the History of an Ideal* (University of North Carolina Press, 2006), pp. 128–44.

53   R. Tomes, *Apocalypse Then: American Intellectuals and the Vietnam War* (New York University Press, 1998), pp. 9–122; Schlesinger, *Bitter Heritage*, pp. 19–79, 102–7.

54   See, for example, N. Chomsky, *American Power and the New Mandarins* (The New Press, 2002), and Kolko, *Politics of War*.

55   Melvin Small, *Antiwarriors: The Vietnam War and the Battle for America's Hearts and Minds* (SR Books, 2002), p. 8; quoted in Westad, *Global Cold War*, pp. 28, 106.

56   Small, *Antiwarriors*, p. 6; M. Isserman and M. Kazin, *America Divided: The War of the 1960s* (Oxford University Press, 2004 – second edition), pp. 23–45; M. Kurlansky, *1968: The Year That Rocked the World* (Vintage Books, 2004), pp. 17–18; Small, Antiwarriors, p. 40.

57   Small, *Antiwarriors*, p. 3; Mayer, *Changing American Mind*, p. 69.

58   J. Micklethwait and A. Wooldridge, *Right Nation: Why America is Different* (Penguin Books, 2005), p. 204–5.

59   J. Heilbrunn, *They Knew They Were Right: The Rise of the Neocons* (Doubleday, 2008), p. 19; quoted in G. Packer, *The Assassin's Gate: America in Iraq* (Farrar, Straus & Giroux, 2006), p. 57; J. Muravchik, 'The Neoconservative Cabal', in I. Stelzer, ed., *Neoconservatism* (Atlantic Books, 2004), pp. 245–9; A. Wald, 'Are Trotskyites Running the Pentagon?', *History News Network*, 23 June 2003.

60   J. Heer, 'Trotsky's ghost wandering the White House Influence on Bush Aides: Bolshevik's writings supported the idea of pre-emptive war', *National Post*, 7 June 2003.

61   Such is the claim made by former Colin Powell aide, Lawrence Wilkerson. For example: '"A Leaderless, Directionless Superpower": An Interview With Lawrence Wilkerson', *Der Spiegel*, 6 December 2005; the claim is also repeated by presidential candidate Ron Paul: 'Neo-CONNED!', House of Representatives, at <http://www.house.gov/paul/congrec/congrec2003/cr071003.htm>, 10 July 2003.

62   M. Gerson, *The Neoconservative Vision: From the Cold War to the Culture Wars* (Madison Books, 1997), pp. 9–22. With respect to social blueprints, Francis Fukuyama highlights the fact that there was a big difference between anti-Communist liberalism, which still accepted the validity of ambitious social programmes, and neoconservatism, which did not: F. Fukuyama, *After the Neocons: America at the Crossroads* (Profile Books, 2006), pp. 16–20.

63   Gerson, *Neoconservative Vision*, pp. 112–3; S. Halper and J. Clarke, *America Alone: Neoconservatives and the Global Order* (Cambridge University Press, 2005), p. 11; M. Caputi, *A Kinder, Gentler America: Melancholia and the Mythical 1950s* (University of Minnesota Press, 2005), pp. 1–17, 98–105.

64   Wald, *New York Intellectuals*, pp. 311–12.

65   N. Guilhot, *The Democracy Makers: Human Rights and International Order* (Columbia University Press, 2005), pp. 34–45. See also Leon Trotsky's critique of Stalinism: L. Trotsky, *The Revolution Betrayed: What is the Soviet Union and Where is it Going?* (especially chapter 11), reproduced by the Marxist Internet Archive at <http://www.marxists.org/>.

66   Isserman, *If I Had a Hammer*: pp. 37–42.

67 E. Browder, C. Wright Mills and M. Shachtman, 'Is Russia A Socialist Country?', debate transcribed in *New International: A Monthly Organ of Revolutionary Marxism*, vol. 16, no. 3 (May–June 1950), pp. 145–76, reproduced by the Marxist Internet Archive at <http://www.marxists.org/>.

68 Drucker, *Max Schachtman*, p. 245.

69 L. Trotsky, 'Again and Once More Again on the Nature of the USSR', from *In Defence of Marxism* (London, 1966), pp. 29–39, reproduced by the Marxist Internet Archive at <http://www.marxists.org/>.M. Shachtman, 'The Soviet Union and the World War', *New International*, vol. 6, no. 3 (April 1940), pp. 68–72, reproduced by the Marxist Internet Archive at <http://www.marxists.org/>.

70 Isserman, *If I Had a Hammer*, pp. 44–50; quoted in Guilhot, *Democracy Makers*, p. 35; Drucker, *Max Schachtman*, pp. 174–6, 249; Guilhot, *Democracy Makers*, p. 43.

71 Author interview with Peter Drucker.

72 M. Shachtman, *Race and Revolution* (Verso, 2003).

73 For more on Meany's attitude to race and labour, see P. Buhle, *Taking Care of Business: Samuel Gompers, George Meany, Lane Kirkland, and the Tragedy of American Labor* (Monthly Review Press, 1999), pp. 168–9, 189.

74 Drucker, *Max Schachtman*, p. 288, 303–4; M. Isserman, *The Other American: The Life of Michael Harrington* (Public Affairs, 2000), pp. 298–300; S. Diamond, *Roads to Dominion: Right-Wing Movements and Political Power in the United States* (Guilford Press, 1995), pp. 192–4; Drucker, *Max Schachtman*, pp. 307–8.

75 Author interview with Peter Drucker.

76 P. Selznick, 'The Moral Realism of Irving Kristol', in I. Kristol, C. DeMuth and W. Kristol, *The Neoconservative Imagination: Essays in Honor of Irving Kristol* (American Enterprise Institute, 1995), pp. 19–35.

77 M. Lind, 'A Tragedy of Errors', *Nation*, 23 February 2004.

78 M. Ledeen, *Freedom Betrayed: How America Led A Global Democratic Revolution, Won the Cold War, And Walked Away* (American Enterprise Institute, 1996); J. Laughland, 'Flirting With Fascism', *American Conservative*, 30 July 2003; Ledeen, *Freedom Betrayed*, pp. 1–6.

79 S. Hersh, 'Selective Intelligence', *New Yorker*, 12 May 2003; M. Boot, 'Myths About Neoconservatism', in I. Stelzer, ed., *Neoconservatism*, p. 51; F. Fukuyama, *After the Neocons: America at the Crossroads* (Profile Books, 2006), pp. 22–3; P. Berkowitz, 'What Hath Strauss Wrought?', *Weekly Standard*, vol. 8, issue 37 (2 June 2003).

80   K. Weinstein, 'Philosophic Roots: The Role of Leo Strauss And the War in Iraq', in Stelzer, *Neoconservatism*.

81   S. Holmes, *The Anatomy of Antiliberalism* (Harvard University Press, 1993); S. Horton, 'Will the Real Leo Strauss Please Stand Up?', *Harpers Magazine*, 21 January 2008; S. Horton, 'The Letter', *Balkinization*, 16 July 2006.

82   See Guilhot, *Democracy Makers*, pp. 65–9; Djilas explained the basis of the 'New Class' theory by suggesting that social relations in the Soviet Union

> resemble state capitalism . . . industrialization is effected not with the help of capitalists but with the help of the state machine . . . Ownership is nothing other than the right of profit and control. If one defines class benefits by this right, the Communist states have seen, in the final analysis, the origin of a new form of ownership or a new ruling and exploiting class.

Milovan Djilas, *The New Class: An Analysis of the Communist System* (Thames & Hudson, 1957), p. 35. The argument, structurally similar to Shachtman's 'bureaucratic collectivism' theory, was adapted by neoconservatives to suggest that such a bureaucratic class was developing in the United States and formed the basis of the 'New Left'.

83   This is typical of the glib handling of complex sociological arguments from those who, like Irving Kristol, prefer experts to intellectuals. There is, after all, the question of whether one's having been born with a talent is the basis for desert; whether all talents distribute themselves across the same 'bell curve' in the same fashion; and whether the distribution of wealth actually corresponds in some structurally isomorphic fashion to the distribution of talent.

84   Friedman, *Neoconservative Revolution*, pp. 129–32.

85   Dorrien, *Neoconservative Mind*, pp. 91–3.

86   Gerson, *Neoconservative Vision*, p. 114; N. Podhoretz, *Why We Were in Vietnam* (Simon & Schuster, 1982), pp. 10–19, 108, 174–6.

87   N. Podhoretz, 'My Negro Problem – and Ours', *Commentary*, February 1963, pp. 93–101. 'Letters from Readers', *Commentary*, May 1963, pp. 430–8.

88   Ehrman, *Rise of Neoconservatism*, pp. 37–8.

89   D. Cesarani, *Koestler: A Biography* (Arrow Books, 1999), pp. 33–61, 235–43.

90   Gerson, *Neoconservative Vision*, pp. 123–5, 304, 296; Dorrien, *Neoconservative Mind*, p. 166; Friedman, *Neoconservative Revolution*, p. 125; Ehrman, *Rise of Neoconservatism*, pp. 128–9.

91   J. Mearsheimer and S. Walt, *The Israel Lobby and US Foreign Policy* (Allen Lane, 2007), pp. 128–32.

92   D. Lazare, 'Lobbying Degree Zero', *Nation*, 22 October 2007.

93   A. Kapeliouk, 'Israel on Kosovo', *Le Monde Diplomatique*, May 1999; R. Aldrich, 'America Used Islamists to Arm the Bosnian Muslims', *Guardian*, 22 April 2002. See also J. Blom and P. Romijn, 'Srebrenica – a safe area', *Netherlands Institute for War Documentation*, 2002, and Boot, 'Myths about Neoconservatism', p. 47.

94   Friedman, *Neoconservative Revolution*; Heilbrunn, *They Knew They Were Right*, pp. 10–15.

95   Ehrman, *Rise of Neoconservatism*, p. 40.

96   Kristol's views on welfare are outlined at length in his *Neoconservatism: The Autobiography of an Idea* (The Free Press, 1995); Halper and Clarke, *America Alone*, pp. 53–4.

97   G. Horne, *Fire This Time: The Watts Uprising and the 1960s* (University Press of Virginia, 1995), pp. 230–1; the full text of Moynihan's report is available at the US Department of Labor website: <http://www.dol.gov/>; P. Hill Collins, 'A Comparison of Two Works on Black Family Life', *Signs*, vol. 14, no. 4 (University of Chicago Press, 1989), pp. 875–884.

98   W. Ryan, *Blaming the Victim* (Pantheon Books, 1971); Gerson, *Neoconservative Vision*, pp. 99–109; Ehrman, *Rise of Neoconservatism*, pp. 70–83; D. Moynihan, 'The United States in Opposition', *Commentary*, March 1975, available at <http://www.commentarymagazine.com/>.

99   Ehrman, *Rise of Neoconservatism*, pp. 83–94; D. Moynihan, *Pandaemonium: Ethnicity in International Politics* (Oxford University Press, 1993), p. 200.

100   At one point, Moynihan implied that affirmative action was totalitarian, arguing that it was similar to 'the sorting out of human beings for the death camps of Hitler's Germany'. Buhle, *Taking Care of Business*, p. 189.

101   Ehrman, *Rise of Neoconservatism*, pp. 83–94; G. Hodgson, *The Gentleman From New York: Daniel Patrick Moynihan, A Biography* (Houghton Mifflin, 2000), pp. 223–59. Moynihan's remarks on East Timor are discussed by Noam Chomsky in the foreword to José Ramos-Horta's memoirs, *Funu: The Unfinished Saga of East Timor* (Red Sea Press, 1987), p. xiii.

102   See G. Horne, *From The Barrel of a Gun: The United States and the War Against Zimbabwe, 1965–1980* (University of North Carolina Press, 2001); Gerson, *Neoconservative Vision*, pp. 93–4.

103   L. Briggs, *Reproducing Empire: Race Sex, Science, and US Imperialism*

in Puerto Rico (University of California Press, 2002), pp. 1–10. As Matthew Frye Jacobson argues, the depiction of America as a 'nation of immigrants', especially since the 1960s, has served a highly conservative ideological function. The 'displacement of Plymouth Rock by Ellis Island in our national myth of origins' obscures the violent reality of white supremacy in America's racial past and present. See M. Jacobson, *Roots Too: White Ethnic Revival in the Post-Civil Rights Era* (Harvard University Press, 2006).

104　Moynihan, *Pandaemonium*, p. 36; Friedman, *Neoconservative Revolution*, pp. 142, 165.

4: A Courageous Retreat

1　A. Johnson and K. Makiya, 'Putting Cruelty First: An Interview with Kanan Makiya', *Democratiya*, January–February 2006.

2　L. Gehlen and J. Heisterkamp, 'Bin Laden, Dostoevsky and the reality principle: an interview with André Glucksmann', *Open Democracy*, 31 March 2003.

3　M. Christofferson, *French Intellectuals Against the Left: The Antitotalitarian Movement of the 1970s* (Berghahn Books, 2004), pp. 89, 37–40, 30–4.

4　Author interview with Philippe Cohen. For further details on Lévy's period as a Marxist, see P. Cohen, *BHL: une biographie* (Fayard, 2005), pp. 77–100. Lévy remarks that, as late as 1978 (one year after his famous anti-Marxist text), 'I was still something of a Marxist, and vaguely leftist'; Bernard-Henri Lévy, *Adventures on the Freedom Road: The French Intellectuals in the 20th Century* (Harvill Press, 1995), pp. 295–6. See also Lévy's own brisk reminiscence of the Maoist movement, in ibid., pp. 45–6.

5　Dominique Lecourt, for example, maintains that 'the young Bernard-Henri Lévy was a brilliant figure, who . . . was never himself a Marxist or a Maoist'. D. Lecourt, *The Mediocracy: French Philosophy Since 1968* (Verso, 2001), p. 49.

6　Cohen, *BHL*, pp. 210–14; author interview with Philippe Cohen.

7　Quoted in Cohen, *BHL*, p. 214; Christofferson, *French Intellectuals*, p. 97.

8　B.-H. Lévy, *Barbarism With a Human Face* (Harper & Row, 1977), pp. 3–11, 148, 147, 187–9; Christofferson, *French Intellectuals*, p. 188; Lévy, *Barbarism*, p. 190.

9　A. Glucksmann, *The Master Thinkers* (Harvester Press, 1977), p. 288.

10　'A Conversation With André Glucksmann', *Swiss Review of World Affairs*, September 1993.

11　Glucksmann, *Master Thinkers*, pp. 267–8.

12 J. Bourg, *From Revolution to Ethics: May 1968 and Contemporary French Thought* (McGill-Queens University Press, 2007), p. 251; see D. Ibárruri, 'Reply to the Enemies, Slanderers and Wavering Elements', *Communist International*, vol. xiv, no. 11 (November 1937), pp. 808–13, reproduced by the Marxist Internet Archive at <http://marxists. catbull.com/archive/ibarruri/1937/08/10.htm>.

13 Bourg, *From Revolution to Ethics*, p. 53.

14 Christofferson, *French Intellectuals*, p. 187; A. Badiou, *Ethics: An Essay on the Understanding of Evil* (Verso, 2002), p. 13; Christofferson, *French Intellectuals*, p. 187.

15 The 'new philosophers' were energetically promoted in the mass media, a fact enjoyed and cultivated by Lévy, who went on to make his name as a columnist and pundit. Christofferson, *French Intellectuals*, pp. 191–7.

16 Christofferson, *French Intellectuals*, pp. 189–90; P. Anderson, *In The Tracks of Historical Materialism* (Verso, 1983), p. 32.

17 Lecourt, *Mediocracy*, p. 61; J. Bachrach, 'Philosopher-Prince, Brand New; To Be Bright, Beautiful and French in a Wicked World', *Washington Post*, 4 May 1978; 'France: Those magnificent Marx-haters', *Economist*, 20 August 1977; 'Text of Reagan's Address to Parliament on Promoting Democracy', *New York Times*, 9 June 1982.

18 Quoted in K. Ross, *May '68 and its Afterlives* (University of Chicago Press, 2002), pp. 162–3; Lévy, *Adventures*, p. 41.

19 Quoted in K. Ross, 'Ethics and the Rearmament of Imperialism: The French Case', in J. Wasserstrom, G. Grandin, L. Hunt, and M. Young, eds, *Human Rights and Revolutions* (Rowman and Littlefield, 2005 – second edn), pp. 158–9.

20 Ross, 'Ethics and the Rearmament of Imperialism', p. 156; A. Sa'adah, *Contemporary France: A Democratic Education* (Rowman & Littlefield, 2003), p. 285.

21 G. Webb, *Dark Alliance: the CIA, the Contras, and the Crack Cocaine Explosion* (Seven Stories Press, 1998).

22 Cohen, *BHL*, pp. 161–72; G. McArthur, 'Exiles form Anti-Communist Resistance International', *Associated Press*, 16 May 1983; D. Hoffman, 'Europeans Lobby For Aid to "Contras"; Churchill's Grandson Urges Funds' Release', *Washington Post*, 19 April 1985; Ross, 'Ethics and the Rearmament of Imperialism', pp. 168–9; K. Coogan and K. Vanden Heuvel, 'An InterNation Story: U.S. fund for Soviet dissidents; Center for Democracy funds from National Endowment for Democracy for English translation of periodical Glasnost', *Nation*, 19 March 1988.

23 J. Steele and T. Jenkins, 'Slaughter at the Cooperatives', *Guardian*, 15 November 1984.

24 Quoted in W. LeoGrande, *Our Own Backyard: the United States in*

Central America, 1977–1992 (University of North Carolina Press, 1998), p. 413; author interview with Philippe Cohen.

25   S. McBride, '"New Philosopher"; Bernard-Henri Lévy', *Christian Science Monitor*, 20 January 1983.

26   J. Vinocur, 'Europe's Intellectuals and American Power', *New York Times*, 29 April 1984.

27   D. Cohen, 'Trouble on the right', *Atlantic Monthly*, February 1985; Ross, 'Ethics and the Rearmament of Imperialism', p. 168; J. Steele, 'French aid agency is accused of bias', *Guardian*, 6 February 1986; M. Ikonicoff, 'Making the Most of Multinational Capital', *Manchester Guardian Weekly*, 4 August 1985.

28   J. Kirkpatrick, 'Dictatorship and Double Standards', *Commentary*, November 1979; quoted in G. Grandin, *Empire's Workshop: Latin America, the United States and the Rise of the New Imperialism* (Metropolitan Books, 2006), p. 106; Grandin, *Empire's Workshop*, p. 106; J. Mann, *Rise of the Vulcans: The History of Bush's War Cabinet* (Penguin, 2004), p. 126.

29   Grandin, op cit: 100–105.

30   N. Guilhot, *The Democracy Makers: Human Rights and International Order* (Columbia University Press, 2005), pp. 32, 49, 65, 84–93.

31   Berman discusses his anarchist background in A. Johnson, 'Interrogating *Terror and Liberalism*: An Interview with Paul Berman', *Democratiya*, 24 May 2006.

32   Berman, 'Visitor's view of Nicaragua', *Mother Jones*, vol. 11, no. 2 (February 1986), pp. 21–8, 55.

33   Quoted in A. Cockburn, 'Beat The Devil: Michael meets Mr. Jones, Michael Moore fired from Mother Jones', *Nation*, 13 September 1986.

34   A. Jones, 'Radical Magazine Removes Editor, Setting Off A Widening Political Debate', *New York Times*, 27 September 1986.

35   R. Grossman, '"The Blood of the People": The Guardia Nacional's Fifty-Year War Against the People of Nicaragua, 1927–1979', in C. Menjívar and N. Rodríguez, *When States Kill: Latin America, the US, and Technologies of Terror* (University of Texas Press, 2005), pp. 61–2; H. Vanden and G. Prevost, *Democracy and Socialism in Sandinista Nicaragua* (Lynne Rienner Publishers, 1993), pp. 23–49; Vanden and Prevost, *Democracy and Socialism*, p. 90; Grossman, '"Blood of the People"', p. 59; H. Sklar, *Washington's War on Nicaragua* (South End Press, 1988), p. 36; R. Cox, *Power and Profits: US Policy in Central America* (University Press of Kentucky, 1994), p. 120; figure quoted in A. Stein 'The Undermining of the Sandinista Revolution', *American Political Science Review*, vol. 91, no. 4, (1997), p. 992; see W. Gordon West's critical study, 'The Sandinista Record on Human Rights in

Nicaragua', *Droit et Société*, 22, (1992); The Americas Watch Committee, 'Human Rights in Nicaragua 1986', *Americas Watch*, February 1987; J. Steele and T. Jenkins, 'Vote of Confidence in the Sandinistas', *Manchester Guardian Weekly*, 11 November 1984; T. Jenkins, 'Contra threat to take reprisals against voters: Rebels oppose elections in Nicaragua', *Guardian*, 2 November 1984.

36   W. Robinson, *Promoting Polyarchy: Globalization, US Intervention, and Hegemony* (Cambridge University Press, 1996), pp. 222–3; P. Berman, 'Nicaraguans See A Real Chance for Revolution', *Oregonian*, 2 March 1990.

37   Johnson, 'Interrogating Terror and Liberalism'.

38   P. Berman, 'In Search of Ben Linder's Killers', *New Yorker*, 23 September 1996, pp. 62–3.

39   N. Chomsky, *Deterring Democracy* (Vintage, 1992), p. 305; C. Smith, *Resisting Reagan: The US Central America Peace Movement* (University of Chicago Press, 1996), p. 357; Chomsky, *Deterring Democracy*, p. 299; Robinson, *Promoting Polyarchy*, p. 226; R. Beamish, 'Bush Will Lift Trade Embargo if Nicaraguan Opposition Candidate Wins', *Associated Press*, 8 November 1989; Robinson, *Promoting Polyarchy*, pp. 235–6, 220, 238.

40   Berman, 1996, 'In Search of Ben Linder's Killers', pp. 66–9; A. Armony, 'Producing and Exporting State Terror', in Menjívar and Rodríguez, *When States Kill*, p. 83.

41   A. Cockburn, 'Beat the Devil: Berman and Linder', *Nation*, 11 November 1996.

42   P. Berman, 'Letters', *Nation*, 9 December 1996. Berman argues:

> In a better world, the White House, too, would be dominated by social democrats and liberals . . . White House Republicans were over-interventionist early in this century and dispatched the Marines to Nicaragua, which was a calamity. They were under-interventionist in the 1950s and failed to support the anti-Somoza conspiracies of Mrs. Chamorro's husband, Pedro Joaquin Chamorro. The Republican record in the 1980s is too grim to mention, except to recall that the trials in Washington are still going on.

Paul Berman, 'For Mrs. Chamorro, The Honeymoon's Over', *New York Times*, 28 February 1990.

43   A. Johnson, 'Putting Cruelty First: An Interview with Kanan Makiya (Part 1)', *Democratiya*, January–February 2006; G. Packer, *The Assassins' Gate: America in Iraq* (Faber & Faber, 2006), pp. 69–70.

44   Packer, *Assassin's Gate*, p. 70; J. Shklar, 'Putting Cruelty First', *Daedalus*, 1982, reproduced in *Democratiya*, Spring 2006. Makiya acknowledges this debt in the introduction to the second edition of his book, *Republic of Fear: The Politics of Modern Iraq* (University of California Press, 1998), p. xxix. In the following, I rely on the original 1989 version of his book, also published by the University of California Press under Makiya's pseudonym of Samir al-Khalil.

45   Shklar, *Putting Cruelty First.*

46   M. Walzer, 'On Negative Politics', in B. Yack, ed., *Liberalism Without Illusions: Essays on Liberal Theory and the Political Vision of Judith N. Shklar* (University of Chicago Press, 1996), pp. 17–19; C. Robin, *Fear: The History of a Political Idea* (Oxford University Press, 2004).

47   As it is described by Stephen Holmes, 'Ordinary Passions in Descartes and Racine', in Yack, *Liberalism Without Illusions*, p. 95.

48   Al-Khalil, *Republic of Fear*, pp x–xi, xiv, xviii, 3–20.

49   Ibid., pp. 40, 46–72.

50   Ibid., pp. 74–97,149–205.

51   N. Ayubi, *Overstating the Arab State: Politics and Society in the Middle East* (I.B. Tauris, 1995), p. 362–7.

52   For a discussion of these, see F. Jabar, *The Shiite Movement in Iraq* (Saqi, 2003).

53   See Peter Gowan's criticisms in P. Gowan, 'The Gulf War, Iraq, and Western Liberalism', *New Left Review* I/187 (May–June 1991).

54   M. Dowd, 'War in the Gulf: White House Memo; Bush Moves to Control War's Endgame', *New York Times*, 23 February 1991.

55   'The Operation Desert Shield/Desert Storm Timeline', American Forces Press Service News Articles, Department of Defense, 8 August, 2000; F. Halliday, *The Middle East in International Relations: Power, Politics and Ideology* (Cambridge University Press, 2005), p. 58; M. Farouk-Sluglett and P. Sluglett, *Iraq Since 1948: From Revolution To Dictatorship* (I.B. Tauris, 2003), pp. 284–7.

56   Z. Brzezinski, *Second Chance: Three Presidents and the Crisis of American Superpower* (Perseus Books, 2007), pp. 58–9.

57   For a discussion of these, see N. Chomsky, *Deterring Democracy*, (Vintage, 1992), pp. 190–3.

58   In October 1990, 69 per cent of the American public felt that the UN sanctions campaign should be given more time. At that point, only 46 per cent of Americans favoured war if the sanctions failed, with 48 per cent against. In November, 70 per cent counselled against going to war. Two days after mid-term elections resulted in a Democratic-controlled Congress, Bush sent an additional 200,000 troops and 1,200 tanks to the Gulf. The total coalition presence at that point was 450,000. By mid-

November, the number of Americans who felt Bush had been too quick to get military forces involved rose to 47 per cent, and the number feeling he had tried hard enough to get a diplomatic solution fell from 51 per cent to 38 per cent. R. Sobel, *The Impact of Public Opinion on US Foreign Policy Since Vietnam* (Oxford University Press, 2001), pp. 145–8.

59   A. Kitty, *Don't Believe It: How Lies Become News* (Disinformation, 2005), pp. 143–6.

60   Bush Sr. first made the comparison with Hitler in his White House address on 8 August 1990. Adam Kelliher, 'American forces arrive in Saudi Arabia', *United Press International*, 8 August 1990. British foreign secretary Douglas Hurd had made the comparison days before: John Keegan, 'How to Stop the Madman's March', *Courier-Mail*, 7 August 1990; 'Appeasement does not work', was Bush Sr.'s habitual recourse. The media usually followed suit. From 2 August 1990 until the war's end on 28 February 1991, there were at least 118 articles comparing Saddam Hussein and Hitler in the major English-language press on a simple LexisNexis search. Talk of a nuclear weapons programmes became a theme as support for the war started to slump in late 1990. Defense Secretary Dick Cheney explained in November 1990 that Saddam was making 'steady progress' on developing a nuclear weapons programme, while Brent Scowcroft explained that Bush had decided to emphasize Iraq's closeness to developing a nuclear weapon to show that the United States could not wait 'a year or two years' for the economic sanctions to resolve the crisis peacefully. At the time, a study by the Congressional Research Service concluded that Iraq lacked the means to produce the weapons-grade plutonium needed to make a nuclear warhead, and it would require five to ten years to acquire sufficient materials to make even crude weapons. S. Kurkjian, 'Support rises for a war to defuse a nuclear Iraq', *Boston Globe*, 26 November 1990.

61   S. Shuaib, 'Desert Bloom', *News Statesman and Society*, 31 August 1990.

62   See B. Warren, *Imperialism: Pioneer of Capitalism* (Verso, London, 1980); Halliday's favourable reception can be found in 'Imperialism and the Middle East', *MERIP Reports*, no. 117, 'Debt and Development', September 1983, pp. 19–23. A. Sivanandan replied to Warren's argument by castigating the 'racial arrogance' of Warren and much of the European Left. 'Where in colonial capitalism', he demanded to know, 'was there even a suggestion of political democracy except at its end? When did the colonies ever enjoy "the moral and cultural standards" of capitalism: "equality, justice, generosity, independence of spirit and mind, the spirit of inquiry and adventure, opposition to cruelty, not to mention

political democracy"?' See A. Sivanandan, *Communities of Resistance: Writings on Black Struggles for Socialism* (Verso, 1990), pp. 163–6. Halliday would later argue that the Left ought to have supported the occupation of Iraq for the same reasons that he feels it ought to have supported the occupation of Afghanistan: the foes of the occupation were not on the side of progress. See D. Postel, 'Who is Responsible? An Interview with Fred Halliday', *Salgamundi*, November 2005.

63   F. Halliday, 'No Rest for the Wicked', *New Statesman and Society*, 10 August 1990, and 'The left and the war', *New Statesman and Society*, 8 March 1991.

64   F. Halliday, 'The war of ideas', *New Statesman and Society*, 22 March 1991; F. Halliday and N. Geras, 'Letters', *New Statesman and Society*, 12 April 1991; R. Blackburn, 'The war of ideas', *New Statesman and Society*, 22 March 1991.

65   A LexisNexis search yields a mere five references to Makiya's book in the English-language news before the war began, and sixty-four from the invasion of Kuwait until the end of the war.

66   A. Cockburn, 'Beat the Devil: The wonderful world of books – Kuwait public relations influence on book publishing', *Nation*, 22 October 1990; J. Miller and L. Mylroie, *Saddam Hussein and the Crisis in the Gulf* (Random House, 1990) – for more on Mylroie's support for Hussein, see K. Silverstein, 'Laurie Mylroie's Song of Saddam', *Harper's Magazine*, 28 August 2007; S. al-Khalil, 'Arabs must fight to deny Saddam victory in defeat', *Manchester Guardian*, 30 September 1990, and 'Allied forces should liberate the Iraqi people', *St Petersburg Times*, 28 March 1991; Packer, *Assassin's Gate*, pp. 71–8.

67   M. Ignatieff, 'The tyrant counts on our tender hearts', *Observer*, 9 December 1990; 'The risks of a battle that can't be won', *Observer*, 27 January 1991; and 'One good deed in a dirty world', *Observer*, 10 February 1991; P. Berman, 'Protesters are fighting the last war', *New York Times*, 31 January 1991; and *A Tale of Two Utopias: The Political Journey of the Generation of 1968* (W.W. Norton & Company, 1996).

68   'A Conversation with André Glucksmann', *Swiss Review of World Affairs*, September 1993.

69   C. Hitchens, 'Realpolitik in the Gulf: A Game Gone Tilt', *Harper's Magazine*, January 1991, reproduced in C. Hitchens, *For the Sake of Argument* (Verso, 1993), pp. 75–7; C. Hitchens, 'Churchillian Delusions', *Nation*, February 1991, reproduced in *For the Sake of Argument*, pp. 84–6, and C. Hitchens, 'Befriending the Kurds', *Nation*, July 1991, reproduced in *For the Sake of Argument*, pp. 91–3.

70   C. Hitchens, 'No End of a Lesson', *Nation*, March 1991, reproduced in Hitchens, *For the Sake of Argument*, pp. 87–9.

71   P. Gowan, 'Neoliberal Theory and Practise for Eastern Europe', *New Left Review* I/213 (September–October 1995); J. Stiglitz, *Globalization and Its Discontents* (Penguin Books, 2002), pp. 153–9; J. Lester, *Modern Tsars and Princes: The Struggle for Hegemony in Russia* (Verso, 1995), p. 45.

72   See T. Garton Ash, *The Polish Revolution: Solidarity, 1980–82* (Yale University Press, 2002).

73   Quoted, Andy Zebrowski, 'Obituary: Jacek Kuron', *Socialist Review*, July 2004.

74   Author interview with Peter Gowan.

75   Ibid.

76   S. Woodward, *Balkan Tragedy: Chaos and Dissolution After the Cold War* (The Brookings Institution, 1995), pp. 47–66, 74; L. Silber and A. Little, *The Death of Yugoslavia* (Penguin Books/BBC, 1996), p. 73.

77   L. Benson, *Yugoslavia: A Concise History* (Palgrave Macmillan, 2004), pp. 136–8; D. Guzina, 'Kosovo or Kosova – Could It Be Both? The Case of Interlocking Serbian and Albanian Nationalisms', in F. Bieber and Ž. Daskalovski, eds, *Understanding the War in Kosovo* (Routledge, 2003), pp. 32–3; Woodward, *Balkan Tragedy*, p. 71.

78   Author interview with Catherine Samary.

79   A. Cockburn, 'Beat the Devil: Mighty was the Rose; Lieutenant General Sir Michael Rose, United Nations commander in Bosnia-Herzegovina', *Nation*, 9 May 1994; M. Collon, *Poker Menteur* (EPO, 1998), p. 268. For more detail on the role of the PR firm Ruder Finn, see D. Johnstone, *Fool's Crusade: Yugoslavia, NATO and Western Delusions* (Pluto Press, 2002), pp. 68–71.

80   'Independence Rally', Press Association, 11 August 1991; S. Baxter, 'Finally, Labour starts to consider Bosnia: Labour Party stand on Yugoslavian civil war', *New Statesman & Society*, 11 December 1992; J. Hardy, 'Foot Calls for Mercy Mission to Dubrovnik', Press Association, 10 November 1991; B. Magaš, *The Destruction of Yugoslavia* (Verso, 1993), p. 316; A. Glucksmann, 'A Moral Pearl Harbor', *Le Monde*, 12 December 1991; A. Finkielkraut, 'Power but no Glory: Yugoslav blood is seeping through the cracks in European union and France's hands aren't entirely clean', *Guardian*, 4 September 1992; R. Joseph Golsan, *French Writers and the Politics of Complicity: Crises of Democracy in the 1940s and 1990s* (Johns Hopkins University Press, 2006), pp. 102–22.

81   Woodward, *Balkan Tragedy*, p. 75; D. MacDonald, *Balkan Holocausts? Serbian and Croatian Victim-centred Propaganda and the War in Yugoslavia* (Manchester University Press, 2002), p. 99; M. Glenny, *The Fall of Yugoslavia* (Penguin, 1994), p. 63; quoted in M. Parenti, *To Kill*

A Nation: The Attack on Yugoslavia (Verso, 2000), pp. 41–2; MacDonald, *Balkan Holocausts?*, pp. 99–100; E. Stitkovac, 'Croatia: The First War', in J. Udovicki and J. Ridgeway, eds, *Burn This House: The Making and Unmaking of Yugoslavia* (Duke University Press, 1997), pp. 154–5; W. Bartlett, *Croatia: Between Europe and the Balkans* (Routledge, 2003), p. 36.

82   J. Udovicki and E. Stitkovac, 'Bosnia and Herzegovina: The Second War', in Udovicki and Ridgeway, *Burn This House*, p. 174; M. Ignatieff, 'Shame on all us good Europeans', *Observer*, 22 September 1991; M. Ignatieff, *The Warrior's Honor: Ethnic War and the Modern Consciousness* (Chatto & Windus, 1998), p. 17; M. Shields and R. Novak, 'Bush's Deadline', *Capital Gang*, CNN, 14 March 1992; C. Hitchens, 'Appointment in Sarajevo', *Nation*, September 1992, reproduced in *For The Sake of Argument*, pp. 148–55; and 'Our Shame and Bosnia's Bitter Harvest', *Evening Standard*, 24 November 1992.

83   P. Bruckner, 'Will we survive Yugoslavia?', *Le Monde*, 28 May 1992; M. Ignatieff, 'The show that Europe missed', *Independent*, 22 November 1995. As Alain Badiou points out, there is a certain amount of relish in this:

> if it is a matter of ethical principles, of the victimary essence of Man, of the fact that 'rights are universal and imprescriptable,' why should we care about the length of the flight? . . . In this *pathos* of proximity, we can almost sense the trembling equivocation, halfway between fear and enjoyment of finally perceiving *so close to us* horror and destruction, war and cynicism.

Badiou, *Ethics*, p. 34.

84   Andrew Bell, 'French At Odds Over Mitterrand's Mercy Dash', *Guardian*, 29 June 1992.

85   Cohen, *BHL*, pp. 173–4.

86   Ibid., pp. 174–81.

87   Ibid., p. 181.

88   Author interview with Philippe Cohen.

89   Cohen, *BHL*, pp. 182–3.

90   M. Ignatieff, 'How many Romeos and Juliets lie dead in Sarajevo's rubble?', *Globe and Mail*, 29 June 1992; C. Lane, 'When Is It Genocide?', *Newsweek*, 22 August 1992; E. Vulliamy, 'Shame of camp Omarska', *Guardian*, 7 August 1992; P. Maass, *Love Thy Neighbour: A Story of War* (Vintage, 1997), p. 5; J. Miller, 'Death-camp scoop made the world sit up', *Sunday Times*, 9 August 1992; P. Knightley's 28 December 1998 account, reproduced in Alexander Cockburn, 'Storm

Over Brockes' Fakery', *Counterpunch*, 5/6 November 2005. The confession is related in Bernard Kouchner's book 'Les guerres de la paix', translated in D. Johnstone, 'Srebrenica Revisited', *Counterpunch*, 12 October 2005.

91   M. O'Kane, 'Save Sarajevo, Mr Major', *Guardian*, 22 May 1992; C. Samary, *Yugoslavia Dismembered* (Monthly Review Press, 1995), p. 87.

92   P. Corwin, *Dubious Mandate: A Memoir of the UN in Bosnia, Summer 1995* (Duke University Press, 1999); ibid., p. 231.

93   In this fashion, the US negotiator, Richard Holbrooke, claims that the US 'came to intervene' 'belatedly' and only in such a way as to end the war. See Holbrooke, *To End A War* (Modern Library, 1998), pp. xv–xvii.

94   Corwin, *Dubious Mandate*, p. 8.

95   See, for instance, C. Hitchens, 'Our Shame and Bosnia's Bitterest Harvest'; C. Hitchens, 'Betrayal Becomes Farce: In Bosnia, the Final Act Is Our Own Pathetic Complicity', *Washington Post*, 15 August 1993.

96   N. Malcolm, *Bosnia: A Short History* (New York University Press, 1994), p. 219; Samary, *Yugoslavia Dismembered*, p. 95; Woodward, *Balkan Tragedy*, p. 253; K. Hudson, *Breaking the South Slav Dream: The Rise and Fall of Yugoslavia* (Pluto Press, 2003), p. 107.

97   R. Kumar, *Divide and Fall? Bosnia in the Annals of Partition* (Verso, 1999), p. 54; Woodward, *Balkan Tragedy*, pp. 283, 305–9; D. Binder, 'US Policymakers on Bosnia Admit Errors in Opposing Partition in 1992', *New York Times*, 29 August 1993; Woodward, *Balkan Tragedy*, pp. 305–6; R. Aldrich, 'America used Islamists to arm the Bosnian Muslims', *Guardian*, 22 April 2002; T. Marshall, 'The Hidden Army of Radical Islam', *Sky News*, March 2006.

98   T. Cushman and S. Mestrovic, eds, *This Time We Knew: Western Responses to Genocide in Bosnia* (New York University Press, 1996).

99   Thus, Richard Holbrooke sets the figure at 'close to three hundred thousand'. See Holbrooke, *To End A War*, p. xv.

100 E. Tabeau and J. Bijak, 'War-related Deaths in the 1992–1995 Armed Conflicts in Bosnia and Herzegovina: A Critique of Previous Estimates and Recent Results', *European Journal of Population/ Revue européenne de Démographie*, vol. 21, nos 2–3 (June 2005), pp. 187–215, and see note 12; E. Herman and D. Peterson, 'The Dismantling of Yugoslavia: A Study in Inhumanitarian Intervention (and a Western Liberal-Left Intellectual and Moral Collapse)', *Monthly Review*, vol. 59, no. 5 (October 2007); see the Research and Documentation Centre website: < www.idc.org.ba/presentation>.

101 M. Hoare, in B. Magaš and I. Zanix, eds, *The War in Croatia and Bosnia-Herzegovina, 1991–1995* (Frank Cass, 2001), p. 309; 'Serb official says mass grave discovered in northwestern Bosnia', *BBC*

Monitoring Europe, 21 February 2006; J. Fish, 'Sarajevo Massacre Remembered', *BBC News*, 5 February 2004.

102   '"Brutal crimes" of Bosnia Muslims', *BBC News*, 2 December 2003; 'Bosnia leader was war crimes suspect', *BBC News*, 22 October 2003; M. Corder, 'Bosnian Muslim's War Crimes Trial Starts', *Associated Press*, 9 July 2007; 'Niset Rami convicted of war crimes against civilians and sentenced to 30 years long term imprisonment', *Court of Bosnia and Herzegovina*, 17 July 2007, available at <www.sudbih. gov.ba/?id=457&jezik=e>.

103   The judgment in the Radovan Krstic trial describes this narrative – although it contextualizes the attack on Visnjica as a response to Serb aggression, and minimizes it as 'relatively low intensity' with 'some houses' burned and 'several people' killed. In fact, forty were killed, and other villages were also attacked. See Prosecutor vs Radislav Krstic, 'Judgment', Paragraph 30, available at <www.un.org/icty/krstic/ TrialC1/judgement/index.htm>.

104   <www.un.org/icty/krstic/Appeal/judgement/krs-aj040419e.pdf>; M. Simons, 'Court Declares Bosnia Killings Were Genocide', *New York Times*, 27 February 2007; 'Court clears Serbia of genocide', *BBC News*, 26 February 2007; 'Highest U.N. court rules Serbia failed to prevent genocide in Bosnia', *Associated Press*, 26 February 2007.

105   See, for example, K. Southwick, 'Srebrenica as genocide? The Krstic decision and the language of the unspeakable; Radislav Krstic', *Yale Human Rights and Development Law Journal*, 1 January 2005.

106   Kumar, *Divide and Fall?*, p. 38.

107   'Tanjug reports Muslim shelling of Serbian victims' exhumation', *BBC Summary of World Broadcasts*, 22 February 1993; R. Reynolds, 'Village of Kravica Devastated in Bosnian War', *CNN*, 23 March 1993; J. Darnton, 'We Suffer, Too, Serbs in Bosnia Cry', *New York Times*, 22 April 1993; 'Brutally betrayed by trusted protectors', *Scotsman*, 13 July 1994; R. Block, 'Elusive "terrorist" general is main quarry of Serbs', *Ottawa Citizen*, 13 July 1995; Southwick, 'Srebrenica as genocide?'; Woodward, *Balkan Tragedy*, p. 293; 'Human Losses in Boznia and Herzegovina, '91–'95, Research and Documentation Centre <http://www.idc.org.ba/7, accessed 18 June 2007.

108   Kumar, *Divide and Fall?*, 1999: pp. 1–2, 32–3; D. Chandler, *Bosnia: Faking Democracy After Dayton* (Pluto Press, 2000), pp. 34–65.

109   Quoted in S. Halimi and D. Vidal, 'Media and disinformation', *Le Monde Diplomatique*, March 2000.

110   T. Friedman, 'Stop the Music', *New York Times*, 23 April 1999.

111   J. Freedland, 'War in Europe: The left needs to wake up to the real world. This is a just war', *Guardian*, 26 March 1999, and 'A long war requires patience, not a search for the door marked "Exit"', *Guardian*, 14 April 1999; D. Goldhagen, 'German lessons', *Guardian*, 29 April

1999; M. Tanner, 'I watched as "TV Slobbo" turned into voice of hate,' *Independent*, 24 April 1999.

112   P. Starobin, 'The Liberal Hawk Soars', *National Journal*, 15 May 1999; S. Sontag, 'Why Are We in Kosovo?', *New York Times*, 2 May 1999.

113   M. Ignatieff, *Virtual War: Kosovo and Beyond* (Vintage, 2001), pp. 7, 41, 79, 46; N. Chomsky, *The New Military Humanism: Lessons From Kosovo* (Pluto Press, 1999), pp. 81–5.

114   Christopher Hitchens, 'Bloody blundering: Clinton's cluelessness is selling out Kosovo', *Salon.com*, 5 April 1999; Hitchens repeated this argument on the Charlie Rose show, 28 April 1999.

115   S. Abramsky, 'Christopher Hitchens – columnist', *Progressive*, February 1997. In fact, matters are slightly more complicated. The direct military intervention was the culmination of successful indirect intervention through the CIA-supported FRAPH death squads, signalling the defeat of the radical Lavalas movement and its acceptance of Washington's preferred policies. Jean-Bertrand Aristide's refusal to accept the policies of his opponent, who had lost the 1991 elections, was what precipitated Washington's mobilization of the death squads in the first place. See P. Hallward, *Damming the Flood: Haiti, Aristide, and the Politics of Containment* (Verso, 2007), pp. 39–57.

116   R. Southan, 'Free Radical', *Reason,* November 2001.

117   J. Pilger, 'What Really Happened at Rambouillet? And What Else Is Being Kept under Wraps by Our Selective Media', *New Statesman*, 31 May 1999; G. Kenney, 'Rolling Thunder: the Rerun', *Nation*, 14 June 1999; J. Benner, 'War Criminal, Ally, or Both?', *Mother Jones*, 21 May 1999; V. Zimonjic, 'Former Kosovan PM goes on trial for KLA's ethnic cleansing crimes', *Independent*, 6 March 2007; 'Kosovo clashes "ethnic cleansing"', *BBC News*, 20 March 2004; Parenti, *To Kill A Nation*, pp. 160–1; H. Smith, 'Angry Kosovars call on "colonial" UN occupying force to leave', *Guardian*, 19 October 2003; 'Mission impossible?', *Economist*, 10 July 1999.

118   Quoted in V. Fouskas, *Zones of Conflict: US Foreign Policy in the Balkans and the Greater Middle East* (Pluto Press, 2003), p. 49.

119   D. Briscoe, 'U.S. raises genocide issue on Kosovo', *Associated Press*, 1 April 1999; 'Human Rights, Humanitarian Groups Call for Use of Force to Prevent Genocide in Kosovo', *US Newswire*, 1 April 1999; D. Rieff, *At the Point of a Gun: Democratic Dreams and Armed Intervention* (Simon & Schuster, 2005), p. 123.

120   D. Pearl and R. Block, 'Despite Tales, the War in Kosovo Was Savage, but Wasn't Genocide', *Wall Street Journal*, 31 December 1999.

121   G. Kraja, 'U.N.-run court in Kosovo says acts committed during Milosevic's regime in Kosovo were not genocide', *Associated Press*

Worldstream, 7 September 2001; S. Power, *'A Problem from Hell'*: *America and the Age of Genocide* (Harper Perrenial, 2007), pp. 470–2; C. Samary, 'The case against the Hague court', *Le Monde Diplomatique*, April 2002; see M. Ignatieff, 'Counting the Bodies in Kosovo', *New York Times*, 21 November 1999.

122 D. Chandler, *From Kosovo to Kabul: Human Rights and International Intervention* (Pluto Press, 2002).

123 Chandler, *From Kosovo to Kabul*, p. 51; Freedland, 'War in Europe'; Chandler, *From Kosovo to Kabul*.

124 Ministry of Defense, 'The Future Strategic Context of Defense', 2001, available at <www.mod.uk/NR/rdonlyres/7CC94DFB-839A-4029–8BDD-5E87AF5CDF45/0/future_strategic_context.pdf>.

125 P. Wood, 'The Downfall of Milosevic', *BBC News*, 1 April 2001.

126 M. Ignatieff, *Blood and Belonging* (Vintage, 1994), pp. 1–2, 3–7.

127 Ibid., pp. 8–9.

128 Ibid, p. 9.

129 On this point, see D. McNally, 'Imperial Narcissism: Michael Ignatieff's Apologies for Empire', in C. Mooers, ed., *The New Imperialists: Ideologies of Empire* (Oneworld, 2006), pp. 87–109.

130 Ignatieff, *Blood and Belonging*, pp. 35–6, 54–5, 58, 3, 4, 10–11, 12–14, 49–51, 45.

131 Ignatieff, *Warrior's Honor*, pp. 6–7.

132 Not so far. And let us note that Ignatieff's claim itself involves historical revisionism: the claim that 10,000 Kosovar Albanians had been killed by the Serbian forces was first made in early April, not at the end of the war in May. The US government was suggesting that this many had been killed prior to or in the early days of US bombing, not throughout the war.

133 M. Ignatieff, *Empire Lite: Nation-Building in Bosnia, Kosovo and Afghanistan* (Vintage, 2003), pp. 2, 3, 7, 17, 23, 45–75; Regarding the origins of the claim of 10,000 killed during the war, see 'Are Kosovars returning willingly?', *Associated Press*, 8 April 1999. On the 100,000 claim, see F. Haq, 'Annan Boosts UN Role in Peace Efforts', *Inter Press Service*, 19 April 1999:

> David Scheffer, U.S. ambassador-at-large for crimes against humanity, claimed that some 100,000 Kosovar males are unaccounted for and added, 'You're actually looking at the possibility of tens of thousands of Kosovars who not only are at risk but also may actually have perished at this stage.'

The claim of 100,000 deaths has disappeared into the memory hole, but the claim of 10,000 deaths is still widely repeated, though it has

absolutely no basis in reality. For example, see G. Kraja, 'U.N. delegation tours Kosovo before Security Council decision on independence',
Associated Press, 28 April 2007; I. Hajdari, 'Kosovo poised for independence, UN envoys told', *Agence-France Presse*, 27 April 2007.

134   Ignatieff, *Empire Lite*, pp. 119–23.

Conclusion: The Apotheosis of Human Barbarism

1   S. Holmes, *The Matador's Cape: America's Reckless Response to
      Terror* (Cambridge University Press, 2007), p. 170.

2   Author interview with Rony Brauman.

3   S. Power, '*A Problem From Hell': America and the Age of Genocide*
      (Harper Perennial, 2003). Power consistently underestimates or ignores
      the crimes of Western states and overestimates the crimes of official
      enemies. So, while Power's history goes back as far as 1915, it does not
      include any reference to Vietnam or Guatemala, for example. Though
      it includes a lengthy exposition of the massacre of 8,000 Bosnian
      Muslim males in Srebrenica, it makes no mention of extensive crimes
      killing up to 100,000 in El Salvador, and 50,000 in Nicaragua. It
      casually describes US policy in respect of the Indonesian invasion of
      East Timor as simply one of 'looking away', whereas in fact the US was
      deeply involved in the invasion. Similarly, she cites a figure of 2 million
      'slaughtered' by the Khmer Rouge, which is in fact false. Arguably, 2
      million people did die, although this is at the higher end of the range of
      estimates, and some of this total was the direct result of genocidal
      violence, but the total figure includes deaths that the Khmer Rouge
      bears responsibility for because of its social policies rather than only
      those 'slaughtered' by them. Possibly, Power's estimate is based on a
      false figure supplied in 1978 by Jean Lacouture – a figure that was
      rapidly discredited, but was nevertheless popularized by mainstream US
      commentators. Power briefly discusses the US support for the Khmer
      Rouge during the 1980s, but substantially underestimates both the scale
      of that support and the number of deaths caused by the US bombing of
      Cambodia during the early 1970s, which she describes as 'tens of thou-
      sands', whereas in fact the correct figure was at least 100,000 by 1973,
      and somewhere between 500,000 and 1 million deaths resulting in total.
      In fact, as Ben Kiernan points out, Kissinger instructed the army to
      launch 'a massive bombing campaign in Cambodia. Anything that flies
      on anything that moves', an instruction that makes the bombing
      campaign effectively genocidal. And again, while Power discusses
      Saddam Hussein's genocidal violence in light of a failure of the US to
      try to prevent it, she does not discuss the genocidal sanctions regime.
      Power, '*A Problem From Hell'*, pp. 94, 146–7, 152–4; B. Kiernan,

'Coming to Terms With the Past: Cambodia', *History Today*, no. 9, vol. 54 (1 September 2004). For a summary of arguments over the Cambodian genocide, see E. Kissi, 'Genocide in Cambodia and Ethiopia', in R. Gellately and B. Kiernan, eds, *The Specter of Genocide: Mass Murder in Historical Perspective* (Cambridge University Press, 2003), pp. 307–23. Michael Vickery's classic account estimates 700,000 deaths above the normal rate: M. Vickery, *Cambodia: 1975–1982* (Silkworm Books, 2002). For a detailed examination of US support for the Khmers after 1979, see T. Fawthrop and H. Jarvis, *Getting Away with Genocide? Elusive Justice and the Khmer Rouge Tribunal* (Pluto Press, London, 2005). For figures on mortality resulting from the bombing of Cambodia, see Vickery, *Cambodia*. On Lacouture and similar controversies over the Cambodian genocide, see N. Chomsky and E. Herman, *After the Cataclysm: Postwar Indochina and the Reconstruction of Imperial Ideology* (Spokesman, 1979), pp. 135–294.

4   M. Ignatieff, ed., *American Exceptionalism and Human Rights* (Princeton University Press, 2005), p. 7.

5   Denis Halliday, the former United Nations Humanitarian Co-ordinator in Iraq, has said that the imposition of sanctions on Iraq constitutes 'genocide' because 'it is an intentional programme to destroy a culture, a people, a country – economic sanctions are known to do that'. A. Howeidy, 'Death For Oil: An Interview With Dennis Halliday, Ex-UN Assistant Secretary-General Heading The UN Humanitarian Mission In Iraq', *Al-Ahram Weekly*, 19 July 2000. Hans Von Sponeck, Halliday's successor, commenting on the way that sanctions deprived Iraqis of clean water, medicines and electricity, which was responsible for thousands of deaths a month, said, 'Make no mistake, this is deliberate. I have not in the past wanted to use the word genocide, but now it is unavoidable' – quoted in J. Pilger, *The New Rulers of the World* (Verso, 2003), p. 62. Lawrence J. LeBlanc, *The United States and the Genocide Convention* (Duke University Press, 1991), pp. 34–5; W. Patterson, ed., *We Charge Genocide: The Crime of Government Against the Negro People* (International Publishers, 1970).

6   A. de Waal and B. Conley-Zilkic, 'Reflections on How Genocidal Killings Are Brought to an End', at webforum 'How Genocides End', 22 December 2006: <howgenocidesend.ssrc.org/de_Waal/>. This website provides invaluable information on the often neglected empirical background to this question: <howgenocidesend.ssrc.org/>.

7   See J. Lobe, 'War Hawks Spread Wings for Post-Vote Campaign', *Inter-Press Service*, 4 November 2002; P. Wolfowitz, 'Clinton's First Year', *Foreign Affairs*, January/February 1994.

8   Nick Cohen argues that 'Wolfowitz is a conservative who, during his career, has championed democracy in the Philippines and Indonesia, feminism in Iran and opposition to Saddam Hussein in Iraq, causes that were once the preserve of the liberal-left'. See 'When giving to the poorest just lines the pockets of the rich', *Observer*, 17 September 2006. For Anne Clwyd's account of Wolfowitz, see 'How a Labour rebel became friends with US hawks', *Guardian*, 23 June 2003. On Wolfowitz's role in Indonesia, see J. Winters, 'Wolfowitz's Jakarta Years: Suharto Apologist, Economic Cronyist', *Joyo*, 29 March 2005; T. Shorrock, 'Paul Wolfowitz: A man to keep a close eye on', *Asia Times*, 21 March 2001. On his role in the Philippines, see J. Mann, *Rise of the Vulcans: The History of Bush's War Cabinet* (Penguin, 2004), pp. 128–34.

9   On East Timor, Turkey and Colombia, see N. Chomsky, *Rogue States: The Rule of Force in World Affairs* (Pluto Press, 2000). On Haiti, see P. Hallward, *Damming the Flood: Haiti, Aristide and the Politics of Containment* (Verso, 2008). See also Christopher Cramer, *Civil War Is Not A Stupid Thing: Accounting for Violence in Developing Countries* (Hurst & Co., 2006), p. 56. On the intellectual resuscitation of imperialism, see B. Bush, *Imperialism, Race and Resistance: Africa and Britain, 1919–1945* (Routledge, 1999), pp. 1–3. See also S. Shalom, *Imperial Alibis: Rationalising US Intervention After the Cold War* (South End Press, 1993), p. 111; A. de Waal, *Famine Crimes: Politics and the Disaster Relief Industry in Africa* (James Currey, 1997), p. 65.

10   See M. Shaw, *War and Genocide: Organised Killing in Modern Society* (Polity Press, 2003) and *What is Genocide?* (Polity Press, 2007). Shaw argued for a long time that militarism was under retreat in Western societies, which permitted a less critical attitude to such military interventions as did occur. See Shaw's *Post-Military Society: Militarism, Demilitarization and War at the End of the Twentieth Century* (Temple University Press, 1991), and also *The New Western Way of War* (Polity Press, 2005), in which he finds the new 'Western' way of limited, risk-averse war under threat, particularly in the case of Iraq.

11   W. Shawcross, *Sideshow: Kissinger, Nixon and the Destruction of Cambodia* (Simon & Schuster, 1979). Later, Shawcross was to represent his book as a discussion of Khmer Rouge atrocities, whereas it was in fact a discussion of US atrocities. See discussion in N. Chomsky, *World Orders: Old and New* (Pluto Press, London, 1996).

12   Alex de Waal cites the resistance of the people of the Nuba Mountains. See A. de Waal, *Famine That Kills: Darfur, Sudan* (Oxford University Press, 2005), p. xix, and 'Averting Genocide in the Nuba Mountains, Sudan', 'How Genocides End', 22 December 2006: <howgenocidesend. ssrc.org/de_Waal2/>.

13   G. Achcar, *The Clash of Barbarisms: September 11 and the Making of the New World Order* (Monthly Review Press, 2002), pp. 22–4.

14   N. Chomsky, 'The Afghanistan Food Crisis', *ZNet*, 4 September 2005; A. Benini and L. Molton, 'Civilian Victims in an Asymmetrical Conflict: Operation Enduring Freedom', *Journal of Peace Research*, vol. 41, no. 4 (2004); M. Herold, 'A Dossier on Civilian Victims of United States' Aerial Bombing of Afghanistan: A Comprehensive Accounting' at <www.cursor.org/stories/civilian_deaths.htm>; J. Steele, 'Forgotten Victims', *Guardian*, 20 May 2002.

15   Amnesty International, 'Refugees From Afghanistan: The world's largest single refugee group', 1 November 1999; UNHCR, 'Feature: Afghan refugees who are reluctant to return', *Reliefweb*, 6 October 2003, available at <http://www.reliefweb.int/>; K. Allen, letter published in *Amnesty International News*, 23 June 2003; 'Afghanistan's maternal and child mortality rates soar', *Medical News Today*, 6 August 2005; 'Afghanistan's maternal and child mortality rates soar', UNICEF Press Release, 4 August 2005; 'Afghanistan: Mortality Rates Remain High For Mothers, Newborns', *Radio Free Europe*, 10 May 2006; 'State of the World's Mothers 2007: Saving the Lives of Children Under 5' (Save the Children, May 2007).

16   Quoted in M. Mann, *Incoherent Empire* (Verso, 2003), p. 138.

17   M. Benjamin, 'When is an accidental civilian death not an accident?', *Salon.com*, 30 July 2007.

18   'Afghan power brokers: International fundraiser in chief', *Christian Science Monitor*, 10 June, 2002; 'Afghanistan's civilian deaths mount', *BBC News*, 3 January, 2002; 'Afghan leader says US bombed civilians', *BBC News*, 3 February 2002; K. Connolly and R. McCarthy, 'New film accuses US of war crimes', *Guardian*, 13 June 2002; 'Afghan: U.S. bomb hits wedding party', *CNN*, 1 July 2002; M. Herold, 'Attempts to Hide the Number of Afghan Civilians Killed by US Bombs Are An Affront To Justice', 8 August 2002; B. Dehghanpisheh, J. Barry and R. Gutman, 'The Death Convoy of Afghanistan', *Newsweek*, 26 August 2002; 'US bombing kills Afghan children', *BBC News*, 7 December 2003; 'Afghans understand deaths – U.S.', *CNN*, 7 December 2003; P. Constable, 'U.S. troops shot at Afghans after crash: Military says soldiers fired in self-defense', *Washington Post*, 1 June 2006; 'Afghanistan: Reject Known Abusers as Police Chiefs, Time for President Karzai to Show He Is a Genuine Reformer', *Human Rights Watch*, 4 May 2006; 'Afghanistan woman stoned to death', *BBC News*, 23 April 2005; L. Sadid, 'Suicide an option for desperate war-widows, UNIFEM Survey revealed: "65 per cent of the 50,000 widows in Kabul see suicide as the only option to get rid of their miseries and desolation"', *Indo-Asian News Service*, 14

August 2006; H. Zada, '"Attack of Police" to Girl's Dormitory in Balkh', BBC Persian (translated by RAWA), 5 June 2006: <www.rawa.org/balkh.htm>; Human Rights Watch, *The Status of Women in Afghanistan*, October 2004; 'Gulbar is Burnt by Her Husband', RAWA report, 26 January 2006: <www.rawa.org/burning_p.htm>; J. Huggler, 'Women's lives "no better" in the new Afghanistan', *Independent*, 1 November 2006; D. Campbell and S. Goldenberg, 'Afghan detainees routinely tortured and humiliated by US troops', *Guardian*, 23 June 2004; J. Brecher and B. Smith, 'Senate Vote Advances President's Effort to Kill War Crimes Act', *Nation*, 22 September 2006; quoted in C. Lamb, 'Death Trap', *Sunday Times Review*, 9 July 2006.

19   C. Hitchens, *A Long Short War: The Postponed Liberation of Iraq*, Plume, 2003; C Hitchens, 'What Happens Next in Iraq', *Mirror*, 26 February 2003; H. Porter, 'Democracy is not in the war plans', *Observer*, 16 March 2003; J. Borger, 'US plans military rule and occupation of Iraq', *Guardian*, 12 October 2002; R. Cornwell, 'Turf War Rages in Washington Over Who Will Rule Iraq', *Independent*, 5 April 2003; O. Morgan, 'Man who would be "king" of Iraq,' *Observer*, 30 March 2003; D. Dehl, 'Iraq's U.S. Overseer Is Praised by Rumsfeld', *New York Times*, 2 May 2003; N. Klein, 'Baghdad year zero: Pillaging Iraq in pursuit of a neocon utopia', *Harper's Magazine*, September 2004; E. Herring and G. Rangwala, *Iraq in Fragments: The Occupation and Its Legacy* (Hurst & Co., 2006), pp. 222–36; D. Whyte, 'The Crimes of Neoliberal Rule in Occupied Iraq', *British Journal of Criminology*, no. 47 (2007).

20   H. Docena, 'How the US got its neoliberal way in Iraq', *Asia Times*, 1 September 2005.

21   Herring and Rangwala *Iraq in Fragments*, pp. 127–60. This 'pattern of "fragmented clientelism"' is 'characteristic of countries in transition, such as Russia in the 1990s', according to P. Le Billon, 'Corruption, Reconstruction and Oil Governance in Iraq,' *Third World Quarterly*, vol. 26, nos 4–5 (2005), pp. 685–703; S. Murray, 'Senate Endorses Plan to Divide Iraq: Action Shows Rare Bipartisan Consensus', *Washington Post*, 26 September 2007. On Iraqi opposition to partition, see 'Iraqis' Own Surge Assessment: Few See Security Gains', *ABC News*, 10 September 2007. On Maliki's rejection of the plans, see 'Iraqi PM rejects partition plan', *Associated Press*, 28 September 2007. H. Cooper, 'Biden plan for "soft partition" of Iraq gains momentum', *International Herald Tribune*, 30 July 2007.

22   'Biden to Iraqi pols: "I Don't Know Who the Hell They Think They Are"', *ABC News*, 1 October 2007.

23   G. Burnham, R. Lafta, S. Doocy and L. Roberts, 'Mortality after the
      2003 invasion of Iraq: a cross-sectional cluster sample survey', *Lancet*,
      11 October 2006, available at < www.thelancet.com/webfiles/
      images/journals/lancet/s0140673606694919.pdf>; T. Susman, 'Poll:
      Civilian death toll in Iraq may top 1 million', *Los Angeles Times*, 14
      September 2007; Opinion Research Business, Press Release, 'More than
      1,000,000 Iraqis murdered', 14 September 2007, available at
      <www.opinion.co.uk/Newsroom_details.aspx?NewsId=78>;
      <www.opinion.co.uk/Documents/TABLES.pdf>; O. Bennett-Jones,
      'Iraqi deaths survey "was robust"', *BBC News*, 26 March 2007.

24   Michael Hirsh and John Barry, 'The "Salvador Option"', *Newsweek*,
      14 January 2005.

25   Paul Wolfowitz testified before the Senate Armed Services Committee
      that the SPC was 'entirely' an 'Iraqi invention': 'Testimony as delivered
      to the Senate Armed Services Committee: hearing on military opera-
      tions in Iraq and Afghanistan', US Department of Defense Speeches, 3
      February 2005. However, General David Petraeus takes credit for having
      formed the commandos himself: 'Gangs of Iraq: Interview General
      David Petraeus', *PBS*, 11 October 2006. And there is no controversy at
      all over whether the US military commands the SPC.

26   Todd Clark describes the SPC as a response to the need for 'organized
      counterinsurgency' in the professional journal of the US Army's
      'Armor' branch at Fort Knox: 'Forging the sword: conventional U.S.
      Army forces advising host nation; HN forces', *Armor*, 1 September
      2006.

27   See, for example A. MacDonald, 'US Sends in Secret Weapon: Saddam's
      Old Commandos', *Reuters*, 27 November 2004; 'Iraq's Death Squads',
      Washington Post, 4 December 2005; K. Septunga, 'US forces arrest
      "death squad" suspects', *Independent*, 27 March 2006; K. Silverstein,
      'The Minister of Civil War', *Harper's Magazine*, 1 August, 2006; S.
      Tavernise, 'Iraq Suspends Police Brigade In Baghdad', *New York
      Times*, 5 October 2006; testimony of Gerald F. Burke, former major,
      Massachusetts State Police and former senior advisor to the Iraqi
      Police, reproduced in full in 'Veterans, Experts Testify About the Bush
      Administration's Conduct in War in Iraq', *US Newswire*, 12 October
      2006; A. Al-fadhily and D. Jamail, 'Iraq: Public Sceptical Government
      Can Reel in Death Squads it Backed', *IPS*, 19 October 2006. See also the
      testimony of US Army Major Charles Miller, who advised the comman-
      dos for a year: S. Inskeep, 'Riding Herd on the Iraqi Police's Dirty "Wolf
      Brigade"', *National Public Radio*, 28 March 2007. Recent incidents of
      alleged SPC death-squad activity include reported involvement in the
      kidnapping of five Britons: T. Moynihan, 'Vicar Helping in Hostage

Crisis Leaves Iraq', *Press Association*, 11 July 2007; A. Johnson, M. Woolf and R. Whitaker, 'Britain's private army in Iraq', *Independent on Sunday*, 3 June 2007.

28   K. Sengupta, 'Operation Enduring Chaos', *Independent on Sunday*, 29 October 2006; N. Turse, 'The Secret Air War in Iraq', *Nation*, 24 May 2007. It later emerged that 2007 had seen massive peaks in aerial bombardment. A. Cordesman, 'US Airpower in Iraq and Afghanistan: 2004–2007', *Centre for Strategic and International Studies*, 13 December 2007, available at <www.csis.org/media/csis/pubs/071213_oif-oef_airpower.pdf>.

29   S. Elworthy, 'Background: the situation in Fallujah', in J. Holmes, *Fallujah: Eyewitness Testimony from Iraq's Besieged City* (Constable, 2007), pp. 1–25; M. Marqusee, 'A name that lives in infamy', *Guardian*, 10 November 2004. Eyewitness reporter Jo Wilding describes US attacks on civilians and ambulances: J. Holmes, *Fallujah*, pp. 30–64. Major General Richard Natonski later conceded that, though Abu Musab al-Zarqawi's presence had been suggested, they had never expected him to be there: 'Fallujah invasion called success', *Associated Press*, 15 November 2004.

30   'Leadership Failure: Firsthand Accounts of Torture of Iraqi Detainees by the U.S. Army's 82nd Airborne Division', *Human Rights Watch*, vol. 17, no. 3 (September 2005); <www.aclu.org/torturefoia/released/032505/index.html>. Witnesses told BBC *Newsnight* that it was drummed into their heads that 'they're not humans, they're just "hajis"', and if one wanted to take a pop at an Iraqi, it was simple enough to drop a shovel near where they lay dead, so that it would appear that they were insurgents – BBC *Newsnight*, 30 March 2006. Fifty individual witnesses described atrocities and casual killings in C. Hedges and L. Al-Arian, 'The Other War: Iraq Vets Bear Witness', *Nation*, 9 July 2007.

31   'War and Occupation in Iraq', *Global Policy Forum*, June 2007, at <www.globalpolicy.org/security/issues/iraq/occupation/report/full.pdf>.

32   N. Geras, 'Failure in Iraq', *Normblog*, 15 October 2006. On Geras's earlier writing against standing by, see *The Contract of Mutual Indifference: Political Philosophy After the Holocaust* (Verso, 1998). In this deeply pessimistic account of human society, Geras outlines the thesis that a norm of human conduct is indifference to suffering, one which was most dramatically illustrated by those who stood by without protest and permitted the judeocide to take place. The extent of general human indifference, Geras argues, ranges from the minor to the extreme, from misfortune to genocide. Against the 'contract of mutual indifference', which effectively nullifies our claimed rights, he proposes that the 'queen of all virtues' is 'not to remain a bystander in the face

of preventable or remediable suffering'. Geras is obviously alert to the possibilities of such a philosophy when calling for the empire to commit itself to charity and humanitarianism. Yet, in the face of preventable suffering inflicted by the American empire, Geras would rather be a bystander and keep his mouth shut. Perhaps this is better than actually having demanded such actions as caused that suffering, which raises the possibility of another royal virtue: namely, not to make things any worse than they already are. See also <www.eustonmanifesto.org/>.

33 Author interview with Gary Younge.

34 S. McLemee, 'Euston . . . We Have a Problem', *Inside Higher Ed*, 24 May 2006.

35 A. Johnson, 'Jackson's new deal for social democrats', *Guardian*, 22 September 2007; M. Gove, 'All hail the new anti-Islamist intelligentsia', *Spectator*, 27 January 2007.

36 J. Paul, 'Boycott opponents hit back with big London meet', *Jerusalem Post*, 13 July 2007. For information on the boycott call, see the 'Palestinian Campaign for the Academic and Cultural Boycott of Israel' website: <www.pacbi.org>; see 'UCU response to boycott vote', 30 May 2007, on the UCU website: <http://www.ucu.org.uk/index.cfm?articleid=2595>; M. Gerstenfeld, 'Boycott battle won. The war goes on', *Jerusalem Post*, 2 October 2007.

37 P. Hennessy, 'Anti-Kerry remarks by Labour MP put Blair on the spot', *Telegraph*, 31 October 2004; O. Kamm, 'The liberal case for returning Bush to the White House', *The Times*, 10 July 2004.

38 T. McElvey, 'Interventionism's Last Hold-Out', *American Prospect*, 15 May 2007; D. Reiff, 'A New Age of Liberal Imperialism?' reproduced in D. Rieff, *At the Point of a Gun: Democratic Dreams and Armed Intervention* (Simon & Schuster, 2005), pp. 35–57, 92–3; D. Rieff, 'The Darfur Deception', *Los Angeles Times*, 7 October 2007.

39 Quoted in K. Ross, 'Ethics and the Rearmament of Imperialism: The French Case', in J. Wasserstrom, G. Grandin, L. Hunt and M. Young, eds, *Human Rights and Revolutions* (Rowman & Littlefield, 2005 – second edition).

40 Author interview with Rony Brauman.

41 P. Beinart, 'A Different Country', *New Republic*, 3 May 2007.

42 J. Victor, 'Ignatieff Loses Bid for Party Leadership', *Harvard Crimson*, 4 December 2006; M. Ignatieff, 'Getting Iraq Wrong', *New York Times*, 5 August 2007; 'MPs narrowly vote to extend Afghanistan mission', *CTV.ca*, 17 May 2006.

43 J. Hari, 'The North Korean regime is the worst on earth - and should be overthrown', *Independent*, 18 April 2003.

44 Author interview with Johann Hari.

45   Author interview with Vivek Chibber.

46   The Solidarity Center is a department set up by the AFL-CIO union federation to influence labour struggles outside America. It is mainly funded by the US government, and has generally been seen as assisting its foreign policy goals. See K. Scipes, 'It's Time To Come Clean: Open the AFL-CIO Archives on International Labor Operations', *Labor Studies Journal*, vol. 25, no. 2 (Summer 2000), pp. 4–25; K. Scipes, 'Labor Imperialism Redux?: The AFL-CIO's Foreign Policy Since 1995', *Monthly Review*, vol. 57, no. 1 (May 2005); S. Rodberg, 'The CIO without the CIA: Inside the AFL-CIO's Solidarity Center', *American Prospect*, Summer 2001.

47   Author interview with Liza Featherstone.

48   Z. Eisenstein, *Sexual Decoys: Gender, Race and War in Imperial Democracy* (Zed Books, 2004).

49   G. Packer, *The Assassin's Gate: America in Iraq* (Farrar, Straus & Giroux, 2006), p. 77; McElvey, 'Interventionism's Last Hold-Out'; Packer, *Assassin's Gate*, pp. 66–8, 78–97, 451.

50   K. Makiya still maintains that de-Baathification was 'right in principle' but 'mishandled'. M. Young, 'Three Years, Few Regrets', *Reason*, 6 April 2006.

51   Beinart, 'A Different Country'.

52   Packer, *Assassin's Gate*, p. 59.

53   P. Berman, 'Paul Berman Response', *Dissent*, Spring 2007.

54   Debate with George Galloway at Baruch College, New York, hosted by Amy Goodman, 14 September 2005; C. Hitchens, 'The Lancet's Slant: Epidemiology meets moral idiocy', *Slate.com*, 16 October 2006; C. Hitchens, 'The Case For Regime Change', in T. Cushman, ed., *A Matter of Principle: Humanitarian Arguments for War* (University of California Press, 2005), p. 38; C. Hitchens, 'A Death in the Family', *Vanity Fair*, November 2007.

55   I. Parker, 'He Knew He Was Right', *New Yorker*, 16 October 2006.

56   Author interview with Corey Robin.

57   C. Hitchens, 'Facing the Islamist Menace', *City Journal*, Winter 2007; C. Hitchens on *The Laura Ingraham Show*, 8 November 2005.

58   Amin was, for example, attacked by a fellow student in an interview for David Horowitz's *Front Page* magazine. J. Glazov, 'UK Student Warned to Stop Protesting Jew-Hatred', *FrontPageMag.com*, 27 June 2005. The MP who called for Amin to be charged was the Labour member for Walsall North, David Winnick. See Hansard, 'Written Answers for 21 March 2005', available at <http://www.publications.parliament.uk/pa/cm200405/cmhansrd/vo050321/text/50321w03.htm>.

59   Author interview with Dominique Vidal. See also D. Vidal, 'Self-censorship in France', *Le Monde Diplomatique*, December 2002.

60   P. Bruckner, 'How French', *New Republic*, 21 November 2005.

61   D. Mishani and A. Smotriez, 'What Sort of Frenchmen Are They?', *Haaretz*, 17 November 2005.

62   M. Borton, 'Some on left support Sarkozy for French presidency', *International Herald Tribune*, 31 January 2007; H. Samuel, 'French thinkers abandon "archaic" Royal', *Daily Telegraph*, 19 February 2007; 'France's new government: a study in perpetual motion', *Economist*, 24 May 2007.

63   Kouchner later admitted this failure: 'UN "failed" Kosovo Serbs', *BBC News*, 12 January 2001; 'Iran scorns French warning of war', *BBC News*, 17 September 2007.

64   'France eyes "neutral" military role in Chad conflict', *Reuters*, 2 February 2008; 'Disbelief at Chad's voter figures', *BBC News*, 5 May 2006; '2006 presidential election concluded in Chad', *ElectionGuide*, 5 May 2006.

65   H. Samuel, 'Sarkozy attacks "immoral" heritage of 1968', *Daily Telegraph*, 1 May 2007. As Serge Halimi argues, Sarkozy learned a great deal here from the American Right: 'The Reinvention of France's Right-Wing: What Sarkozy Learned About Politics from the US . . . and From Antonio Gramsci', *Counterpunch*, 8 June 2007.

66   B.-H. Lévy, *Ce grand cadavre á la renverse* (Grasset, 2007).

67   Author interview with Serge Halimi.

68   P. Cohen, 'Vive les comités BHL 2012!', *Marianne 2*, 9 October 2007.

69   M. Ignatieff, *The Lesser Evil: Political Ethics in an Age of Terror* (Princeton University Press, 2005).

70   A. Rabinbach, 'Totalitarianism Revisited', *Dissent*, Summer 2006.

71   See, for example, I. Kershaw, *The Nazi Dictatorship: Problems of Perspective and Interpretation*, (Arnold, 2000 – fourth edition), pp. 23–6. Richard J. Evans argues that the similarities between Nazism and Stalinism were substantially outweighed by the differences in the origins and social forces that made up the regimes: R. Evans, *The Coming of the Third Reich* (Penguin, 2003), pp. xxvi–xxvii. Robert O. Paxton criticizes totalitarianism theory for missing the specificities of the regimes:

> Stalin ruled a civil society that had been radically simplified by the Bolshevik Revolution, and thus he did not have to concern himself with autonomous concentrations of inherited social and economic power. Hitler (totally unlike Stalin) came into power with the assent and even insistence of traditional elites, and governed in strained but effective association with them. In Nazi Germany the party jostled with the state bureaucracy, industrial

and agricultural proprietors, churches and other traditional elites
for power. Totalitarian theory is totally blind to this fundamental
character of the Nazi governing system, and thus tends to fortify
the elites' postwar claim that Hitler tried to destroy them.

R. Paxton, *The Anatomy of Fascism* (Penguin, 2004), p. 212.

72 Author interview with Enzo Traverso.

73 See D. Losurdo, 'Towards a Critique of the Category of Totalitarianism', *Historical Materialism* 12.1 (April 2004); J. de Maistre, quoted in D. Losurdo, *Hegel and the Freedom of Moderns* (Duke University Press, 2004), p. 63; E. Traverso, *The Origins of Nazi Violence* (New Press, 2003), pp 21–3; author interview with Enzo Traverso. See also, E. Traverso, ed., *Le totalitarisme, Le XX siècle en débat* (Seuil, 2001).

74 A. Rabinbach, 'Moments of Totalitarianism', *History and Theory* 45 (February 2006), p. 74.

75 'Statement of Principles', *Euston Manifesto*, 29 March 2006.

76 See, for example, A. Johnson, 'Why I am not a Marxist', <http://normblog.typepad.com>, 16 July 2007.

77 J. Herf, R. Berman, T. Cushman, R. Just, R. Lieber, A. Markovits and F. Siegel, 'American Liberalism and the Euston Manifesto', *Euston Manifesto*, available at <http://eustonmanifesto.org/>, 12 September 2006; Rabinbach, *Dissent* and 'Totalitarianism Revisited'.

78 Far from Saddam throwing the weapons inspectors out, US Ambassador Peter Burleigh, acting on instructions from Washington, told Richard Butler to withdraw the inspectors in late 1998, in order to protect them from planned US–UK air-strikes: D. Hiro, *Neighbors, Not Friends: Iraq and Iran After the Gulf Wars* (Routledge, 2001), p. 161. Far from being 'stronger', Saddam's weapons capacity at that time was seriously degraded, and he showed no ability to resist US attacks on Iraq. Scott Ritter, the former weapons inspector, described the regime as being between 90 and 95 per cent disarmed: C. Lynch, 'Ex-U.N. Inspector Ritter to Tour Iraq, Make Documentary', *Washington Post*, 27 July 2000.

79 P. Berman, *Terror and Liberalism* (W.W. Norton & Co., 2003), pp. 3–15. One might also pause at this point to comment on the slipperiness of Berman's 'anti-totalitarian' metaphor – initially, we are told that 1991 is 1939; then it becomes, in the space of nine pages, World War I, and 2003 becomes 1939. This, even though Saddam was much weaker in 2003 than in 1991, at which point he was almost a continent weaker than Adolf Hitler was in 1939.

80 When it comes to impressionism, it is hard to beat Berman's discussion

of Chomsky's writing on Cambodia in the late 1970s. Unable to seriously engage with Chomsky's critique of the overstating of Khmer atrocities compared to the understating of Washington-backed Indonesian atrocities in East Timor, he asserts that

> Well-known journalists reported one set of data, but Chomsky assembled immense supplies of alternative data, which he drew from the recollections of random tourists, wandering church workers, and articles in little known left-wing magazines . . . He showed that genocide had never occurred; and, conversely, he showed that, if genocide did occur, it was the fault of the American military intervention, which had driven the Cambodians mad.

P. Berman, *Terror and Liberalism*, p. 148. In fact, Chomsky's critique, co-written with Edward Herman, differs from Berman's description of it in a number of ways: 1) it did not simply provide 'alternative data', but pointed out the inconsistencies and flaws in the sourcing of the 'well-known journalists'; 2) it did not rely on 'random tourists', 'wandering church workers' and 'little known left-wing magazines' for its 'alternative data'. It did not present 'alternative data'. Its critique relied almost wholly on reports in reputable Western newspapers and magazines, as well as that 'wandering church worker', Father Ponchaud, who was cited quite frequently by the Western press. Where Chomsky and Herman do offer figures, these emerge from Ponchaud and the State Department; 3) the critique did not seek to show whether genocide had or was occurring in Cambodia, and nor did it say that the US was exclusively to blame, but rather that its share of the blame for the catastrophe through its murderous bombing campaign was being neglected in Western press coverage. See N. Chomsky and E. Herman, *After the Cataclysm: Postwar Indochina and The Reconstruction of Imperial Ideology: The Political Economy of Human Rights, Volume II* (Spokesman Books, 1979), pp. 135–294.

81   A. Johnson, 'Interrogating Terror and Liberalism: An Interview with Paul Berman', *Democratiya*, 24 May 2006; Berman, *Terror and Liberalism*, p. 208,124–8.

82   Theodor Adorno and Max Horkheimer explored the input of modernity, rationalism and scientism in the Nazi death camps in T. Adorno and M. Horkheimer, *Dialectic of Enlightenment* (Verso, 2002). See also E. Traverso, 'Production line of murder', *Le Monde Diplomatique*, February 2005.

83   N. Cohen, *What's Left? How the Liberals Lost Their Way* (Fourth Estate, 2007), p. 62.

84   Speech by General Sir Richard Dannatt, 'Military Leaders Forum',
      International Institute for Strategic Studies, 21 September 2007. Recording
      available at <http://www.iiss.org/conferences/military-leaders-forum/
      general-sir-richard-dannatt/>.
85   D. Francis, *Rethinking War and Peace* (Pluto Press, 2004), pp. 13–15.
86   M. Bhadrakumar, 'Afghanistan: Why NATO cannot win', *Asia Times*,
      30 September 2006; K. Sengupta, 'Afghanistan: Campaign against
      Taliban "causes misery and hunger"', *Independent*, 6 September 2006;
      A. Jones, 'Why It's Not Working in Afghanistan', *TomDispatch.com*,
      September 2006; S. Shahzad, 'A voice for the Afghan insurgency', *Asia
      Times*, 15 June 2007; 'British colonial forces suffered heavy defeats in
      Afghanistan in the 19th century when Britain tried to win over
      Afghanistan's tribes and make their lands a protective buffer against
      perceived Russian designs on British India. . .' quoted in K. Roberts,
      'Rumsfeld arrives in Afghanistan', *Scotsman*, 11 July 2006; Senlis
      Council, *Field Notes, Afghanistan Insurgency Assessment, The Signs of
      an Escalating Crisis: Insurgency in Helmand, Kandahar and Nangarhar*
      (7 April 2006): <www.senliscouncil.net/modules/publications/011_
      publication/documents/insurgency_assessment_field_report>. See also
      the International Crisis Group's report, 'Countering Afghanistan's
      Insurgency: No Quick Fixes', *Asia Report*, no. 123, 2 November 2006:
      <www.crisisgroup.org/home/index.cfm?action=login&ref_id=4485>.
      The policy is being implemented by Dyncorp, the same organization
      that was deployed to attack coca farms in Colombia, where it is accused
      of engaging in widespread military activities targeting the rebels
      against Colombia's repressive government. See D. Shearer, *Private
      Armies and Military Intervention*, Adelphi Paper No. 316 (Oxford
      University Press, 1998); P. Singer, *Corporate Warriors: The Rise of the
      Privatized Military Industry* (Cornell University Press, 2003), pp. 88–
      100; The Permanent People's Tribunal Session on Colombia, 'Hearing
      on Biodiversity, Humanitarian Zone, Cacarica', 24–27 February 2007:
      <www.colectivodeabogados.org/IMG/pdf/dyncorp_acu_eng.pdf>;
      '"Martyrdom culture" not major cause of Afghan suicide attacks, UN
      reports', *UN News Service*, 10 September 2007: <www.un.org/apps/
      news/story.asp?NewsID=23749&Cr=afghan&Cr1=>.
87   'AP count: Afghan deaths up 55 percent compared to 2006',
      International Herald Tribune, 4 October 2007; C. Johnson and J.
      Leslie, *Afghanistan: The Mirage of Peace* (Zed Books, 2005), pp. 82–3;
      N. Ghufran, 'The Taliban and the Civil War Entanglement in
      Afghanistan', *Asian Survey*, vol. 41, no. 3 (May–June 2001), pp. 462–87.
88   J. O'Malley, 'Afghan Girls' Struggle for Schooling', *MERIP Middle East
      Report*, 6 July 2000; S. Kolkhatkar and J. Ingalls, *Afghanistan:*

Washington, Warlords, and the Propaganda of Silence (Seven Stories Press, 2006), pp. 114–5; 'Afghanistan: Signs of a Major Shift', *Stratfor*, 3 October 2007.

89   C. Hitchens, 'A few words of fraternal admonition to "Norm" Finkelstein', Hitchens Web, September 2003: <users.rcn.com/peterk. enteract/fink.html>; C. Hitchens, 'Beating a Dead Parrot,' *Slate.com*, 31 January 2005.

90   N. Geras, 'Out of Tune', <http://normblog.typepad.com/>, 19 March 2005; J. Weintraub, 'Some thoughts on the terrorist strategy of the Iraqi "insurgency"', <http://normblog.typepad.com/>, 15 March 2005; K. Pollitt, '2,4,6,8! This Beheading is Really Great!', *Nation*, 13 January 2007.

91   A. Hashim, *Insurgency and Counter-Insurgency in Iraq* (Cornell University Press, 2006); L. Napoleoni, *Insurgent Iraq: Al-Zarqawi and the New Generation* (Constable & Robinson, 2005); Z. Chehab, *Iraq Ablaze: Inside the Insurgency* (I.B. Tauris, 2006); Herring and Rangwala, *Iraq in Fragments*; A. Shadid and S. Fainaru, 'Militias on the Rise Across Iraq', *Washington Post*, 21 August 2005; 'Measuring Stability and Security in Iraq', June 2007, Report to Congress, In accordance with the Department of Defense Appropriations Act 2007 (Section 9010, Public Law 109–289): <www.defenselink.mil/pubs/pdfs/9010–Final-20070608.pdf>; M. Junaid Alam, 'Does the Resistance Target Civilians? According to US Intel, Not Really,' *LeftHook*, 16 April 2005; F. Kaplan, 'Western Targets: The Iraqi insurgency is still primarily an anti-occupation effort', *Slate.com*, 9 February 2006; 'Iraq violence: Facts and figures', *BBC News*, 17 August 2006; W. Pincus, 'CIA Studies Provide Glimpse of Insurgents in Iraq,' *Washington Post*, 6 February 2005; E. Knickmeyer and J. Finer, 'Iraqi Sunnis Battle To Defend Shiites', *Washington Post*, 14 August 2005; A. Hashim, 'Iraq's Chaos: Why the insurgency won't go away', *Boston Review*, October–November 2004; M. Schwartz, 'Schwartz on Why the Military Is Failing in Iraq,' *TomDispatch.com*, 5 March 2005; 'New Poll Says Majority of Iraqis Approve of Attacks on U.S. Forces: An Overwhelming Majority Think U.S. Forces Are Provoking Conflict', *ABC News*, 27 September 2006; 'Allawi May Offer Iraq Insurgents Amnesty', *Associated Press*, 5 July 2004.

92   See briefing slides from military commanders boasting about propaganda successes, reprinted in 'Leverage Xenophobia', *Washington Post*, 10 April 2006. For the full account of the propaganda drive by intelligence agencies and others on Abu Musab al-Zarqawi, see N. Davies, *Flat Earth News* (Chatto & Windus, 2008), pp. 205–57.

93   M. Ignatieff, *The Lesser Evil: Political Ethics in an Age of Terror*

(Edinburgh University Press, 2005), p. 12; C. Hitchens, '"Evil": Scoff if you must, but you can't avoid it', *Slate.com*, 31 December 2002; Makiya, 'Putting Cruelty First'.

94   Interview with Kanan Makiya, 'Faith and Doubt at Ground Zero', *PBS Frontline*, Winter 2002.

95   Ibid.

96   Paul Berman, 'Under the Bridge; Brooklyn Dispatch', *New Republic*, 24 September 2001.

97   See, for example, C. Hitchens, 'Realism in Darfur: Consider the horrors of peace', *Slate.com*, 7 November 2005; N. Cohen, 'How the UN lets genocidal states get away with murder', *Observer*, 29 October 2006.

98   De Waal, *Famine That Kills*, p. 89. The best account of the Darfur conflict to date is J. Flint and A. de Waal, *Darfur: A Short History of a Long War* (Zed Books, 2005). See also M. Mamdani, 'The Politics of Naming: Genocide, Civil War, Insurgency', *London Review of Books*, 8 April 2007.

99   Quoted in A. McSmith, 'Blair hit by Lebanon backlash as minister admits ceasefire "mistake"', *Independent*, 14 September 2006; 'PM "says Israel pre-planned war"', *BBC News*, 8 March 2007; C. Brown and F. Elliott, 'Just hot air? Bush and Blair refuse to call for ceasefire', *Independent*, 29 July 2006.

100   S. Wilson and E. Cody, 'Israel, Hezbollah Intensify Ground Conflict in Lebanon', *Washington Post*, 21 July 2006; A. Pfeffer, 'IDF preparing for civil administration in Lebanon', *Jerusalem Post*, 23 July 2006; 'UN appalled by Beirut devastation', *BBC News*, 23 July 2006; M. Hason, 'Northern Command chief: Don't count the casualties', *Yedioth Ahronoth*, 21 July 2006; L. Ohrstrum, 'Latest targets of air blitz: milk and medicine', *Lebanon Daily Star*, 19 July 2006; '"Many dead" in Israeli raids', *ABC Australia News*, 19 July 2006; 'Israel pounds Lebanon again', *Sydney Morning Herald*, 20 July 2006; E. O'Loughlin, 'Grim proof ordinary folk are dying in the killing zone', *Sydney Morning Herald*, 20 July 2006; R. Fisk, 'Lebanon's pain grows by the hour as death toll hits 1,300', *Independent*, 17 August 2006; H. Hendawi, 'Day 22: Bloodiest Day for Israel . . . 1 Million Displaced in Lebanon So Far. . .', *Associated Press*, 3 August 2006; 'Statement by Ambassador Dan Gillerman, Permanent Representative During the open debate on "The Situation in the Middle East"', United Nations Security Council, New York, 30 July 2006; *Human Rights Watch*, 'Fatal Strikes: Israel's Indiscriminate Attacks Against Civilians in Lebanon,' vol. 18, no. 3(E) (August 2006), p. 3; 'Israeli soldiers use civilians as human shields in Beit Hanun', *B'Tselem*, 20 July 2006.

101   M. Walzer, 'The Ethics of Battle: War Fair', *New Republic*, 31 July

2006; N. Geras, 'The rights and wrongs of Israel's military action', <http://normblog.typepad.com/>, 26 July 2006. For his stance on the targeting of civilians, see N. Geras, *Discourses of Extremity: Radical Ethics and Post-Marxist Extravagances* (Verso, London, 1990). The Human Rights Watch report, 'Civilians under Assault: Hezbollah's Rocket Attacks on Israel in the 2006 War', August 2007, briefly acknowledges Israel's placement of military facilities in civilian areas: <hrw.org/reports/2007/iopt0807/index.htm>. This was reported during the war, but not widely. See J. Cook, 'Israel, Not Hizbullah, is Putting Civilians in Danger on Both Sides of the Border', *Counterpunch*, 3 August 2006. Both military personnel and weapons were placed in civilian areas. Young soldiers recalled firing at Hezbollah missiles from within Kibbutzes and residing in these throughout the war. See E. Ashkenazi, 'IDF takes responsibility for Kfar Giladi deaths', *Haaretz*, 21 December 2007, and J. Vasagar, '"When it comes to firing the gun, it's a massive shock. It's what you don't see in the movies."', *Guardian*, 23 November 2006. An extensive report by the EU-funded Arab Association for Human Rights, 'Civilians in Danger' (December 2007), describes how 'the most intensive attacks during the war were ones that were surrounded by military installations, either on a permanent basis or temporarily during the course of the war'. Missiles and weaponry were fired from military installations less than half a kilometre from civilian areas. See <www.arabhra.org/HraAdmin/UserImages/Files/LebanonWarReportFinalEng.doc>.

102 N. Geras, E. Garrard and S. Lappin, 'Open Letter to Jews for Justice for Palestinians', <http://normblog.typepad.com/>, 15 August 2006.

103 C. Hitchens, 'The Politics of Sabotage', *Wall Street Journal*, 18 July 2006; C. Hitchens, 'Islamism Goes Mainstream: My Evening With Tariq Ramadan', *Slate.com*, 11 September 2007.

104 C. Hitchens on 'The Charlie Rose Show', *PBS*, 4 May 2007. The claim was widely repeated in neoconservative publications: S. Hayes, 'Saddam's Philippines Terror Connection, And Other Revelations from the Iraqi Regime Files', *Weekly Standard*, vol. 11, issue 26 (27 March 2006); 'Study Discounts Hussein-Al Qaeda Link', *Washington Post*, 11 March 2008.

105 J. Brinkley, 'Ex-C.I.A. Aides Say Iraq Leader Helped Agency in 90's Attacks', *New York Times*, 9 June 2004.

106 B. Ross and C. Isham, 'The Secret War Against Iran', *ABC News*, 3 April 2007; S. Shahzad, 'The legacy of Nek Mohammed', *Asia Times*, 24 July 2004; Z. Hussain, 'Al-Qaeda's New Face', *Newsline*, August 2004; A. Dareini, 'Explosion Kills 11 Elite Iranian Guards', *Associated Press*, 14 February 2007; A. Bright, 'Sunni rebels claim deadly terror

attack in Iran', *Christian Science Monitor*, 14 February 2007; 'Iran Sunni rebels video shows killing of officer: TV', *Reuters*, 11 April 2006; 'Sunni group vows to behead Iranians', *Washington Times*, 26 October 2006; W. Lowther and C. Freeman, 'US funds terror groups to sow chaos in Iran', *Sunday Telegraph*, 25 February 2007; G. Dinmore, 'US Marines Probe Tensions among Iran's Minorities', *Financial Times*, 23 February 2006. It was also reported that the Pentagon had been directing funding and support to the Mujahedeen-e Khalq, an opposition group that had been supported by Saddam Hussein's Iraq and carried out numerous attacks on Iranian soil, and which has repeatedly been used as a source by US officials for 'intelligence' indicating Iranian nuclear weapons programmes and involvement in Iraqi terrorism. L. Alexandrovna, 'On Cheney, Rumsfeld order, US outsourcing special ops, intelligence to Iraq terror group, intelligence officials say', *Raw Story*, 13 April 2006; A. Russell, 'Briefing frenzy in Washington over Iran nuclear fear', *Daily Telegraph*, 21 November 2004; R. Wright and K. Richburg, 'Powell Says Iran Is Pursuing Bomb: Evidence Cited of Effort to Adapt Missile', *Washington Post*, 18 November 2004; S. Hersh, 'The Next Act', *New Yorker*, 27 November 2006.

107 A. Memmi, *The Colonizer and the Colonized* (Earthscan Publications, 2003), p. 137; A. Michnik, 'We, the Traitors', *Gazeta Wyborcza*, 28 March 2003; 'Hitchens gives reasons for regime change', 'Lateline', *ABC*, 30 June 2003.

108 M. Ignatieff, *Maclean's*, 23 June 2003.

109 'UK restates nuclear threat', *BBC News*, 2 February 2003; A. Johnson, 'Interrogating Terror and Liberalism'.

110 Though Ahmadinejad's remarks were translated in Western newspapers as 'Israel must be wiped off the map', Farsi speakers have repeatedly challenged this translation. See J. Steele, 'Lost in Translation', *Guardian*, 14 June 2006. The *New York Times* made a partial retraction and partial defence of its mistranslation: E. Bronner, 'Just How Far Did These Words Against Israel Go?', *New York Times*, 11 June 2006. Even the pro-Israel propaganda outfit, the Middle East Media and Research Institute, upholds the alternative translation. See 'Special Dispatch Series – No. 1013', *MEMRI*, 28 October 2005. The Iranian government has, of course, repeatedly denied that Ahmadinejad's remarks should be construed as a call to annihilate Israel. See 'Ahmadinejad misunderstood, says Iran', *Daily Times* (Pakistan), 22 February 2006. Ahmadinejad's clarification for *Time* magazine was that it was a call for the abolition of Zionism through a Palestinian referendum: Scott MacLeod, 'We Do Not Need Attacks', *Time*, 17 September 2007. This is the position outlined by Ayatollah Khameini:

'Leader's Speech to Government Officials on the Eid-al-Fitr', 4 November 2005: <www.khamenei.ir/EN/Speech/detail.jsp?id=2005 1104A>. To take one example of extensively reported remarks, see R. Wright, 'Iranian Leader: Tehran Has No Need for Nuclear Bomb', *Washington Post*, 24 September 2007; M. Mazzetti, 'U.S. Says Iran Ended Atomic Arms Work', *New York Times*, 3 December 2007.

111 See J. Muravchik, 'Bomb Iran', *Los Angeles Times*, 19 November 2006; N. Podhoretz, 'The Case for Bombing Iran', *Commentary*, June 2007; 'FACTBOX-New U.N. sanctions resolution on Iran', *Reuters*, 3 March 2008.

112 David Nason, 'Clooney, Bolton strange bedfellows on Darfur', *Australian*, 16 September 2006; <www.miafarrow.org/>; 'Cheadle acts to stop Darfur genocide', *CNN*, 4 May 2007; J. Vargas, 'In "Darfur Is Dying," The Game That's Anything But', *Washington Post*, 1 May 2006; R. Powell, 'Steven Spielberg boycotts Chinese Olympics', *Daily Telegraph*, 26 February 2008. Ted Kennedy co-sponsored legislation with a Republican senator calling for international military intervention in Darfur with Nato support. See Senator Gordon Smith's press release, 'On The Eve of Global Day for Darfur, Smith and Kennedy Announce New Plan for Peace in Darfur', 15 September 2006: <gsmith.senate.gov/public/index.cfm?FuseAction=PressReleases.Detail&PressRelease_id=244&Month=9&Year=2006>; J. McCain and B. Dole, 'Rescue Darfur Now', *Washington Post*, 10 September 2006. See, 'Darfur: Another Problem From Hell', Council on Foreign Relations, 21 September 2004, and S. Power, 'Why Can't We?', *Nation*, 23 May 2006. Notably, as Obama's advisor, Power has been swift to allay Israeli fears that her crusading fervour might cause her to favour 'imposing' a peace settlement. See S. Rosner, 'Obama's top adviser says does not believe in imposing a peace settlement', *Haaretz.com*, 4 March 2008. For the role of evangelicals in the campaign to save Darfur, see A. Cooperman, 'Groups Plan Rally on Mall To Protest Darfur Violence: Bush Administration Is Urged to Intervene in Sudan', *Washington Post*, 27 April 2006. The National Association of Evangelicals is among the leading components of the coalition. See G. Beckerman, 'US Jews Leading Darfur Rally Planning,' *Jerusalem Post*, 27 April 2006; <www.aicongress.org/>. On Zainab al-Suwaij's pro-war activism, see 'The Opportunity Before Us: A Conversation with Zainab Al-Suwaij', Ethics and Public Policy Center, 24 June 2003: <www.eppc.org/publications/pubID.1592/pub_detail.asp>.

113 Flint and de Waal, *Darfur: A Short History of a Long War*.

114 Author interview with Alex de Waal. The coalition experienced a setback when its advertisements demanding forceful military intervention and a

no-flight zone were criticized by aid groups for potentially making a bad situation catastrophic. They also attacked the coalition for claiming in some of its advertising to represent aid groups working in Sudan – in fact, Save Darfur is exclusively a lobbying outfit. See S. Strom and L. Polgreen, 'Darfur Advocacy Group Undergoes a Shake-Up', *New York Times*, 2 June 2007.

115   J. Gettleman, 'Business and Islam: Allies Against Anarchy in Somalia', *New York Times*, 18 September 2006; see C. Barnes and H. Hassan, 'The Rise and Fall of Mogadishu's Islamic Courts', Chatham House Briefing Paper, April 2007: <www.chathamhouse.org.uk/files/9130_bpsomalia0407.pdf>; J. Gettleman, 'As Somali Crisis Swells, Experts See a Void in Aid', *New York Times*, 20 November 2007; C. Maynes, 'Relearning Intervention', *Foreign Policy*, no. 98 (Spring 1995), p. 98.

116   For more on the breaches of the Geneva conventions, see Alex de Waal, 'US War Crimes in Somalia', *New Left Review*, I/230, July–August 1998,

116   Author interview with Alex de Waal.

117   E. Meiksins Wood, 'Democracy as Ideology of Empire', in C. Mooers, ed., *The New Imperialists: Ideologies of Empire* (Oneworld, 2006); Herring and Rangwala, *Iraq in Fragments*; R. Limbaugh, 'EIB Interview: President George W. Bush', 'The Rush Limbaugh Show', 1 November 2006, <http://www.rushlimbaugh.com>.

118   M. Yates, 'A Statistical Portrait of the U.S. Working Class', *Monthly Review*, vol. 56, no. 11 (2006); R. Brenner, *The Economics of Global Turbulence: The Advanced Capitalist Economies from the Long Boom to Long Downturn, 1945–2005* (Verso, 2006), pp. 330–1; J. Peters, 'Job Growth in July Is the Slowest in Months', *New York Times*, 3 August 2007; see C. Johnson, *The Sorrows of Empire: Militarism, Secrecy and the End of the Republic* (Verso, 2004).

Afterword

1   Richard Seymour, 'Humbling the hawks', *Socialist Worker*, 31 March 2009.

2   Domenico Losurdo, *Liberalism: A Counter-History* (Verso, 2011); on the relationship between classical liberalism, neoliberalism and the anti-democratic right, see William E. Scheuerman, *Carl Schmitt: The End of Law* (Rowman & Littlefield, 1999); and Renato Christi, *Carl Schmitt and Authoritarian Liberalism: Strong State, Free Economy* (University of Wales Press, 1998).

3   Arguably, these exclusion clauses are structured around the founding liberal commitment to 'property rights' which, we noted in Chapter 1, were devised from inception in such a way as to exclude non-Europeans from ever exercising them. Further, if the realisation of property rights

entails the global spread of capitalist markets, it also demands the creation of national states as the main strategic bases from which said markets are organized and defended. It thus tends to create classes of property owners who are nationally constituted but globally oriented. The result is that, as Woodrow Wilson put it, 'since trade ignores national boundaries and the manufacturer insists on having the world as a market, the flag of his nation must follow him, and the doors of the nations which are closed must be battered down' (see Chapter 2). Put briefly, a liberal world system is also an imperialist system.

4　On Gramsci and intellectuals, see Antonio Gramsci, 'The Intellectuals', in Quintin Hoare and Geoffrey Nowell Smith, eds, *Selections from the Prison Notebooks of Antonio Gramsci* (Lawrence & Wishart, 1971), pp. 5–23; also Peter Thomas, 'Gramsci and the Intellectuals', in *Marxism and Intellectuals* (Palgrave Macmillan, 2007), available at brunel.academia.edu.

5　'Most US aid to Egypt goes to military', *Daily Telegraph*, 29 January 2011; Ewen McAskill, 'Egypt protests: US resists calls to cut military aid', *Guardian*, 4 February 2011.

6　See David McNally, *Global Slump: The Economics and Politics of Crisis and Resistance* (PM Press, 2010).

7　Massimo Calabresi, 'James Jones: Obama's National Security Surprise', *Time*, 1 December 2008; Yochi J. Dreazen and Siobhan Gorman, 'Scowcroft Protégés on Obama's Radar', *Wall Street Journal*, 24 November 2008; Yaakov Lappin, 'Obama advisor raises concerns', *Ynet*, 16 September 2007; see Zbigniew Brzezinski, *Second Chance: Three Presidents and the Crisis of American Superpower* (Basic Books, 2007).

8　Laura Rozen, 'Slaughter confirms HRC State Department post', *Foreign Policy*, 21 January 2009; Susan E. Rice, Anthony Lake and Donald M. Payne, 'We Saved Europeans. Why Not Africans?', *New York Times*, 2 October 2006; Susan Rice, 'Don't Let Up After South Sudan's Independence', *Daily Beast*, 14 June 2011; Sheryl Gay Stolberg, 'Still Crusading, but Now on the Inside', *New York Times*, 29 March 2011.

9　Madeleine K. Albright and William S. Cohen, 'Commentary: Leadership key to preventing genocide', *CNN.com*, 10 December 2008.

10　David E. Sanger and Peter Baker, 'New U.S. Strategy Focuses on Managing Threats', *New York Times*, 27 May 2010.

11　On the demobilization of the anti-war movement, see Michael T. Heaney and Fabio Rojas, 'The Partisan Dynamics of Contention: Demobilization of the Antiwar Movement in the United States, 2007–2009', *Mobilization: An International Journal*, vol. 16, no. 1 (March 2011).

12　Roger Cohen, 'Middle East Reality Check', *New York Times*, 8 March 2009.

13 'Americans Closely Divided Over Israel's Gaza Attacks', *Rasmussen Reports*, 31 December 2008.

14 Nick Palmer, 'Israel's friends must say "stop"', *Guardian*, 1 January 2009.

15 'Gaza residents "terribly trapped"', BBC News, 4 November 2008.

16 Quoted in Norman G Finkelstein, '*This Time We Went Too Far': Truth and Consequences of the Gaza Invasion* (OR Books, 2010), p. 52.

17 Andrea Becker, 'The slow death of Gaza', *Guardian*, 24 November 2008; 'Israel's detention of UN expert "unprecedented" – rights chief', *UN News Centre*, 16 December 2008.

18 Fatah's acquiescence was perhaps epitomized in the Palestinian Authority's (PA) withdrawal of support for the UN report on Operation Cast Lead, which lambasted Israel's actions. The PA claimed to be under severe pressure from Israel, with the threat of economic sabotage mooted. See 'Outrage as UN discusses Gaza report', Al Jazeera, 7 October 2009. Later reports in the Israeli newspaper *Maariv* claimed that Fatah had caved in over threats by Israeli officials to release footage of PA officials urging Israel to continue Operation Cast Lead, the better to weaken their rivals. Translation reproduced at 'Oh, People of Palestine,/If not bullets,/Pray tell,/Where are your shoes?', Norman Finkelstein.com, 6 October 2009.

19 Amira Hass, 'How we like our leaders', *Haaretz*, 30 December 2008.

20 'Israel says mortar may have been fired from Israeli-hit UN school', *Agence France-Presse*, 18 September 2011; 'Statement of the UN Humanitarian Coordinator for the occupied Palestinian territory Mr. Maxwell Gaylard, 6 Jan 2009', *Reliefweb*, 6 January 2009; Tim McGirk, 'UN: No Hamas Fighters in Bombed Gaza School', *Time*, 7 January 2009. For a sense of the targets of Israel's aggression during the invasion, invariably described as 'Hamas' targets, see Jamie Stern-Weiner, ' "This is an all-out war against the civilian Palestinian population in Gaza"', *The Heathlander*, 6 January 2009.

21 'Red Cross: Israel breaking int'l law, letting children starve in Gaza', Reuters, 8 January 2009.

22 Heather Sharp, '"This is an all-out war against the civilian Palestinian population in Gaza"', *BBC News*, 5 January 2009

23 'Israel warns Hezbollah war would invite destruction', Reuters, 3 October 2008 (emphasis added); see also Valentina Azarov, 'No lessons learned: Israeli military plans to intensify the use of indiscriminate and disproportionate force in its next armed conflict', *International Law Observer*, 9 October 2008.

24 'Human Rights in Palestine and Other Occupied Arab Territories: Report of the United Nations Fact-Finding Mission on the Gaza

Conflict', UN Human Rights Council, Twelfth Sessions, Agenda Item 7, 15 September 2009.

25   Lynn Sweet, 'President-elect Obama first press conference. Transcript', *Chicago Sun-Times*, 7 November 2008; Michael D. Shear, 'Obama's "One President" Philosophy Is Not One-Fit-All', *Washington Post*, 31 December 2008; Glenn Kessler, 'Obama Clarifies Remarks on Jerusalem', *Washington Post*, 5 June 2008.

26   Christopher Hitchens, 'Bad Timing', *Slate*, 5 January 2009.

27   See D. D. Guttenplan's commentary in his review of Hitchens' biography, *Hitch-22*; 'Changing Places', *Nation*, 28 July 2010.

28   Benny Morris, 'Why Israel Feels Threatened', *New York Times*, 29 December 2008. Morris explains with respect to the 1948 ethnic cleansing of Palestinians: 'Under some circumstances expulsion is not a war crime. I don't think that the expulsions of 1948 were war crimes. You can't make an omelet without breaking eggs. You have to dirty your hands ... if he [David Ben-Gurion] was already engaged in expulsion, maybe he should have done a complete job. I know that this stuns the Arabs and the liberals and the politically correct types. But my feeling is that this place would be quieter and know less suffering if the matter had been resolved once and for all. If Ben-Gurion had carried out a large expulsion and cleaned the whole country – the whole Land of Israel, as far as the Jordan River. It may yet turn out that this was his fatal mistake. If he had carried out a full expulsion – rather than a partial one – he would have stabilized the State of Israel for generations.' Quoted in Baruch S. Kimmerling, 'Benny Morris's Shocking Interview', *History News Network*, 26 January 2004.

29   Paul Berman, *The Flight of the Intellectuals* (Melville House, 2009); for a sensible review, see Andrew F. March, 'Arguments: *The Flight of the Intellectuals* and Tariq Ramadan', *Dissent*, 25 May 2010.

30   Michelle Sief, 'Gaza and After: An Interview with Paul Berman', *The Z Word*, March 2009.

31   Bernard-Henri Lévy, 'Choses vues dans la Géorgie en guerre', *Le Monde*, 20 August 2008; 'BHL n'a pas vu toutes ses "choses vues" en Géorgie', Rue89.com, 22 August 2008; 'Pandora: Bernard-Henri Lévy, French gift to Georgia', *Independent*, 18 August 2008.

32   Bernard-Henri Lévy, 'Reportage from Israel/Gaza', *Huffington Post*, 20 January 2009; Sefi Hendler, 'Feisty on all fronts', *Haaretz*, 27 May 2010.

33   Attila Somfalvi, 'Bernard-Henri Lévy: Israel secular miracle', *Ynet*, 31 May 2010

34   George Orwell, 'Not Counting Niggers', *Adelphi* (July 1939), republished online at orwell.ru. Not by accident, Orwell was also prescient

about the Palestine question, opposing Zionist claims to that country, and noting that 'few English people realise that the Palestine issue is partly a colour issue and that an Indian nationalist, for example, would probably side with the Arabs'. Quoted, Pankaj Mishra, 'The west will not prevent a Palestinian state's eventual birth', *Guardian*, 14 September 2011.

35   Henry Samuel, 'Bernard-Henri Lévy caught out by fake philosopher', *Daily Telegraph*, 9 February 2010.

36   He would be elected leader in May 2009, a seemingly catastrophic move as Ignatieff lost his own seat in the 2011 federal elections in the Liberals' worst electoral performance in their history.

37   In a speech to the Canadian Jewish Congress in May 2009, he responded to Conservative bids for Jewish votes by complaining: 'It is beyond reckless for political leaders to try to score points by branding one another as "anti-Israel" . . . My party will never claim to be the only genuine defenders of Israel in Canadian politics because I don't want my party to be alone in the defence of Israel. I want all parties to be genuine defenders of Israel.' Quoted, 'Michael Ignatieff's speech to the Canadian Jewish Congress', *Blogging Canadians*, May 2009. See also Sheldon Gordon, 'Where have all of Canada's Jewish Liberals gone?', *Haaretz*, 24 December 2009.

38   'CIC Reports on Canadian View of Gaza War', Canada–Israel Committee, 17 March 2009; 'Ignatieff says Israel must be allowed to defend itself from Hamas attacks', *The Canadian Press*, 8 January 2009.

39   'Israeli minister warns of Palestinian "holocaust"', *Guardian*, 29 February 2008.

40   Amnesty International UK, Broederlijk Delen (Belgium), CAFOD (UK), CCFD Terre Solidaire (France), Christian Aid (UK and Ireland), Church of Sweden, Diakonia (Sweden), Finn Church Aid (Finland), Medical Aid for Palestinians, medico international (Germany), Medico International Schweiz (Switzerland), Mercy Corps, MS ActionAid Denmark, Oxfam International, Trocaire (Ireland), and United Civilians for Peace (a coalition of Dutch organizations – Oxfam Novib, Cordaid, ICCO, and IKV Pax Christi), 'Failing Gaza: No rebuilding, no recovery, no more excuses: A report one year after Operation Cast Lead', December 2009.

41   There are only a small number of original sources for such claims, none of them reliable. One is Jean-Louis Bruguière, whose evidence on the IHH to the 2001 trial of Assad Rehman was dismissed as hearsay. Another is the Intelligence and Terrorism Information Centre (ITIC), an Israeli think-tank linked to the Ministry of Defence. As the *Mavi Marmara* embarked on its mission to Gaza, the ITIC claimed to have

reliable information indicating that in the past IHH had links with global jihad'. The basis for its claim was a paper by Evan Kohlmann, itself based on Bruguière's claims as well as French prosecution testimony against Islamist suspects. These claims, then, would appear to be sensationalist at best, drawing on thin material to make weighty claims. But the image of terrorists descending on Gaza, possibly bearing arms or some other deadly cargo, was used to justify what took place next. 'United States of America v. Ahmed Ressam, CR 99-666-JCC, Reporter's Transcript of Proceedings, April 2, 2001', available at seattletimes. nwsource.com. Evan F Kohlmann, 'The Role of Islamic Charities in International Terrorist Recruitment and Financing', DIIS Working Paper no. 2006/7, available at diis.dk; Kohlmann, who has been dubbed a 'hand for hire' in the 'guilty-verdict industry' and a 'whore of the court', due to his willingness to testify against nearly every defendant in US terrorism trials, seems to take prosecution claims at face value. See the sympathetic interview with Kohlmann at Wesley Yang, 'The Terrorist Search Engine', *New York News and Features*, 5 December 2010.

42   Robert Mackey, 'Reporters Dispute Israeli Account of Raid', the Lede blog, *New York Times*, 3 June 2010; for live footage, see Ali Abuminah, 'Footage proves indiscriminate Israeli live fire at Mavi Marmara passengers in Gaza Flotilla', AliAbuminah.posterous.com, 13 June 2010; for a comprehensive rundown of developments in evidence since the raid, see Ali Abuminah, 'Israel's attack on the Gaza Freedom Flotilla: Looking back a year later', *Electronic Intifada*, 31 May 2011.

43   'Report of the international fact-finding mission to investigate violations of international law, including international humanitarian and human rights law, resulting from the Israeli attacks on the flotilla of ships carrying humanitarian assistance', UN Human Rights Council, 15th Session, Agenda Item 1, 27 September 2010.

44   Max Blumenthal, 'Under Scrutiny, IDF Retracts Claims About Flotilla's Al Qaeda Links', MaxBlumenthal.com, 3 June 2010.

45   Max Blumenthal, 'IDF Releases Apparently Doctored Flotilla Audio; Press Reports As Fact', MaxBlumenthal.com, 4 June 2010.

46   Belén Fernández, 'Sinking the Mavi Marmara', Al Jazeera, 30 August 2011.

47   Omar Barghouti, *Boycott Divestment Sanctions: The Global Struggle for Palestinian Rights* (Haymarket, 2011), p. 205.

48   David Grossman, 'A Puppet on a String', *Haaretz*, 2 June 2010.

49   Seth Freedman, 'Israel had no choice over Gaza flotilla', *Guardian*, 1 June 2010.

50   The view that Arabs are happy to sacrifice their children is a stubbornly

resistant one. British actress Maureen Lipman asserted during the invasion of Lebanon that while human life is 'not cheap to the Israelis', it is 'quite cheap' to Arabs, because 'they strap bombs to people and send them to blow themselves up' (whereas Israel only blows other people up). Maureen Lipman, *This Week*, BBC One, 14 July 2006.

51   Christopher Hitchens, 'Israel and Turkey: It's Complicated', Slate.com, 7 June 2010; still harping on the same theme a year later, Hitchens did not forget to remind the world that Free Gaza activists were at best credulous fools and at worst in bed with Hamas. Christopher Hitchens, 'Boat People', Slate.com, 4 July 2010.

52   Bernard-Henri Lévy, 'It's time to stop demonizing Israel', *Haaretz*, 8 June 2010.

53   Howard Jacobson, 'Why Alice Walker shouldn't sail to Gaza', CNN, 24 June 2011

54   Alexei Sayle, 'Alexei Sayle on Gaza & Israeli Violence', YouTube, 2 January 2009.

55   Sameer Yacoub, 'Invasion led to spike in Iraq widows', Associated Press, 19 September 2011.

56   BHL even hinted that he bore some of the credit since 'The motor of this revolution . . . was the internauts, the web surfers, users of Twitter, Facebook, YouTube and others . . . They are the Anonymous, this group of hackers supported by my review, *La Règle du jeu*, who, when they realized the cyberpolice were about to reduce the space of this cyberresistance to nothing, attacked the regime's official sites and blocked the State machine. Bernard-Henri Lévy, 'The Lessons of Tunisia', *Huffington Post*, 19 January 2011; Bob Mitchell, 'Ignatieff says democracy is only acceptable outcome in Egypt', *Star*, 30 January 2011.

57   Scott Malcomson, 'A Free-for-All on a Decade of War', *New York Times*, 7 September 2011.

58   In 2007, Berman attempted to render his position thus: 'I approved on principle the overthrow of Saddam. I never did approve of Bush's way of going about it. In the run-up to the war, I became, on practical grounds, ever more fearful that, in his blindness to liberal principles, Bush was leading us over a cliff.' In fact, he approved both in principle and in practice, and devoted much of his energy to supporting the war both before its prosecution and well into the occupation. Paul Berman and Ian Buruma, 'His Toughness Problem – and Ours: An Exchange', *New York Review of Books*, 8 November 2007.

59   Dan Murphy, 'Joe Biden says Egypt's Mubarak no dictator, he shouldn't step down ...', *Christian Science Monitor*, 27 January 2011.

60   'Blair says leak of Palestine papers "destabilising" for peace process', *Guardian*, 28 January 2011; Chris McGreal, 'Tony Blair: Mubarak is

"immensely courageous and a force for good"', *Guardian*, 2 February 2011. The fact that Mubarak's support for Israel was so important to his international sponsorship, and that pro-Palestine activism was among the tributaries building up to his downfall, would tend to make nonsense of liberal columnist Nick Cohen's claim that the revolutions 'had nothing to do with Palestine'. Nick Cohen, 'Our absurd obsession with Israel is laid bare', *Observer*, 27 February 2011.

61   'Tony Blair talks to Newsnight – Part 2', *Newsnight*, 2002, available at BBC.com.

62   In fact, Ghannouchi represents one of the most pluralist and democratic Islamist currents in the world, and the reason for his exile is that his party was the subject of some bloody repression, particularly in the early 1990s. On al-Nahda, see Francois Burgat and William Dowell, *The Islamic Movement in North Africa* (University of Texas Press, 1993); Linda G. Jones, 'Portrait of Rashid Al-Ghannoushi', *Middle East Report*, no. 153 (July–August 1988). The fear of Islamist resurgence is still being used to justify potential restrictions on democracy in post-revolutionary Tunisia. Rachel Linn, 'Tunisia must hold its nerve for democracy's sake', *Guardian*, 11 August 2011.

63   Christopher Hitchens, 'At the Desert's Edge', *Vanity Fair*, July 2007.

64   Christopher Hitchens, 'Tunisia, the Arab world's most civilized dictatorship', *National Post*, 18 January 2011. A better analysis of the reasons for the revolution would focus on the twin crises of global capitalism and of regional authority. The region's dictatorships had experienced a dramatic narrowing of their social base as a result of neoliberal policies involving weakened trade unions, the privatization of public goods, deregulation and cuts to social security programmes, well before the recession. The result was a transfer of wealth to an increasingly narrow elite. The dictator Ben Ali was primarily responsible for introducing such policies into Tunisia. Despite his pledge to democratize the country, he reinforced these policies with increased repression. Combining rigged elections and interference in the country's trade union federation (long a partner of the ruling party, going back to their cooperation in the anti-colonial movement) with torture and the use of military courts, Ben Ali took out one opposition force after another – the trade union left, the communists and the Islamists. As the regime's base of support narrowed, the internal security apparatus was expanded. The decomposition of the regime resulted from three weak points: the continued existence of a trade union movement that, though wholly co-opted, had latent power that was unleashed during the revolt; the desire of the army to hold to its 'constitutional' role and avoid direct involvement in repression; and the existence of elite factions who were

not wholly integrated into the regime and could thus break from it. For background on the origins of the Ben Ali dictatorship, its repression and neoliberal policies, see Clement Henry Moore, 'Tunisia and Bourguibisme: Twenty Years of Crisis', *Third World Quarterly*, vol. 10, no. 1, (January 1988); Karen Pfeifer, 'How Tunisia, Morocco, Jordan and even Egypt became IMF "Success Stories" in the 1990s', *Middle East Report*, no. 210 (Spring 1999); L. B. Ware, 'The Role of the Tunisian Military in the Post-Bourguiba Era', *Middle East Journal*, vol. 39, no. 1 (Winter 1985); Christopher Alexander, 'Authoritarianism and Civil Society in Tunisia', *Middle East Report*, no. 205 (Winter 1997); Christopher Alexander, 'Tunisia's protest wave: where it comes from and what it means', *Foreign Policy*, 3 January 2011.

65   'Iran opposition says 72 killed in vote protests', *Agence France-Presse*, 3 September 2009; 'Tunisia protests against Ben Ali left 200 dead, says UN', BBC News, 16 May 2009. It may be added that while Ben Ali never achieved less than 90 per cent of the vote – a fact which Hitchens acknowledged made him 'nervous' – Ahmadinejad's arguably rigged election result in 2009, with his campaign claiming 62 per cent of the votes, was not typical of Iranian elections. Further, US officials maintain that Ahmadinejad's fraud exaggerated his victory, and that he would have won without it. See Christopher Dickey, 'The Supreme Leader', *Daily Beast*, 19 July 2009.

66   Christopher Hitchens, 'What I Don't See at the Revolution', *Vanity Fair*, April 2011. Hitchens was not lacking in sympathy for the revolutionaries. He took heart from the absence of mass Islamist movements rushing to take power, saluting the 'really admirable solidity and maturity, both in their civic conduct and in their demands' of the revolutionaries. Christopher Hitchens, 'Egypt: Islamism Meets Realism', available at secularhumanism.org. But he asserted that Egypt lacked 'a genuine opposition leader' and its political parties were 'emaciated hulks' with the exception of the Muslim Brotherhood. This account was exaggerated and unfairly condescending. Egyptian civil society had been developing and maturing under the despot's integument over the preceding decade, beginning with pro-Palestine and anti-war activism, building to a remarkably broad coalition of liberals, socialists and Islamists by 2005. There followed the first eruptions of an organized and independent labour movement whose strikes inspired the April 26 movement. This coalition, with the labour movement proving important in the later stages, broke the Mubarak dictatorship and its backers. Egyptians were not, after all, *so* unlettered and unversed in the language of civil society.

67   Ali Abdullatif Ahmida, *Forgotten Voices: Power and Agency in Colonial and Postcolonial Libya* (Routledge, 2005), pp. 67–83; Roger Owen,

State, Power and Politics in the Making of the Modern Middle East (Routledge, 1992), pp. 53–5; Nazih N. Ayubi, *Over-stating the Arab State: Politics and Society in the Middle East* (I.B. Tauris, 2006), p. 257.

68   On the Lockerbie bombing and Libya, see the investigative reportage by Paul Foot, 'Lockerbie: The Flight from Justice', a special report from *Private Eye* (Pressdam, 2001).

69   Lisa Anderson, 'Rogue Libya's Long Road', *Middle East Report*, no. 241 (Winter 2006); Ray Takeyh, 'The Rogue Who Came in From the Cold', *Foreign Affairs*, May/June, 2001.

70   Laura Rozen, 'Among Libya's lobbyists', Politico, 21 February 2011; Ed Pilkington, 'US Firm Monitor Group Admits Mistakes over $3m Gaddafi Deal', *Guardian*, 4 March 2011; Anthony Giddens, 'My chat with the colonel', *Guardian*, 9 March 2007.

71   Anthony Shadid and Kareem Fahim, 'Opposition in Libya Struggles to Form a United Front', *New York Times*, 8 March 2011.

72   Richard Seymour, 'Libya's spectacular revolution has been disgraced by racism', *Guardian*, 30 August 2011; David Enders, 'Empty village raises concerns about fate of black Libyans', *McClatchy*, 13 September 2011; Kim Septunga, 'Rebels settle scores in Libyan capital', *Independent*, 27 August 2011; Patrick Cockburn, 'Libyans don't like people with dark skin, but some are innocent', *Independent*, 30 August 2011; Jason Koutsoukis, 'Africans targeted as rebels hunt mercenaries', *Age*, 6 March 2011; Gert Van Langendonck, 'In Tripoli, African "mercenaries" at risk', *Christian Science Monitor*, 29 August 2011; 'Libyan rebels rounding up thousands of black citizens and immigrants', *Associated Press*, 1 September 2009.

73   'Gaddafi Graffiti In Libya', NPR, 17 April 2011; Nouri al-Misrahi, a former regime official, and Ibrahim Dabbashi, the former ambassador, were both early sources for these rumours. See Bernard Namunane, 'Kenya: "Dogs of War" Fighting for Gaddafi', *Daily Nation* (Nairobi), 25 February 2011; Andrew McGregor, 'Special Commentary: Can African Mercenaries Save the Libyan Regime?', *Jamestown Foundation*, 23 February 2011; on Libya's immigration policies, see 'Rights on the Line', *Human Rights Watch*, 12 December 2010; on rebel agreements with Italy, see 'Vendetta per raid a Brega, minacce a Italia e Nato', Ansa.it, 13 May 2011; and 'Libia, gli insorti: "Fermeremo l'immigrazione e rispetteremo i trattati con l'Italia"', *Blitz quotidiano*, 29 March 2011.

74   Jihad Taki, 'Libyan Ambassador to UN urges international community to stop genocide', *Global Arab Network*, 21 February 2011; Mohammad Abbas, 'Libya rebels form council, oppose foreign intervention', *Reuters*, 27 February 2011; 'No foreign intervention, Libyans tell West', Agence France-Presse, 1 March 2011.

75   Julian Borger, 'Nato weighs Libya no-fly zone options', *Guardian*, 8 March 2011; 'Libya: UK and French no-fly zone plan gathers pace', BBC News, 8 March 2011; Murray Brewster, 'Canada sending warship to Libya', *The Canadian Press*, 1 March 2011; Akhtar Jamal, 'US, UK, French forces land in Libya', *Pakistan Observer*, 28 February 2011.

76   Stephen M. Walt, 'Hints of Realism?', *Foreign Policy*, 9 March 2009.

77   Josh Rogin, 'Anne-Marie Slaughter accuses Obama of prioritizing oil over values', *Foreign Policy*, 16 March 2011.

78   Anne-Marie Slaughter, 'Interests vs. Values? Misunderstanding Obama's Libya Strategy', *New York Review of Books* blog, 30 March 2011.

79   By far the best source on torture, war and civil liberties in the Obama era is Glenn Greenwald's column in Salon.com. See, for example, his bravura resume of the Obama administration, 'Robert Gibbs attacks the fringe losers of the left', Salon.com, 10 August 2008.

80   On French manoeuvring, see 'Sarkozy's Libyan surprise', *Economist*, 14 March 2011; on BHL's involvement, see Kim Willsher, 'Libya: Bernard-Henri Lévy Dismisses Criticism for Leading France to Conflict', *Observer*, 27 March 2011; on French belligerence vs. US reticence, see Richard McGregor and Daniel Dombey, 'Foreign Policy: A Reticent America', *Financial Times*, 23 March 2011; Penny Hollinger and Peter Spiegel, 'Paris calls for targeted Libyan air strikes', *Financial Times*, 10 March 2011.

81   On the Economic Development Board, see Stanley Reed, 'Libya Is Open for Business', *Business Week*, 14 March 2007; on Jibril's pitch for a broad alliance with the US during his time in the regime, see the Wikileaks cable published as '08TRIPOLI917' published in the *Telegraph*: 'Head of Libya's Economic Development Board: U.S.–Libya Relations Not Just About Oil', *Daily Telegraph*, 31 January 2011.

82   Helene Cooper and Steven Lee Myers, 'Obama Takes Hard Line With Libya After Shift by Clinton', *New York Times*, 18 March 2011; Glenn Thrush, 'Day after saying no second term, a big win for Hillary Clinton', *Politico*, 17 March 2011.

83   Pepe Escobar, 'Exposed: The US–Saudi Libya deal', *Asia Times*, 2 April 2011. Former British diplomat Craig Murray also states that: 'A senior diplomat in a western mission to the UN in New York, who I have known over ten years and trust, has told me for sure that Hillary Clinton agreed to the cross-border use of troops to crush democracy in the Gulf, as a quid pro quo for the Arab League calling for Western intervention in Libya.' 'The Invasion of Bahrain', CraigMurray.org.uk, 14 March 2011.

84   Peter John Cannon, 'The Welcome Return of Interventionism', The Henry Jackson Society, 1 April 2011.

85   Julio Godoy, 'France: Corrupt Relations With African Dictators?', *Terra Viva Europe*, 17 February 2009; Eric Conan, 'Exclusif: le livre qui peut ruiner Kouchner', *Marianne 2*, 30 January 2009; Lizzy Davies, 'Cash from dictators for France's "Mr Clean"', *Guardian*, 5 February 2009; Christopher Caldwell, 'Communiste et Rastignac', *London Review of Books*, vol. 31, no. 13 (9 July 2009); Robert Zaretsky, 'Kouchner's new-found borders', *Le Monde Diplomatique*, September 2010.

86   Bernard Kouchner, 'Libya: The morality of intervention', *Guardian*, 24 March 2011.

87   Christopher Hitchens, 'The Iraq Effect', Slate.com, 28 March 2011.

88   Christopher Hitchens, 'American Inaction Favors Qaddafi', Slate.com, 7 March 2011

89   Kim Willsher, 'Libya: Bernard-Henri Lévy dismisses criticism for leading France to conflict', *Observer*, 27 March 2011; Steve Erlanger, 'By His Own Reckoning, One Man Made Libya a French Cause', *New York Times*, 1 April 2011; Robert Marquand, 'How a philosopher swayed France's response on Libya', *Christian Science Monitor*, 28 March 2011 Bernard-Henri Lévy, 'Sarkozy, Libya and Diplomacy of Extreme Urgency', *Huffington Post*, 12 March 2011. As for BHL's propensity for self-promotion, French television broadcast footage of the *philosophe* repeatedly trying to get into camera shots featuring Cameron and Sarkozy, but being bundled away by handlers every time. See 'BHL se fait virer deux fois de la tribune à Tripoli', YouTube, 19 September 2011; Marcelo Svirsky, 'An open letter to Bernard-Henri Lévy', *Le Monde Diplomatique*, 17 March 2011.

90   See Clay Claiborne, 'No Libyans allowed at ANSWER Libya Forum', *Daily Kos*, 23 June 2011; Michael Fiorentino and Jeremy Tully, 'A disservice to the antiwar movement', SocialistWorker.org, 12 July 2011; and ANSWER's defence, 'ANSWER LA responds to attack on Eyewitness Libya forum', ANSWER Coalition, 24 June 2011

91   See, for example, Lance Selfa, 'Libya's revolution, US intervention, and the left', *International Socialist Review*, no. 77 (May–June 2011); also see my article, 'Imperialism and revolution in the Middle East', *Socialist Review*, May 2011.

92   Gilbert Achcar, 'Libyan Developments', *ZNet*, 19 March 2011; Gilbert Achcar, 'Libya: a legitimate and necessary debate from an anti-imperialist perspective', *ZNet*, 25 March 2011; Gilbert Achcar, 'NATO's "conspiracy" against the Libyan revolution', *Jadaliyya*, 16 August 2011; Juan Cole, 'An Open Letter to the Left on Libya', *Informed Comment*, 27 March 2011.

93   'Western, Arab nations say Gaddafi must go', Reuters, 13 April 2011; 'Pragmatism rules in Libyan stalemate', Channel 4 News (UK), 26 July

2011; 'We are edging towards the partition of Libya', *Daily Telegraph*, 27 July 2011.

94   Kim Septunga, 'Libyan rebels have conceded ground since bombing began', *Independent*, 27 July 2011.

95   'Gen.: US troops not ideal, but may be considered in Libya', CBS News, 7 April 2011.

96   Laura Rozen, 'Polls show American public not sold on Libya intervention', *Envoy*, 18 March 2011; Jodie Ginsberg and Avril Ormsby, '60% oppose Libya bombing', Reuters, 21 March 2011.

97   Tony Karon reported as early as April that negotiations were underway. See Tony Karon, 'Libya Peace Negotiations Are Already Underway', *Time*, 4 April 2011.

98   Patrick Cockburn, 'Amnesty questions claim that Gaddafi ordered rape as weapon of war', *Independent*, 24 June 2011.

99   'Libyan deputy ambassador to the UN: "What's happening is genocide"', BBC News, 21 February 2011; Chris McGreal, 'Gaddafi's army will kill half a million, warn Libyan rebels', *Guardian*, 12 March 2011.

100   Patrick Cockburn, 'Amnesty questions claim that Gaddafi ordered rape as weapon of war', *Independent*, 24 June 2011.

101   Alan J. Kuperman, 'False pretense for war in Libya?', *Boston Globe*, 14 April 2011; Rod Nordland, 'Libya Counts More Martyrs Than Bodies', *New York Times*, 16 March 2011; David Enders, 'Prisons grow as rebels pursue their enemies and questions arise about the missing', *McClathy*, 18 September 2011.

102   Alex Thomson, *Channel 4 News*, 29 August 2011; Kim Septunga, 'Rebels settle scores in Libyan capital', *Independent*, 27 August 2011.

103   See 'Blair says leak of Palestine papers "destabilising" for peace process', *UTV News*, 28 January 2011.

INDEX

Boot, Max 9, 154, 160
Bosnia 193–205, 210, 211, 212, 214,
    219, 220, 226, 231, 240, 241
Bourdieu, Pierre 249
Bourg, Julian 169
Bourguiba, Habib 58, 59
Bourne, Randolph 104
Bowman, Isaiah 102
Boxer Rebellion 42, 89
Brailsford, H.N. 74
Brauman, Rony 218, 231–3
Brazil 82–3, 84
Bremer, Paul 225
Bricmont, Jean 2
British Empire, the 23–35, 50, 64, 73–7,
    83, 94–5, 110
    Marx on 36–7, 38
    and the Second Boer War 39–43
    and the turn to America 65–9
    wars on China 42
Bronstein, Lev Davidovich 155
Brooke, Francis 188
Browder, Earl 124, 148
Brown, H. Rap 157
Bruckner, Pascal 11, 167, 171, 197, 247–8
Bryan, William Jennings 95–6
Brzezinski, Zbigniew 173, 186–7, 251
Buchez, Philip 43
Buckley, William F., Jr 4, 162
Bukharin, Nikolai 110–11
Burke, Edmund 27
Burnham, James 124, 160
Bush, George, Sr 186
Bush, George W. 4, 7, 9, 10, 11, 13, 17,
    137 179, 180, 209, 224–5, 249,
    252, 258, 263
Bush, Laura 236
Buttinger, Joseph 142
Byroade, Henry 126

Calhoun, John C. 83, 95
California 82
Callinicos, Alex 240, 242
Cambodia 140, 169, 219, 222
Camus, Albert 71–2
Canada 41
Cannon, James 147, 148
Capra, Frank 114
Cardignac, Louis (General) 38
Caribbean, the 126–7

Carlyle, Thomas 27, 31, 85
Carnegie, Andrew 95
Carter administration 163
Carter, Graydon 7
Casanova, Laurent 73
Castoriadis, Cornelius 251
Castro, Fidel 127
Catholic Church 44
CCF (Congress for Cultural Freedom)
    121
Çeku, Agim 208
Central America 117, 173, 174, 176, 177,
    178, 179, 239
Central Europe, and post-war revolutions
    57–8
Cerovi, Stanka 198
Chad 175, 248
Chalabi, Ahmed 11, 188, 237, 239, 268
Chalabi, Salem 237
Chamberlain, Joseph 35, 39–40
Chamorro, Edgar 173, 174
Chamorro, Violeta 179, 180
Chandler, David 205, 210
Chavez, Linda 160, 163
Cheney, Dick 189, 237
Chesler, Phyllis 236
Chibber, Vivek 235
China 5, 42, 45, 89, 91, 106, 112, 130,
    133, 137, 138, 163, 170
    see also PRC
Chirac, Jacques 172, 244–5
Chomsky, Noam 10, 177, 231, 253
Christianity 15, 31
Christofferson, Michael Scott 166
Churchill, Ward 36
Churchill, Winston 4
CIA (Central Intelligence Agency) 2, 68,
    76, 120, 128, 133, 156, 174, 180,
    188, 257, 263
civil rights movement 143, 150, 157
Clavel, Maurice 172
Clemenceau, Georges 98
Clifford, Clark 129
Clinton, Bill 4, 5, 116, 153, 197, 202–3,
    206, 209, 210, 220, 239–43
Cockburn, Alexander 242
Cohen, Francis 167
Cohen, Nick 10, 18, 19, 229, 234, 254
Cohen, Philippe 174, 199, 250
Cohn-Bendit, Daniel 189